A DIFFERENT LIGHT

חַג הַחֲנֻכָּה

Hanukkah Delight

(A little girl from Indiana, 1953, photographed by Rita Kurtz Lewis, Beit Hatefutsot Photo Archive)

**The David and Rae Finegood Institute for Diaspora Education and
the Charles and Valerie Diker Family Resource Center for Jewish Continuity
at the
Shalom Hartman Institute in Jerusalem**

Moritz Daniel Oppenheim, Germany, 1886

Language Editors and Consultants — Marcelle Zion and Jeni Friedman

Illustrator — Tanya Zion   Graphic Design — Joe Buchwald Gelles

Published by **Devora Publishing**
40 East 78th Street Suite 16 D
New York, NY 10021
Tel: 1-800-232-2931
Fax: 212-472-6253
pop@netvision.net.il
ISBN hb 1-930143-25-7, pb 1-930143-31-1
Printed in Hong Kong

The Shalom Hartman Institute
P.O.B. 8029, Jerusalem, Israel 93113
Tel: 972-2-5675320
Fax: 972-2-5611913
zionsacs@netvision.net.il
© 2000 by Noam Zion
www.hartmaninstitute.com
LC 99-76450

A DIFFERENT LIGHT

THE HANUKKAH BOOK OF CELEBRATION

A how-to guide to a creative candle lighting ceremony: blessings, songs, stories, readings, games and cartoons to engage adults, teenagers and children on each of the eight nights

BY NOAM SACHS ZION AND BARBARA SPECTRE

A sequel to

A Different Night:
The Family Participation Haggadah

THE HANUKKAH BOOK OF CELEBRATION

Table of Contents

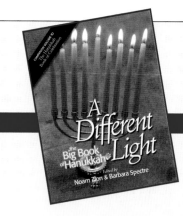

also in this holiday series of **A DIFFERENT LIGHT**

the companion volume to THE BOOK OF CELEBRATION *is*

THE BIG BOOK OF HANUKKAH: PERSPECTIVES AND PROFILES

Pluralist Perspectives on the Festival of Lights

I. Multiple Jewish Identities, Multiple Versions of Hanukkah: A Pluralism of Interpretation

How different communities and denominations find their particular identity symbolized in the light of the Menorah including Jewish Renewal, Reform, Reconstructionist, Habad, and Secular Zionist

Gallery: The Children's Festival of Lights

II. The Historians' Hanukkah: Recalling the Worst Jewish Civil War

Gallery: Elephants at War with the Jews

III. The Philosophers' Hanukkah: Where Hellenism and Judaism Differ

Gallery: Warrior Menorahs

IV. The Rabbis' Hanukkah: Rabbinic Reflections on the Warrior, the Zealot, the Martyr and the Family Peacemaker

V. The Scientists' and the Kabbalists' Thoughts on Lights and Lamps

Exploring the scientific understanding of physical light and the Jewish understandings of the symbolic light of the Menorah

Gallery: Temple Menorahs and Traditional Hanukkiot

Profiles in Modern Jewish Courage

VI. Profiles in Modern Jewish Courage

Yoni Netanyahu (the Raid on Entebbe), Chana Szenes (Israeli paratrooper in Hungary), Januscz Korczak (father of the orphans in Warsaw), teenage tzedakah heroes, two civil rights rabbis in Atlanta and in Buenos Aires, and Righteous Gentiles

for Passover

for customizing one's own seder

A DIFFERENT NIGHT

• **The Family Participation Haggadah**
• **The Leader's Guide**

DEDICATIONS   חֲנוּכַּת הַסֵּפֶר

The many people who worked on this Hanukkah project as writers, editors, consultants
and sponsors would like to dedicate this book to several very special forebears:

In honor of the 80th birthday of Rabbi Moses Bertram Sachs,
רב משה בנימין הלוי
affectionately known as Opa Moshe and Buddy,
and in memory of his wife Frances Rose Sachs

from his family, friends, and students:
by Noam and Marcelle, Mena and Marc, Sharon and Jerry, and all the grandchildren

Bunny Rosenthal with Eddie and Ellen, Roy and Leslee, Lynn and Billy, and Leonard and
Lainy Sachs and family; Henry and Bella Muller; Henriette and Avi Sonnenberg-Zion;
Mel and Judy Sykes, Earl Schwartz, Jeremy Kraff and Morris Rosenfeld, Sandy and Ken
Brown, Jerry and Gali, Merle and Anna Hillman; David and Linda, Stanley and Jean
Estrin; Sally and David Lowenfeld, Miriam and Forrest Foss, Kass and Joan Lipnick
Abelson, Michael and Hedy Milgrom, Albert J. Winn and Scott Portnoff; Jack and
Barbara Blumberg (Am Echad Congregation, Waukegan), Leonard and Rivian Silesky,
Walter Silesky, Racha and Charles Marks, Esta and Jerry Gold, Betty Kohn and family and
the B'nai Emet Synagogue in St.Louis Park, Minnesota; and the Jerusalemites Sarah
Fienberg, Irvin and Betty Beiner, Jack and Rose Hoffmitz, Marcia Abrams, Arnold
Sullum, Ray Kaplan, Dorothy S. Kripke, Margie and Moshe Tutenauer, Will and Miriam
Shuchat, Jack J. and Rhoda Cohen, Avraham and Leona Feder, Harry and Annie Allen and
the Moreshet Yisrael Synagogue.

In honor of my husband, Phil, our children, David, Michal and Guy,
Levi and Galia and our grandchildren, Omri and Tamar

from Barbara Spectre

In honor of Paul, Rachel and Laura Wiener
and the many joyous Hanukkahs we shared

from David and Sheila Wiener, their parents

In memory of Grandfather
Samuel Chazankin,
שמואל חזנקין ז״ל
from Gloria **זהבה** and Mark **משה מרדכי**
Bieler and family

In honor of the 80th birthdays
of Harry and Marilyn Saltzberg

from Marc **מרדכי** Saltzberg

Harper's Magazine, NY, 1890 (Beit Hatefutsot Photo Archive)

INTRODUCTION AND USER'S GUIDE
FOR THE HANUKKAH BOOK OF CELEBRATION
RITUALS, RETELLING AND CELEBRATING

There is, of course, no "Seder" Hanukkah or "Haggadah" for Hanukkah in the sense that there is one for Pesach. Nor did the Rabbis or the authors of this book intend for you to have a long, sit-down ritualized meal like the Passover Seder or to read aloud an extensive religious text like the Haggadah. Hanukkah is and should remain much more informal and modest in its family celebration.

Still there is a place for a limited "Seder" with brief readings in order to help us choreograph the half hour or so we spend around the Menorah every evening. This will lend it sanctity and substance as well as creativity and variety. In this book you will find ideas for a beautiful, simple candle lighting or for a Hanukkah dinner or party. Our target audience is not only parents of young children (see *Parental Guidelines for Celebrating with Young Children* in Chapter II, page 116), but also thoughtful adults and teenagers, because Hanukkah is not "for children only." We have outgrown a merely "pediatric Hanukkah" and we need a more mature and an even more entertaining version. Especially in North America, which is sometimes suffused with the commercialized "holiday spirit," Jews need a Festival of Lights that satisfies us spiritually, emotionally and intellectually. This *Hanukkah Book of Celebration* — along with its companion volume, *The Big Book of Hanukkah* — will empower you to celebrate in old and new ways. You can use it to customize candle lighting, gift giving and socializing over latkas to fit your needs. This how-to book is a **learning experience** for the uninitiated, as well as for those who thought they already knew what "little" there was to know about this "kids' holiday." This learning will be enjoyable, an experiment in growth, just as our previous book in this holiday series —

The Family Participation Haggadah: A Different Night — enlivened the seders of tens of thousands. Similarly, *A Different Light* will give you more pleasurable options and illumination for each of the eight days without losing the easy-going flexibility of Hanukkah.

Very simply put, our Seder Hanukkah is composed of three parts: **Rituals, Retelling, and Celebration**. The **rituals** are the traditional blessings (with transliteration) as well as medieval and modern songs. For those most frequently asked questions about exactly how and when to light the candles, see the survey of traditional views in *Questions and Answers: How to Light Right* (page 236).

In addition, we have written original *Spiritual Meditations* to accompany the candle lighting. These poems express the desire for personal and family rededication.

The **retelling** involves a kind of "haggadah" or "megillah" that attempts to fill the biggest gap in the Rabbinic development of Hanukkah. What has been missing is a storytelling centerpiece to a holiday that commemorates an external threat to our survival, a heroic human response, and a Divine rescue. Unlike Purim and Pesach, Hanukkah, the last of the holidays created by the Rabbis, lacks both a text and elaborate symbolic and theatrical rituals to make the memory come alive. The candles are meant to "publicize the miracles," but there are no props and narratives to accomplish this.

Therefore, we have created a *Maccabees' Megillah* — a brief history of the Maccabees told as a series of dramatic stories. The stories — drawn from the historic *Books of the*

Maccabees — are built on striking characters like Antiochus (called by his contemporaries the "Maniac"), like Hannah (the mother of seven martyrs whose eloquence was in words as well as in deeds), like Mattathias (the rebel priest and his five sons, especially Judah), and like Judith (whose erotic charms led General Holofernes to lose his head). By editing and abbreviating the historical *Books of the Maccabees* and the popular Rabbinic retellings of Judith, we offer readable, intriguing and dramatic — sometimes melodramatic — accounts of villains and heroes/heroines of the Maccabean era.

These eight brief historical readings may be read aloud, one per night, with the lighting of each candle. Please note that the language and content of the **Maccabees' Megillah** is most appropriate for teenagers and adults, while younger children should be read one of the many children's stories readily available in many stores. For children's cartoons and a recommended book, music and resource list see *Chapter II: Family and Friends, Food and Fun*, on page 113. For an easy guide to the historical background of Hanukkah — separating historic fact and legend — see *Questions and Answers: Getting the History of Hanukkah Right — Facts or Legends?* (page 243). For greater historical depth see *The Historians' Hanukkah* in the companion volume, **The Big Book of Hanukkah**.

Besides the ancient tales of the *Maccabees' Megillah*, we have provided **Profiles in**

NAVIGATING THIS BOOK:
THE MENU BAR

Within Chapter I, **The Hanukkah Ceremony**, there is a "menu bar" on each right-hand page (see example at right). The solid red section shows where you are; the lighter red shows where you have already been or are going.

Within Chapter II, **Family and Friends, Food and Fun**, there is a tab on each spread showing the resources for celebration: cartoons, recipes, games, gift giving and so on.

THE HANUKKAH CEREMONY

Brachot

Songs

Maccabee Megillah

Profiles

Spiritual Meditation

Modern Jewish Courage, stories that may be read aloud each night. Inspired by President John F. Kennedy's *Profiles in Courage* which is devoted to American models of heroic moral action, we have collected stories from modern Jewish history. The style of the profiles is *not* at all like encyclopedia entries in the *Who's Who* of Jewish celebrities. Rather, these biographical narratives portray moments of challenge, decision and action that are the substance of moral dramas. These stories offer insight into the inner struggles of individuals who are called upon to be courageous. At the same time, they inspire us by describing ingenious battles of wit and will against the enemies of humankind.

In our judgement, these men and women, while very human and fallible, are worthy of admiration and emulation. On Hanukkah we seek to celebrate Jewish heroism, not to debunk myths, but we hope these selections reflect nuanced heroes worthy of respect from mature readers. While physical and moral courage is in no way limited to a particular nation, the occasion — Hanukkah — has led us to focus almost exclusively on Jewish courage. For an expanded version of *Profiles in Modern Jewish Courage* see the companion volume, **The Big Book of Hanukkah**.

We suggest you consider structuring your own Seder Hanukkah with:

Rituals:
Candlelighting, Blessings and Songs
(10- 15 minutes)

Retelling:
Maccabees' Megillah and Profiles in Modern Jewish Courage
(10-15 minutes)

Celebration:
Gift giving, games, food
(30 minutes or more)

Right after Chapter I, **The Hanukkah Ceremony**, with its rituals and retelling, it is time to celebrate. In Chapter II, entitled **Family and Friends, Food and Fun: Gambling, Gift Giving, Games and Gelt**, you will find extensive ideas for children and adults as well as some reflections on the dilemmas of Hanukkah and Christmas. There is also a suggestion for organizing the gelt and gift giving to emphasize giving as well as receiving and giving of oneself as well as of one's material resources.

Finally, in Chapter III, **Hanukkah for Today**, contemporary Jewish thinkers reflect on the significance of the holiday for us. In particular we recommend the opening essays by our teacher Rabbi David Hartman who inspired and initiated the creation of this pluralistic series of holiday books.

We wish you a joyful Hanukkah with greater variety and more fun than ever before, both for the adults and teenagers as well as the younger children. May **A Different Light** serve to publicize the meaning of the Maccabean revolt for our generation.

Noam Zion and Barbara Spectre

Marc Chagall, Lighting Hannukah Candles, 1946
(© ADAGP, Paris, 2000)

BRACHOT בְּרָכוֹת

BLESSINGS FOR THE HANUKKAH CANDLES

THE
HANUKKA
CEREMO

Brache

Songs

Maccabe
Megilla

Profile

Spiritua
Meditatic

Before saying the blessings, the menorah needs to be set up with as many candles (oil or wax) as nights, in addition to one extra candle — the **shamash**. Generally the candles are **inserted** in the menorah **starting from the right** of the one lighting the candles. Each night another candle is added to the left. However the candles are **lit beginning from the left-most candle**, the "newest" one representing the added miracle of that night. Before actually lighting the candles, the blessings are sung. For the many simple and complex questions that arise regarding candle lighting according to traditional Jewish law, see the appendix **Questions and Answers: How to Light Right** (page 236).

CANDLE LIGHTING הַדְלָקַת נֵרוֹת

First Blessing

Baruch ata Adonai,	בָּרוּךְ אַתָּה יהוה	Blessed are You Adonai,
Eloheinu melech ha-olam,	אֱלֹהֵינוּ מֶלֶךְ הָעוֹלָם	our God, Ruler of the World,
Asher kidshanu	אֲשֶׁר קִדְּשָׁנוּ	who made us holy
b'mitzvotav	בְּמִצְוֹתָיו	through your commandments
V'tzivanu,	וְצִוָּנוּ	and commanded us
l'hadlik ner shel Hanukkah.	לְהַדְלִיק נֵר שֶׁל חֲנֻכָּה.	to light the Hanukkah Light.

Second Blessing

Baruch ata Adonai,	בָּרוּךְ אַתָּה יהוה	Blessed are You Adonai,
Eloheinu melech ha-olam,	אֱלֹהֵינוּ מֶלֶךְ הָעוֹלָם	our God, Ruler of the World,
Sheh-asah nissim	שֶׁעָשָׂה נִסִּים	who made miracles possible
la'avoteinu,	לַאֲבוֹתֵינוּ	for our ancestors
bayamim ha-heim,	בַּיָּמִים הָהֵם	in those days
Ba-z'man ha-zeh.	בַּזְּמַן הַזֶּה.	at this same season.[1]

Third Blessing — for the First Night Only

Baruch ata Adonai,	בָּרוּךְ אַתָּה יהוה	Blessed are You Adonai,
Eloheinu melech ha-olam,	אֱלֹהֵינוּ מֶלֶךְ הָעוֹלָם	our God, Ruler of the World,
She-heh-chi-yanu,	שֶׁהֶחֱיָנוּ	who has kept us alive
v'ki-y'manu,	וְקִיְּמָנוּ	and enabled us
V'higiyanu,	וְהִגִּיעָנוּ	to reach
La-z'man ha-zeh.	לַזְּמַן הַזֶּה.	this season of life.

---

1. In the earliest prayerbooks from Babylonia (Saadia Gaon, 9th century CE) and from France (Machzor Vitri, 11th century CE) there is an added prayer: "Just as You made miraculous victories possible for our ancestors in those days at this season, so may You do the same for us in our days."

Lighting Shabbat Candles, for Friday Evening only

נֵרוֹת שַׁבָּת

On Friday evening we light Shabbat candles **after** lighting the Hanukkah candles. Traditionally Hanukkah candles are lit before sundown with their blessings and then Shabbat candles are lit with their blessing and then, and only then, is it traditional to begin Hanukkah songs, gifts and games. The following blessing is said after lighting the Shabbat candles (usually with eyes covered):

Baruch ata Adonai,	בָּרוּךְ אַתָּה יהוה	Blessed are You Adonai,
Eloheinu melech ha-olam,	אֱלֹהֵינוּ מֶלֶךְ הָעוֹלָם	our God, Ruler of the World,
Asher kidshanu	אֲשֶׁר קִדְּשָׁנוּ	who made us holy
b'mitzvotav	בְּמִצְוֹתָיו	through your commandments
V'tzivanu,	וְצִוָּנוּ	and commanded us
l'hadlik ner shel Shabbat.	לְהַדְלִיק נֵר שֶׁל שַׁבָּת.	to light the Shabbat Light.

Havdalah on Saturday Night only

הַבְדָּלָה

On Motzaei Shabbat (Saturday evening after sundown) **before** lighting the Hanukkah candles, we celebrate the transition from Shabbat to the six days of labor that begin as the stars come out. Using a havdalah candle (a braided candle or simply any two candles whose wicks are held together), spices (a variety is best like cinnamon, cloves, perfumes and so on) and a cup of wine (though milk or orange juice or any beverage, other than water, is adequate), we recite the following blessings:

הִנֵּה אֵל יְשׁוּעָתִי, אֶבְטַח וְלֹא אֶפְחָד, כִּי עָזִּי וְזִמְרָת יָהּ יהוה, וַיְהִי לִי לִישׁוּעָה: וּשְׁאַבְתֶּם מַיִם בְּשָׂשׂוֹן, מִמַּעַיְנֵי הַיְשׁוּעָה: לַיהוה הַיְשׁוּעָה, עַל עַמְּךָ בִרְכָתֶךָ סֶּלָה: יהוה צְבָאוֹת עִמָּנוּ, מִשְׂגָּב לָנוּ אֱלֹהֵי יַעֲקֹב סֶלָה: יהוה צְבָאוֹת אַשְׁרֵי אָדָם בֹּטֵחַ בָּךְ: יהוה הוֹשִׁיעָה, הַמֶּלֶךְ יַעֲנֵנוּ בְיוֹם קָרְאֵנוּ:

All together while raising the cup:

לַיְּהוּדִים הָיְתָה אוֹרָה וְשִׂמְחָה וְשָׂשׂוֹן וִיקָר: כֵּן תִּהְיֶה לָּנוּ. כּוֹס יְשׁוּעוֹת אֶשָּׂא וּבְשֵׁם יהוה אֶקְרָא:

"The Jews had light and joy and honor" [in the days of Esther and Mordechai].[2] So may it be for us. I raise my cup of rescue and call on God's name.[3]

Blessing over the Wine (but do not yet drink):

בָּרוּךְ אַתָּה יהוה, אֱלֹהֵינוּ מֶלֶךְ הָעוֹלָם, בּוֹרֵא פְּרִי הַגָּפֶן.

Blessed are you, Adonai, our God, Ruler of the World, who creates the fruit of the vine.

Blessing over the Spices (then smell and offer to everyone):

בָּרוּךְ אַתָּה יהוה, אֱלֹהֵינוּ מֶלֶךְ הָעוֹלָם, בּוֹרֵא מִינֵי בְשָׂמִים.

Blessed are you, Adonai, our God, Ruler of the World, who creates various kinds of spices.

Blessing over the Flame (then everyone examines the play of light and shadow on one's hand):

בָּרוּךְ אַתָּה יהוה, אֱלֹהֵינוּ מֶלֶךְ הָעוֹלָם, בּוֹרֵא מְאוֹרֵי הָאֵשׁ.

Blessed are you, Adonai, our God, Ruler of the World, who creates the lights of fire.

Conclude:

בָּרוּךְ אַתָּה יהוה, אֱלֹהֵינוּ מֶלֶךְ הָעוֹלָם, הַמַּבְדִּיל בֵּין קֹדֶשׁ לְחֹל, בֵּין אוֹר לְחֹשֶׁךְ, בֵּין יִשְׂרָאֵל לָעַמִּים, בֵּין יוֹם הַשְּׁבִיעִי לְשֵׁשֶׁת יְמֵי הַמַּעֲשֶׂה. בָּרוּךְ אַתָּה יהוה, הַמַּבְדִּיל בֵּין קֹדֶשׁ לְחֹל.

Now drink the wine and extinguish the flame.

Blessed are you, Adonai, our God, Ruler of the World, who differentiates between the holy and the secular, between light and dark, between Israel and the nations, between the seventh day and the six days of creation. Blessed are you, Adonai, who differentiates between holiness and dailiness.

---

2. Esther 8:16   3. Psalms 116:13

HA-NEIROT HALLALU

הַנֵּרוֹת הַלָּלוּ

"THESE LIGHTS RECALL THE MIRACULOUS VICTORIES"

After lighting the candles it is traditional to declare these candles holy. The verses below, "HaNeirot," stipulate that these lights may be used for only one purpose — to commemorate these miraculous victories, but not to provide light for everyday use.

Haneirot hallalu,	<div dir="rtl">הַנֵּרוֹת הַלָּלוּ</div>	These lights
Anach-nu madlikim,	<div dir="rtl">אֲנַחְנוּ מַדְלִיקִין</div>	are lit to recall
Al ha-nissim,	<div dir="rtl">עַל הַנִּסִּים</div>	the miracles
V'al ha-niflaot,	<div dir="rtl">וְעַל הַנִּפְלָאוֹת</div>	the wonders
V'al ha-t'shuot,	<div dir="rtl">וְעַל הַתְּשׁוּעוֹת</div>	the rescues
V'al ha-milchamot,	<div dir="rtl">וְעַל הַמִּלְחָמוֹת</div>	and the victories
She-asita la-avoteinu,	<div dir="rtl">שֶׁעָשִׂיתָ לַאֲבוֹתֵינוּ</div>	that You granted our ancestors
Ba-yamim ha-heim	<div dir="rtl">בַּיָּמִים הָהֵם</div>	in those days
Ba-z'man ha-zeh	<div dir="rtl">בַּזְּמַן הַזֶּה</div>	at this season
Al y'dei	<div dir="rtl">עַל יְדֵי</div>	through [Your envoys],
Kohanecha ha-k'doshim.	<div dir="rtl">כֹּהֲנֶיךָ הַקְּדוֹשִׁים.</div>	the holy priests [the Maccabees].
V'chol sh'monat	<div dir="rtl">וְכָל־שְׁמוֹנַת</div>	For all eight
Y'mei Hanukkah,	<div dir="rtl">יְמֵי חֲנֻכָּה</div>	days of Hanukkah
Ha-neirot hallalu kodesh heim	<div dir="rtl">הַנֵּרוֹת הַלָּלוּ קֹדֶשׁ הֵם</div>	these candles are sanctified
V'ein lanu r'shut	<div dir="rtl">וְאֵין לָנוּ רְשׁוּת</div>	and no one may
l'hishtameish ba-hem	<div dir="rtl">לְהִשְׁתַּמֵּשׁ בָּהֶם</div>	use them
ela lir-otam bilvad,	<div dir="rtl">אֶלָּא לִרְאוֹתָם בִּלְבָד,</div>	except to look at them, and to
k'dei l'hodot u-le'hallel	<div dir="rtl">כְּדֵי לְהוֹדוֹת וּלְהַלֵּל</div>	be reminded to thank and praise
l'shim-cha ha-gadol	<div dir="rtl">לְשִׁמְךָ הַגָּדוֹל</div>	Your great name
al nisecha, v'al nifl'otecha,	<div dir="rtl">עַל נִסֶּיךָ וְעַל נִפְלְאוֹתֶיךָ</div>	for all your miraculous
v'al y'shu-ah-techa.	<div dir="rtl">וְעַל יְשׁוּעָתֶךָ.</div>	rescues.

SONGS: TRADITIONAL AND MODERN

MAOZ TZUR
THE ROCK OF MY RESCUE

מָעוֹז צוּר

1. The Rock of my Rescue

My God, You are the Rock of my Rescue[4]
and it is lovely to praise You.
Restore my House of Prayer,
where I will offer you thanks.
When you prepare the destruction of the enemy
who threatens us (like a barking dog),
then I will sing a song for the
Hanukkah (Rededication) of the Altar.

Maoz tzur y'shu-ah-ti,
L'cha na-eh l'shabei-ach
Tikkon beit t'filati
V'sham todah n'zabei-ach
L'eit tachin mat'bei-ach
Mi-tzar ha-m'nabei-ach
Az egmor b'shir mizmor
Hanukkat ha-miz'bei-ach

מָעוֹז צוּר יְשׁוּעָתִי
לְךָ נָאֶה לְשַׁבֵּחַ.
תִּכּוֹן בֵּית תְּפִלָּתִי
וְשָׁם תּוֹדָה נְזַבֵּחַ.
לְעֵת תָּכִין מַטְבֵּחַ
מִצָּר הַמְנַבֵּחַ.
אָז אֶגְמוֹר בְּשִׁיר מִזְמוֹר
חֲנֻכַּת הַמִּזְבֵּחַ.

4. *Psalms 31:3*

2. The Rescue from Pharaoh (1200 BCE)

Oh, my soul is sated with trouble[5]
Reducing my strength to nothing, consumed with grief.[6]
My life was embittered with hard labor
enslaved by Egypt's Empire.[7]
But with God's great (outstretched) arm,
God took out his treasured people.[8]
Then Pharaoh's army
sank in the depths of the Red Sea like a stone.[9]

רָעוֹת שָׂבְעָה נַפְשִׁי
בְּיָגוֹן כֹּחִי כָּלָה
חַיַּי מֵרְרוּ בְקֹשִׁי
בְּשִׁעְבּוּד מַלְכוּת עֶגְלָה.
וּבְיָדוֹ הַגְּדוֹלָה
הוֹצִיא אֶת הַסְּגֻלָּה,
חֵיל פַּרְעֹה וְכָל זַרְעוֹ
יָרְדוּ כְאֶבֶן בִּמְצוּלָה.

5. *Psalms 8:4*　　6. *Psalms 31:11*　　7. *Exodus 1:14*　　8. *Exodus 19:5*　　9. *Exodus 15:5*

3. The Rescue from Babylonia (539 BCE)

Despite the fact that God brought me to his Holy Place,
Even there I found no peace.
Along came a persecutor who exiled me,
for I sinned by worshipping foreign gods.
I drank poisoned wine[10]
and almost passed from this world.
Then came the end of Babylonia and the rise of Zerubavel[11]
and at the end of 70 years of exile[12] I was rescued.

דְּבִיר קָדְשׁוֹ הֱבִיאַנִי
וְגַם שָׁם לֹא שָׁקַטְתִּי
וּבָא נוֹגֵשׂ וְהִגְלַנִי
כִּי זָרִים עָבַדְתִּי
וְיֵין רַעַל מָסַכְתִּי
כִּמְעַט שֶׁעָבַרְתִּי
קֵץ בָּבֶל זְרֻבָּבֶל
לְקֵץ שִׁבְעִים נוֹשַׁעְתִּי.

10. *Psalms 60:5*　　11. the leader of the return to Zion, 538 BCE
12. as prophesied by *Jeremiah 25:12-13*

The most popular (Ashkenazi) song for Hanukkah is *Maoz Tzur*, written by MORDECHAI whose name is spelled out in the initial letter of each stanza (an acrostic). Each stanza refers to a different rescue in Israel's history.

THE HANUKKAH CEREMONY

Brachot

Songs

Maccabees Megilla

Profiles

Spiritual Meditations

4. The Rescue from Haman (5th C. BCE)

Cutting down a tree to hang Mordechai is what Haman, descendant of King Agag of Amalek, requested from King Ahashverosh of Persia. However it became his snare and stumbling block, so Haman was hung and his arrogance was stilled. You raised up Mordechai while wiping away his enemy's name. Haman's many sons were hung on that tree.

כְּרוֹת קוֹמַת בְּרוֹשׁ
בִּקֵּשׁ אֲגָגִי בֶּן הַמְּדָתָא
וְנִהְיְתָה לּוֹ לְפַח וּלְמוֹקֵשׁ
וְגַאֲוָתוֹ נִשְׁבָּתָה.
רֹאשׁ יְמִינִי נִשֵּׂאתָ
וְאוֹיֵב שְׁמוֹ מָחִיתָ;
רֹב בָּנָיו וְקִנְיָנָיו
עַל הָעֵץ תָּלִיתָ.

5. The Rescue from Antiochus (164 BCE)

Against me the Greeks gathered, back in the days of the Hasmoneans. Into my walls they broke and polluted all my oils. Yet from the remaining cruses a miracle was made for the people of the roses.[13] The Rabbis established eight days of song and Hallel.

יְוָנִים נִקְבְּצוּ עָלַי
אֲזַי בִּימֵי חַשְׁמַנִּים.
וּפָרְצוּ חוֹמוֹת מִגְדָּלַי
וְטִמְּאוּ כָּל הַשְּׁמָנִים;
וּמִנּוֹתַר קַנְקַנִּים
נַעֲשָׂה נֵס לַשּׁוֹשַׁנִּים.
בְּנֵי בִינָה יְמֵי שְׁמוֹנָה
קָבְעוּ שִׁיר וּרְנָנִים.

13. *Song of Songs* 2:2

6. The Messianic Redemption

Bare Your holy arm (ready for war)[14] and hasten the Millenium, Time of Redemption.[15] Avenge your servant's blood (spilled in Crusade and pogrom) by the wicked nation (Christian Europe), for the rescue is too long delayed for us. There seems no end to the days of evil's rule. Repel the Red One[16] in the shadow of the cross and raise up for us the seven shepherds.[17]

חֲשׂוֹף זְרוֹעַ קָדְשֶׁךָ
וְקָרֵב קֵץ הַיְשׁוּעָה
נְקוֹם נִקְמַת דַּם עֲבָדֶיךָ
מֵאֻמָּה הָרְשָׁעָה
כִּי אָרְכָה לָנוּ הַשָּׁעָה
וְאֵין קֵץ לִימֵי הָרָעָה
דְּחֵה אַדְמוֹן בְּצֵל צַלְמוֹן
הָקֵם לָנוּ רוֹעִים שִׁבְעָה.

14. *Isaiah* 52:10   15. *Daniel* 8:19

16. The Red One, Esau's descendants, may refer to the German Crusader Barbarosa who was the Holy Roman Emperor in the 12th C. who, like his colleague Richard the Lion Heart, was red haired.

17. Our messianic redeemers are the seven shepherds referred to in *Micah* 5:4 who will defeat the enemies of Israel. They include David in the center, Adam, Seth, and Metushelach to the left and Abraham, Jacob and Moses to the right (see *Talmud Bavli Sukkah* 52b).

MORDECHAI'S LYRICS: THE CRYPTIC LAST STANZA AND THE UNIDENTIFIED RED ONE

Mordechai, the Ashkenazi poet who lived before the 13th century in Crusader Germany, wrote this Hanukkah song (whose stanzas begin with an acrostic of his name). The song reviews God's past rescues of our people from Pharaoh, Nebuchadnezar, Haman and Antiochus and looks forward to the messianic redemption from the final evil world kingdom as prophesied by the prophet Daniel. After the defeat of the Greeks, the Rabbis looked forward to the demise of the final world empire that had burned the Temple, that is, Rome, identified symbolically with Esau, the Red One, father of Edom (the "Red People," in Hebrew). Later Rome was identified with Roman Catholic Christianity and with the medieval German kings who claimed the throne of the Holy Roman Empire and prepared for the Crusades to reconquer Jerusalem.

Some scholars[18] argue that the cryptic last verse refers to a specific Christian King. The "Red One" of *Maoz Tzur*, they claim, refers to the red-bearded Frederick of Germany, who led the Third Crusade to recapture Jerusalem from Salah-a-din, the Turkish military genius who had taken it from the Crusaders after almost 100 years of Christian rule (1099-1187).[19] The Jews had every reason to fear the revival of the Crusades that had brought widespread pogroms, forced conversions, cancellation of debts, and pillage. They had every reason to pray for the defeat of the Red One who would have reestablished the Christian rule of Jerusalem that had involved the massacre of its Jews and a prohibition on further Jewish residence after the First Crusade.

Ultimately, the Red One drowned in Asia Minor during one of the battles, while his fellow Crusader King, red-haired Richard the Lion Hearted, arrived in the Holy Land by sea. Eventually, he too was unsuccessful in conquering Jerusalem and returned to England. King Richard and Robin Hood[20] are heroic figures in English medieval myths and in American children's stories where Richard's treacherous brother Prince John is the villain. However for the Jews, it was Richard and Frederick, the "Red Ones," who were the villains whose defeat, it was hoped, would open the messianic age.

A GERMAN CHRISTIAN MELODY

The popular tune for *Maoz Tzur* is borrowed from a folksong. It is written in a major chord. This shift from music in the minor to the major chord is typical of the changes of style reflecting the German Protestant revolt against Catholic Gregorian chants. The song was used as a military marching song (1504) and then (1523) set to the words of a Christian hymn by Martin Luther, founder of the Reformation. The lyrics read *"Nun freut euch lieben Christen gemein — Now be joyful you dear Christians altogether."* Later, the tune was adopted by German Jews who took it to

Venice. There a Catholic composer who visited the synagogue picked it up and reused it in Italy, for Italian dance numbers.[21]

---

18. Yom Tov Levinsky, *Sefer HaMoadim: Hanukkah*
19. See *The Big Book of Hanukkah*, Chapter I, the subsection, "The Christian Cult of the Maccabees."
20. Historians identify the origins of the legends of Robin Hood with an earlier period in English history, but his legends are later woven into the historical period of Richard and John during the Crusades.
21. L. Levi from *Sefer HaMoadim: Hanukkah*

*The Seal of Richard the Lion Heart,
the red-haired English Crusader King.*

The Holiness of the Candles:
Haneirot Hallalu

The Halachic warning *"Hanerot Hallalu"* is derived from the late Talmudic Tractate *Soferim*. The point is to warn the family **not** to use the light of these 36 Hanukkah candles (lit over 8 days, not counting the *shamash*). In fact, some versions of this section include exactly 36 words after the opening phrase: "Hanerot Halla**lu**," which can be understood playfully as "these candles are LU = 30 + 6." The Hebrew and Greek letters function also as numbers, so words can be translated into numbers using a system called "gematria."[22]

The holiness of the candles derives from their being dedicated to recalling the Divine miracle of rescue from the Greeks and the lighting of the Temple menorah at the original Rededication of the Temple by the Maccabees.[23] Unlike Shabbat candles which are meant to light up the meal at the table and to create a peaceful, sociable atmosphere, Hanukkah candles are placed at the doorway or windowsill as symbols for passersby. Since this is their purpose, unlike other lamps in the house, their light may not be used. As the *Shulchan Aruch* rules: "One may not use the Hanukkah candle even for another holy task like studying Torah [or making *havdalah* on Saturday evening of Hanukkah]. However, some rabbis [from Provence, France] permit secondary holy uses."[24]

22. Maharshal, see Daniel Sperber, *Minhagei Yisrael*, Vol. 5 p. 19
23. Sperber, p. 38-39   24. *Shulchan Aruch, Tur Orach Hayim* 673:1; Sperber, p. 24

The Vaad HaTzala Relief Organization distributes menorahs in a Displaced Persons camp in Germany, December 5, 1948.

(Haus der Bayerischen Geschichte)

A Personal Meditation on *Maoz Tzur*   BY ISMAR SCHORSCH

smar Schorsch, rabbi and historian, Chancellor of the Jewish Theological Seminary, offers an alternative reading of Maoz Tzur in the light of his family's flight from Nazi Germany:

Family history has graced me with a special affection for the holiday of Hanukkah. Fifty years ago, back in the fall of 1938, it literally marked a moment of redemption. As the last rabbi of Hanover, my father, along with thousands of other German Jews, was interned by the Nazis on the still unimaginable night of *Kristallnacht*. Several weeks later a visa to England, secured through the good offices of Joseph H. Hertz, the Chief Rabbi of the British Empire, managed to effect his release, and like our ancestors in Egypt, we left Germany in haste, by plane, on the first day of Hanukkah. My father was fond of recounting that in that fateful year we lit the first candle in Germany and the second in England. I had just turned three a month before and our dramatic flight was to become my only tangible memory of Germany.

The conjunction of Hanukkah with our personal escape from Nazi tyranny prompted my father later on to enliven our celebration of the festival with a lusty rendition of the traditional hymn, *Maoz Tzur*. While the practice among American Jews generally is to sing only the first stanza, and maybe the fifth, we sang all five, skipping only the sixth and final stanza. The poem's theme of redemption seemed to offer a poignant comment on our family's experience. Thus, in time, I developed an existential interest in the poem, spiced by the curious omission of its final stanza. When questioned, my father would simply declare that the stanza was a later and inferior addition.

[The last stanza, so often rewritten or censored, is in fact, a later addition.] The addition of the sixth stanza is an unabashed messianic plea for divine retribution upon Israel's Christian oppressors, often left untranslated by the modern prayerbooks that deign to print it. The sixth stanza begins with an acrostic: "strong" = "*Hazak*." It involves a theological reflection on the fragility of redemption from Israel's historic oppressors. Each celebration — including Hanukkah — is undermined by the rise of a new, wicked empire. Only the redemption engineered by God's "bared arm" offers triumph and the end of history.[25]

25. *Judaism* No. 148:4, Fall 1988, p. 45

The prayerbook's summary of the miraculous victory of the Hasmoneans is traditionally recited as part of the blessing after eating and in the Amidah prayers during the eight days of Hanukkah. Interestingly enough, only the military victories that enabled the rededication of the Temple are mentioned, not the miracle of the cruse of oil, the Talmudic legend.

[Thank you God,] for the miracles,	עַל הַנִּסִּים
for the liberation from the foreign yoke and for the rescues,	וְעַל הַפֻּרְקָן וְעַל הַגְּבוּרוֹת
for the heroism and for the military victories	וְעַל הַתְּשׁוּעוֹת וְעַל הַמִּלְחָמוֹת
that You did for our ancestors	שֶׁעָשִׂיתָ לַאֲבוֹתֵינוּ
in those days at this season [and in our own era].	בַּיָּמִים הָהֵם וּבַזְּמַן הַזֶּה.
In the days of Mattathias, son of Yochanan	בִּימֵי מַתִּתְיָהוּ בֶּן־יוֹחָנָן
[High Priest[26]], the Hasmonean, and his children,	[כֹּהֵן גָּדוֹל] חַשְׁמוֹנַאי וּבָנָיו
the evil Greek kingdom	כְּשֶׁעָמְדָה מַלְכוּת
[of Antiochus IV of Greater Syria]	יָוָן הָרְשָׁעָה
set out to make the Jewish people	עַל עַמְּךָ יִשְׂרָאֵל
forget your Torah	לְהַשְׁכִּיחָם תּוֹרָתֶךָ
and violate your laws.	וּלְהַעֲבִירָם מֵחֻקֵּי רְצוֹנֶךָ.
You acted with great mercy	וְאַתָּה בְּרַחֲמֶיךָ הָרַבִּים
and stood up for Israel in its time of trouble.	עָמַדְתָּ לָהֶם בְּעֵת צָרָתָם
You argued their case, You vindicated them,	רַבְתָּ אֶת־רִיבָם, דַּנְתָּ אֶת־דִּינָם,
and You avenged their wrongs.	נָקַמְתָּ אֶת־נִקְמָתָם,
You handed over the strong into the hands of the weak,	מָסַרְתָּ גִבּוֹרִים בְּיַד חַלָּשִׁים,
the many to the few,	וְרַבִּים בְּיַד מְעַטִּים,
the corrupt to the pure,	וּטְמֵאִים בְּיַד טְהוֹרִים,
the guilty to the innocent,	וּרְשָׁעִים בְּיַד צַדִּיקִים,
the arrogant to those loyal to the Torah.	וְזֵדִים בְּיַד עוֹסְקֵי תוֹרָתֶךָ.
Thereby You made a great and holy name	וּלְךָ עָשִׂיתָ שֵׁם גָּדוֹל וְקָדוֹשׁ בְּעוֹלָמֶךָ,
for Yourself and You brought great redemption	וּלְעַמְּךָ יִשְׂרָאֵל עָשִׂיתָ תְּשׁוּעָה גְדוֹלָה
and liberation to Your people.	וּפֻרְקָן כְּהַיּוֹם הַזֶּה.
Then Your children reentered	וְאַחַר כֵּן בָּאוּ בָנֶיךָ
the Holy of Holies,	לִדְבִיר בֵּיתֶךָ וּפִנּוּ אֶת־הֵיכָלֶךָ
purified Your Sanctuary	וְטִהֲרוּ אֶת־מִקְדָּשֶׁךָ,
and lit the lights in Your Temple courtyard.	וְהִדְלִיקוּ נֵרוֹת בְּחַצְרוֹת קָדְשֶׁךָ
They enacted these eight days of Hanukkah,	וְקָבְעוּ שְׁמוֹנַת יְמֵי חֲנֻכָּה אֵלּוּ,
dedicated to thanking You and to praising Your great name.	לְהוֹדוֹת וּלְהַלֵּל לְשִׁמְךָ הַגָּדוֹל.

26. Historically speaking, Mattathias did not descend from High Priests. His sons' victories led to their recognition as the Hasmonean High Priests.

CONTEMPORARY YIDDISH AND NORTH AMERICAN SONGS FOR HANUKKAH

OH HANUKKAH

Oh Hanukkah, Oh Hanukkah
Come light the menorah.
Let's have a party,
We'll all dance the hora.

Gather round the table,
We'll give you a treat —
S'vivon to play with,
Latkes to eat.

And while we
Are playing
The candles are burning low.
One for each night,
They shed a sweet light,
To remind us of days long ago.

אוי, חנוכה

אוי, חנוכה, אוי, חנוכה,
אַ יום־טוב אַ שיינער,
אַ לוסטיקער, אַ פריילעכער,
ניטאָ נאָך אַזוינער!

אַלע נאַכט אין דריידל
שפּילן מיר,
פרישע הייסע לאַטקעס
עסן מיר.

געשווינדער,
צינדט, קינדער,
די חנוכה־ליכטעלעך אָן.
זאָל יעדער באַזונדער
באַזינגען דעם וווּנדער
און טאַנצן פריילעך אין קאָן.

OY, KHANIKE[27]

Oy, khanike, oy, khanike,
A yontef a sheyner,
A lustiker, a freylekher,
Nito nokh azoyner!

Ale nakht in dreydl
Shpiln mir,
Frishe heyse latkes
Esn mir.

Geshvinder,
Tsindt, kinder,
Di khanike-likhtelekh on.
Zol yeder bazunder
Bazingen dem vunder
Un tantsn freylekh in kon.

---

27. Yiddish from *Yontefdike Teg, Song Book for the Jewish Holidays*, Workmen's Circle, 1985.
    The English version is not a literal translation.

I HAVE A LITTLE DREIDEL

I have a little dreidel,
I made it out of clay.
And when it's dry and ready,
Then dreidel I shall play.

Chorus:
  Oh dreidel, dreidel, dreidel,
  I made it out of clay;
  And when it's dry and ready,
  Then dreidel I shall play.

It has a lovely body,
With leg so short and thin.
And when it gets all tired,
It drops and then I win.

(Chorus again)

My dreidel's always playful,
It loves to dance and spin,
A happy game of dreidel,
Come play, now let's begin.

(Chorus again)

LIGHT ONE CANDLE[28]

by Peter Yarrow

Light one candle for the Maccabee children, for thanks that their light didn't die.
Light one candle for the pain they endured, when their right to exist was denied.
Light one candle for the terrible sacrifice, justice and freedom demand.
But light one candle for the wisdom to know when the peacemakers' time is at hand.

Chorus: Don't let the light go out.
It's lasted for so many years.
Don't let the light go out.
Let it shine through our love and our tears.

Light one candle for the strength that we need to never become our own foe.
Light one candle for those who are suffering the pain we learned so long ago.
Light one candle for all we believe in, that anger not tear us apart.
Light one candle to bind us together, with peace as a song in our heart.

What is the memory that's valued so highly, that we keep it alive in this flame?
What's the commitment to those who have died, when we cry out "they've not died in vain"?
We have come this far always believing that justice will somehow prevail.
This is the burden, this is the promise and this is what we will not fail.

---

28. "Light One Candle" (© 1983, Silver Dawn Music) was written for Peter Yarrow's singing group, Peter, Paul and Mary, for a Christmas concert in Carnegie Hall that fell on the third night of Hanukkah. Peter's reflections on folk music, social activism and his Jewish heritage appeared in an interview by Rahel Musleah that appeared in Hadassah magazine, Nov. 1994, p. 44. Permission requested.

THIS LITTLE LIGHT OF MINE

The light that shines is the light of love —
Lights the darkness from above.
It shines on me and it shines on you,
Shows what the power of love can do.
I'm gonna shine my light both far and near.
I'm gonna shine my light both bright and clear.
If there's a dark corner in this land,
I'm gonna let my little light shine!

Some say "It's dark, we cannot see"
But love lights up the world for me.

Some say "Turn around and just go hide"
But we have the power to change the tide.

Some call life a sad old story
But we see a world that's bound for glory.
The real power is yours and mine,
So let your little light shine!

Chorus: This little light of mine, I'm gonna let it shine!
Let it shine, let it shine, let it shine!

— *American folksong*

Folk Music and Freedom   BY PETER YARROW[28]

I believe as a Jew and as a human being that I have an ethical imperative to look at any circumstance that deprives people of their liberty. That's what fuels me. That's why I write the songs, why I sing the songs.

Folk music is a people-to-people expression. It doesn't say, "Look how brilliant a performer that person is." It says, "You can do this too." Its power is that it allows inclusiveness. It lets people realize we are together, that we care about each other. In acknowledging that, we say we all matter and that we can change the way things are. The whole idea of empowerment, the importance of that moment of finding a sense of togetherness, is for me a very Jewish concept.

CONTEMPORARY ISRAELI SONGS FOR HANUKKAH[29]

MEE Y'MALEIL

Mee y'maleil g'vurot Yisrael
Otan mee yimneh?
Hein b'khol dor yakum ha-gibor
Go-eil ha-am. (2x)

Sh'ma!
Ba-yamim ha-heim ba-z'man ha-zeh.
Makabi moshiyah u-fodeh
Uv'yameinu kol am Yisrael,
Yit'ached yakum v'yi-ga-el.

מִי יְמַלֵּל[30]

מִי יְמַלֵּל גְּבוּרוֹת יִשְׂרָאֵל,
אוֹתָן מִי יִמְנֶה?
הֵן בְּכָל דּוֹר יָקוּם הַגִּבּוֹר,
גּוֹאֵל הָעָם

שְׁמַע!
בַּיָּמִים הָהֵם בַּזְּמַן הַזֶּה
מַכַּבִּי מוֹשִׁיעַ וּפוֹדֶה.
וּבְיָמֵינוּ כָּל עַם יִשְׂרָאֵל
יִתְאַחֵד יָקוּם וְיִגָּאֵל!

WHO CAN RETELL

Who can retell the heroic deeds of Israel?[31]
Who can count them?
In every age, a hero arises
to redeem the people.

Listen!
In those days at this season
Judah the Maccabee rescued us.
Now in these days all the people of Israel
must unite and rise to redeem themselves.

---

29. Songs reprinted by permission of ACUM.
30. Words and music by Menashe Ravina, 20th C. Israel.
31. The verse from *Psalms* read originally "Who can retell the heroic deeds of God" but it has been rewritten to reflect the secular nationalist views of the Zionist pioneers.

MY CANDLE
(NURSERY SCHOOL SONG)

On Hanukkah I will light my little candle and sing my songs.

נֵר לִי

נֵר לִי, נֵר לִי,
נֵר לִי דַּקִּיק.
בַּחֲנֻכָּה
נֵרִי אַדְלִיק.
בַּחֲנֻכָּה
נֵרִי יָאִיר.
בַּחֲנֻכָּה
שִׁירִים אָשִׁיר.
בַּחֲנֻכָּה
נֵרִי יָאִיר.
בַּחֲנֻכָּה
שִׁירִים אָשִׁיר.

NER LI

Ner li, ner li,
Ner li dakik.
Ba-Hanukkah
Neri adlik.
Ba-Hanukkah
Neri Ya-ir,
Ba-Hanukkah
Shirim ashir.
Ba-Hanukkah
Neri ya-ir
Ba-Hanukkah
Shirim ashir

MY HANUKKAH MENORAH[32]

I have a "hanukkiya"
that laughs with fire
and whispers to me about
the little cruse of oil.

---

32. Music by Sh. Gluzman and words by N. Melamed.

חֲנֻכִּיָּה לִי יֵשׁ

חֲנֻכִּיָּה לִי יֵשׁ,
צוֹחֶקֶת בָּה הָאֵשׁ.
וְשָׂחָה לִי בַּלָּאט,
עַל כַּד קָטָן אֶחָד.
חֲנֻכִּיָּה שֶׁלִּי
אוֹרֵךְ לִי – הַעֲלִי!

MY DREIDEL

Dreidel, spin, spin, spin!

Hanukkah is a happy holiday for the people.

A great miracle happened there.

---

33. Words by Levin Kipnis. Music by N. Varsano

סְבִיבוֹן סֹב סֹב סֹב

סְבִיבוֹן סֹב סֹב סֹב
חֲנֻכָּה הוּא חַג טוֹב
חֲנֻכָּה הוּא חַג טוֹב
סְבִיבוֹן סֹב סֹב סֹב.
חַג שִׂמְחָה הוּא לָעָם
נֵס גָּדוֹל הָיָה שָׁם
נֵס גָּדוֹל הָיָה שָׁם
חַג שִׂמְחָה הוּא לָעָם.

S'VIVON, SOV, SOV, SOV!

S'vivon, sov, sov, sov!

Hanukkah, hu chag tov;

Hanukkah, hu chag tov;

S'vivon, sov, sov, sov.

Chag simcha hu la-am

Nes gadol haya sham;

Nes gadol haya sham;

Chag simcha hu la-am.

THESE DAYS OF HANUKKAH

We celebrate

the dedication

of our Temple

day and night.

We spin the dreidel,

we eat donuts (*sufganiyot*)

and light so many candles.

יְמֵי הַחֲנֻכָּה

יְמֵי הַחֲנֻכָּה חֲנֻכַּת מִקְדָּשֵׁנוּ
בְּגִיל וּבְשִׂמְחָה מְמַלְּאִים אֶת לִבֵּנוּ
לַיְלָה וָיוֹם סְבִיבוֹנֵנוּ יִסֹּב
סֻפְגָּנִיּוֹת נֹאכַל בָּם לָרֹב.
הָאִירוּ הַדְלִיקוּ
נֵרוֹת חֲנֻכָּה רַבִּים
עַל הַנִּסִּים וְעַל הַנִּפְלָאוֹת
אֲשֶׁר חוֹלְלוּ הַמַּכַּבִּים.

Y'MEI HA-HANUKKAH

Y'mei Ha-Hanukkah hannukat mikdasheynu

B'geel u'vesimcha m'mal-im et libeynu.

Lai'la vayom, svivoneiynu yisov

Sufganiyot nochal bam larov.

Ha-iru, hadliku

Neirot Hanukkah rabim

Al Hanissim v'al hanifla-ot

Asher chollelu Ha-Maccabim!

ONE LITTLE CRUSE

One little cruse (jug) of oil

Gave its light for eight whole days.

The whole people were amazed

It replenished itself.

Then everyone declared:

That is a miracle!

If it hadn't been for that one cruse of oil,

Our Temple would not have been filled with light.

כַּד קָטָן

כַּד קָטָן, כַּד קָטָן,
שְׁמוֹנָה יָמִים שַׁמְנוֹ נָתַן
כָּל הָעָם הִתְפַּלֵּא
מֵאֵלָיו הוּא מִתְמַלֵּא.
כָּל הָעָם אָז הִתְכַּנֵּס
וְהִכְרִיז: אַךְ, זֶהוּ נֵס!
אִלּוּלֵא כַּד זֶה נִשְׁאַר
מִקְדָּשֵׁנוּ לֹא הוּאַר.

KAD KATAN

Kad Katan (2x)

Shmona yamim, shamno natan

Kol ha-am, hit-palei

Mei-eilav hu hit-malei.

Kol ha-am az hit-kaneis

V'hichriz: ach, zehu neis!

Ee-lu-lei kad ze nishar

Mikdasheinu lo hu-ar.

ANU NOSIM LAPIDIM[35]

אָנוּ נוֹשְׂאִים לַפִּידִים

WE ARE CARRYING TORCHES

Anu nosim lapidim	אָנוּ נוֹשְׂאִים לַפִּידִים	We are carrying torches
b'lei-lot afei-lim	בְּלֵילוֹת אֲפֵלִים	through dark nights
dorchim ha-shvi-lim	דּוֹרְכִים הַשְּׁבִילִים	We tread along paths
mi-tachat rag-leinu	מִתַּחַת רַגְלֵינוּ	Beneath our feet.
u-mi asher lev lo	וּמִי אֲשֶׁר לֵב לוֹ	Whoever has heart,
ha-tzamei la-or	הַצָּמֵא לָאוֹר	Whoever is thirsty for the light
yi-sa et einav	יִשָּׂא אֶת עֵינָיו	Let them raise their eyes
v'li-bo ei-leinu la-or	וְלִבּוֹ אֵלֵינוּ לָאוֹר	And their hearts to the light
v'ya-vo!	וְיָבוֹא!	Let them come!
Neis lo kara lanu	נֵס לֹא קָרָה לָנוּ.	A miracle never happened to us.
pach shemen lo matzanu	פַּח שֶׁמֶן לֹא מָצָאנוּ.	No vessel of oil did we find.
la-emek halachnu	לָעֵמֶק הָלַכְנוּ.	Rather, we descended to the valley
heh-hara alinu	הֶהָרָה עָלִינוּ.	And we climbed the mountain.
mayanot orot	מַעְיָנוֹת הָאוֹרוֹת	We discovered wellsprings
ha-genuzim gi-li-nu	הַגְּנוּזִים גִּלִּינוּ.	of hidden light.
neis lo kara lanu	נֵס לֹא קָרָה לָנוּ.	A miracle never happened to us.
pach shemen lo matzanu	פַּח שֶׁמֶן לֹא מָצָאנוּ.	No vessel of oil did we find.
ba-sela chatzavnu ad dam	בַּסֶּלַע חָצַבְנוּ עַד דָּם	We quarried in the stone until we bled.
Va-y'hi or!	וַיְהִי אוֹר.	"Let there be light"[36]

35. By Aharon Zeev (lyrics) and Mordechai Zeira (music)   36. *Genesis* 1:3

בָּאנוּ חֹשֶׁךְ לְגָרֵשׁ

בָּאנוּ חֹשֶׁךְ לְגָרֵשׁ.
בְּיָדֵינוּ אוֹר וָאֵשׁ
כָּל אֶחָד הוּא אוֹר קָטָן
וְכֻלָּנוּ – אוֹר אֵיתָן.
סוּרָה חֹשֶׁךְ!
הָלְאָה שְׁחוֹר!
סוּרָה – מִפְּנֵי הָאוֹר!

EXPELLING THE DARKNESS[34]

With fire in our hands we have

come to chase away the darkness.

Each of us has a small light

but together we are a powerful light.

Away with darkness — here

comes the light.

---

34. Sara Levi-Tana wrote this Secular Zionist nursery
school song that celebrates the power of human
beings to dispel darkness.

Anu Nosim Lapidim — No Miracles Happened Here

This militant secularist song was sung by the Zionist pioneers who believed that the belief in supernatural miracles (like the legend of the cruse of oil and the messiah who will come on a white donkey) prevented Jews from trying to redeem themselves. Thus the song argues that only when Divine miracles were denied, would human beings find the light that is within and create their own world saying, in God's stead, *"Let there be light."* Not prayer but pioneering sweat and blood in the valleys and mountains of Eretz Yisrael in the early 20th Century reveal the inner cruse of oil that can illuminate the Jewish future.

This song was central to the Zionist public celebration of Hanukkah in the pre-state period. The Independence Day celebrations after 1948 have absorbed and displaced the public processions of pre-state Hanukkah. Independence Day evening begins on Mount Herzl with the lighting of 12 torches by 12 citizens representing the history of Zionism. At that time this song *"We are carrying torches"* is still sung, though religious Zionists have objected to its polemical wording.

14

The Maccabees' "Megillah"

The "Bar Kochba (B.K.)/ HaKoach" Jewish athletics club of Berlin (1902) was one of many Jewish sports organizations at the turn of the century seeking, on one hand, to emulate the non-Jewish and often anti-semitic sports fraternities and, on the other, to revive Jewish pride. Clubs were named after ancient military heroes, like the Maccabees and Bar Kochba, the tough guerrilla fighter who led the last revolt against Roman rule in 132 CE (Bildarchiv Preussicher Kulturbesitz, Berlin).

The Maccabees' "Megillah"

These eight selections from the Books of the Maccabees and other historical and midrashic sources have been edited to read aloud, primarily for teenagers and adults. You may wish to read them while the candles burn on each of the eight nights of Hanukkah. For young children we suggest reading one of the many children's versions available in bookstores or libraries or retelling the story orally (See ideas and cartoons suggested in Chapter II, page 119).

IN PURSUIT OF ACCEPTANCE AT ALL COSTS

THE TURNCOAT HIGH PRIEST JASON (174-171 BCE)

THE HANUKKAH CEREMONY

Brachot

Songs

Maccabees Megillah

Profiles

Spiritual Meditations

In the days before the Maccabees, the Jews were content to live in a small mountain province up in the hills of Jerusalem where they kept the Torah, the official constitution of Judea. The traditional High Priest served in the Temple but also ruled over all the local affairs in Judea. In international affairs, Judea was ruled by the heirs of Alexander the Great, whose capital was in Antioch, Syria. Cities and provinces that chose to abandon their traditional laws and to follow the Greek ways of Alexander were invited to participate in the excitement of the Olympics and the spectacle of pagan worship as well as in the international trade that enriched the leaders of the provinces.

Below is a partisan history, written by the Maccabees, of the way a new brand of High Priest rose to power and voluntarily introduced Greek customs into Jerusalem, especially sports competition.

LET'S MAKE A NEW COVENANT

In those days there arose out of Israel lawless men.[1] They persuaded many, saying, **"Let us go and make a covenant with the nations around us, for ever since the time we became separated from the nations, many misfortunes have overtaken us."**[2]

Jason [one of these ambitious assimilationists] **obtained the high priesthood through corruption** by promising the king, Antiochus, 360 talents of silver.[3] Besides this he promised to pay 150 more, for the authority to set up a **gymnasium** and a training place for youth and to enroll the people of Jerusalem as citizens of Antioch [the new name given to Jerusalem in honor of Antiochus].

When the king had consented, Jason immediately brought his own people over to the **Greek way of living**. He introduced new customs contrary to the Torah and willingly established a gymnasium right under the acropolis [the high plateau of the city where the public buildings are found], and he made the finest of the young men wear the broad-brimmed Greek sunhat. The cultivation of Greek fashions and the adoption of foreign customs reached such a pitch because of the excessive wickedness of this impious Jason — who was no high priest at all [as far as the Maccabees were concerned]. Even the priests no longer had their heart and soul in the service on the altar, but rather disdained the sanctuary and neglected the sacrifices. Whenever the competition of the discus-throwing was announced, they hurried to take part in the unlawful exercises in the wrestling school. Regarding as worthless the things their ancestors valued, the priests now considered Greek standards the finest.

THE RELIGIOUS DILEMMA OF THE JEWISH OLYMPIANS

Being accepted by the majority culture of the Greeks required the young Jews to make many compromises. Involvement in Greek sports was the benchmark of acceptance. But in those days the Olympics were a religious as well as an athletic event. To participate in the games meant to compete in the nude. However the Jewish sportsmen were afraid that the Greeks would see that the Jews were circumcised and would ridicule this "primitive, barbaric" ritual, as they called it. Many young men would do anything to avoid this shame and they submitted to a painful operation of "un-circumcision." Some wanted to play in the games but not to worship idols. This is the story of their dilemma:

Now the Olympic games, which were held every four years [among teams from the Greek cities], were being hosted in Tyre [in Lebanon] and the king was present. So the

---

1. The people interested in assimilation are called "lawless," as the Maccabees called them, because these Jews wanted to repeal the law of the Torah, the covenant with God, the constitution of Judea.   2. *I Maccabees* 1:11

3. A talent, a weight measure of gold or silver, is equal to 60 mina. Each mina is 100 drachma and each drachma is 6 obol. A talent is approximately 25-40 kilograms.

vile Jason sent envoys from Jerusalem who were **citizens of Antioch** [the new name for Jerusalem] to carry three hundred silver drachmas for the **sacrifice to Hercules** [the deified patron of the Olympics]. But even those who carried it thought it should not be used for a pagan sacrifice, as that was not fitting, but should be spent in some other way. So this money, intended by its sender [Jason the High Priest] for the sacrifice to Hercules, was used to outfit ships [as a gift to the monarch].[4]

---

4. *I Maccabees* 4: 7-20

The Jewish Steeple Chase at the Maccabiah in Israel
(Central Zionist Archives, Jerusalem)

Greek Olympic Horse Racing
(5th century BCE vase)

Hercules the Greek Hero and the Disney Hero

By virtue of the Disney cartoon epic, Hercules has been confirmed as an American child's hero. However, the Jews had a very ambivalent attitude to the ancient Hercules to whom they were asked to make sacrifices at the Greek Olympics. The Greek mythological figure is quite different from the Disney version.

Hercules, known in Greek as Heracles, was believed to have been born to a human mother and a divine father, Zeus. Therefore Zeus' divine spouse Hera, who was jealous of this relationship, tried over and over to kill Hercules. Even in his crib he had to strangle two serpents she sent to kill him. As an adult he was tested by 12 "labors" including subduing a lion, a hydra, a boar, a hind and a bird. Traditionally he is considered the founder of the Olympics and his symbols are the lion skin cape, the hood, the club, the bow and arrows. After his death, the half-god Hercules became a full god. He is the primary "hero" — a semi-divine status. The royal family of Alexander the Great claimed descent from Hercules. The mythological story of the Greek gods reveals the depth of jealousy and violence within the family. Interestingly enough in promoting Hercules as a hero for American children, Disney's version turned Hera, Zeus and Hercules into a happy family. Baby Hercules is portrayed as a sweet baby threatened by the god Hades, rather than endangered by his own family's adultery, jealousy and vengeance.

Hercules is received into heaven. A winged figure of Victory (Nike) presents him with a garland, and the god Zeus looks on, bearing his winged thunderbolt and sceptre. Hercules has his traditional attributes: a club, bow and lionskin.

(From an amphora made in Athens, c. 470-450 BCE.)

The Olympics and the Maccabiah — An Ironic Imitation?

The original Maccabees rejected the temptation of Jews to participate in the Greek Olympics. Yet when the modern Olympics were renewed, the latter-day self-styled heirs of the Maccabees — modern Zionists — were anxious to develop Jewish sports as part of our national revival and to create a parallel to the Olympics called the Maccabiah. To some, especially the Ultra-Orthodox, the games called the "Maccabiah" are a travesty to the memory of the Maccabees. However, the ancient Olympics were very different in spirit from the modern Olympics and their Jewish counterpart, the Maccabiah. The ancient Olympics were pagan festivals and under the heirs to Alexander the Great they helped unite all Greek-speaking peoples to the exclusion and denigration of "barbarians" of other national loyalties. In the modern period the Olympics are religiously neutral and the national pride of each delegation is honored and reinforced.

The **ancient Olympics** originated from the Greek sports competition held in Olympia, Greece, from 776 BCE to 395 CE. It began with a footrace the length of a stadium and developed into a seven-day celebration in honor of Zeus whose sacred mountain was Mount Olympus. It included the discus throw, footrace, pentathlon, wrestling, long jump and chariot racing (in the hippodrome — *hippo* is horse and *drome* is arena). The ancient discus weighed somewhere between the modern discus (4.4 lb) and the modern shot put (16 lb).

The Olympic games were held every four years at Mount Olympus sometime between August 6 and September 19, and were protected by a Pan Hellenic truce, so contestants of warring cities could compete. Similar games were held in other cities like Tyre. The traditional founder of the Olympics was Hercules (Heracles). Originally "amateurs" competed — only free-born Greek males. Their victory earned them an olive wreath and the praise of poets and sculptors. Later professional athletes competed and won monetary awards.

The Tenth Maccabiah:
A Running Star of David

(Dan Reisinger, designer of the Maccabiah emblem for the 10th Maccabiah, by courtesy of the designer)

The purpose of the Olympics[5] during the Hellenist period of Antiochus was to turn the elites of various ethnic groups ruled by the Greek kings into soldiers and citizens devoted in body and mind to the Seleucid monarchy in Damascus. Training for the Olympics took place in the gymnasium where sports and Greek culture were mixed in a fiercely competitive atmosphere. Jews who needed to compete in the nude voluntarily underwent a reverse circumcision called an "epispasm" to stretch the remaining skin to cover the penis. Gymnasium studies and regional Olympics involved the worship of Zeus and the deified Hercules as well as the ruler Antiochus, who considered himself a manifestation (*epiphanes*) of the sun-god.

The **modern Olympics** were revived in 1896 CE, under the patronage of the King of Greece in Athens. The modern **Maccabiah** was promoted by the Zionist Joseph Yekutiel who convinced Meyer Dizengoff, Mayor of Tel Aviv, to build Israel's first sports stadium and then convinced the Zionist Maccabiah sports clubs around the world to come to Eretz Israel to hold the first World Jewish Olympics in 1932. Five hundred participants from 23 countries came in 1932 and 1700 Jewish sports people participated in the Maccabiah in 1935, at a time when Jews were excluded from the Olympics held in Nazi Germany in Berlin, 1936.

---

5. **Greek sports** events were called *"agones"* (as in "agony") meaning contests, which provided individuals a chance to achieve glory and immortality, while **Roman sports** events were called "ludi" (meaning spectator games) to entertain the public. In Rome the *hippodrome* (for chariot racing) and *Circus Maximus* (for horse racing) held 250,000 spectators. Rome loved violent "games" best, especially gladiators fighting animals, wrestling on the *pancratium* (an all-out bout with kicking, no holds barred except biting and gouging eyes). Generally Greeks looked up to Olympic athletes who competed naked, while Romans looked down on sports performers who stripped naked to compete in public. The most violent Roman "sports" were competitions to the death by gladiators. Most of the gladiators were captured enemy soldiers who could only win their freedom if they survived 100 days of mortal combat. Only 88 survived in 400 years of bloody "games" that were provided for free by the Caesar to their male citizens as part of a policy of bread and circuses to keep the populace happy.

THE
HANUKKA
CEREMON

Bracho

Songs

Maccabe
Megilla

1st Candl
Assimilati

A Religious Dilemma:
Yom Kippur and Sandy Koufax

The United States has often been a melting pot that subtly pressures individuals to pursue competitive success through conformity. Minority religious scruples have not always been appreciated. But certain individual competitors who have shown the courage not to compromise their beliefs, have taught the West to be more tolerant of difference. The British movie *Chariots of Fire* dramatizes the dilemma of an observant Christian runner from Scotland (1924) who refuses to compete on Sunday. A real-life sportsman faced such a decision on a highly publicized day in his life — the famous Jewish pitcher, Sandy Koufax, at the World Series in 1965 on Yom Kippur.

A 6-foot-2 left-handed pitcher, Sandy Koufax was a slow starter for the Brooklyn and later the Los Angeles Dodgers. In 1961, he showed the first consistent signs of greatness, striking out a National League record 269 batters. Then, in his final five seasons, he dominated, producing the remarkable record of 111-34 with a 2.02 earned-run average over 1,377 innings from 1962 through 1966, leading the league in ERA (earned run average) each year. Koufax won three Cy Young Awards. "Hitting against him is like eating soup with a fork," Pittsburgh Pirates slugger Willie Stargell said.

Koufax pitched a National League record four no-hitters in four consecutive seasons, including a perfect game. Twice he fanned 18 batters in a game, and in 1965 he whiffed 382, a major-league record. In 1963, he won the MVP (Most Valuable Player Award) with a 25-5 record, "I can see how he won 25 games," Yankees catcher Yogi Berra said. "What I don't understand is how he lost five." But in 1964 Koufax developed arthritis in his throwing arm.

In 1965 Koufax recovered and went 26-8 with a 2.04 ERA to win his second Cy Young award and help his team to the World Series. The first game of the World Series fell on Yom Kippur, October 6, 1965, in the Twin Cities, Minneapolis and St. Paul. Despite the pressure to win and the honor of being asked to pitch the opening game of the World Series, Sandy Koufax decided to go to the synagogue rather than to the mound. He pitched the next day and lost. But then he blanked the Minnesota Twins in Games 5 and 7 to give the Dodgers the World Series.

With his lifetime record of 165-87, 2.76 ERA and 2,396 strikeouts in 2,324⅓ innings, in 1972 he became, at 36, the youngest player voted into the Hall of Fame. But his fame among American Jews of the 1960's also rests on his quiet pride in being a Jew and his courage to set priorities — Yom Kippur comes before the World Series.

Sandy Koufax
(Courtesy of National Baseball Hall of Fame Library, Cooperstown, NY)

THE RELIGIOUS PERSECUTION OF THE JEWS IN JUDEA

KING ANTIOCHUS, THE ROYAL "MANIAC" OF THE GREEK DYNASTY IN SYRIA (169-167 BCE)

THE HANUKKA CEREMO

Brach

Songs

Maccabe Megilla

2nd Cand Persecut

ANTIOCHUS PLUNDERS THE TEMPLE AND STEALS THE GOLD MENORAH (169 BCE)

The villain of Hanukkah was King Antiochus IV who considered himself all powerful and even divine, because he was the heir to the 150 year reign of Alexander the Great's empire. In one lightning-ride Alexander had come from Greece (Macedonia) and conquered the whole Middle East from Turkey to Egypt to India (332 BCE). No wonder Alexander and later his heirs considered themselves divine and their culture — the Greek way — the only one worthy of the newly conquered subjects, whatever their traditional way of life had been. On his deathbed, Alexander had divided his kingdom among his officers including Seleucus, ruler of Greater Syria, who was Antiochus' ancestor. (Note that the "Greeks" of the Hanukkah story are actually from Greater Syria and their king's capital is Antioch, not Athens.) Here is the Maccabees' version of what happened when Antiochus IV came to power.

There emerged a wicked offspring [from the dynasty of Seleucus] named **Antiochus Epiphanes**. [In 169 BCE] the wicked Antiochus Epiphanes entered Jerusalem with a large force. **In his arrogance he went into the sanctuary and took the gold altar and the menorah for the light.** He also discovered and plundered the hidden treasuries of silver and gold. Then he massacred many people. There was **great mourning** everywhere throughout Israel. Rulers and elders groaned, girls and young men fainted away, and the beauty of the women faded. Every bridegroom began to lament, and the bride in the bridal chamber grieved.

A CALL FOR UNITY AND BROTHERHOOD

Later the king wrote to his whole kingdom that they should all become one people, and everyone should give up his

Plundering the Temple. Antiochus pays off his debts by stealing the golden ritual objects (169 BCE). The enormous weight of the booty is shown in the posture of the soldiers carrying it, while the violence used against the population is portrayed in the background. The architectural style, of course, reflects the artist's period, not that of Antiochus.

(A 15th century French illuminated copy of Josephus, Wars of the Jews, *Bibliotheque Nationale Paris).*

Antiochus IV

ordinances. Anyone who did not obey the command of the king would die. The king appointed inspectors over all the people, and he ordered the towns of Judah, every one of them, to offer pagan sacrifices. Many of the people who were ready to forsake the Torah joined with them and they did evil in the land, and forced Israel [loyal Jews] to hide in every refuge they could find.[6]

THE DEDICATION OF THE TEMPLE TO ZEUS (167 BCE)

Not long after, the king sent an **old Athenian** to force the Jews to forsake the laws of their ancestors and to cease governing their lives according to the laws of God. [He forced them] to pollute the Temple in Jerusalem and dedicate it to the Olympian Zeus, [god of the heavens]. This most grievously intensified the evil, for the Greeks filled the Temple with riotous revelry, amusing themselves with prostitutes and lying with women within the sacred precincts. **Jews could not keep Shabbat or celebrate the festivals of their ancestors or admit that they were Jews in any way at all.**

On the celebration of the **king's birthday**, they were forced to taste the sacrifices, and when the festival of Dionysus was celebrated, the Jews were compelled to wear wreaths of ivy and march in procession in his honor.[7]

On the fifteenth day of Kislev [167 BCE] Antiochus erected a "dreadful desecration" [which probably refers to an idol of Zeus] upon the Temple's altar, and in the surrounding towns of Judah they built pagan altars. **At the doors of their houses** and in the squares they burned incense and wherever they found scrolls of the Torah, they tore them up and burned them. If anyone was found who possessed a book of the covenant or respected the Torah, the king's decree condemned him or her to death. **On the twenty-fifth of the month they offered a pagan sacrifice upon the altar.**[8]

particular practices. All the peoples [of the empire] assented to the command of the king. The king sent word by written edicts to Jerusalem and the towns of Judah ordering them:

(1) to follow practices foreign to the country and put a stop to all sacrifices at the sanctuary;

(2) to break the Sabbath and profane the festivals; to pollute the sanctuary and the priests;

(3) to build altars and sacred precincts and chapels for idols and sacrifice hogs and ritually impure cattle; and to leave their sons uncircumcised and defile themselves with every profane practice

[The king wanted Israel to] **forget the Torah** and change all their religious

---

6. *I Maccabees* 1: 1-10, 20-21, 24-27, 33-34, 37, 41-53
7. *II Maccabees* 6: 1-7   8. *I Maccabees* 1: 54-61

The Mark of Dionysius — the God of Mania

The festival of Dionysus, celebrated in Jerusalem during the persecutions of Antiochus, was dedicated to the son of Zeus who is reputed to be half-human and half-beast, half male and half female. Simultaneously both young and old, Dionysus is the god of *mania* (ecstasy and madness) as well as of wine. This fluid god of masks, who violates all borders, also became known as the god of the afterlife.

During the Dionysian festivals women often joined in ecstatic dance, carried phallic symbols, dressed in the skin of fawns and wore a wreath of ivy.[9] These women went up into the mountains, where they tore apart wild animals with their bare hands and ate their raw meat.

In the *Third Book of Maccabees* 2:29 a kind of Dionysian "circumcision" is reported. The Greek Egyptian ruler Ptolemy Philopater ordered that all the Jews in Egypt be branded with the Mark of Dionysus — an ivy leaf shaped sign. The Maccabees regarded the worship of this bizarre god as a pollution of Jerusalem.

---

9. In Greece each type of wreath had a different significance. The olive wreath signified an Olympic winner; the rose was for the priests of Aphrodite the goddess of love, and the ivy was reserved for the rites of Dionysus including the theater performances held under his auspices.

Anyone could see how miserable the people were. Two women were arrested for circumcising their children, and they were led publicly about the city with their babies hanging at their breasts, and then thrown from the top of the wall. Others, who had gathered in caves nearby to keep the seventh day in secret, were betrayed and all were burned together because they had refused to defend themselves on their most holy day.[10]

Yet many in Israel stood firm and resolved in their hearts not to eat what was unclean; they preferred death to violating the sacred covenant, and so they died. Israel suffered intensely.[11]

PORTRAIT OF A MADMAN IN POWER
by Emil Schurer[12]

Antiochus IV Epiphanes reigned over Syria from 175-163 BCE. He was by nature a genuine despot, eccentric and unpredictable, at one moment lavishly generous, affectedly fraternizing with the common people, and then again, ferocious and

---

10. *II Maccabees* 6: 10-11   11. *I Maccabees* 1: 62-64

12. From Emil Schurer, *The History of the Jewish People in the Age of Jesus*, p. 146-147, by permission of T. & T. Clark, Ltd., Publishers.

tyrannical, as his treatment of Judea demonstrates. The characteristics outlined by Polybius, the ancient historian, portray the more pleasant aspect of his bizarre personality.

Sometimes Antiochus IV would slip away from the palace, unnoticed by his servants, appearing in the city at one time here, at another time there, sauntering along in the company of one or two others. Very frequently he could be seen in the workshops of the silversmiths and goldsmiths, where he would chat with the artisans and seek to impress them with his love of art. Then he would condescend to engage in familiar conversation with any of the common people he happened to meet, and carouse with strangers of the lowest rank whom he stumbled upon by chance. On learning however, that somewhere young people were holding a drinking bout, he would march in unannounced with horn and bagpipe, so that most of them, being frightened by this strange sight, would take flight. Quite often he would exchange his royal robes for a toga, go to the forum and apply as a candidate for an office. He would then seize some people by the hand and embrace others, asking them to give him their vote. If he succeeded in

obtaining the office and was seated according to custom in an ivory chair, he would take note of the contracts signed in the forum and give his decisions in a serious and conscientious manner.

Reasonable folk, therefore, did not know what to make of him. Some regarded him as a simple and modest man, while others said that he was mad. He acted in a similar fashion when he distributed gifts. To some he gave dice made of bone, to others dates, while another group received gold. When he happened to meet someone whom he had never seen before, he would bestow upon him unexpected presents.

Antiochus used to frequent the public baths, when they were quite full of ordinary citizens, and had vessels with precious perfumes brought to him. When somebody once said to him, "You kings are fortunate to have such ointments of exquisite fragrance," he went the next day, without saying anything to the man, to the place where he bathed, and had a large vessel of the most precious ointment poured over his head. Then everyone [in the public bath] rose and rushed forward to receive a share of this aromatic perfume, but because of the slippery floor, many fell over amid shouts of laughter, and the king himself joined in the mirth.

The ancient historians also emphasize Antiochus' love of luxury and his munificence. Brilliant spectacles, magnificent buildings, regal presents, these were his chief delights. But in everything he inclined towards senseless extremes, so that Polybius spoke of him as *"epimanes"* (maniac) rather than *"epiphanes"* (the god who manifests himself).

The policies and motives of Antiochus remain a matter of controversy. It may be that **Tacitus** [the ancient historian] judged him correctly when he said that **Antiochus wished to take from the Jews their superstitions and to teach them Greek customs**, but that he was prevented by the outbreak of the Parthian (Persian) war from rendering "the detestable nation" more civilized.

The Dancers of Pompeii. Antiochus IV is described as an eccentric man who would "crash" a private party "quite unceremoniously with a fife and a procession of musicians." *(3rd century BCE mosaic from Pompeii, Italy, recovered from the destruction caused by the volcanic eruption of Mount Vesuvius in ancient times)*

The all-conquering imperial Greeks believed they had a universal rational philosophy that no intelligent or humane person could reject. Hence they reacted with venom and violent intolerance to those who maintained their cultural differences.

Ancient Antisemitism and the Jewish Hatred for Humankind

The earliest forms of antisemitism developed in the Hellenist world of Alexander the Great's heirs. Precisely because the all-conquering imperial Greeks believed they had a universal rational philosophy that no intelligent or humane person could reject, they reacted with venom and violent intolerance to those who wished to maintain their cultural and religious differences. Greeks and Romans who heard of the Jews' bizarre customs often attributed to them barbaric rationales. They believed circumcision to be a mutilation of the sacred body and a practice that abnormally increases sexual desire. They considered Shabbat and the Sabbatical year a sign of laziness since the Jews wasted 1/7 of life on inactivity. Pork was forbidden by the Jews, they claimed, because Jews worshiped pigs. In general, the ancient antisemites claimed that dietary restrictions, Shabbat prohibitions and circumcision reflect a peculiar Jewish **misanthropy**, the hatred of humankind, taught by the Torah.

The Greek historian Diodorus reports that Antiochus IV tried to smash the taboos of the Jews in 169 BCE in the most shocking manner:

> Since Antiochus Epiphanes was shocked by such [Jewish] hatred directed against all humankind, he had set himself to break down their traditional practices. Accordingly, he sacrificed a great hog before the idol on the open-air altar and poured its blood over [the Jews]. Then, having prepared the hog's flesh, he ordered that the Jews' holy books, containing the [Torah's] xenophobic [anti-foreigner] laws, be sprinkled with the broth of this meat. The **lamp [menorah]**, which they call undying *[ner tamid]* since it burns continually in the Temple, was to be extinguished. Antiochus ordered that the High Priest and the rest of the Jews be compelled to partake of that meat.

A generation later the royal advisors to Antiochus VII strongly advised the king "to wipe out completely the nation of the Jews, since they alone of all nations avoided dealings with any other people and looked upon all men as their enemies." [13]

---

13. *Diodorus Bibliotheca Historica* XXXIV 1:1-3

The Decrees of Antiochus IV (167 BCE–164 BCE)

1. No Jewish sacrifices may be offered in the Temple of God. Instead, mandatory sacrifices of pigs and impure animals were dedicated to Zeus on the Temple's altar.

2. Pagan temples were to be built throughout Judea.

3. No circumcisions were allowed on pain of death to child, parent and *mohel* (the one who does ritual circumcision).

4. The Torah was to be forgotten and its legal system replaced with Greek law.

5. Shabbat and holidays were to be desecrated.

6. The celebration of the Emperor's birthday was enforced including the eating of sacrifices made in his honor.

7. Participation in Dionysian processions crowned with ivy wreaths was required.

8. It was prohibited to identify oneself as a Jew (including, perhaps, the prohibition of the use of Jewish names) *(see Sidebar entitled "Sticks and Stones")*.

THE HANUKKA CEREMON

Brache

Songs

Maccabe Megilla

2nd Cand
Persecuti

"Sticks and Stones" or "What's in a [German-Jewish] Name?"   BY JERRY MULLER

Antiochus sent an old Athenian to forcibly Hellenize the Jews. One could not "admit being a Jew at all" (II Maccabees 6:6). Some scholars understand that Jewish names were forbidden. Even before this decree many Jews voluntarily adopted double names — one Greek and one Jewish — including Mattathias' five sons such as Judah Maccabeus (Greek for hammer). With this new decree, name changing now became mandatory.

Many Jews in the modern period have changed their names or chosen their children's names in order to ease their social acceptance in Western society. Below is an intriguing review of name changing in Germany in the last two centuries — sometimes mandatory and sometimes voluntary.

Dietz Bering's book, *The Stigma of Names: Antisemitism in German Daily Life, 1812-1933* (1987), serves as an historical refutation of the adage that "sticks and stones may break my bones, but names can never hurt me."

Until the early 19th century, most Jews in central Europe did not have surnames; they were known to one another by their given names and by their patronymic (their father's name) as indeed, Jews continue to be known for religious purposes (when called up to read the Torah). It was the modern, bureaucratic state which demanded that they take permanent surnames, the better to administer them. In Prussia, Jews took surnames in 1812, as part of the process of their admission to citizenship by the reformist government of the day.

Far from being routine matters of registration, requests for the transformation of that most intimate and private possession — one's name — were subject to policy changes within the bureaucracy, the changes which reflected both the willingness and the resistance of Germans to see the Jews integrated into their society.

The desire to change one's name reflected a willingness for assimilation, but also the pressure felt by those with names perceived as "too Jewish." Take for example the plea of Wolff Itzig of Danzig who wrote to the Ministry of the Interior early in the twentieth century and asked to change his surname. "I have enclosed with my petition a number of documents from firms which all declared themselves unable to engage my son since his name was offensive," he wrote.

When Jews were first compelled to adopt surnames, they typically took their patronymic as their permanent surnames (such as Moses, Levy, Hirsch, or Issak) or adopted names that recalled the Hebrew original (such as "Markus" in place of "Mordechai"). Some also changed their first names: but in so doing they chose German names with identical initial letters (such as "Moritz" in place of "Moses"). By the second half of the century, these names too were stigmatized as Jewish, and a new round of name-changing began in which Jews gave up the principle of consonance entirely, in order to adopt names that were entirely inconspicuous. Amongst the most stigmatized of names, Bering shows, was "Isidor," a Greek name adopted by many Jews because of its consonance with the traditional Jewish names Isaac, Israel, or Itzig.

Bering notes that actually few Jews officially tried to change their names, since this was perceived by Jews themselves as a form of abandonment of Jewish identity. Among Jews there was an aversion to name-escapers, which accounts for the frequency of the theme in Jewish humor, second only to that of Jewish apostates [converts to Christianity], who were similarly stigmatized through humor, for what Jews regarded as ignoble opportunism. The thousands of requests for name changes despite this intra-Jewish sentiment testifies to the pressures of anti-semitism felt by Jews with stigmatized names.

[Ironically, there were times when Jews wanted names that were *less* German sounding. In the 20th century a popular German Jewish name was Adolf. However during World War II many German Jewish refugees in England who had been born with the name Adolf, officially changed their first names to dissociate themselves from Nazi Germany. At that time many German Jewish refugees in England were unjustly suspected of being sympathetic with the Nazi enemy and were sent to enemy alien detention camps along with non-Jewish German citizens].

Name Changing in America

"Making-it-in-America" in the early 20th century often involved deliberate self-estrangement and accommodation of one's most precious family heirloom — one's name — to the sometimes snobbish expectations of one's Gentile neighbor. Charles Silberman in *A Certain People* recalls how the New York telephone company once rejected the application of "Prenowitz" but accepted an edited version under "Prentice." Silberman's aunt insisted he change his Jewish sounding last name "Silberman" to something more American. When he refused, she was enraged and argued, "you owe it to your poor parents to do whatever is necessary to become successful." Ironically Charles Silberman's grandfather had already changed his European name from Zarkey to Silberman. As a peddler in the 1870's in Des Moines, Iowa, among farmers of German origin, his grandfather had picked a new name off a label in a haberdashery (hat) shop — "Silberman."

Famous Name Changes in Hollywood

To gain acceptance in the days of the great melting pot in America and even today, popularity-conscious performers often change their names to less Jewish sounding appellations. For example:

Jack Benny from Ben Kubelsky
Eddie Cantor from Israel Iskowitz
George Burns from Nathan Birnbaum
Ed Wynn from Isaiah Leopold
Tony Curtis from Bernie Schwartz
Kirk Douglas from Issur Danielovich
John Garfield from Julius Garfinkle
Peter Lowe from Laszlo Lowenstein
Jill St. John from Jill Oppenheim
Lauren Bacall from Joan Paske
Paul Muni from Muni Weisenfreund
David Copperfield from David Kotkin
Winona Ryder from Winona Horowitz
Barry Manilow from Barry Alan Pincus

Elazar the Scribe is martyred for refusing to eat pork at the command of Antiochus
(Gustav Dore, 19th century France)

THE FIRST RELIGIOUS MARTYRS IN HISTORY:

ELAZAR THE ELDERLY SCRIBE AND HANNAH AND HER SEVEN SONS (167-165 BCE)

When Antiochus decided to force Hellenism on the Jews, he inadvertently created the first recorded example of martyrdom. The Greek word "martyr" means to bear witness. The Greeks wanted the leading Jews — first Elazar and Hannah and later Judah's father Mattathias — to bear witness to their loyalty to the earthly ruler and to meld into the new nation of Greeks. Even though the king had the physical power to force his will on anyone, he wanted people to accept his absolute authority voluntarily. Antiochus' plan was to make an example of the leaders — either they would model obedience voluntarily or they would be tortured until they begged for a quick death. Pigs — the typical Greek sacrifice — would be the test of loyalty.

The description of the confrontation of Antiochus and Elazar is melodramatic and somewhat grisly, typical of the style used in Greek history-writing, which influenced the authors of the Books of the Maccabees.

THE TEST AND THE TASTE OF PORK

Elazar was one of the leading scribes [an expert in the traditional constitution of Judea and a known philosopher], a man of advanced age and fine appearance [with a silver gray beard]. When ordered to eat pork, he refused.

When Antiochus saw Elazar's public refusal, he spoke to him persuasively: "Before I commence inflicting torture upon you, graybeard, I would give you this counsel: eat of the pig's flesh and save yourself. I respect your age and your gray head; but I cannot think you a philosopher when you have so long been an elder and still cling to the religion of the Jews. Why are you disgusted by eating the excellent meat of this animal?"[14]

Elazar responded coolly and defiantly:

"We, Antiochus, who out of conviction lead our lives in accordance with the divine Law, believe no constraint more compelling than our own willing obedience to the Law; and therefore under no circumstance do we deem it right to violate the Law. We do not regard the eating of unclean flesh a small offense. You mock at our philosophy. Yet it teaches us

self-control, so that we rule over all pleasures and desires; and it trains us in **courage**, so that we willingly endure any difficulty. I shall not violate the sacred oaths of my ancestors who swore to observe the Torah, not even if you cut my eyes out and burn my insides. I am neither so decrepit, nor so ignoble, that reason should lose the vigor of youth in the cause of religion. So make ready your torturer's wheel, fan your fires to a fiercer heat. You shall not defile the sacred lips of my old age. Pure shall my [deceased] ancestors welcome me [after death]."[15]

The king ordered the torture to begin in order to break Elazar's will. With his head raised high to heaven the old man suffered a fierce whipping; he was flowing with blood, and his sides were lacerated. He fell to the ground when his body was no longer able to endure the torment; but he kept his reason erect and unbent. Whenever he fell, one of the savage guards kicked him in the side to make him get up. Elazar endured the pain, despised the compulsion, prevailed over the torments, and like a **noble athlete** under blows, outstripped his torturers. With his face bathed in sweat and his panting breath coming hard, his stoutness of heart won the admiration even of his torturers.[16]

Welcoming a glorious death in preference to a life of pollution, Elazar went up of his own accord to the torture wheel. He set an example of how one should be steadfast enough to refuse food, which it is wrong to

---

14. *IV Maccabees 5:4-8*
15. *IV Maccabees 5:14-36*
16. *IV Maccabees 6:6-11*

taste, even for the natural love of life.

Those who were in charge of that unlawful sacrificial meal, because of their long-standing acquaintance with Elazar, took him aside. Privately they urged him to provide his own meat, which he could properly eat, and pretend that he was eating the meat of the sacrifice, as the king had ordered. By doing this he might escape the death penalty, and on account of his lifelong friendship with them, be kindly treated. But Elazar refused [to use this loophole].

"It does not become our time of life to pretend, and so lead many young people to suppose that Elazar, when ninety years old, has gone over to foreign worship, lest they be led astray through me. If I pretend [to eat pork] for the sake of this short and insignificant life, I will defile and disgrace my old age.

For even if for the present I escape human punishment, whether I live or die I shall not escape the hands of the Almighty. Therefore by manfully giving up my life now, I will prove myself worthy of my advanced years, and leave to the young a noble example of how to die willingly and nobly for the sacred and holy laws."

With these words he went straight to the torture wheel, while those who so shortly before had felt kindly toward him became hostile to him, because the words he had uttered were in their opinion mere **madness**. As he was about to die Elazar declared: "Lord, in my soul I am glad to suffer this, because I respect and honor God." And so he died, leaving in his death a model of nobility and a memorial of virtue not only to the young but to the mass of his nation.[17]

HANNAH AND HER SEVEN SONS[18]

"*It is for Your sake that we are slain all day long, that we are thought of as sheep to be slaughtered.*"[19] *This verse refers to the woman [Hannah] and her seven sons.*[20]

Having failed to convince Elazar the old philosopher, Antiochus turned to the seven young sons of Hannah and began to flatter them, on one hand, and to threaten them on the other in order to convince them to bow down to a pagan idol:

"Young men, I admire you and because I pay high honor to such beauty and such a numerous band of brothers, I counsel you against raging with the same madness as that old man who has just been tortured and I urge you to yield to me. Renounce your ancestral Law. Share in the Greek ways, change your way of life, and take pleasure in your youth. If by your stubbornness you

rouse my anger, you will compel me to have recourse to terrible punishments and to destroy you with torture."[21]

[To show he meant business, Antiochus ordered] the guards to bring out torture wheels and instruments for dislocating joints, racks and wooden horses, caldrons and braziers, thumbscrews and iron grips, wedges and bellows: The tyrant then resumed, and said: "Lads, be afraid [of these tortures, but do not fear your Law, for] the Law which you revere will be indulgent to violations committed under pressure."[22]

As each son from the oldest to the youngest was brought before the king and instructed to bow down to the idol, they each refused and were cruelly tortured to death. Thus the executions continued until the turn of the seventh, last and youngest son.

The king said to him: "Your [older] brothers had had their fill of years of life and had experienced happiness; but you are so young, you have had no fill of years and life and have not yet experienced happiness. Bow

17. *II Maccabees* 6:18-31

18. This version of the story of Hannah appears in the Talmud. There, it is attributed to an anonymous woman standing before the Roman Caesar rather than to Hannah who is mentioned in *Maccabees II and IV*. Nevertheless we prefer to use this Talmudic adaptation of the Maccabean story of Hannah (*II Maccabees* 7) because it is so much less gory than the original.

19. *Psalms* 44:23   20. *Lamentations Rabbah* 1

21. *IV Maccabees* 8:5-9 (excerpts)   22. *IV Maccabees* 8:13-14

yourself before the image and I will bestow favors upon you."

[The seventh and youngest son] replied: "You are of no account and so are God's enemies. A human being lives today and is dead tomorrow, rich today and poor tomorrow; but the Holy One, blessed be He, lives and endures for all eternity."

The king said to him, "Look, your brothers lie dead before you. [Here is your last chance], I will throw my ring to the ground in front of the idol. [Bend down and] pick it up, so that everyone will think that you have obeyed my command."

The boy answered, "Woe unto you, O Emperor! If you are afraid of what human beings might think, even though they are the same as yourself, shall I not fear the supreme

Hannah and her Seventh Son refuse to bow to Antiochus (II Mac. 7:37)
(Gustav Dore, 19th century France)

The boy answered, "Woe unto you, O Emperor! If you are afraid of what human beings might think, even though they are the same as yourself, shall I not fear the supreme King of kings, the Holy One, blessed be He, the God of the universe?"

THE
HANUKK.
CEREMO

Brach

Song

Maccab
Megilla

3rd Cand
Martyr

King of kings, the Holy One, blessed be He, the God of the universe?"

The king asked him: "Does the universe have a God?"

He replied, "Shame on you, King! Do you, then, see a world without a Master!"

The Emperor asked: "Why doesn't your God save you from me in the same manner that He rescued [Daniel from the lion's den and] Hananiah, Mishael, and Azariah from the furnace into which the Babylonian King Nebuchadnezzar threw them?"

The boy answered, "The Holy One, blessed be He, will avenge our blood on you!" The king ordered him to be put to death, however, the child's mother said to the king, "By the life of your head, O Emperor, give me my son that I may embrace and kiss him." They gave her seventh son to her, and she bared her breasts and fed him. She said to the king, "By the life of your

head, O Emperor, put me to death first and then slay him."

[The king refused and then] the mother threw herself upon the child and embraced and kissed him. She said to him: "My son, go to our father Abraham and tell him, 'This is what my mother has to say to you, Abraham, do not boast of [your righteousness] in building an altar and offering up your only son [Isaac], for I have offered seven sons in one day. Yours was only a test, but mine was in earnest.'" While she was embracing and kissing him, the Emperor gave an order and they killed him in her arms.

After a few days the woman became mentally unstable and fell from a roof and died. A voice from heaven proclaimed, "A happy mother of children;"[23] but the Holy Spirit cried out: "For these things I weep."[24]

---

23. *Psalms* 113:9   24. *Lamentations Rabbah* 1.16.50 and *T.B. Gittin* 57b

Divine Vengeance:
Antiochus's Tortuous Bowel Movements (164 BCE)

With historic and poetic justice we can contemplate the fate of Antiochus who called himself "Theos Epiphanes" (god is manifest) but who died like all men. Antiochus forced the Jews to celebrate his royal birthday (II Maccabees 6) in the Temple, yet he himself died just after the Temple was recaptured by Judah and purified (164 BCE).

Antiochus was on a distant military expedition when he heard of the Maccabean success:

Antiochus in his arrogance said, "When I get there, I will make Jerusalem the common graveyard of the Jews." But the All-seeing Lord, the God of Israel, struck him down with an incurable but unseen blow, for he had hardly uttered the words when he was seized with an incurable pain in his bowels and sharp internal torments. This was very just, for he had tormented the bowels of others with many unusual tortures. Yet Antiochus did not desist at all from his insolence, but he was more and more filled with arrogance, breathing fire in his fury against the Jews, and giving orders to hasten the journey.

But it happened that he fell out of his chariot as it was rushing along, and was racked with pain in every part of his body from the fall. And the man who just now presumed to command the waves of the sea, in his

superhuman boastfulness, and thought he could weigh the mountain heights in his scales, was flat on the ground. He had to be carried in a litter — making the power of God manifest to all men; so that worms swarmed from the impious creature's body. While he was still alive in anguish and pain, his flesh began to fall off, and because of the stench, the whole army turned away from his filth in disgust. The man who, shortly before, had thought he could touch the stars of heaven, no one could now bear to carry, because of his **intolerable stench**.

So broken in spirit, Antiochus began for the most part to give up his arrogance, and under the whip of God to attain some knowledge, for he was tortured with pain every instant. And when he could not even endure his own stench, he confessed: **"It is right to submit to God, for humans are mortal. One should not speak arrogantly and think oneself God's equal."**

So the murderer and blasphemer, after the most intense sufferings, such as he had inflicted on other people, ended his life most pitiably, up in the mountains, in a foreign land.[25]

---

25. *II Maccabees* 9:4-12, 28

"God forbid that we should abandon the Torah!"

THE HANUKKA CEREMO

Brach

Songs

Maccabe
Megilla

4th Cand
Mattathi

4th Candle

THE FIRST REBEL

MATTATHIAS THE LOYAL PRIEST AND HIS FIVE SONS (167-166 BCE)

In those days [of religious persecution by King Antiochus], a priest named **Mattathias** moved from Jerusalem, and settled in Modiin [a provincial town]. He had five sons, John, Simon, Judah called Maccabeus, Elazar, and Jonathan. When he saw the blasphemous things that were going on in Judea and Jerusalem, he said with a heavy sigh, "Why was I born to witness the ruin of my people and the ruin of the Holy City, and to sit by while it is being given up to its enemies, and its Temple to aliens?" Mattathias and his sons tore their clothes in mourning.

Later, the king's officers who were forcing the people to give up their religion, came to the town of **Modiin**, to make them offer an idolatrous sacrifice. When many Jews, among them Mattathias and his sons, gathered together, the king's messengers said to Mattathias:

"You are a leading man, great and distinguished in this town, surrounded with sons and brothers; now be the first to come forward and carry out the king's command as all the peoples, all the men of Judea and those who are left in Jerusalem have done. Then

> When Mattathias learned of [the massacre], he said, "If we all do as our brothers have done and refuse to fight [on Shabbat], the Greeks will very soon wipe us off the face of the earth."

you and your sons will be counted among the Friends of the King and will receive silver, gold and many royal commissions."

Then Mattathias answered and said in a loud voice: "Even if all the peoples in the king's dominions listen to him and forsake each of them the religion of their ancestors, **I and my children and my siblings will live in accordance with the covenant of our ancestors**. God forbid that we should abandon the Torah and the ordinances. We will not listen to the message of the king, nor depart from our religion to the right hand or to the left."

When Mattathias finished speaking, a Jew went up before everyone's eyes to offer the pagan sacrifice on the altar in Modiin as the king commanded. Mattathias saw him and was filled with zeal. Shaking with emotion and unable to contain his anger, Mattathias ran up and slaughtered him upon the altar. At the same time Mattathias killed the king's officer who was trying to compel them to sacrifice, and tore down the altar. Thus he showed his zeal for the Torah, just as **Pinchas [the zealous priest]** did.[25] Then Mattathias cried out in a loud voice in the town, **"Let everybody who is zealous for the Torah and stands by the Covenant follow me."** And he and his sons fled to the mountains and left all they possessed in the town.

DEATH ON SHABBAT IN THE WILDERNESS

[Due to the persecution] many seekers for justice went down into the wilderness to settle with their children, their wives and their cattle, because their hardships had become so severe. News reached the king's agents and the Greek forces that were in Jerusalem that people who had disregarded the king's order had gone down to the hiding places in the wilderness. The soldiers pursued them in force, overtook them, pitched their camp opposite [the mountain caves where they hid] and prepared **to attack them on Shabbat**.

The Greeks said to the Jews, "Enough! Come out and do as the king commands, and you will live." The refugees [from religious persecution] replied, "We will not come out nor do as the king commands and break the Sabbath."

Then the Greeks hastened to attack them, while the Jews made no response; they did not throw a stone at them nor block up their hiding places, for they said, "Let us all die guiltless. We call heaven and earth to witness that you destroy us unlawfully. [But we will not violate the laws of Shabbat by conducting war on this holy day]."

So the Greeks attacked them on the Shabbat, and the Jews died with their children and their cattle — a thousand people.

A RADICAL RELIGIOUS REFORM [26]

When Mattathias and his friends learned of [the massacre], they grieved bitterly and said to one another: **"If we all do as our brothers have done and refuse to fight [on Shabbat] against the pagans, for our lives and for what we believe is right, they will very soon wipe us off the face of the earth."** On that day they reached this decision: **"If anyone attacks us on Shabbat, let us fight against them and not all die, as our brothers died in the hiding places."**[27]

---

25. *Numbers 25*
26. The Talmudic Rabbis later argued that these martyrs who refused to violate Shabbat even for self-defense had misunderstood God's intent. *"Pikuach Nefesh,"* saving a life in threatening situations, always takes precedence over Shabbat observance. (See David Dishon's essay, "To be a Martyr or a Warrior? Self-Defense on Shabbat" in Chapter VI of *The Big Book of Hanukkah*).
27. *I Maccabees 2: 29-41*

THE FIRST GENERAL IN THE GUERRILLA WAR AGAINST THE GREEKS

JUDAH THE HAMMER (166 BCE-161 BCE) — THE FEW AGAINST THE MANY

THE HANUKKA CEREMO

Brach

Song

Maccabe Megilla

5th Cand Judah

MATTATHIAS' DEATH BED SPEECH

When the time drew near for Mattathias to die, he said to his sons: "Arrogance and reproach have now grown strong; it is a time of disaster and hot anger. Now, my children, you must be zealous for the Torah and give your lives for the covenant of our ancestors.

"Judah Maccabeus has been a powerful fighter from his youth; he will be your captain and conduct the people's warfare. You must gather about you all who observe the Torah, and avenge the wrongs of your people." Then Mattathias blessed them and he was gathered to his ancestors.[28]

THE GUERRILLA BATTLE BEGINS

Judah Maccabeus with some nine others withdrew to the wilderness and kept himself alive in the mountains as wild animals do. They lived on what grew naturally, rather

---

28. *II Maccabees 49-50, 66-67*

Judah leads his men to reclaim Jerusalem (I Mac. 4:37)
(Julius Schnor, 19th century Germany)

Elazar, Judah's brother, tries to bring down the war elephant of the Greek General
(Gustav Dore, 19th century France)

than participating, along with the rest [of the people who remained in the settled areas under Greek occupation], in the desecration of that which was holy.[29]

Judah Maccabeus and his followers secretly entered the villages and called on their kinsmen to join them. By enlisting those who had clung to Judaism, they mustered as many as six thousand. [The Maccabees] called upon the Lord to look upon His people who were so oppressed, to have pity on the Temple, which had been profaned by impious persons, and to have mercy on the city which was being destroyed.

"Listen, God," they prayed, "and pay attention to the blood that cries out. Remember the lawless destruction of the innocent babies and the blasphemies uttered against Your name. Show your hatred to the wicked."

As soon as Maccabeus organized his forces, the Greeks found him unstoppable. He would go unexpectedly to [Greek occupied] towns and villages and set fire to them. He recovered strategic positions and put to flight many enemies. Judah found the **nights** especially favorable for such attacks. The country rang with talk of his courage.[30]

29. *II Maccabees* 5: 27   30. *II Maccabees* 8:1-7

Elazar and the Elephant

Like any superpower the Greeks had superior technology including their super-tank, the Indian elephant; however, the edge in personal daring and cunning belonged to the Maccabees.

When the king heard [of the defeat of his armies], he was angry, so he gathered all his friends, the officers of his army, and those in charge of the cavalry. His forces numbered 100,000 infantry, 20,000 cavalry, and 32 elephants trained for war. The Indian drivers showed the **elephants** the juice of grapes and mulberries to incite them to battle. They distributed the animals among the *phalanxes* [the infantry's assault formation] and stationed with each elephant a thousand men in armor with brass helmets on their heads, and five hundred choice horsemen. On each elephant there was an ingeniously constructed fortified tower manned by several powerful fighters.

When Judah and his army advanced to battle, his brother **Elazar** saw that one of the animals was dressed with royal armor, and stood higher than all the other animals. He thought that the king was on that elephant. **Thus he [decided to] give his life to save his people and won everlasting renown for himself.** Fighting his way through the *phalanx*, to his right and to his left, he slipped under the elephant, stabbed it underneath and killed it. Then it fell to the earth upon him, and Elazar died there.

General Nicanor and his men advanced with trumpets and battle songs, while Judah and his men met the enemy with prayers. Thus fighting with their hands and praying to God with their hearts, Judah's men inflicted no less than thirty-five thousand casualties and were greatly encouraged by God's obvious aid.

When the battle was over, and they were returning joyfully, they recognized Nicanor, lying dead in his armor. There was shouting and excitement, and [the Maccabees] blessed God the Heavenly Sovereign.

They hung Nicanor's head from the citadel, a clear and conspicuous proof to all of the Lord's help. And they all decreed by popular vote of the people, never to let this day go by without observing it. Let **[Nicanor Day]** be celebrated on the thirteenth day of the twelfth month — which is called in Aramaic Adar — the day before Mordechai's day [Purim].[31]

JUDAH'S FIRST BIG VICTORY (165 BCE)

[The Greeks] saw that this man was gaining ground little by little, and that his successful advances were becoming more frequent.[32] **Nicanor and Gorgias**, powerful men, "Friends of the King," gathered forty thousand men and seven thousand horses to go to Judea, for the king had ordered that Judea be destroyed. They set off with all their forces, and they encamped near Emmaus in the plain. The Greek merchants of the country heard about the army and came to the camp with vast amounts of gold and silver to purchase Judeans [who would certainly be captured and sold into slavery by the Greek armies].

Judah and his brothers saw that the situation was very grave. They knew that the king had ordered the army to utterly destroy the people [of Israel].[33] Judah went out with very few men to meet him. But when the Judeans saw the army coming towards them, they said to Judah: **"How can we, few as we are, fight against such a strong army? Besides we are faint, for we have had nothing to eat today** [since according to biblical custom soldiers in a religious war must fast during the battle]."

Judah said: "It is easy for the many to fall into the hands of the few. There is no difference in the sight of God between saving you by the hand of many or few, for **victory in war does not depend upon the size of the force, but strength comes from heaven**. They come against us full of *hubris* (arrogance) and lawlessness, to destroy us, our wives and our children, and to plunder us. But we are fighting for our lives and our laws. God himself will crush them before our eyes. So you must not be afraid of them."[34]

Judah said, "Prepare yourselves and be brave men and be ready in the morning to fight these pagans who are gathered together against us, to destroy us and our sanctuary, for it is better for us to die in battle than to witness the ruin of our nation and our holy places."

At daybreak, Judah appeared in the plain with three thousand men, though they did not have

31. *II Maccabees* 15:26-29, 34-36

32. *II Maccabees* 8:8   33. *I Maccabees* 3:38-42
34. *I Maccabees* 3:16-22

THE HANUKKA CEREMO

Brach

Song

Maccabe Megilla

5th Cand
Judah

the armor and swords they wished. They saw the enemy camp strongly fortified, with expert horsemen patrolling it. But Judah said to the men who were with him:

"**Do not be afraid of their numbers**, and do not fear their attack. Remember how our ancestors were saved at the **Red Sea**, when Pharaoh pursued them with an armed force. So now let us cry to heaven. Perhaps God will accept us and remember his covenant with our ancestors, and crush this camp before us today. **Then all the nations will know that there is One who redeems Israel.**"

Then the aliens lifted up their eyes and saw the Judeans coming against them, and they came out of the camp to battle. Judah's men sounded the trumpets and attacked, and the Greeks broke and fled to the plain. [The Maccabees] returned singing and blessing heaven, *"For God has been good, for his mercy endures forever."* So Israel had a great victory and they were saved that day.[35]

35. *I Maccabees* 3:58-60; 4:6-14, 24-25

The Science of Warfare: Imperial Armies versus Rebel Guerrillas

The core of the Hellenistic imperial armies was the "phalanx" (256 soldiers with shields and 8 meter long spears marching as a block of 16 soldiers in 16 rows). Cavalry rode on each side of the phalanx, while ancient "tanks" — fighter elephants — served as the advance forces breaking through enemy lines and causing terror and panic.

Judah identified the classical weaknesses of this imperial army, however formidable. It was limited to flat plains, not the mountains of Judea, to daylight battles, not night raids, and to similarly organized rival armies, not guerrilla forces. Since the soldiers were hired by their generals and drawn from a hodgepodge of nations, their chief motivation was the spoils they earned in addition to the personal loyalty they felt towards their commanders.

Therefore the Maccabees used hit-and-run guerrilla tactics staged in the mountains and aimed to kill the commanders of the army in daring direct hits. For example, Elazar, Judah's brother, was crushed to death in a suicide mission to stab the Greek general's elephant in its belly. While the Judean arms consisted initially of clubs, slingshots, daggers and homemade swords, the Maccabees soon confiscated the sophisticated arms of the many fallen Greek Syrian soldiers and used them effectively against the invaders.

The Defeat and Death of Judah "the Hammer"

When King Demetrius [a successor of Antiochus] heard that Nicanor and his troops had fallen in battle, he sent Bacchides and Alcimus into the land of Judea again with 20,000 men and 2,000 horses, while Judah was encamped at Elasa, and had only 3,000 select men with him. When the Jews saw that the number of the enemy troops was great, they were greatly terrified and many slipped out of the camp; not more than eight hundred men were left. Judah saw that his army had dwindled away, and that the battle was imminent. He was troubled, for he had no time to rally them and in desperation he said to those who were left, "Let us rise up against our opponents; perhaps we can succeed in fighting against them."

Judah's soldiers tried to dissuade him, saying: "We certainly cannot; but let us save our lives now, and come back with our brothers and fight against them; we are so few." Judah said: "I will never do that, **I will never run from them. If our time has come, let us die bravely for our brothers, and not leave a stain upon our honor.**"

The Greek military *phalanx* advanced on the two sides, and sounded their trumpets. Judah's men also sounded their trumpets, and the earth shook with the shout of the armies; the battle raged from morning till evening. Then Judah fell and the rest fled. Jonathan and Simon took their brother Judah and buried him in the tombs of their ancestors in Modiin. They wept over him, and all Israel lamented greatly, saying, **"What a hero is fallen, the Savior of Israel."**[35]

36. *I Maccabees* 9:1, 4-10, 13-14, 19-21

Judah smashing the pagan statue erected in the Holy of Holies by the Greeks (164 BCE)
(medieval print of the Book of Maccabees, courtesy of the Library of the Jewish Theological Seminary of America)

THE
HANUKK
CEREMO

Brach

Song

Maccab
Megilla

6th Cane
First
Hanukk

6th Candle

THE FIRST HANUKKAH

FROM DESECRATING TO DEDICATING THE TEMPLE (25 KISLEV /DECEMBER 164 BCE)

Only three years after Antiochus had erected an idol in the Temple and desecrated the altar with sacrifices of pig on the 25th of Kislev in 167 BCE, Judah's miraculous victories over the Greek army allowed him to reconquer the Temple. Even though the War of Independence against the Greek Syrians would continue for another 25 years, the Rededication of the Temple, not political sovereignty, became the focus of celebration then and thereafter for generations. By reading carefully both the story from the Book of Maccabees and the Talmudic legends we will discover two different reasons for celebrating Hanukkah for eight days, several different names for the holiday and the reason that it begins, not coincidentally, on the 25th of Kislev.

Judah and his brothers said [in 164 BCE], **"Now that our enemies are crushed, let us go up to purify the sanctuary and rededicate it."** So the whole army gathered together, and they went up to Mount Zion. They found the sanctuary desolated, the altar polluted, the doors burned up, and weeds growing in the courts as they do in a forest or on some mountain. Judah's men tore their clothes [as a sign of mourning], covered themselves with ashes, sang songs of lament, and fell on their faces on the ground. They sounded the shofar and cried out to heaven. Then Judah appointed priests that were without blemish and adherents of the Law, and they purified the sanctuary.

Why did Judah wave a palm branch on the First Hanukkah?

The reasoning may be derived both from Greek and Jewish tradition. In the Greek world the goddess Nike carries a palm branch as a sign of victory. But of course the primary explanation seems to be the Maccabees' attempt to make up for their missed celebration of the autumn festival of Sukkot usually held two months earlier. However at that time the Temple was still occupied by the Greeks. (Centuries later, Christianity mandated the carrying of palm branches on Palm Sunday in the spring to celebrate Jesus' resurrection, his victory over death).

The Festival of Lights and Freedom of Worship

It took a long time to agree on a name for the eight-day celebration which the Rabbis more than a hundred years later, called "**Hanukkah**" — meaning the **Dedication of the altar and the Temple**. Josephus, the first century Jewish historian, is the first to call it the **Festival of Lights** and to connect it explicitly to the right of freedom of religion:

> We call [the holiday] the **Festival of Lights**, giving this name to it, I think, from the fact that the right to worship appeared to us [like a flash of light] at a time when we hardly dared hope for it.[39]

39. Josephus, *Jewish Antiquities* 12.7 , 100 CE

Judah's men made a **new menorah** and lit its lamps. Then they arose early on **the twenty-fifth day of the ninth month**, that is the month of **Kislev** (approximately on December 25, 164 BCE), and offered sacrifice, according to the Law, upon the new altar which they had made. **At the very time and on the very day the Greeks had polluted the Temple [three years earlier]**, it was rededicated with songs and harps, lutes and cymbals. All the people fell on their faces and blessed heaven, which had prospered them. They celebrated the **rededication of the altar for eight days**.[37]

[Like the eight-day celebration of Sukkot] they celebrated in high spirits for **eight days** and recalled how but a little while before, during the Sukkot festival they had been wandering in the mountains and caverns like wild animals. Now carrying a *thersos* [a branch wrapped in ivy] and the seasonal *lulav* [palm branches], they praised God who had succeeded in purifying his own place — the

Temple. They passed a public ordinance and decreed that the whole Jewish nation should observe these days every year.[38]

37. *I Maccabees* 4: 36-42, 50-56   38. *II Maccabees* 10: 6-8

The Miracle of the Self-Igniting Water

While the Books of the Maccabees never mention the Talmudic legend of the cruse of pure oil that burned in the Temple Menorah for eight days, Second Maccabees does recall an even greater miracle. It follows the tradition that every dedication of a Temple in Jewish history is accompanied by a mysterious lighting of the new altar.

When Moses and Aaron dedicated the portable mishkan (tabernacle/tent of meeting) in the desert, fire descended from Heaven.[40] Later, Solomon prayed and fire descended on the altar during the dedication of the First Temple.[41] But most interesting is the story of the dedication of the new altar in the Second Temple (516 BCE) which is inaccurately credited to Nehemiah (450 BCE) by the author of Second Maccabees quoted below. Nehemiah's self-igniting "water" is reported in a letter sent by the Maccabees to the Diaspora Jews in Egypt (125 BCE).

Note that "Hanukkah" has a different name in the Book of Maccabees. It is called the "Delayed Sukkot Festival." Sukkot is the eight-day holiday associated not only with the harvest festival but also with the original dedication of the First Temple by Solomon. Now Judah's rededication of the Temple is also celebrated with an eight-day holiday with the same name.

"To the Jewish brothers in Egypt, from the Jewish brothers in Jerusalem and the land of Judea who send greetings and wish you perfect peace.

Since we are about to celebrate the purification of the Temple on the twenty-fifth day of the month of Kislev, we think it necessary to inform you, so that you too may observe this delayed **Sukkot festival**. [It is also the **festival of] the kindling of the fire**, when Nehemiah, who [according to the historian of *Second Maccabees*] rebuilt the [Second] Temple and the altar, first offered sacrifices. For when our ancestors were being taken (by the Babylonians into exile 586 BCE), the pious priests of that day took some of the fire on the altar and hid it safely in the hollow of an empty cistern, so that the place remained unknown to anyone. Many years later, when it pleased God, Nehemiah was commissioned by the king of Persia [450 CE], and sent the descendants of the priests who had hidden the fire to get it. When they reported back that they could not find any fire but **only muddy water**, he ordered them to draw some water and bring it with him. When the offerings to be sacrificed had been put in place, Nehemiah ordered the priests to sprinkle the "water" on the wood and on the offerings that were laid on it. When this was done and some time had passed, the sun, which had been clouded over, came out and shined on it and a great blaze was kindled, so that they all were amazed.

Then the priests started singing Psalms. When the sacrifices were consumed, Nehemiah ordered them to pour the "water" that was left on large stones. When this was done, a flame was kindled. Nehemiah's people called this *Nephtar*, which is translated "Purification" but most people call it *Nephthai*. ["Nephtar" means oil and may refer to petroleum].[42]

---

40. *Leviticus* 8:24   41. *I Kings* 8
42. *II Maccabees* 1:1, 18-22, 30-32, 36

THE HANUKKAH CEREMONY

Brachot

Songs

Maccabee Megillah

6th Candle First Hanukkah

THE LEGENDARY MIRACLE OF THE CRUSE OF OIL AND THE MAKESHIFT TEMPORARY MENORAH

Why are lamps kindled during Hanukkah?

The Eight Hollow Rods. At the time that the sons of the Hasmonean High Priest triumphed over the kingdom of Greece, they entered the Temple and found there eight rods of iron which they hollowed out and then kindled wicks in the oil which they had poured into its grooves [creating a menorah].[43]

The Eight-Day Cruse. The twenty-fifth of [Kislev] is the day of Hanukkah. For eight days mourning is forbidden. Why? When the Greeks entered the Temple, they defiled all the oils that were there. When the House of the Hasmoneans prevailed and won a victory over them, they searched and found only one cruse [of oil] with the seal of the High Priest that was not defiled. It had only [enough oil] to burn for one day. A miracle happened, and there was light from it for eight days. In the following year they established eight festival days.[44]

---

43. *Midrash Pesikta Rabbati* 2.1
44. *Babylonian Talmud, Megillat Taanit* 9

A WOMAN'S PROTEST AGAINST ABUSE

MATTATHIAS' DAUGHTER IGNITES
THE MACCABEAN REVOLT AGAINST
THE FIRST NIGHT "PRIVILEGES" OF THE GREEK VICEROY

A MEDIEVAL MIDRASH[45]

In some Sephardic communities the seventh night of Hanukkah is dedicated to Jewish women. Therefore our readings suggested for the 7th and 8th candles describe two legendary Jewish heroines associated traditionally with Hanukkah — Hannah daughter of Mattathias and Judith who beheaded Holofernes. Neither legend is historically credible but both present a powerful image of a Jewish heroine. The selection below reflects an ancient and medieval feudal custom of "first night privileges" — the right of the feudal lord to sleep with his subject's bride on her wedding night.

The legendary tale of Hannah daughter of Mattathias portrays her — rather than her father — as the one who incited the Maccabees to act. The initial cause of the revolt was, according to the tale below, not only religious persecution but the sexual exploitation of brides under the infamous "first night privileges."

*Note that "Hannah of the seven sons who were martyred" is **not** the same as "Hannah daughter of Mattathias" in this folktale and that her bridegroom, Elazar the Hasmonean, is not portrayed as Mattathias' son as he is in the Book of the Maccabees. Medieval midrash often recalls historical details differently than history books do. Whatever its historical veracity, it is a wonderful story.*

The Greeks plotted: "Come let us invent [harsh] new decrees that will cause the Jews to reject their God and believe in our gods."

First they decreed that **everyone with a door needed to inscribe on the door bolt the words, *"Israel has no relationship to the God of Israel."*** All violators of the decree would be pierced by the sword. When Israel heard the decree, they tore out their doors in order to evade its implementation. As a result, without doors, the Jews had no honor, [for a house without a door offers no dignity and no privacy]. Everyone can go in and out at will, whether during the day or at night, so Jews could no longer eat nor drink nor sleep with their spouses in dignity. Jews could not sleep securely night or day just as was predicted in the Biblical curse *"you shall be afraid day and night."*[46]

Since the Greeks saw that the Jews persevered despite the first decree, they added a second decree that **everyone was forbidden to let his wife go to the mikveh**. (The mikveh is the ritual bath at which she purifies herself after her menstrual period which is a prerequisite, according to the Torah, for having sexual relations with her husband.) A husband who violates the decree would be pierced by a sword. Anyone who sees a woman going to mikveh (and informs on her husband) earns the right to marry her and enslave her children. When the Jews heard this second decree, the Jewish couples decided to avoid [the temptation to have] intercourse without ritual immersion by separating from their spouses completely.

Since the Greeks saw that the Jews seemed impervious to their previous decrees, they legislated an even more bitter decree — **"first night privileges."** Every Jewish bride should go from her *chuppah* (her marriage celebration) directly to the local Greek official to have sexual relations with him for the first night and only return to her husband subsequently.

When Israel heard this most awful decree, they grew weak and many refrained from becoming engaged, preferring to grow old as virgins. This decree continued for three years and eight months until the wedding night of Hannah, the daughter of Mattathias the

---

45. This reading is a composite of two versions of this midrash composed in 10th/11th century Europe and found in A. Jellinek's anthology, *Beit HaMidrash* 8.
46. *Deuteronomy* 28

priest, who married Elazar the Hasmonean. On her day of joy they placed her on a bridal chair and all the great personages of Israel attended the wedding feast. As they sat down to eat, Hannah rose from her bridal chair, clapped her hands together (a gesture of

---

Hannah rose from her bridal chair, clapped her hands together, tore off her bridal wreath and tore her clothes. She stood exposed before all of Israel, before her father, her mother and her bridegroom.

---

mourning in those days), tore off her bridal wreath and tore her clothes. She stood exposed before all of Israel, before her father, her mother and her bridegroom.

When Judah and his brothers saw her exposed in public, they were ashamed and cast their glances down to the ground and tore their clothes in mourning. Then they were filled with anger and declared: "*Take her out and burn her*,[47] for she dared to appear naked in public, but do it so that the Greek government does not hear, lest the whole community be endangered."

Then Hannah rose to accuse her judges: "Listen my brothers and cousins. If you are so zealous over [my immodest behavior in] appearing naked before this righteous audience — though I did not sin sexually — then why aren't you zealous about my purity when you yourselves are handing me over to be exploited by this uncircumcised Greek? Will I be disgraced more before my brothers and friends than when **you desecrate me and take me to sleep with the Greek ruler**? Shouldn't you learn from the brothers of Dinah, daughter of Jacob, who was raped and held hostage by the prince of Shechem? Dinah's brothers, Shimon and Levi — even though there were only two of them — showed they were zealous for their sister's honor and they endangered their lives to sanctify God's name. With God's help, they invaded a big city like Shechem in order to rescue her and avenge themselves on the men

of the city. Aren't you ashamed, since you are **five** brothers — Judah, Yochanan, Elazar, Jonathan and Simon along with another 200 young priests? Trust God and He will help you!" Then Hannah prayed aloud to God and wept: "Master of the Universe, if you will not have mercy on us, then at least defend the honor of your holy name which is identified with Israel and avenge us today!"

As soon as Judah and his friends heard this, they took counsel to slay the Greek magistrate. They dressed Hannah in royal apparel and made a *chuppah* of myrtle which they carried from the house of the Hasmoneans to the house of the magistrate. The musicians played lyres and harps and the singers sang and danced until they arrived at the home of the magistrate.

As soon as the magistrate heard this, he said to his officers and courtiers, "See the leaders of Israel, the seed of Aaron the priest, how happy they are to do my will. They are deserving of great honor." He commanded his officers and courtiers to exit. Judah and his friends, along with Hannah, entered and cut off the magistrate's head. They plundered everything which was his and slew his officers and courtiers. The Jews who were in the city were terror-stricken on behalf of those brave youths. A voice from Heaven went forth and said, "The lamb, which went forth to do battle with Antiochus, has been victorious." The youths returned, closed the gates, did *teshuvah* (repentance) and busied themselves with Torah and Righteous Deeds.

---

47. "Take her out and burn her" is an application of the law that a priest's daughter who becomes a prostitute should be burned (*Leviticus* 21:9). It is a direct quote from the story of Judah and Tamar (*Genesis* 38:24). There, Tamar dresses as a prostitute, sleeps with her father-in-law Judah in order to keep his seed alive. In the story Tamar is in the right since Judah has refused — against the law — to marry his third son to Tamar who was widowed of his first sons. When Tamar becomes pregnant from Judah, he pounces on the occasion to decree that she be "taken out and burned" as an adulteress. Yet in the end Tamar reveals that Judah is the father of her child and Judah admits his error — "She was more righteous than I."

THE
HANUKK
CEREMC

Brach

Son

Maccab
Megill

7th Can
Mattath
Daugh

Judith escapes with General Holofernes' Head (Judith 13:22)

(Gustav Dore, 19th century France)

A WOMAN WARRIOR

JUDITH CONFRONTS HOLOFERNES
MA'ASEH YEHUDIT: A HANUKKAH MIDRASH

**THE
HANUKK
CEREMO**

Brach

Song

Maccab
Megilla

8th Can
Judith

*A*n ancient Jewish historical romance, which became a famous theme in European art (see pages 189-190), tells about a beautiful, pious and wealthy widow, Judith, who surprised the men of her generation and saved Israel from the Greek King Holofernes. Jews have retold this story on Hanukkah. It became an excuse to eat cheese dishes and to include women in the mitzvah of candle lighting on Hanukkah on an equal basis since women, by virtue of Judith, played a central role in the redemption celebrated on Hanukkah. There is no historical basis for this tale nor is there any connection between King Holofernes and Antiochus; however this story was originally written in the era of the Persians or the Greeks in Eretz Yisrael. Here is an abbreviated medieval version of the tale.[48]

HOLOFERNES' SIEGE OF JERUSALEM

Holofernes, king of Greece, was a great and mighty king, who conquered many nations and powerful kings, destroyed their castles and burned their palaces. In the tenth year of his reign he decided to go up to Jerusalem, the holy city and conquer it. The king said, "The children of Israel who are in Jerusalem *differ in their religion and do not practice the religion of the king.*[49] They are filled with malice; fraud and deceit never leave their marketplace. Arise and let us go and attack them, so that the name Israel is no longer remembered."

Holofernes [besieged the city and] found the water sources which lay outside the city [and blocked them.] The next day Holofernes commanded [his army] to go forth to battle. The people under arms were 120,000 foot soldiers, 12,000 horsemen, and 92,000 archers gathered as a mighty force

against the children of Israel. When the Israelites in Jerusalem saw the multitudes, they sat down on the ground, placed ashes on their heads, and cried out to the Lord. *"The soldiers were seized with trembling, like a woman in the throes of labor."*[50] They then entered the Temple of the Lord and worshiped the Lord in weeping and *with a great and bitter outcry."*[51]

The people of Israel assembled before their king, Uzziah — all the men, women and youths together and said: "Isn't it better for us to worship God and be slaves to Holofernes, than to die of thirst and to see our sons and daughters die before our eyes?"

When the outcries and the weeping ended, Uzziah arose, his eyes over-flowing with tears. He said to them: *"Be strong and of good courage,*[52] my brothers, and hope for mercy from the Lord. Perhaps God will relent of His anger and give glory to His name. If after five days God does not deliver us, then we will [surrender to Holofernes]."

JUDITH'S SECRET PLAN

News of these matters reached the widow Judith, a woman of such great piety that she had prepared in the upper story of her house a separate room for prayer. She was a very beautiful woman who found favor in the eyes of everyone who saw her.

When she heard that Uzziah intended to turn the city over in five days, she sent for the priests. When they came to her, Judith asked: "What is this? Does Uzziah intend to turn over the city to the enemy, if the Lord does not deliver us within five days? Who is he that he should test the Lord?"

---

48. This translation is abbreviated and adapted from Bernard H. Mehlman and Daniel F. Polish, *Journal of Reform Judaism*, Winter, 1979, reprinted by permission.

  The medieval midrashic text of *Ma'aseh Yehudit* made its first printed appearance in the Kabbalist collection *Hemdat Yamim* (Livorno, 1793). The translation follows the text of A. Jellinek, *Bet Ha-Midrash*, volume 11. It is based on *Judith* the Hellenist historical romance preserved in the Septuagint and the Christian Bible. This version reflects a medieval reworking with many Biblical allusions.

49. based on *Esther 3:8*   50. *Psalms 48:7*   51. *Esther 4:1*   52. *Psalms 31:25a*

Judith
by Artemisia Gentileschi

The renaissance Italian artists, Orazio and his daughter, Artemisia, were often commissioned to portray Judith. They emphasize the female conspiracy against the male aggressor. Not only are these women defending their nation in the name of God but they are also punishing masculine brutality against women.

(based on Judith: Sexual Warrior *by Margarita Stocker)*

"I will pray to the Lord on your behalf and you also pray to the Lord for me that God fulfill my plan to avenge the Israelites upon the Greeks. At nightfall my maiden Amta and I will leave the city. Do not question me about where I am going."

Then Judith entered her prayer-room, put on sackcloth and ashes, placed dust on her head and prostrated herself before the Lord. With fasting and crying she poured out her heart.

Lord, God of my ancestor Shimon [son of Jacob], who took sword in hand to take revenge on the strangers who defiled and raped Dinah his sister.

Cast Your eye on the camp of this evil enemy and let their sword enter their own heart and let their bows be shattered. Let this evil one who vexes us, King Holofernes, be ensnared by his eyes to love me and be smitten with desire for me.

Give my soul strength to resist him and give me power to destroy him; *"Let the wicked fall into their nets while I alone come through."*[53] Thus your great name will

be remembered for the Lord our God handed over Holofernes into the hands of a woman[54] [as Yael defeated General Sisera as he slept in her tent — by hammering a tent peg through his forehead].

You, O Lord, have always hated the arrogant kingdom. You attend to the cry of the needy and deliver.

JUDITH'S WEAPONS: WINE AND CHEESE

When Judith finished praying, she removed her widow's garb and the sackcloth. She washed her body and anointed herself with myrrh and plaited her hair and placed a diadem on her head. She donned fine and gilded clothing, jewelry, purses, crescents, and signet rings. She beautified herself with all manner of cosmetics and twenty-four adornments.

The Lord gave her splendor and great beauty to find favor in the eyes of all who saw her. Judith gave a jug of **milk**, a skin of **wine**, a flask of oil, meal, bread and **cheese** to Amta, her servant, and went on her way out of the gates of the city.

At dawn, when they were coming down from the mountain, some of Holofernes' guards seized her, and asked her, "Where did you come from? Where are you going?" Judith answered them: "I am an Israelite woman and I have fled under cover from the city. I know that the people of Israel are delivered over to your hand. Therefore, I thought I would take myself to Holofernes' camp to reveal to him the secrets of the people and to instruct his army how to conquer the city without losing even one soldier."

When the men who seized her heard her words, they looked at her appearance and her beauty and were impressed by it. They were amazed by the pleasantness of her words, by her counsel and knowledge. They said to her: "You are blessed with discernment, that you

---

53. *Psalms* 141:10   54. *Judges* 4:9

have saved yourself from death and were wise enough to come to our lord. Be assured that when you present yourself to him it will go well with you and you will find favor and mercy in his eyes."

They brought her to the king. As soon as she came before him and he saw her beauty and splendor, a fire of lust burned within him and the king was smitten with desire. All of the officers, courtiers and nobles who had been sitting before the king said: "Who could loathe the Hebrew people who have women as beautiful as this, and who would not do battle to possess them?" Judith, seeing the king seated on his royal throne, prostrated herself, but the courtiers raised her up, for thus was the king's command. Then the king

> Judith approached the head-post of his bed and drew his sword, the sword of Holofernes himself, which was hanging on the post. She grasped him by the hair of his head and said: "Strengthen me, O Lord God." She struck his neck repeatedly until his head was severed and gave the head of Holofernes to her maiden, to place it in her sack.

said to her: "Rejoice and do not fear, for I do not wish the death of any that desire to serve me. I would not have raised my swords and my spears against your people if they had not rejected me. Now tell me why you fled from them and chose to come to us?"

Judith told them: "We have sinned before the Lord our God. Therefore, God spoke to the people through the prophets to punish them for their sins. That is why the Israelites are afraid of you — for they have sinned before the Lord their God and so the famine is great among them."

The king ordered that she be brought to his treasure house and served food from his table. Judith replied to him: "Your servant cannot eat what you have ordered to be given me, lest a catastrophe befall me [for this is not considered ritually pure for our religion].

I shall eat what I have brought with me."

Judith asked permission to leave the camp at nightfall and at dawn, in order to pray to the Lord her God daily. "I, Judith your servant, will be unable to worship the Lord my God, here with you [in a pagan army camp]. So I shall go out of the camp three times a day to pray to the Lord my God. I shall prostrate myself before my God, and He will tell me when He will recompense them for their sins and evil actions. Then I will come and tell you. I will lead you through all the courtyards of Jerusalem, and all the community of Israel shall be like a flock which has no shepherd. 'No dog shall snarl'[55] at you. For all of this has been told me in a divine vision." So Holofernes commanded his men to permit her to come and go as she wished in order to pray to her God. So she left the camp every night to immerse herself in a pool of water and to pray.

A NIGHT IN HOLOFERNES' TENT

On the third day the king made a great feast for all his officers and courtiers. He said to his eunuch, the keeper of his harem: "Go, see if you are able to entice or convince this Judith that I come to her." So the eunuch went to Judith and said to her: "Do not be ashamed, do not cringe when you come to my lord. It will go well for you when you eat and drink with him." Judith answered him: "Who am I that I should withhold from my lord anything that pleases him? I shall do all that is worthy in his sight, for whatever my lord the king wishes shall be my delight all the days of my life."

So she put on splendid clothing and went and stood before him. When the king saw her beauty, he was immediately smitten with love for her. He said to her: "Eat your bread in joy and drink your wine in joy, for you have found favor in my eyes." Judith answered him: "I will drink, my lord, for today I am happier than any day in my life."

---

55. *Exodus* 11:7

Judith and her Maidservant with the Head of Holofernes
by Orazio Gentileschi

So she sat down and ate. *"Then she opened a skin container of milk"*[56] and she drank and also gave the king to drink. The king rejoiced in her exceedingly and he drank much wine, more wine than he had ever drunk in his life.

After this all the servants of the king retired to their posts and the king's eunuch closed the door behind Judith and the king. So Judith was alone in the tent with King Holofernes who was fast asleep on his bed. She ordered Amta to station herself outside, to stand guard in front of the tent.

Judith approached the head-post of his bed and drew his sword, the sword of Holofernes himself, which was hanging on the post. She grasped him by the hair of his head and said: "Strengthen me, O Lord God." She struck his neck repeatedly until his head was severed and gave the head of Holofernes to her maiden, to place it in her sack.

Then the two of them went out, as was their custom, to pray. They traversed the whole camp and none said a word to them or cried out after them, for so the king had commanded. When they had gone around the valley, they came to the gates of the city. Judith called to the guards on the walls from afar in a happy voice: "Open the gates, for God is with us, He has brought great salvation for Israel."

When the people of the city heard her voice, they all gathered, young and old, and went out to greet them in gladness and with song[57] and with praises and thanks to the Lord. They lit **candles** in all the streets of Jerusalem and in the courtyards.

BY THE HAND OF A WOMAN: A MAN HAS LOST HIS HEAD

Judith went up to a high place and silenced the people, saying:

"Praise the Lord, O Jerusalem, who acts righteously through His handmaiden. The Lord handed over this enemy of Israel into the hand of a woman on this night."

Then Uzziah, chief of Israel, said to her: *"Blessed are you of the Lord[58] above all women. Blessed are you more than the women of the tent.[59]* May the memory of your splendid deed not depart from the mouth of all who remember the mercies of the Lord forever. For you did not spare yourself in the time of your people's trouble and sorrow." And all the people answered: "Amen and Amen."

Judith said to all the people: "Hear me, my brothers and my people. Hang this head at the top of our walls. When the sun rises, each of you take your weapons and go forth with a battle cry. At sunrise they hung the head of the enemy and troubler of Israel on the top of the walls. Then every man took his weapon in hand and went forth, giving war cries and shouting mightily.

When the [Greek] watchmen saw this, they went to the tent of their king Holofernes. They gave a great cry at the door of the tent to awaken him. When the officers and captains came, they said to the eunuchs: "There is no

56. *Judges* 4:19   57. *Genesis* 31:27
58. *Ruth* 3:10   59. *Judges* 5:24

time to hesitate! Go, wake up the king, for the mice have come out of their holes, challenging us to battle." Then the king's eunuch, the keeper of the harem, entered Holofernes' tent, stood before the curtains of his bed and clapped his hands, [thinking]

Judith of Bethulia
(a still from the film by D. W. Griffiths)

perhaps he is asleep and will awake. For he thought that he was still sleeping with Judith. But when he did not sense anything, he approached the bed and turned back the curtains. He saw the body of Holofernes sprawled on the ground, wallowing in his own blood, headless. Then he let out a cry, sobbing. He rent his clothes. He entered Judith's tent but did not find her. So he went out to the people and said to them: "One single Hebrew woman did this great wrong." When the soldiers heard that their leader was slain and dead, all sense left them and they fled in fear and terror.

After this great salvation the people celebrated this deliverance for three months. For the rest of Judith's life no adversary arose against Israel. After her death the land was tranquil for many years. *"And all the children of Israel enjoyed the **light** in their dwellings."*[60]

60. *Exodus* 10:23

THE HANUKKA CEREMON

Brach

Song

Maccabe
Megilla

8th Cand
Judith

The Modern Judith of Nicaragua (1970s) BY JOE KIRCHBERGER[61]

In the Bible, there is a tradition of strong and courageous heroines which contradicts the cliche of female weakness and timidity. [But] no other woman in biblical tradition has been so honored as Judith was with the statement that "no fear was in Israel when Judith was alive."

This bloody story at first meant little to me; it seemed to me overloaded with pious sentiments and charged with a strange notion of heroism. But my displeasure disappeared when I heard a contemporary story, which seemed to breathe the same spirit. In Nicaragua under the dictator Somoza, a woman in the liberation movement performed an analogous deed in the 1970s. General Vega, a member of the tyrant's ruling party and an infamous torturer for the secret service, had cast his eye on a beautiful lawyer, Nora Astorga, and tried to seduce her.

One day she let him know by phone that she was ready to cooperate and he should prepare to receive her. Her plan was to capture the drunken general with the help of resistance fighters and to exchange him for imprisoned freedom fighters. But her lover, refusing

all preliminaries such as cognac or other refreshment, flung himself upon the woman as she entered, dragged her upon the bed and left her no choice but to alarm the hidden guerrillas. In the ensuing shooting the general was killed. Later, after the Sandinista rebels came to power and Nora Astorga was designated Nicaragua's ambassador in Washington, this story was published by the media. This modern Judith was morally condemned.

[However, in my judgment] this Judith, too, subordinated her personal concerns to the liberation of her people. She too used her sexual appeal as a weapon. She too demonstrated strategic wisdom, determination and courage. As it was said of Judith, "there was no fear in Israel as long as Judith was alive," one can probably say of this unusual Central American woman that, for a short while, she diminished the fear of the poor people in her country.

61. From Dorothy Solle and Joe H. Kirchberger, *Great Women of the Bible in Art and Literature*, 1994, William.B. Eerdmans Publishing Co., Grand Rapids, MI. Reprinted by permission of the publisher; all rights reserved (p. 213).

Martha Graham, The Mistress of Modern Dance and Judith (1935 CE)

What I did not permit in the dance studio was any discussion of politics or religion. But there was a time for that, and a place, too. Late in 1935, I received an invitation to dance with my company at the International Dance Festival that was part of the 1936 Olympic Games to be held in Berlin. The invitation was signed by Rudolf Laban, president of the Deutsche Tanzbuhne, by the president of the organization committee of the Eleventh Olympic Games, and by the Reichminister of Volksaufklarung und Propaganda — Dr. Joseph Goebbels.

Actually, before the formal invitation arrived I received a call from the German Embassy in Washington. I was asked if I owned a shortwave radio because a message beamed directly to me from Berlin would come the next day. I went to hear the message read by Goebbels. He said that when the borders of Europe were one for all time another great celebration would be held in Germany, but for now the great artists of the world would join with each other in Germany, and my name was read. The formal invitation arrived, late in 1935. It never entered my mind even for a second to say yes. How could I dance in Nazi Germany? I replied:

"I would find it impossible to dance in Germany at the present time. So many artists whom I respect and admire have been persecuted, have been deprived of the right to work for ridiculous and unsatisfactory reasons, that I should consider it impossible to identify myself, by accepting the invitation, with the regime that has made such things possible. In addition, some of my concert group would not be welcomed in Germany. They are Jewish."

When I was told they would be perfectly immune, I said, "And do you think I would ask them to go?" The Germans said, in that case they would ask an inferior dance company to represent the United States. I said, "Do. But just remember this: I hold the official invitation and I will publish it across the country to show that Germany had to take second best." No American dance company went to the festival.

After the war in Berlin, I was found on a list of those to be "taken care of" when Germany would control the United States. I took it as a great compliment. And when I later performed in Berlin's new Philharmonic Hall, I took as my solo [dance the theme of] a triumphant biblical Jewish heroine, *Judith*, with a score by a Jewish composer, William Schuman.

Jessie Owens (1913-1980), the American track and field athlete who excelled in the sprint, hurdles and long jump. In May, 1935, he broke six world records in less than one hour. At the 1936 Berlin Olympics (shown here) he won four gold medals. The Nazi leader Hitler is said to have stormed out of the stadium in disgust at the black athlete's triumph.

ON THE BEAUTY OF SPORTS

If the Olympic Games were being held now you would be able to see for yourself why we attach such great importance to athletics. No one can describe in mere words the extraordinary pleasure derived from them and which you yourself would enjoy if you were seated among the spectators feasting your eyes on the prowess and stamina of the athletes, the beauty and power of their bodies, their incredible dexterity and skill, their invincible strength, their courage, ambition, endurance and tenacity. You would never stop applauding them.

— LUCIAN, 2ND CENTURY CE

Profiles in Modern Jewish Courage

*Natan Sharansky,
Chess Master and
Minister of Industry and Trade
(Israel Government Press Office)*

Only a life lived for others is a life worthwhile.
— ALBERT EINSTEIN

**Mature your minds with great thoughts;
to believe in the heroic makes heroes.**
— BENJAMIN DISRAELI

Profiles in Modern Jewish Courage

*In addition to reading about the historic heroism of the Maccabean period in the **Maccabees' Megillah**, we recommend that a short profile about modern Jewish courage be read aloud. The eight selections below include military as well as spiritual heroism, amazing acts in times of war and exemplary deeds in times of peace, by women, men and teenagers alike. All of the characters chosen for these Hanukkah readings are Jews, except for one incredible woman, a righteous gentile from the Netherlands who saved Jews and non-Jews during the Holocaust. The first two selections are directly related to Hanukkah and the others deal with courage in different realms.*

*Some of these stories may not be appropriate for young children, in particular the story of Levi Yitzchak; however others such as the stories of the Bar Mitzvah projects will appeal to them. For further readings in Jewish courage see the expanded Profiles in Modern Jewish Courage in the companion volume, **The Big Book of Hanukkah**. It includes stories about Chana Szenes, Yoni Netanyahu, and several tzedakah and civil rights heroes.*

FEAR NO EVIL

HANUKKAH IN THE SOVIET GULAG (RUSSIA, 1980S)

by Natan Sharansky[1]

THE
HANUKKA
CEREMO

Brach

Song

Maccab
Megilla

Profile

Spiritu
Meditatio

On November 2, 1986, Sharansky crossed the bridge between East and West Berlin to freedom. He flew to Israel where he was greeted as a hero.

The holiday of Hanukkah was approaching. At the time, I was the only Jew in the prison zone, but when I explained that Hanukkah was a holiday of national freedom, of returning to one's own culture in the face of forced assimilation, my friends in our "kibbutz" decided to celebrate it with me. They even made me a wooden menorah, decorated it, and found some candles.

In the evening I lit the first candle and recited a prayer that I had composed for this occasion. Tea was poured, and I began to describe the heroic struggle of the Maccabees to save their people from slavery. For each *zek* [a prisoner in the Soviet Gulag] who was listening, this story had its own personal meaning. At one point the duty officer appeared in the barracks. He made a list of all those present, but did not interfere.

On each of the subsequent evenings of Hanukkah I took out my menorah, lit the candles, and recited the appropriate blessing. Then I blew out the candles, as I didn't have any extras. Gavriliuk, the collaborator whose bunk was across from mine, watched and occasionally grumbled, "Look at him, he made himself a synagogue. And what if there's a fire?"

On the sixth night of Hanukkah the authorities confiscated my menorah with all my candles. I ran to the duty officer to find out what had happened.

Natan (Anatoli) Sharansky was arrested in 1977 for his Zionist activism, his insistence on the right of Russian Jews to make aliyah to Israel. However he was accused of the much more serious crime of treason, for spying for the United States. He sat in prison from 1977 to 1986 including eight years in a Soviet prison camp in Siberia. After continuous public protest in the West, spearheaded by his wife Avital, Natan Sharansky was released in a spy exchange between the US and the USSR in 1986. After making aliyah and establishing a Russian immigrant party in 1996, he became Israeli Minister of Industry and Trade and later of the Interior.

His memoirs of the Soviet period are filled with sparkling anecdotes about the power of the few against the many — the power that derives from "fearing no evil" and laughing in the face of oppression. The phrase, "fear no evil," is taken from the little book of Psalms, which he carried with him through his long imprisonment.

---

1. *Fear No Evil* by Natan Sharansky, p. 305-308, reprinted by permission of Random House, © 1988 by Natan Sharansky.

"The candlesticks were made from state materials; this is illegal. You could be punished for this alone and the other prisoners are complaining. They're afraid you'll start a fire."

I began to insist. "In two days Hanukkah will be over and then I'll return this 'state property' to you. Now, however, this looks like an attempt to deny me the opportunity of celebrating Jewish holidays."

The duty officer began hesitating. Then he phoned his superior and got his answer: "A camp is not a synagogue. We won't permit Sharansky to pray here."

I was surprised by the bluntness of that remark, and immediately declared a hunger strike. In a statement to the procurator general I protested against the violation of my national and religious rights, and against KGB [Russian secret police] interference in my personal life.

When you begin an unlimited hunger strike, you never know when or how it will end. Are the authorities interested at that moment in putting a swift end to it, or don't they give a damn? In a few weeks a commission from Moscow was due to arrive in the camp. I didn't know this at the time, but the authorities, presumably, were very aware of it, which probably explains why I was summoned to Major Osin's office two days later, in the evening.

Osin was an enormous, flabby man of around fifty, with small eyes and puffy eyelids, who seemed to have long ago lost interest in everything but food. But he was a master of intrigue who had successfully overtaken many of his colleagues on the road

Anatoly Sharansky's Final Statement in the Soviet Court[2]
presented before being sentenced on trumped-up charges for treason and espionage, July 14, 1978

Sharansky addressed his first remarks to those who were not in the courtroom, his wife Avital who emigrated to Israel and the Jewish people:

"During my interrogation the chief investigators threatened me that I might be executed by a firing squad, or imprisoned for at least fifteen years. But if I agreed to cooperate with the investigation for the purpose of destroying the Jewish emigration movement, they promised me freedom and a quick reunion with my wife.

"Five years ago, I submitted my application for exit to Israel. Now I am further than ever from my dream. It would seem to be cause for regret. But it is absolutely the other way around. I am happy. I am happy that I lived honorably, at peace with my conscience. I never compromised my soul, even under the threat of death.

"I am happy that I helped people. I am proud that I knew and worked with such honorable, brave and courageous people as Sakharov, Orlov, Ginzburg, who are carrying on the traditions of the Russian intelligentsia [in defending human rights in the Soviet Union]. I am fortunate to have been witness to the process of the liberation of Jews of the USSR.

"I hope that the absurd accusation against me and the entire Jewish emigration movement will not hinder the liberation of my people. My near ones and friends know how I wanted to exchange activity in the emigration movement for a life with my wife Avital, in Israel.

"For more that two thousand years the Jewish people, my people, have been dispersed. But wherever they are, wherever Jews are found, every year they have repeated, *'Next year in Jerusalem.'* Now, when I am further than ever from my people, from Avital, facing many arduous years of imprisonment, I say, turning to my people, my Avital, *'Next year in Jerusalem.'*

"Now I turn to you, the court, who were required to confirm a predetermined sentence: **To you I have nothing to say.**"

When in 1986 Sharansky was finally released in an exchange of spies and was reunited with his wife Avital, his first words to her recalled the final words of his declaration in the Soviet court, "Next Year in Jerusalem." He is reputed to have said, with his inimitable sense of humor, "Sorry for being late."

2. Reprinted by permission of Minister of the Interior Natan Sharansky.

Jews in Durban, South Africa, demonstrate for the release of Natan Sharansky, Prisoner of Zion, on the 2nd anniversary of his imprisonment (1979).
(*Durban Daily News, courtesy of the Beit Hatefutsot Photo Archive, Tel Aviv*)

**THE HANUKK
CEREMO**

Brach

Song

**Maccab
Megilla**

Profile

1st Cand
Natan
Sharans

to advancement. During my brief time in the camp he had weathered several scandals and had always managed to pass the buck to his subordinates. I could see that he had enjoyed his power over the *zeks* and liked to see them suffer. But he never forgot that the *zeks* were, above all, a means for advancing his career, and he knew how to back off in a crisis.

Osin pulled a benevolent smile over his face as he tried to talk me out of my hunger strike. Osin promised to see to it personally that in the future nobody would hinder me from praying, and that this should not be a concern of the KGB.

"Then what's the problem?" I said. "Give me back the menorah, as tonight is the last evening of Hanukkah. Let me celebrate it now, and taking into account your assurances for the future, I shall end the hunger strike."

"What's a menorah?"

"Candlesticks."

But a protocol for its confiscation had already been drawn up, and Osin couldn't back down in front of the entire camp. As I looked at this predator, sitting at an elegant polished table and wearing a benevolent smile, I was seized by an amusing idea.

"Listen," I said, "I'm sure you have the menorah somewhere. It's very important to me to celebrate the last night of Hanukkah. Why not let me do it here and now, together with you? You'll give me the menorah, I'll light the candles and say the prayer, and if all goes well I'll end the hunger strike."

Osin thought it over and promptly the confiscated menorah appeared from his desk. He summoned Gavriliuk, who was on duty in the office, to bring in a large candle.

"I need eight candles," I said. (In fact I needed nine, but when it came to Jewish rituals I was still a novice.) Gavriliuk took out a knife and began to cut the candle into several smaller ones. But it didn't come out right; apparently the knife was too dull. Then Osin took out a handsome inlaid pocketknife

Sharansky, the Israeli Cabinet Minister Revisits his Cell in Russia, January 30, 1997[3]

In 1997 Natan Sharansky, now an Israeli cabinet minister, revisited Russia where he had once been imprisoned and then expelled. On this trip he was able to fulfill two major personal goals: visiting the prison cell where he had sat in Moscow and fulfilling a childhood dream.

"When I was young, I dreamed of being a chess champion and having my games published in the Soviet press. Today I made it! Komsomolskaya Pravda published my game with Kasparov." (That was the game Mr. Sharansky won from the world champion, Gary Kasparov, when Mr. Kasparov played a simultaneous match with 25 Israelis in Jerusalem on Oct. 5, 1996).

"Now I've really closed the circle. I sat in the punishment cell [as a free man], I met with 1,000 Russian Jews and my game was published."

The visit to Lefortovo's prison cell had been reluctantly agreed to by Russian authorities, although Mr. Sharansky's request for another trip to the Perm labor camp in Siberia where he served much of his term was denied.

"They had the cell totally cleaned, as I expected. What struck me was how much smaller my cell was than I remembered. I guess things grow bigger in your memory. It was a bit different — they took the cover off the window, and there was a bit of light, and there was a radio. But the prison was still oppressively silent."

Before leaving, Mr. Sharansky left five copies of his book, *Fear No Evil*, which describes his ordeal in Soviet prisons and camps, for the Lefortovo library. "I warned them that their democracy will be judged by whether prisoners see these books or not."

"They asked me why I wanted to sit in the punishment cell today. Was I a masochist? I said no, the cell was the point of my victory, where I felt the strongest. And right from there I went to a meeting with the Jewish community at the House of Cinema. They had distributed 500 tickets, but 1,000 people came and 100 more hid behind the walls. That transition from the cell to the gathering, it was remarkable."

3. Based on quotes from Natan Sharansky that appeared in Serge Schmemann, "Sharansky Revisits His Cell," NY Times, January 30, 1997.

and deftly cut me eight candles.

"Go, I'll call you later," he said to Gavriliuk. Gavriliuk simply obeyed orders. He was a fierce, gloomy man, and this sight must have infuriated him.

I arranged the candles and went to the coatrack for my hat, explaining to Osin that "during the prayer you must stand with your head covered and at the end say 'Amen.'" He put on his major's hat and stood. I lit the candles and recited my own prayer in Hebrew, which went something like this: "Blessed are You, Adonai, for allowing me to rejoice on this day of Hanukkah, the holiday of our liberation, the holiday of our return to the way of our fathers. Blessed are You, Adonai, for allowing me to light these candles. May you allow me to light the Hanukkah candles many times in your city, Jerusalem, with my wife, Avital, and my family and friends."

This time, however, inspired by the sight of Osin standing meekly at attention, I added in Hebrew: "And may the day come when all our enemies, who today are planning our destruction, will stand before us and hear our prayers and say 'Amen.'"

"Amen," Osin echoed back. He sighed with relief, sat down and removed his hat. For some time we looked silently at the burning candles. They quickly melted, and the hot wax was spread pleasantly over the glass surface of the table. Then Osin caught himself, summoned Gavriliuk, and brusquely ordered him to clean it up.

I returned to the barracks in a state of elation, and our kibbutz made tea and merrily celebrated the end of Hanukkah. Naturally, I told them about Osin's "conversion," and it soon became the talk of the camp. I realized that revenge was inevitable, but I also knew they had plenty of other reasons to punish me.

A Menorah in an apartment window overlooking the town hall of Kiel, Germany, bedecked with its Nazi flag (c. 1933-1939)

(Bildarchiv Preussicher Kulturbesitz, Berlin)

THE
HANUKKA
CEREMO

Brach

Song

Maccab
Megilla

Profile

2nd Cand
Hugo
Gryn

2nd Candle

MY FATHER'S SPIRITUAL HEROISM

THE MARGARINE MENORAH (GERMANY, 1944)

by Rabbi Hugo Gryn[4]

MY DEFINITION OF HEROISM

At age 13, Hugo Gryn was deported to Auschwitz with his father. After the war, he became a leading Reform rabbi in London and a well-known participant in BBC broadcasts such as "The Moral Maze." In a broadcast about Hanukkah on December 13, 1976, Rabbi Gryn recalled a special Hanukkah menorah and his father's unique spiritual heroism.

At the end of this week, Jews and Jewish communities will celebrate the festival of Hanukkah. It is our festival of light and it recalls the heroism of

4. A transcript of the BBC talk show, December 13, 1976 reprinted in *European Judaism* volume 11 no. 1 (p. 4-5) under the title "Suffering: Four Meditations," Winter 1976-1977, with the permission of the Gryn family.

the Maccabees.

Was there any comparable heroism during World War II in the midst of the Nazi persecution of the Jews? If heroism can only be vindicated by victory, as the Maccabees' was, the answer is "no." But if you can agree with **my definition of heroism**, that it is achieved **when the spirit of an individual or of a group of people triumphs over a surrounding barbarism, and emerges, not merely triumphant, but still civilized and with human dignity intact**, then there were many such acts of heroism.

"I DISCOVERED GOD IN GERMANY"

I discovered God in Germany. You may think this is a strange thing to say, but when I was a teenager in Nazi concentration camps in Germany, I discovered God. Not the God of my childhood. I lost him, or lost sight of him, around the crematoria of Auschwitz. I prayed that he "do something" and when he did not, I turned my back on him as well. But later, in the slave labor camps, and, I suppose, in retrospect too, when I saw more clearly the different ways in which the human spirit can respond to people and events, I rediscovered God.

Irritability and brutalization could only be suppressed through intellectual and emotional effort.

In the camps there was "a regression to primitiveness," that is to say, our interests became restricted to the most immediate and urgent needs. Food and water and sleep. Because there was hardly any food, and crowded conditions combined with vermin plus 14 hours of work a day, gave little chance for sleep, we were in the main apathetic and irritable.

Disillusionment brought a quick decline of bodily defenses. All thinking was concentrated on a simple and single point: Get through today! Survive another day! Irritability and brutalization could only be

suppressed through intellectual and emotional effort. If you could not do this you became less, considerably less, than a civilized human being.

It became a **choice**: to fit into the surroundings and swim with the tide — this was towards primitiveness. Or to struggle against a dreadful environment and swim against a powerful tide. I began to see it then, and see it much more clearly now: **it was a matter of spiritual effort**.

The **miracle of Hanukkah** stems from the victory of the few over the many. A small handful of pious Jews stood up to the might of the empire of Antiochus Epiphanes and prevailed. This happens so rarely that it is in the category of miracles. And the motto of the festival is a line from the prophet Zechariah: *"Not by power, nor by might — but by My spirit, says the Lord."*[5]

The legacy of the Maccabees was a very "Jewish" kind of faith. There are several kinds of faith and there is probably an appropriate time for all of them, though, personally, I don't trust the fanatic's sort. But there is faith through which a man accepts his lot; there is a simple faith in divine providence, or reliance on authority. There is also faith, which is a compound of trust and hope. No matter what today may be like or the odds — this faith urges that there is a partnership between the divine and the human, and that salvation or redemption in this world, in the here and now, is possible and not merely a pious pipe-dream.

MY FATHER'S MIRACLE

I did not learn this lesson in a theological college but in a miserable little concentration camp grotesquely called *"Lieberose"* (Lovely Rose) in German Silesia. It was the cold winter of 1944 and although we had nothing like calendars, my father, who was my fellow prisoner there, took me and some of our friends to a corner in our barrack. He

---

5. *Zechariah* 4:6, from the Haftorah for Shabbat Hanukkah.

The Heroic Scientists   BY HUGO GRYN

Let me tell you about a book which is virtually unknown in our country, and which illustrates most movingly what I mean by spiritual heroism. It is called *Maladie de Famine*, published in Warsaw in 1946, a few months after the war. It is a detailed, scientific study of starvation.

In the Autumn of 1940, the Nazis herded half-a-million Jews into the Warsaw ghetto. A year later all food reserves were completely exhausted. The daily ration dwindled to about 800 calories and starvation had become one of the main killers in the ghetto. A poorly equipped hospital tried to cope, but the doctors soon realized not only the extent, but also the hopelessness of the situation. At this point, in February 1942, a group of 33 Jewish doctors, scientists and medical students made a heroic decision. They would study and record the effects of starvation both on their patients and on themselves. They met every month to coordinate their work and knew that it could come to a sudden end through their own or their patients' deportation to one of the extermination camps. (In fact, not a single doctor survived.)

By the Spring of 1943, when the population of the ghetto was reduced to 40,000 due to starvation, epidemics and deportation, they decided to smuggle the manuscript (meticulously illustrated by graphs, charts and some haunting photographs) to a non-Jewish professor at Warsaw University. As soon as Poland was liberated, the American Jewish Joint Distribution Committee had the Yiddish and Polish texts translated into French (considered the language of civilized Europe) and printed on cheap brownish paper.

I look at my much-thumbed copy now, and I wonder about the purpose of its authors. Why did they work so hard? 3,658 autopsies and tens of thousands of examinations and tests were performed, all in their off-duty hours. I am convinced that it was done in order to give both their lives and their deaths a measure of significance. They knew that never in human experience had there been destruction on such a vast scale. They also knew starvation to be a universal problem. Dr. Emil Apfelbaum, in his study of the circulatory system in extreme hunger, wrote: "The organism which is destroyed by prolonged hunger is **like a candle which burns out**, life disappears gradually without a visible shock to the naked eye."

Why do I think of this book as heroic? Because it represents **the triumph of the human spirit over human barbarism**. Neither Hitler's name nor the word "Nazi" is ever mentioned in it. There is no note of self-pity. It is a legacy by scientists to fellow scientists which has yet to be properly appreciated. Moreover, it is a classic testament to human self-respect and dignity.

THE
HANUKK
CEREMO

Brach

Song

Maccab
Megilla

Profile

2nd Can
Hugo
Gryn

announced that it was the eve of Hanukkah, produced a curious-shaped clay bowl, and began to light a wick immersed in his precious, but now melted, margarine ration. Before he could recite the blessing, I protested at this waste of food. He looked at me — then at the lamp — and finally said: "You and I have seen that it is possible to live up to three weeks without food. We once lived almost three days without water: but **you cannot live properly for three minutes without hope!**"

Here was the legacy of the Maccabees transmitted to me by my father, and it was at that moment, I think, that I first began to understand clearly the meaning of the distinctly Jewish component of my heritage.

I would like to be able to end with a story of another miracle. I would like to — but I can't. Unless it is that our guards, who seemed to have eyes and guns in the back of their heads, did not see our little celebration. But that could be because the margarine had more water in it than fat, and after some spluttering and smoke the little flame went out. Nor did my father survive. But I like to think that his spirit, which went back through Judah the Maccabee and the prophet Zechariah all the way to Abraham, is in me, too, and, with a bit of luck and hope, has gone into my children. That, too, is a miracle of sorts.

The Wassink Family and their "Hidden Treasure" 50 Years later.

In the picture in the center with the tie is the ten-year-old boy, now 60, Wim Wassink, to the left the English pilot who was hidden under their roof, and to the right Wim's older brother and one of the two Jewish girls who also hid with them. The sacred memorabilia of the family include the pot for making stew, the framed Dutch translation of the Biblical verse of hospitality, "Blessed are you when you come in and when you go out," the scale model of the original house and one board from the original attic on which Sallie Zion had carved a poem during the war.

(Reproduced by permission of Wim Wassink, Eibergen, The Netherlands)

2nd Candle (alternative reading)

THE RIGHTEOUS GENTILES

THE BIBLE AND HEROIC HOSPITALITY (NETHERLANDS, 1945)[6]

by Wim Wassink

*Wim Wassink, a devout Christian living in a little town in the Netherlands, often finds himself recalling a great family moment demonstrating his **mother's courage and toughness**. His family was instrumental in saving the only Jewish family in his village that survived World War II, the Zion family.*

The Zion family lived in Russia before coming to the Netherlands. When Emperor Napoleon invaded Russia in the early 1800's, his military government forced all citizens to take last names. In Augustova near Minsk, their family was called into the military office to pick a last name. The date was immediately after Tisha B'Av, the day when Jews remember the destruction of the First and Second Temples. The family had just been to the synagogue where they prayed and wept as they remembered the destruction of Zion, the poetic name for Jerusalem. So they chose the last name — "Zion." In 1852, the Zion family left Russia and settled in the Netherlands, in a village called Eibergen.

In 1940, the Germans invaded Holland and in 1941, the Jews of Holland were ordered by the Nazis to report for "resettlement." The Zion family had three brothers and three sisters who decided to go underground. Even though Jews had little social contact with their Calvinist-Protestant neighbors, Jews were aided by the ministers of the Calvinist church, Puritans, in the underground movement.

Even before the war, one of the Dutch ministers would go across the border from Holland to Germany to try to convince the German Calvinists to oppose the Nazis. Soon, the German ministers, who wanted to prove their loyalty to the Nazis, refused to allow him to speak at their services. Even after the Nazis invaded Holland, this minister, who was called "Frits de Zwerver" (Fritz the Wanderer), continued to go from church to church in the Netherlands to arouse opposition to the Nazis. He travelled on his bicycle, but since all the rubber had been confiscated by the Germans, his bike had wooden wheels. When this minister came to Eibergen, Wim Wassink's family attended that church service. Below Wim retells the story of his family's involvement in saving the Zion brothers.

---

6. The *Leader's Guide* to *The Family Participation Haggadah: A Different Night* by Noam Zion and David Dishon (p. 49-50).

One Sunday morning Frits arrived in our church in Eibergen and walked to the podium (the most important part of the Calvinist service was the sermon preached from the Bible). Even though there were pro-Nazi Dutch officials sitting in the front row, he opened his Bible to Exodus 1:15-22 and read the story of the midwives in Egypt who saved the Hebrew male children from drowning. Then he asked the congregation and they replied: "Who is the Pharaoh today?" "The Nazis!" "Who are the babies who have to be hidden?" "The Jews!" "Who are the midwives today? We are! It is our job to outsmart the Pharaohs, to have the courage of the midwives and to protect the Jews and all those being persecuted." Then he got on his bicycle and went to the next village. The people were inspired by Frits de Zwerver, who encouraged them to organize an underground movement. Many members of our church participated, and hid Jews in their houses. (Since Dutch architecture emphasizes large roofs on houses, Jews and other refugees often hid *"ondergedoken"*/submerged under the roof in an attic).

necessary they would go up a rope ladder, which could be folded and pulled up. The ladder was hidden behind a large embroidered wall hanging, traditional in Calvinist homes. It was embroidered in Dutch with the Biblical words:

בָּרוּךְ אַתָּה בְּבֹאֶךָ
וּבָרוּךְ אַתָּה בְּצֵאתֶךָ

Blessed are You When You Come In and When You Go Out!

THE HANUKK CEREMO

Brach

Song

Maccab Megilla

Profile

2nd Can Wassink

During this period, Sallie Zion and his brother were hidden by these righteous gentiles in some 40 different places. When the person protecting him would say, "I can't hide you any more," he would have to find another hiding place. Sometimes he was told ahead of time that they would have to leave in a day or a week. Then someone would come from the underground, usually at night, on a bicycle, and take him and his brother to a safe house and hide them under the roof or in the closets and barns.

The last place Sallie Zion and his brother stayed was at our home, the Wassink family. We lived in a kind of large farmhouse on the outskirts of town. We could see people coming across the fields to the house; one of us children would be the lookout stationed in the living room, so we could alert the people who were hiding whenever danger approached. Sallie and his brother were hidden under the roof, a triangular space about three feet by six feet. (Sallie Zion carved a poem he wrote on one of the beams from the roof, which I still have).

Since we were on the outskirts of the town, they did not need to hide during the day. They were able to help with the household tasks, but always stayed indoors. When

Hidden with Sallie Zion and his brother were two Jewish girls, 16 and 18 years old, as well as a Russian pilot, a Canadian pilot and a British pilot who had been shot down and taken in by the family. Also hidden was my oldest brother and a first cousin who had been called up to work in a German factory and did not want to go. All were hidden in one very narrow area.

A couple of days before the liberation of the village from the Nazis in March, 1945, a lookout for our family reported that 13 Nazis and two Dutch collaborators were approaching. Quickly all the illegals hid under the roof. In order to remove all signs of the hidden illegals, my mother cleared away extra cutlery, dishes and chairs. She turned to my older sister, gave her the stolen ration cards used to purchase extra food and told her to hide them in the barn in an old stove. Then she turned to me, Wim, and told me to go visit relatives, but not to run lest I arouse suspicion.

As I nonchalantly twirled a stick in the air, the Nazis spotted me and told me to come with them into the house; it was about 11 a.m. The Nazis searched the house. One of them came to the kitchen and saw a large, black pot on the stove. He turned to my mother and pointed to the big pot, saying "too much food" (implying that the quantity of food showed that she was feeding extra mouths — the hidden illegals they had come to arrest). My mother stood up stoically and held her two fingers forming "V" in a victory sign and said, "This big pot is enough for two days" (meaning that the food was only for her nuclear family but it was a portion for several days). Incidentally, the iron pot contained a carrot stew whose orange color is the national color of the Dutch Queen, symbol of the resistance to the Nazi occupation.

While the Nazis continued their search, our family sat down for lunch in full view of

---

Then one of the Germans took me out to the pigsty. "We know there are people hiding here. If you don't tell us where, we will throw you in with the pigs." I thought, "Pigs are certainly better than Nazis."

---

the German soldiers. In a Calvinist household everyone sits down for their big meal at lunch, a prayer is said and the Bible is read. The prayer my mother recited in Dutch was "May the evil Nazis be struck by blindness, just as the evil people of the Biblical city of Sodom were struck by blindness when they came to molest the guests taken in by Lot."[7] While we were eating, the Nazis continued their search and even measured the inside and outside of the house to see if there was any space unaccounted for. However, they measured the length and not the width. The hiding place under the attic was, luckily, in the width of the house. The Nazis even went to the attic with a lantern. It shone on the hidden people through a crack, but when the Nazi held the lantern and tried to look through, the light of the lantern blinded him, so in a way, my mother's prayer came true.

Then one of the Germans took me out to the pigsty. "We know there are people hiding

---
7. *Genesis* 19:11

here. If you don't tell us where, we will throw you in with the pigs." I thought, "Pigs are certainly better than Nazis." The soldier began beating me, and I screamed. My older brother, one of the people in hiding, got upset and wanted to come down and help me. However, the Russian pilot, Alex, took a pillow and shoved it over my brother's head until he calmed down. I did not reveal anything.

After the beating, my mother turned to the officer and pointed to me. "Look how you have beaten him! Look at his bloody nose!" The officer apologized and told the German who had beaten me to go to the yard, pump some water and wash my face. Then the Nazi officer told our family we would have to leave our house. He put up a sign declaring the house off limits. At night the underground came to extricate the people hiding in the attic. Several days later the Allies arrived in the vicinity of Eibergen. Outside the village Sallie Zion spied the incoming English tanks, showed them how to get across a low spot in the river since all the bridges had been bombed. He rode into town seated on a British tank. His neighbors and friends who had not seen him since he went underground in August, 1941, rubbed their eyes and said, "I told you Sallie Zion went to England during the war."

On Dutch liberation day, May 5, the Wassink clan and all those they helped, like to get together. They pull out the old iron pot and sometimes eat carrot stew. The embroidery of "Blessed are You When You Come In and When You Go Out" (which once covered the rope ladder leading to the hideaway) hangs on the wall next to the framed, yellowing Nazi poster instructing everyone that this house is off limits and everyone must evacuate it. Though after the war the old house itself was razed, a scale model was constructed (like a dollhouse) showing the secret spaces. The family sits together on those occasions and the young members ask the elders to retell the story in detail, so that it shall never be forgotten.

Two Special Bar Mitzvah Projects
Yigal Allon and David Levitt

Here we have examples of two young boys' courage in two countries and in two different eras. For both of them, their parents encouraged them to take a large step toward manhood. While for us they may seem like exceptional heroes, from their own point of view they were just trying to do what responsible adults like their parents had modeled for them.

THE HANUKK. CEREMO

Brach

Song

Maccab
Megilla

Profile

3rd Cand
Yigal
Allon

A FATHER TESTS HIS SON (ERETZ YISRAEL, 1931)
BY GENERAL YIGAL (PEIKOVITZ) ALLON[8]

In 1948 General Yigal Allon, at age 29, became one of the youngest generals in the fledgling State of Israel. Among other military assignments, Allon headed the elite unit of the Haganah, the Palmach, that included the young Yitzchak Rabin. Later he would become Deputy Prime Minister (1967-1974); however in this context we are interested in his youth. Yigal was born in Israel in 1918 to a Zionist pioneer family. In an age when the Diaspora Jews who made aliyah were trying to refashion themselves in the image of a new type of Israeli, a sabra — a farmer, not a shopkeeper, and a fighter, not a weakling — Yigal's father represented a new kind of hero for his son. His parents named him Yigal because it reflected their national hopes — "Yigal" means "He will redeem [his people]." In the memoir below, we see a little boy describing the heroism of his father as well as the father finding a ritual that would initiate his son into a responsible manhood and ultimately a national career. This is the story of how a great Israeli leader "celebrated" a unique Bar Mitzvah and how that event shaped his identity and changed his name.

FATHER'S FEARLESSNESS (1925)

[During the British mandate in Israel] it was with good reason that the older settlements in the Galilee and other regions of Israel surrounded themselves with protective walls. The Jewish farms were fruitful and thriving, and there was no lack of hostile, aggressive elements who were always ready to lay hands on Jewish life and property, whether their motives stemmed from greed or nationalism.

More than once during my childhood, I was an eyewitness to real physical combat in

General Yigal Allon, 1948 *(Courtesy of Allon Museum)*

which my father employed the tactics of a wrestler against Arabs who had trespassed on his property. I particularly remember one hard fight:

As we approached the field we saw two Arabs sitting by the road while their horses munched the ears of our cut barley. My father boiled with indignation at the audacious encroachment on his land. My father raised

8. Yigal Allon, *My Father's House* (copyright by the author, 1976) (pp. 72-82), translated by Reuven Ben-Yosef, and reprinted by permission of W.W. Norton and Co., NY.

his voice and demanded that they get their horses out of the field at once. If they had stood up and taken their horses and gone, the incident would have ended without a quarrel. But one of them had a loose tongue and he greeted my father with a round of Arab curses. My father jumped off the wagon while it was still moving. I stopped the mules and ran after him, in case he needed help — I was seven or eight years old at the time — and when I arrived he was already wrestling with one of them, while the other tried to get a hold on him from behind. The time had come for me to intervene in what might be described as my first engagement in battle: I gathered up some pebbles and began throwing them at the other Arab. I was careful not to hit my father, but I didn't hit the Arab either.

"Why didn't you draw the pistol?" I asked him. He replied: "A shot might have resulted in the Arab's death, and the killing of an Arab starts off a blood feud that could go on for many years."

It took my father two minutes to pin down the first Arab, with whom he was wrestling; then, with an unexpected, unorthodox move, while still bent over his out-stretched, screaming opponent, he grabbed the other Arab's legs in one hand and laid him flat as well. It goes without saying that my father had a pistol in his pocket, but he didn't draw it.

"Why didn't you draw the pistol?" I asked him afterwards and he replied: "A shot might have resulted in the Arab's death, and the killing of an Arab starts off a blood feud that could go on for many years. Since we have to live here, we should use our hands, so long as it's possible. The pistol is for when you have no choice, when your life is in danger." I remember that not only as an example of personal courage — and my father was renowned for his courage throughout the Galilee — but also as my first lecture on the considerations involved in the use of arms. Even when tempers raged my father knew how to control himself and behave as the situation demanded, doing no more than was necessary. Since he was so brave, I often asked him if he was never afraid. **"The man who's never afraid is a fool,"** he would reply. **"The trick is to know how to control fear."**

It wasn't by speeches that my father educated us, but by his personal example.

MY BAR MITZVAH TEST: "NOW YOU ARE A MAN" (1931)

When I attained the Bar Mitzvah age of thirteen, my father summoned me to the grain shed at the rear of the yard and said: "Although you have put on tefillin you haven't yet fulfilled all the principal commandments; you've become a man, and from now on you're going to have your own weapon." As he spoke he pried open a metal can and took out a semiautomatic Browning pistol, wrapped in a woolen napkin. "It was mine; from now on it's yours. You're going to clean it and take care of it. You already know how to use it. There's no license for it and its place is here in the shed, behind the wheat bin." I was very excited. This was the day I'd dreamed about, longing for the time I'd have my own personal weapon like my brothers, and, needless to say, my father. I was still in the grip of my excitement when he added: "Tonight you're going out to guard what's left of the sorghum harvest in the Balut field, since we haven't had time to bring it in to the barn yet."

That distant field, at the northern end of the village lands, had, as did all our other fields, an Arab name: *Balut*, meaning oak tree. In the middle of its two sections, in a rocky spot, grew our sturdy, beautiful oaks.

As I said, I was perfectly thrilled. I put on a knowing, courageous air and just after sunset took out my very own pistol, hid it in my shirt and set out to the north, in the direction of the Balut field. For the first time in my life I was the sole guard of a field, alone beneath the starry sky through which a full moon of

Prime Minister David Ben-Gurion of Israel and his young General, Yigal Allon (1948)
(The Defense Ministry Press, Zahal Album, courtesy of Beit Hatefutsot, Photo Archive, Tel Aviv)

THE
HANUKK
CEREMO

Brach

Song

Maccab
Megilla

Profile

3rd Cand
Yigal
Allon

autumn drifted. The farther I got from the village, the greater was my fear.

I reached the field. At once I installed myself beneath an oak tree, behind a large rock. Little by little the tension lessened and I began to get used to the darkness and solitude. My ears opened to receive the stirrings of the night: the gusts of wind among the leaves and bushes, the shrill chirp of the crickets and the sound of the frogs croaking at a little distance by a muddy spring. If I had a prayer in my heart it was only that the thieves should refrain that night from trying to filch the remains of our harvest.

After midnight I heard caravans passing on the path next to the field. Thank God they didn't try to fill their sacks with our crops. But later, it might have been two o'clock, I made out three men on horseback straying from the path and invading the field. Less than fifty meters away from me, they

dismounted and began filling their sacks with sorghum. Their attitude suggested utter confidence: they spoke aloud and one of them even cracked a joke, his two friends laughing. The test was on.

Before my departure, my father had told me that if thieves should approach, I was first to let them get on with their work and only later to sound a warning in Arabic; if my cry didn't faze them, I was to fire a shot in the air. "But remember," he warned me, "be careful not to hit them. Don't be a hothead. Take aim only if they try to get close to you."

I followed his instructions to the letter. I overcame my fear. Papa's orders helped but so did logic: they were standing while I lay behind a rock, and even though it was not the best sort of cover, my situation was better than theirs; they didn't know I existed and I had the advantage of surprise. So I did two things at once: I raised my voice, rather a childish voice to which I tried to give a mature ring as far as possible — after all I was thirteen! — and I yelled "*Andak!*" (Arabic for "Beware, Watch Out") and at the same time I cocked my pistol with a metallic click, so as to frighten them. I hoped the horsemen would let go of the sacks, jump on their horses and flee for their lives.

To my amazement, which was mixed with dread, they took up positions in the field and one of them responded with a battle cry. For the first time in actual combat I pulled the trigger. The pistol fired properly, into the air, of course. The response was a rattle of

---

The then Prime Minister and Minister of Defense, David Ben-Gurion, had decreed with his characteristic resolve that we change our foreign names to Hebrew ones, before they were made public.

---

weapons but no shots. What now, I asked myself, what next? Should I aim at them? And what if one of them is killed? What if I'm killed? Maybe it would be better to withdraw under the cover of darkness? In other words, to flee? Such were the thoughts that rapidly shot through me; but in the same split second I heard all at once, somewhere behind me, a little to the flank, cries and hearty curses in Arabic, with a distinct Russian accent. Immediately after them came rifle shots in the air, above the heads of the horsemen who jumped on their horses and disappeared into the night, leaving their half-full sacks behind. I gave a sigh of relief. Needless to say, the figure darting out at me was Papa's.

Yes, he wanted to test my courage, but he loved me enough — sometimes even too much — to let me go alone. He'd gone after me without my noticing, taken a position in a suitable spot and let me fend for myself. Only when he was sure I was in real danger, did he intervene, and it was his critical intervention, of course, which turned the tide. That night I learned that reserve forces

are a decidedly positive factor, even when the battle is between individuals.

My joy that night was twofold: not only had I passed the test, but Papa saw me pass it. It's hard to imagine how I could have looked him in the face if I hadn't acted as I did.

YIGAL PEIKOVITZ BECOMES GENERAL YIGAL ALLON

Some sixteen years after that event I stood on a lawn at Israel Defense Forces Headquarters in Ramat Gan, for the swearing-in of the first generals in our army. The then Prime Minister and Minister of Defense, David Ben-Gurion, had decreed with his characteristic resolve that we change our foreign names to Hebrew ones, before our promotions were made public. I accepted his demand, but how could I find a name that would please my father and the entire clan, since even in name alone I had no wish to cut myself off from them. What name should I choose now?

Ben-Gurion declared: "HaGiladi" (my *nom de guerre* in the underground had been "Yiftach," the biblical judge Yiftach HaGiladi). I listened to the suggestion but happened to recall that big oak tree in the sorghum field, the tree beneath which I had my first taste of battle. I promised Ben-Gurion an answer by the time our names were to be released to the newscasters. He looked at me and pronounced: "HaGiladi!" and added at once. "You're going to conquer the land of Gilad [in Transjordan]." "I'll decide before the newscast," I repeated.

In the meantime I talked it over with my wife Ruth, and together we decided: **Allon** [*Allon* means oak tree or *Balut* in Arabic]. The note [I wrote] reached the newscaster a minute before his announcement and settled the matter. Hearing my new name for the first time on the air, my older brothers immediately guessed what had determined their kid brother's choice. As for Papa, though he refused to change his name, he was pleased with mine, since *Allon (Balut)* was a part of his own land.

David Levitt, volunteering at the Tampa Bay Harvest, distributing food to the homeless.

(courtesy of the Levitt family)

THE
HANUKK
CEREMO

Brach

Song

Maccab
Megilla

Profile

3rd Cand
David
Levitt

3rd Candle (alternative reading)

ALL THAT FOOD

DAVID LEVITT VS. THE BOARD OF EDUCATION

by Danny Siegel[9]

Danny Siegel is a poet and Jewish educator who has devoted his life to illuminating the phenomenon of human beings giving of themselves to other human beings. He calls these people "Tzedakah heroes" and he is their storyteller as well as one of their important fundraisers. Here is a talk he gave about a 12 year old American boy who aroused his wonder and admiration.

This is about food. Massive quantities of edible food; so much food you couldn't possibly picture it all together in one place; food from the public school cafeterias and food from kids' lunches. Uneaten food. David Levitt's idea was to donate the school leftovers to hungry people. That was his Bar Mitzvah project.

I know, I know. I've heard all the groans and laughs when I mention David's project to my audiences. "Why would anyone ever want to donate such horrible food to soup kitchens and shelters?" In those same lectures, though, once the laughing stops, everyone begins to listen carefully to David's idea. We say, "Why not?" And we say, "Aside from the cafeteria food, think of all the food kids brought in their lunches, never touched, apples and muffins and pretzels and juices they thoughtlessly tossed in the garbage."

THE WAY IT WAS

David wrote, called, and petitioned the school board of Pinellas County, Florida, to have the schools' food donated to shelters and soup kitchens. He had been warned by "Older, Wiser People," that others had tried and failed and that he certainly didn't have a chance to succeed. He wasn't yet 12 years old when he first wrote to Dr. J. Howard Hinesley, who was the superintendent of the district's schools at that time. This is his letter to Dr. Hinesley:

9. Danny Siegel, *Heroes and Miracle Workers* (1997) (p. 11-18) is founder of Ziv Tzedakah Fund (384 Wyoming Avenue, Milburn, NJ 07041, Tel 201-763-9396 Fax 201-275-0346 naomike@aol.com) which supports Tzedakah heroes in North America and Israel. David Levitt, 9603 108th Ave., N., Largo, FL 33773, 727-398-1766, e-mail: celebrate9@aol.com, Website: at Giraffe Project Site www.Giraffe.org/giraffe/levitt.htm. Contributions made out to: "Help for the Harvest." Reprinted by permission of authors.

Dear Dr. Hinesley:

I am a sixth grade student at Osceola Middle School. I am also a year away from my Bar Mitzvah. This means not only am I studying hard at middle school, but I also need to study Hebrew. It is also important for me to try to do something useful in my community.

I am very concerned about hungry and homeless people in our area. I read an article in Parade Magazine a few months ago about an organization called "Kentucky Harvest," which has grown into "Harvest USA."

In 1986 Stan Curtis from Louisville, Kentucky, was in a cafeteria line at lunch time. He was just about to order some green beans when a man put down a new pan of beans and took away a pan that was still one-third full. He wondered where those green beans were going and was told that the buffet line had to always look full. The leftover beans would be thrown out. This bothered Stan Curtis so much that he got a group of volunteers together who would take food that would be thrown away and transport it to people who needed it. This is how Kentucky Harvest got started. Two years later Harvest USA was born.

My mom helped me find out if there was a group like Kentucky Harvest here in Pinellas County. It is called Tampa Bay Harvest. I signed up to be a volunteer. I am trying to find places that will donate food for the hungry and homeless.

As part of this project, I went on a field trip to a homeless shelter called "Everybody's Tabernacle" in Clearwater. This is one of the shelters that Tampa Bay Harvest brings food to. We got there at dinner time and there were about 50 people being served. There were all different kinds of people — children, women, and men — black and white. They didn't look like the dirty bums I sometimes see on TV. They looked a lot like you and me.

I was thinking that it would be cool to have the schools in Pinellas County donate leftover cafeteria food to Tampa Bay Harvest. I asked my principal, Mr. Fred Ulrich, if Osceola Middle School could do this. He said that there is a federal law that prevents public schools from donating cafeteria food. I was upset and disappointed to hear this. My mom and I spoke to Tampa Bay Harvest and found out that Kentucky Harvest developed a program with the Louisville, Kentucky, school system by working together to make changes in the state and federal guidelines. I've enclosed detailed information on this project called "Operation Food for Thought." We have also learned that no school system in the State of Florida has tried this program. (Wouldn't it be cool to be the first?) This is a very large project, so I would suggest a small pilot program for one school — something as simple as donating leftover milk.

Do you think we could make this program work in Pinellas County?

Sincerely,

David Levitt

P.S. PLEASE make this happen. **Today is my 12th birthday and this is the best present I could ask for.** Thank you for taking the time to listen to me.

Not so long afterwards, Dr. Hinesley wrote back, "The Pinellas County School District would certainly like to be the first in Florida to accomplish this goal."

David had a couple of things already working in his favor. The most important one was his youth: when he began this project, he hadn't even had his Bar Mitzvah. The first newspaper article I have about him shows him with his braces still showing through the smile. He was of that magic age so many people have forgotten, the time when "impossible" and "change" was an oxymoronic combination of words, distasteful to hear or say, grammatically unacceptable and syntactically false.

THE NEXT TIME I SAW DAVID LEVITT

The next time I saw David was on TV. I turned the set on in the middle of a brief news story and immediately knew that I recognized this kid. It was David, and it was a lengthy piece about how the program had settled into a routine, a smooth-running routine.

What surprised me was that an earlier article I read reported that the schools had donated about 55,000 pounds of food. Now the TV reporter stated 165,000 pounds. The old article said that 52 of the 92 public schools were donating food. This TV special reported that all 92 schools in the county were donating.

THE HANUKK CEREMO

Brach

Song

Maccab Megilla

Profile

3rd Cand
David
Levitt

Songs of Love: John Beltzer's Gift to Kids[10] BY DANNY SIEGEL

It is my belief that meeting mitzvah heroes and being part of their work makes it easier to understand exactly who we ourselves ought to be as human beings. The correct term is really "human doing," not "human being." Who these people are is defined by what they do.

Many of them are locksmiths: they look for the right key to open up the souls of other people. It often takes no more than a hot meal cooked and served with true compassion.

There are times when a new pair of shoes or a beautiful hair-do can make the ultimate difference in someone's life. Sometimes it only takes placing a kitten on a lonely person's lap in order to bring a smile, memories, a renewed sense of hope, and the will to live. At other times, it takes years of pure love. Here is John Belzer's patented approach:

John Beltzer has an ever-growing group of friends, and friends of friends, individuals who are professional song writers and musicians. They write individualized, personalized songs for children dying of cancer. First they gather information about the child: family facts, hobbies, whether they like to draw or play baseball, what color their eyes are, nicknames, anything that can go into a song. They write it,

Dear John,

Please accept this check as a donation to Songs of Love in memory of our son Sam.

You wrote and sang a song for Sam at Easter time. The song brought him many smiles and he listened to it over and over. Sam passed away May 28 and as there were no words to capture the specialness of Sam, your song was played at his funeral in lieu of a eulogy. We hope this donation helps in some small way so that you can continue to bring joy to other sick children.

Fondly,
Michelle and Barry Johnson

orchestrate it, produce it, and send the tape to the child. It is a simple enough idea and a perfect use of the talents of Beltzer's people. They call themselves Songs of Love.

The following letter will give you and indication of just how awesome this project is.

10. Songs of Love, John Beltzer, President, 108-12 65th Road, Forest Hills, NY 11375, phone/fax: 718-997-8482, e-mail: songslove@aol.com. Reprinted by permission.

THE COURAGE TO TELL THE TRUTH

YITZCHAK RABIN (1943 AND 1976)

by Dan Kurzman[11]

> If we have faith, we will succeed.
> If we hold tight to our dreams, our actions will be blessed.
> If we can grit our teeth, bite our lips, hold back the pain, overcome obstacles
>   — we will reach our destination.
> Even if there are difficult moments, they will never be as difficult as others in the past.
> We will continue to have faith, and we will be victorious.
>
> — YITZCHAK RABIN

INTRODUCTION

Yitzchak Rabin (1922-1995), soldier and Prime Minister (1974-1977, 1992-1995), was known for his military courage especially in the War of Independence (1948) as the officer of the Palmach who defended the road to Jerusalem and in the Six Day War (1967) as the Chief of Staff who led Israel to its miraculous victory and the reunification of Jerusalem (1967). As Prime Minister in 1976 he made the decision to send Ehud Barak and Yoni Netanyahu to lead a daring commando rescue of 100 hostages held in Entebbe, Uganda.

In 1992 his political courage was reflected in his decision to break the political taboos on negotiating with Yasser Arafat, whom he considered a merciless Palestinian terrorist, in order to end the cycle of violence in the Middle East. When he concluded the Oslo agreement with the Palestinians, Rabin faced unprecedented personal attacks in which ironically Rabin, the liberator of Jerusalem, was called a traitor and his picture was displayed on posters which artificially dressed him in the uniform of the Nazi SS. Eventually he was assassinated by an extremist right wing religious Zionist law student at the giant peace rally in Tel Aviv on November 4, 1995 (That same Shabbat the Torah reading of Akedat Yitzchak — the sacrifice of Isaac — was read). Rabin was courageous in war and in peace.

However we have chosen a different aspect of his personal integrity — his courage "to come clean," to confess to a misdemeanor unbecoming a political leader. In the modern era of President Nixon's cover up on Watergate and President Clinton's lies about his sexual affairs, Rabin's sense of political ethics is truly exceptional. It recalls the spirit of David confessing his sin with Batsheva to Nathan the prophet. Yet Rabin surpasses them all because his courage led him to resign from political office for a minor violation committed by his wife with whom he maintained complete solidarity, the integrity of a leader was paramount. Dan Kurzman retells two related stories of Rabin's exceptional political honesty and personal loyalty.

RABIN'S FIRST THEFT: PALMACH, 1943

[In 1943 the Haganah (the Israeli underground military organization including its elite forces the Palmach) was broke]. "Only deep faith and inner conviction kept the Palmach together," Yitzchak Rabin would say. Palmach leaders argued that it was essential to preserve a standing Jewish force that could fight the Germans in the war and, if necessary, the Arabs, or even the British, after the war. And since many of the Haganah's men came from the kibbutzim, which backed the Palmach, the Haganah leaders finally compromised. They would place graduates of the kibbutz youth movement in Palmach units that would be based in the kibbutzim. A little more than half their time would be spent on training and the rest on farm work, which would defray about 80 percent of the organization's

---

11. Dan Kurzman, *Soldier of Peace: The Life of Yitzchak Rabin* 1922-1995 © 1998, reprinted by permission of HarperCollins Publishers.

Young Prime Minister Yitzchak Rabin
(Central Zionist Archives, Jerusalem)

THE HANUKKA CEREMO

Brach

Song

Maccabe
Megilla

Profile

4th Cand
Yitzcha
Rabin

expenses. The Palmach thus became a true workers' army.

Rabin was shortly promoted to platoon commander, based in Kibbutz Kfar Giladi near the Lebanese border, where he trained his men in modern military tactics when they weren't working the land. As he tried to overcome the unit's impoverishment by scrounging for every bullet and shell, his zeal on one occasion nearly brought his military career to a startling end.

In the fall of 1943, during a firearms display before some Haganah senior officers at a kibbutz near Haifa, a mortar shell failed to fire. It was placed aside, and after the display Rabin, who had mortars for his platoon but no shells, decided to expropriate it — secretly.

The Haganah leaders had issued strict orders that no one was to carry weapons openly for fear they might be found by the British, jeopardizing the entire organization. So Rabin lugged the mortar shell in his shoulder bag. Then he took a bus so that if the British caught him with the shell, he alone and not other members of his platoon would be blamed. He arrived safely, but a week later was summoned by the Haganah's company commander. "There's a shell missing. Did you take it?"

Rabin would later remark in a statement that would remain valid throughout his life: "Like George Washington faced with the evidence of his cherry-tree crime, I could not tell a lie."

He was reprimanded and then, a few days later, notified that he would be court-martialed. Rabin was devastated. He had hardly begun to fight and he was already in disgrace. For days he "walked around in a trance and couldn't sleep at night." What would his father think of him? Was this how he was honoring his mother's memory?

At his court-martial in a clandestine Haganah office in Haifa, he confessed his crime once more and then explained his motives with the kind of reasoned detail that

---

Rabin was devastated. He had hardly begun to fight and he was already in disgrace.

would help to catapult him to the top in later years.

"Wait outside, please," Rabin was ordered. And as he waited, "the minutes ticked past like an eternity." His destiny was about to be set. Finally, he was called into the room. The sentence: "No promotion for at least a year." As Rabin departed, he heaved a sigh of relief. At least he was still in the Palmach, but he would just have to live with the fact that he would never get very far as a soldier.

LOVE AT FIRST SIGHT, TEL AVIV (1942)

It was a hot day in Tel Aviv, and Rabin, who had come home on leave, strode into Whitman's ice cream parlor on Allenby Street for an ice cream cone. Suddenly, he caught the eye of a pretty brunette who was also waiting for a cone.

"There he was," sixteen-year-old Leah Shlossberg Rabin would wistfully recall. "Just like the description of King David: 'Chestnut hair and beautiful eyes.' Our eyes met. Something about him — his appearance, his walk — captured my heart. He seemed different."

> "It was horrible watching this very private man suffering as he chivalrously stood by Leah. He felt a sense of loyalty that reflected a deep inner-family bond."

Rabin was captivated by Leah's vivacious smile and open personality, which was so contrasted with his own withdrawn nature. He needed someone who had the "chutzpah" to walk up to a stranger and introduce herself, something that he, a tough soldier, found extremely difficult to do. And Leah's extroversion relieved the tension of the blushing introvert.

If Rabin and Leah had disparate characters, they were molded in environments having almost nothing in common. Rabin was raised

in a rigidly austere, egalitarian society that even frowned upon pictures on the wall. Leah, on the other hand, was the daughter of a wealthy upper middle class industrialist from Germany and she had lived in relative luxury. [This teenage relationship across these social gaps grew into a solid marriage that would be tested 35 years later.]

A SCANDAL AND A MOMENT OF TRUTH (1976)

That morning Israeli Journalist Dan Margalit [who was stationed in Washington, D.C.] had received a phone call from his wife in Israel, and she had related to him a strange story. The previous evening she had attended a reception in Tel Aviv, and another guest had told her about something that happened in Washington four years earlier, in 1973, when Rabin was ambassador to the United States. Three people from the Israeli embassy had gone to the Dupont Circle branch of the National Bank, and a clerk had told them proudly: "You know, the wife of Yitzchak Rabin also has an account in this bank."

Dan Margalit smelled a story. In 1976 it was against Israeli law for an Israeli to have a bank account in a foreign bank — a law intended to keep black marketeers from depositing their ill-gotten earnings abroad to avoid paying taxes in Israel. Now its violation could politically damage, or perhaps even topple, a Prime Minister — perhaps the cleanest one in Israel's history.

Margalit went to the bank the next morning, March 14, and told a clerk: "I owe the Rabins $50 and wish to deposit it in their account, but I don't know the number."

"Okay," the clerk replied, "I'll take the check." Margalit gave it to her and noted the account number she wrote on it, repeating it over and over in his mind until he could write it down. He went to his office and filed the story: The Prime Minister and his wife had opened a bank account in the Dupont Circle branch of the National Bank in Washington when he was ambassador and

Yitzchak and Leah Rabin *(Israel Government Press Office)*

and politicians should get back to important matters — and everyone, hopefully, will have learned a good lesson." After all, many Israelis felt, the Rabins had made only a technical error, and the Prime Minister never used either account, bearing responsibility only as a cosigner for them.

But Rabin, according to friends, was furious at Leah, even as he stated that "there could be no question that morally and formally we shared responsibility equally."

Though the treasury officials felt a trial was unwarranted, Attorney General Aharon Barak [insisted Leah Rabin stand trial for a charge punishable potentially by imprisonment]. Rabin felt trapped in a nightmare from which he would never wake. Yes, he had committed an offense and he deeply regretted it. But let them punish him, not just his wife. His career seemed over anyway, and he could no longer lead the fight for peace. Nor was his pain eased by the thought that his disgrace stemmed from money matters when he had been raised to scorn material values. He would not concede, at least in public, that while he was preoccupied with peace and other vital issues, Leah had kindled the nightmare.

"It was horrible watching this very private man suffering as he chivalrously stood by Leah," [commented a friend]. "He felt a sense of loyalty that reflected a deep inner-family bond."

Rabin now made his decision: "**I felt that I had to render my own personal and private account, which demanded consistency and courage.** Friends tried to dissuade me from taking any fateful steps, but a man is always truly alone at such times. And alone, my conscience and I came to three interconnected decisions. I would withdraw my nomination as the candidate for Prime Minister. I would share full responsibility with Leah, and I would try to resign my post as Prime Minister, so that the Labor Party's nominee could fill the post up to the elections."

they never closed it.

"Looking back," Leah would later say, "I now know that I wasn't aware enough of the gravity of my transgression. I looked at it much like I would going through a traffic light when it was amber in the hope of crossing the street before the light turned red. I knew I had to close the account, and I had every intention of doing so during that visit, but the technical obstacle of a timetable simply got in the way.

The Jerusalem Post editorialized: "Mrs. Rabin should admit her error, the treasury should impound the money, and the press

THE
HANUKK
CEREMO

Brach

Song

Maccabe
Megilla

Profile

4th Cand
Yitzcha
Rabin

A Miracle War and a Prayer for Peace: The Chief of Staff of the Six Day War (June, 1967)
BY DAN KURZMAN

It had been weeks since Egypt unilaterally closed the Straits of Tiran placing a sea embargo on Israel's only southern port, Eilat. U.N. troops were expelled by Nasser, President of Egypt, and Egyptian troops massed in the Gaza strip some 40 minutes drive from Tel Aviv. The Israeli reserves were called up and the economy came to a standstill. Relying on the powerful military and political support of the Soviets, the Arabs threatened to drive the Jews into the sea. Jews world over began to talk of a new Holocaust. Israel's government decided to launch a preemptive strike.

"I have so much to say to you, I cannot find the words," [Chief of Staff] Rabin told his pilots in a hoarse, emotional voice on the morning of June 5 as he stood on the airfield where the bombers were poised to launch their historic attack. So he paraphrased Winston Churchill's words: "Never in the field of human conflict has the fate of so many depended on the skill and courage of so few. It is you who will decide the destiny of our people and our state."

And they did. Waves of Israeli planes thundered over Egypt firing cannons on enemy planes lined up on nine airfields and dropping bombs on their runways. In about three hours Egypt had lost almost two hundred supersonic and subsonic fighters, nearly sixty bombers, and more than thirty transport planes. Rabin exulted in his own air force command post and called Leah with the news: "The Egyptian air force is completely destroyed!" he cried.

Israeli aircraft, now free to rain disaster on airfields in Syria, Jordan and Iraq, knocked out an additional one hundred planes or so when the three countries began to attack Israel late in the morning. A total now of about four hundred Arab aircraft [were destroyed in the first few hours of the war]!

Within hours, Israeli paratroopers captured Jerusalem's northern Arab suburbs while other fighters attacked south of the city. "The night of June 5-6 must have been a difficult one for Nasser and Hussein," Rabin would say with mock pity. "Never in their worst nightmares could they have dreamed they would be in such a harrowing position after the first day of fighting. Our forces had made a swift breakthrough in both the Sinai and the West Bank, not to mention the fact that we had totally conquered the skies."

Israel had tried to persuade Jordan's King Hussein to stay out of the war through U.N. and American channels,

---

> "I do not believe that hatred adds anything to fighting capacity. We go forth to war when we are forced to, when there is no other choice."

---

but to no avail. How could he stand by, he felt, while his Arab neighbors were under attack, even if the alternative was national suicide? In fact, there seemed to be no way now for the Arabs to effectively assault Israel, especially with their morale plummeting together with their planes. [Nevertheless, Jordan bombarded West Jerusalem from East Jerusalem and launched its troops. Israel responded,

"Yehezkel," Rabin confided to his driver before telling anyone else, "I'm going to quit." The driver felt he "was about to have a heart attack." He slammed down the brakes and the car ground to a halt. "Don't you dare quit!" he exclaimed.

"Yehezkel," Rabin replied, "it's my wife. I'm not going to leave Leah. I'm not going to walk out on her. I owe it to her."

Yitzchak Rabin had made up his mind, "Tell the radio and television reporters to expect an announcement that evening in Tel Aviv." But Maccabi Tel Aviv would be playing the Italian team that evening in Belgrade for the European Basketball Championship. And all that most Israelis could talk and think about was the game. Perhaps, he could wait another day to make the announcement?

But Rabin would not wait. He wanted to leave. He would make the announcement that night — after the game, which would end about midnight. He would not sour the festive, exciting atmosphere before or during the contest. Anyway, not even the resignation capturing the Old City in two days of very hard fighting].

[After capturing the Old City on June 10, 1967, Rabin] came to the Western, or Wailing, Wall, the very soul of the Jewish people.

Its stones, [Rabin would write later], have a power to speak to the hearts of Jews the world over, as if the historical memory of the Jewish people dwelled in the cracks between those ancient [stones]. For years I secretly harbored the dream that I might play a part not only in gaining Israel's independence but in restoring the Western Wall to the Jewish people. Now that dream had come true and suddenly I wondered why I, of all men, should be so privileged. I knew that never again in my life would I experience quite the same peak of elation.

We stood among a tangle of rugged, battle-weary men who were unable to believe their eyes or restrain their emotions. Their eyes were moist with tears, their speech incoherent. The overwhelming desire was to cling to the Wall, to hold on to that great moment as long as possible. Following the ancient custom, Moshe Dayan, the Defense Minister, scrawled a wish on a slip of paper and pushed it in between two of the stones. I felt truly shaken and stood there murmuring a prayer for peace.

THE PRICE OF VICTORY

However the next day, the tears of the grief-stricken families and friends of about eight hundred fallen soldiers dampened the great outpouring of joy that exploded in Israel as a besieged people suddenly found themselves in control of territory three times the size of the stifling state they knew only six days earlier.

[The other side of the victory reverberated in Rabin's head. When Yitzchak Rabin was asked to speak at the Hebrew University on June 28, 1967, in honor of the liberation of its old campus on Mount Scopus in Jerusalem, this is what the usually tongue-tied, shy general had to say:]

Although [the army's] first task is the military one of maintaining security, it has numerous peacetime roles, not of destruction but of construction and of strengthening the nation's cultural and moral resources. The men in the front lines saw with their own eyes not only the glory of victory, but also the price of victory — their comrades fallen beside them soaked in blood. I know, too, that the terrible price paid by our enemies also touched the hearts of many of our men. **It may be that the Jewish people has never learned and never accustomed itself to feel the triumph of conquest and victory, with the result that these are accepted with mixed feelings.**

There has never been any hatred for the Arabs. Can one fight against enemies without hatred in one's heart? Perhaps in this respect, too, we are different from many other peoples. **I do not believe that hatred adds anything to fighting capacity. We go forth to war when we are forced to, when there is no other choice.**

THE HANUKH CEREMO

Brach

Song

Maccab Megill

Profile

4th Can Yitzcha Rabi

of a Prime Minister could compete for popular interest with a European championship game.

And that evening, Rabin, his aides, and Leah gloomily sat around a table watching the game on television in the Prime Minister's office, counting not the points but the minutes until Rabin would shake the nation out of its merrymaking mood, or intensify its melancholia, depending on the outcome of the contest. Israel took the lead, and the crowd at the game was shouting and cheering, together with all of Israel.

The time ticked on amid a cacophony of sounds that grated on minds throbbing with anguish — the roars from Belgrade, the cries of the guards gathered around a TV set downstairs, the soft sobbing of Leah Rabin, and, late in the evening, Rabin's own voice as he taped a resignation speech for Israel Radio that would be broadcast after the game.

Finally, at about 11 p.m., the chaos on the screen signaled the end of the game. Israel was the European champion, beating the

U.S. President Bill Clinton watches Israel's Prime Minister Yitzchak Rabin shake hands with King Hussein of Jordan during the negotiations for a Peace Treaty. (1994, Israel Government Press Office)

Italians by one point. Almost immediately, cries and cheers rose from the street. It was time to go to the television studio some distance away. Rabin and his party walked downstairs and entered a number of limousines parked outside. The vehicles were soon crawling through celebrating crowds, held up by cars draped in Israeli flags, their horns honking jubilantly. At one crossroads, Rabin bent forward and told his driver to pull

What a pleasure just to see their joy. If only he could feel it.

up to the side of the road until it was clear. Let the people enjoy themselves before they learned the nation was in crisis.

He hadn't seen such elation since the rescue of the Entebbe hostages [on July 4,

1976]. This was only a game, but the victory of tiny Israel over the powers of Europe struck a sensitive nationalistic chord. What a pleasure just to see their joy. If only he could feel it. After Entebbe, the people adored their leader. Now, months later, they were about to learn that he was leaving in disgrace.

And years later, Rabin would comment on that moment [after announcing his resignation]: **"I immediately felt the kind of relief that can only be entertained by a man who knows he has been honest with himself and true to his own conscience."**

"I am prepared to travel to Amman, Damascus and Beirut today or tomorrow," Rabin told the Knesset. "For there is no greater victory than the victory of peace." The words reverberated powerfully through the Knesset on July 13, 1992, as its members, either elated or deeply concerned, listened to Rabin stress the central aim of his second premiership. He was finally in a position to seek a final peace with Israel's neighbors.

"No longer is it true that the whole world is against us. We must overcome the sense of isolation that has held us in its thrall for almost half a century. We must join the international movement toward peace, reconciliation and cooperation that is spreading over the entire globe these days — lest we be the last to remain, all alone, in the station."

> "We who have come from a land where parents bury their children; we who have fought against you, the Palestinians — we say to you today, in a loud and a clear voice: enough of blood and tears. Enough."

[Rabin's advisors] drafted a blueprint of peace that seemed almost revolutionary by past standards. Both [Leah and Yitzchak] Rabin contributed their ideas, and the final draft asked the Israelis to shed their Masada complex and break out of their overprotective shell, to take risks that they had always seen as suicidal. The Arabs were admonished as well: Seize the moment!

In a special message to the Palestinians, Rabin pleaded with barely suppressed passion:

"We have been fated to live together on the same patch of land, in the same country. We lead our lives with you, beside you and against you. You have failed in the war against us. One hundred years of bloodshed and terror against us have brought you only suffering, humiliation, bereavement and pain. You have lost thousands of your sons and daughters, and you are losing ground all the time.

"For 44 years now, you have been living under a delusion. Your leaders have led you through lies and deceit. They have missed every opportunity, rejected all our proposals for a settlement and taken you from one tragedy to another. You have never known a single day of freedom and joy in your lives. Listen to us, if only this once.

"We offer you the fairest and most viable proposal from our standpoint today — autonomy, with all its advantages and limitations. You will not get everything you want. Neither will we. So, once and for all, take your destiny in your hands. Don't lose this opportunity that may never return. Take our proposal seriously — to avoid further suffering, humiliation and grief, to end the shedding of tears and of blood."

RABIN'S AGREEMENT WITH THE PALESTINIANS AT THE WHITE HOUSE (1995)

The dramatic, cadenced plea of Rabin to his Palestinian partners at the memorable White House ceremony is likely to resonate through the ages in the soul of peace lovers everywhere:

"We, the soldiers who have returned from battles stained with blood; we who have seen our relatives and friends killed before our eyes; we who have attended their funerals and cannot look in the eyes of their parents; we who have come from a land where parents bury their children; we who have fought against you, the Palestinians — we say to you today, in a loud and a clear voice: enough of blood and tears. Enough."

LIKE MOTHER, LIKE SON

HEROISM AND HUTZPAH IN A U.S. CHAPLAIN (POSTWAR GERMANY, 1945-1947)

by Rabbi Herbert Friedman[12]

Ambassador Yitzchak Rabin and Prime Minister Golda Meir consult with Rabbi Herbert Friedman in September 1970 in New York City. President Nixon had just requested Israeli military intervention to prevent a Syrian attack on Jordan after King Hussein cracked down on Palestinian terrorists.

True redemption will come to the Jew if he bears his name and every other burden imposed upon him by destiny with gleaming courage and radiant nobleness which, whether or not they evoke the love of the world without, will justify the Jew in his own sight and hallow him anew in the presence of the Eternal, to whom alone he is ultimately accountable.

— RABBI STEPHEN S. WISE, REFORM RABBI AND AMERICAN ZIONIST LEADER

The inability to think in grand sweeps connotes mediocrity and ordinariness. Some people are perfectly satisfied being ordinary. But when one is dissatisfied and bored, relief lies in joining great enterprises outside of oneself.

— RABBI HERBERT FRIEDMAN

MY MEMOIR[13]

I smuggled weapons to Palestine, before Israel was born, thus breaking U.S. arms-embargo laws; led convoys of refugees across hostile European borders to freedom; "liberated" crates of medieval religious documents from U.S. Army custody in Germany and transferred them to a professor in Jerusalem; and

committed similar, illegal or borderline-legal acts long-forgotten between 1945 and 1948.

I was arrested once in my life, in Rumania in 1957, by the secret police, on the charge of being a double spy for the Zionists and the CIA. They released me after four days and immediately expelled me from the country.

I look back on these illegal acts now, amazed at how calm I was, and I wonder from what hidden sources the requisite courage emerged. An inner moral summons, not

12. Rabbi Herbert Friedman, *Roots of the Future*, (1999) (p. 1, 13-16, 58-64, 86, 96-97) is reprinted by generous permission of the author and of the Gefen Publishing House, Jerusalem-New York, gefenbooks@compuserve.com.

13. Rabbi Herbert Friedman (born 1918) is an American Reform Rabbi who served as a Chaplain in the U.S. Army in Germany (1945-1947) and helped in the massive illegal immigration of Jews from Europe to Israel. He later helped found the United Jewish Appeal and the Wexner Heritage Foundation for leadership training.

adrenaline alone, seemed to embolden me to react.

I was a seasoned 14½-year-old when Hitler became Chancellor of Germany and immediately introduced various anti-Jewish regulations. I understood what was happening and who the good and bad guys were. As Zionism was life giving, Nazism was life destroying.

I felt uneasy and disturbed by the silence all around me. No one, including the Jewish community, was responding to the threat. Only one top-echelon Jewish leader of the day, Rabbi Stephen S. Wise, was calling for massive protest meetings — including parades down Fifth Avenue — and a general economic boycott of Germany.

THE
HANUKK,
CEREMO

Brach

Song

Maccab
Megilla

Profile

5th Cand
Herber
Friedma

MY MOTHER —
"WHEN HISTORY KNOCKS, YOU ANSWER!" (U.S.A., 1936)

One day the air cleared for me. History knocked at the front door of our house, and I witnessed a beautiful, moving example of a fitting and personal response to Hitler. The "teacher" was my mother, Rae.

My mother's sense of duty was as strong as any I have ever encountered. Endowed with a keen conscience, she kept herself and everyone around her on the absolute straight and narrow. No task too unimportant, no person too insignificant, no demand too menial — her reputation was such that every cause came to her attention because every supplicant knew that she would respond affirmatively.

At one meeting of the [synagogue] sisterhood, a representative of the U.S. National Refugee Service made an urgent plea for [American Jewish] families to take into their homes German-Jewish children whose parents were willing to let them emigrate to the United States, not knowing if they would ever see those children again.

Of the more than 100 women assembled, all mothers, no more than a dozen raised their hand. My mother stood and announced that she would take three children. God had been good to her, she said, giving her three healthy sons; this was her opportunity to repay. She added without embarrassment that her family was living in a small apartment, with only two bedrooms, because their house had been foreclosed by the bank during the Depression. Hence, she could take only boys, who could sleep mixed in with her sons.

Mother came home with the affidavit forms, placed them under my father's nose at the kitchen table, and told him of her commitment. Signing the forms, as far as she was concerned, was only a formality. He saw it differently, because of the legal obligations his signature would impose. A soft-spoken and gentle man, he explained to her that an affidavit was legally binding and reminded her of their precarious financial situation. The Depression had reduced his earnings to some pitifully small amount, and he could not envision for an instant how they could handle the additional expense for food, clothing, school, etc., for three more persons.

My mother answered him quietly, but with great passion. Even though we were poor, how could we refuse to save Jewish lives if we were given the chance to do so? She was ashamed of the other sisterhood members. All of them should have volunteered, and she would not hesitate to tell them so at the next meeting. "But if we have enough food for five of us," she asked, "why can't we simply make it do for eight? If I must wash shirts every day for six boys instead of three, what's the difference?"

She refused to debate the financial issue. She demanded that he sign. He hesitated. She insisted. The parental argument raged all night — the only time I remember my parents raising their voices in anger and disagreement. She won. In the morning, my father signed the affidavits, and she proudly took them back to the synagogue.

As I mulled over the matter, I decided that my mother's fight with my father symbolized

the whole problem, and the only conclusion was therefore to act according to moral Jewish values, without permitting rationalization, delay or any other diluting factor. [**"When history knocks, you answer!"**]

The only conclusion was to act according to moral Jewish values, without permitting rationalization, delay or any other diluting factor.

THE CIGARETTE SMUGGLERS AND ALIYAH BET (BERLIN, 1945-1947)

A woman's voice, low and inviting, asked if she had the right person. Was I the 9th Division chaplain who had been picking up DPs ["displaced persons" after the war] and bringing them to shelter? On whose orders had I been doing that? Who was paying the inevitable expenses? Was my commanding officer aware of what I was doing? The flood of questions threatened to continue indefinitely, so I interrupted to ask in a formal tone who was speaking, how she had found me, and what she wanted?

The woman offered no reply, so we were at a standoff. It was hers to break, and she did. She asked if I would come to meet her in Room 203 of the Royal-Monceau Hotel in Paris, at my earliest convenience.

Three days later, I knocked on the mystery woman's door at the Royal-Monceau. She was middle-aged, plain, somewhat tough-looking, and all business, with the bearing of someone who has seen much in life. She took a deep breath and asked whether I would agree to work with "them." When I asked who "them" was, she answered in just one word: "Haganah." (The Haganah was the underground armed force of the Jews in Palestine. It defended against Arab attacks and prepared for an eventual struggle for

Left and above: Bericha — The Illegal Immigration of Jewish Refugees. Holocaust survivors were smuggled across borders from Eastern Europe through Germany and over the Alps to ships taking them toward Israel (1945-1948) with the help of Jewish soldiers.

(*Tel Aviv Haganah Historical Archives, courtesy of Beit Hatefutsot, Photo Archive, Tel Aviv*)

THE
HANUKK,
CEREMO

Brach

Song

Maccab
Megilla

Profile

5th Cand
Herber
Friedma

statehood, meanwhile trying to rescue persecuted Jews in Europe and smuggle them into Palestine illegally, against the law of the British mandate.)

Perhaps once in a lifetime, or certainly very rarely, one might be confronted with a question containing enormous consequences, opening a path whose course was absolutely unknown. The question did not permit equivocation. Delay or hesitation was tantamount to refusal. Acceptance had to be instantaneous if it were to be taken as sincere and self-confident. Not knowing what in the world I was getting into, my gut told me to say yes, and I did.

Her real name was Ruth Kluger. She had changed it to Ruth Aliav when the Palestinian Jews started taking Hebrew names in place of their Eastern European Jewish ones. "Aliav" was an abbreviation of the phrase *Aliyah Bet* ("b" and "v" are interchangeable in Hebrew),

meaning "[Second Class] Immigration #2" — the so-called illegal immigration of Jews who were smuggled into Palestine against British regulations, which authorized only a limited legal immigration in order to appease the Arabs. Legal immigration was called *Aliyah Aleph* which provided for the rate of 15,000 visas per year for five years, and zero thereafter. That would never empty the DP camps [in Europe]. Therefore, the Haganah had established a department to evade the British and bring Jews in illegally. Since Ruth had spent many years of her life working on *Aliyah Bet*, she decided to take that phrase as her very name.

On that occasion at the Royal-Monceau, Ben-Gurion was in the next room with Moshe Sneh, commander of the Haganah, working on operational plans. To bring people into Germany, two routes were being set up — a northern one toward Berlin and a southern one toward Munich. The collection point for the former was the Polish border town of Stettin, about 150 miles northeast of Berlin. On trucks, wagons, trains, and their own feet, the Jews would stream from Eastern Europe toward Stettin, guided and nourished by a small band of incredibly dedicated Haganah men and women. Stettin offered holding facilities for several thousand DPs at a time, but if there were no steady stream across the border into Germany,

---

The currency of choice all over Europe at that time was cigarettes. The price for admitting one Jew at the Stettin border crossing was $150, one carton of cigarettes.

Stettin would soon become a mess, and the blockage would affect the flow all the way back to Uzbekistan. [Thousands of Jewish refugees returning from Russia and from the concentration camps in Poland were trying to escape from the Soviet-occupied territories of Eastern Europe in order to get first to Western-occupied sectors of Germany where they were placed in transit camps and then to new homes in Israel].

That's where I came in. The Haganah wanted me to take charge of the route from Stettin into Berlin and get it moving in a steady flow up to 10,000 persons per month. It was an awesome request. But it was also an exciting challenge.

Before returning to Germany, we wanted to see the rescue mission in operation. So we flew to a town called Nachod on the Polish-Czech border. During one long night, we witnessed hundreds of refugees, harassed and hounded, survivors of long years of terror or of wartime slave labor in freezing lumber camps in Siberia, boarding trucks, hunkering down under the tarpaulins, without baggage, without papers, parents holding their hands over the mouths of children so that no accidental cry would escape, fear and fever in all of their eyes.

[Back in Germany,] our plan was to leave Berlin around dusk with two Jewish Brigade men in each truck, taking turns driving and riding shotgun. There were several Bren and Thompson sub-machine guns in each vehicle, as well as carbines and Colts. That may sound a bit melodramatic, but we were driving about 200 kilometers northeast from Berlin to Stettin, through Russian territory, and 200 kilometers back, all in darkness. We were thus vulnerable targets, carrying a fortune in bribes every night. Anyone watching us knew that our route never varied, so it would be simple to set up ambushes.

The currency of choice all over Europe at that time was cigarettes. Under the arches of the Brandenburg Gate, in the heart of Berlin, the black market flourished and established trading values. A pack of 20 cigarettes was stable at $15, or $150 per carton of ten packs. At the army Post Exchange (PX), a carton cost 70 cents, and GIs were allowed one carton per week. A soldier who did not smoke could buy his carton, sell it, take the $149.30 profit.

The price for admitting one Jew at the Stettin border crossing was $150, one carton of cigarettes. At the rate of 300 persons per night, we were talking about $45,000! The task of gathering that many cigarettes for daily trade strained every brain and nerve. Some dedicated soldiers helped, soliciting their comrades for cigarettes and bringing in hundreds of packs every day. The soldiers who contributed out of their weekly ration were among the most generous benefactors the Jewish people has ever had. My father was collecting among his friends back home, and I was receiving many mail sacks full every week. By the time the whole operation wound down, in mid-1947, we had a quarter-million Jews living in 64 camps in Germany and Austria. That represented a seven-fold increase over the 35,000 who had been on German soil two years earlier. It was a major migration. Army and Joint Distribution Committee personnel fed, registered, billeted and cared for the sick among them.

As the days and weeks passed, the question

David Ben-Gurion, leader of the pre-state Jewish community in Israel visiting the Jewish refugee camp, Babenhausen, in Germany (1946). He is accompanied by Chaplain Herbert Friedman, officially of the U.S. Army and unofficially a smuggler of refugees for the Haganah.

Courtesy of Rabbi Herbert Friedman, the uniformed officer on Ben-Gurion's right, who was kind enough to provide this photograph and the stories from his memoir Roots of the Future. (Gefen Publishing Co.)

THE
HANUKKA
CEREMO

Brach

Song

Maccabe
Megilla

Profile

5th Cand
Herber
Friedma

grew more persistent: "When will we get to Palestine?" About two months later, I was able to help supply an answer. David Ben-Gurion, chairman of the Jewish Agency, was in Paris, en route to Switzerland to attend the first World Zionist Congress to be held since 1939. He wanted to visit a refugee camp — not a model operation, but one in which he could see the true, rough fiber of DP life. I obtained permits for him [to visit Babenhausen].

We therefore publicized throughout the DP camp the time and place of Ben-Gurion's appearance. He was the clear and undisputed leader of the Jewish population of Palestine (about 600,000 at that time) and the leader of world Jewry's thrust toward a sovereign state. He was a fighter — the small, cocky, bantam rooster — the charismatic, world-famous symbol of the Zionist force. A visit from him would be incandescent.

For the first time, there were smiles inside the gates of Babenhausen. And then came the inevitable question — poignant, pleading, uncertain, wavering, but persistent: "When, Mr. Ben-Gurion? When will we get to Palestine?"

As Ben-Gurion listened to those questions,

he began to weep, the only time in my long relationship with him I saw that happen. The tears fell slowly. He spoke through them, quietly but firmly. I remember his words almost exactly:

"I come to you with empty pockets. I have no British [entrance] certificates to give you. I can only tell you that you are not abandoned, you are not alone, you will not live endlessly in camps like this. All of you who want to come to Palestine will be brought there as soon as is humanly possible. I bring you no certificates — only hope. Let us sing our national anthem — *Hatikvah* (Hope)."

[Soon Ben Gurion was able to live up to the promise when the State of Israel was declared on May 15, 1948, and the state opened up its borders to refugees even though it was in the midst of a war of survival.]

תפלה

Prayer

RABBI LEVI YITZCHAK OF BERDITCHEV
A HEROIC LAWSUIT AGAINST GOD
by Rabbi Anson Laytner[14]

The Hasidic Rebbe, Levi Yitzchak (1740-1810, Poland and Ukraine), is the most colorful in a long line of Jewish heroes who fight their battles not with humans and not with enemies but with their own God of Israel. Their weapons are words and arguments, not firearms. Like Jacob who earned the name "Israel" (God Wrestler) for his struggle with the angel, a central task of the Jewish leader has been to wrestle with God and to defend the Jewish people from the often justified Divine wrath. "Managing up," the ability to redirect the Divine Boss' displeasure, has been a central Jewish task for a leader starting with Moshe's defense of Israel after the Golden Calf.[15]

Yet, beyond the rear action defense of Israel, there is also the proactive barrister who challenges God, accusing him of failing to live up to God's own covenant. Abraham challenged God over the planned destruction of Sodom, "Will the Judge of the whole earth fail to do justice?"[16] and, during and after the Holocaust, Elie Wiesel (survivor and novelist) did the same. Rabbi Anson Laytner has collected the literary expressions of these heroic verbal contests in a wonderful book from which we bring selections from Levi Yitzchak, the Polish Hasidic master of the confrontationist prayer. Levi Yitzchak

is the Jewish people's ultimate lawyer who brought suit for them against the Master of the Universe for neglecting the needs of Israel, God's people.

Anson Laytner explains:

"Ironically the intimate movements of prayer were the preferred means of confrontation, the natural occasion for such endeavors, when petition could be reinforced with protest. On many an occasion, while leading his congregation in prayers, Levi Yitzchak would interrupt his chanting of the Hebrew and, breaking into the Yiddish tongue, set forth before God the case against Him. These private prayers of protest must have left an indelible mark upon those who eavesdropped. Levi Yitzchak was confirmed in

14. Anson Laytner, *Arguing with God in the Jewish Tradition* (reprinted by permission of the publisher, Jason Aronson, Inc., Northvale, N.J., 1990, p. 179-189)

15. *Exodus* 32   16. *Genesis* 18:25

his role as the champion prosecuting attorney of the Hasidim."

LAWSUIT #1:
CHALLENGING GOD'S THRONE

Once, in the *Musaf* service of Rosh Hashana, when he reached the words *"And Your throne will be established in* **mercy** *and You shall sit upon it in* **truth**,*"* Levi Yitzchak stopped praying [from the prayerbook and began to argue with God about the practical import of those prayers]:

ADDRESS: O Lord.

ARGUMENT: If You want the throne of Your glory to be established so that You may sit upon it in that glory which alone is fitting for the King of kings, then deal *"in mercy"* with Your children and issue decrees for their salvation and consolation. But if You deal with us harshly and issue harsh decrees, Heaven forbid, then Your throne will not be established and You will not sit upon it *"in truth."*

THE THREAT: For the *tzaddikim* [the righteous leaders] of the generation will *not* permit You to sit upon Your throne. You may decree, but they will annul.

Petitioning God and Confessing Our Sins on Yom Kippur by A. Levi (1843-1918)

LAWSUIT #2:
DUSTING OFF GOD'S TEFILLIN

At times, Levi Yitzchak could be more demanding and less loving with God. Once he argued that just as Israel observed all that God commands, God should, at times, do no less than treat Israel in the same manner He has commanded them. By analogy, since a Jew is required to lift up, dust off, and kiss a pair of *tefillin*[17] that have fallen on the ground, so God should act likewise with His people Israel [who have been trampled to the ground by the nations].

In effect Levi Yitzchak said:

ADDRESS: [In our earthly *tefillin* it says, *"Shma Yisrael, the Lord our God, the Lord is* **one**" — our only one whom we love, so if it were to fall on the ground like a lover's necklace with the name of her betrothed, then we would pick it up immediately and kiss it. Otherwise there would be no validity in wearing the *tefillin*/love necklace.]

ARGUMENT: Now Your people, Israel, are the *tefillin* of Your head, for the *tefillin* glorify their wearer, and it is through Israel that You are glorified. For what verse is enclosed in Your *tefillin*? It is a verse of King David: *"Who is like Your people, Israel, God's* **one** *special people on earth."* Lord, Your *tefillin* have fallen to the ground and have lain in the dust of exile and suffering these two thousand years. Why do You not raise them up once again?

THREAT: [If You do not redeem us and raise us from the dust, then I, chief rabbi of Berditchev, will be compelled to publicly reveal that Your *tefillin* are not kosher, for You have not lived up to what it says in them.]

LAWSUIT #3: AN INJUNCTION AGAINST WRITING ON YOM KIPPUR

Sometimes the line between earnestness and humor, between boldness and blasphemy,

---

17. *Tefillin* are ritual leather boxes with texts inserted that are worn on the head and arm.

THE
HANUKKA
CEREMO

Brach

Songs

Maccabe
Megilla

Profile

6th Cand
Levi
Yitzcha

is indistinct. At times it becomes difficult to tell whether Levi Yitzchak was joking with his [Divine Parent] or provoking Him with an insolent slap. On one Yom Kippur when, according to tradition, God inscribes the fate of humanity in the Book of Life, Levi Yitzchak interrupted his prayers to pray:

> **ADDRESS:** Lord of the Universe!

> **ARGUMENT AND PETITION:** It is only allowed according to Your Holy Commandments, that a doctor may write on the Day of Atonement, when, by so doing, he may save a life. Therefore O God, if

You intend to save Israel and inscribe them in the Book of Life, then affix Your signature bearing forgiveness to a prosperous year. But if You mean to condemn them, then I, Levi Yitzchak, Rabbi of Berditchev, forbid You to write on Yom Kippur.

The Talmud states: "Boldness is effective — even against heaven."[18] This was a principle Levi Yitzchak and other tzaddikim practiced, and one he also encouraged others to practice as the story of a simple tailor's Yom Kippur prayer illustrates:

---

18. *T.B. Sanhedrin* 105a

Din-Torah:
Bringing a Lawsuit against the Master of the Universe in the Lodz Ghetto[16] (Poland, 1944)

When the Nazis decreed a seven-day curfew on the Lodz ghetto and deported 22,000 Jews to death camps, the remaining ghetto community was deeply shocked. Among them, a group of Haredi (Ultra-Orthodox) Jews decided to conduct a public *Din-Torah*, a lawsuit against God, and they chose a unique individual to be their prosecutor, Alter Schneor.

Alter Schneor was a teacher in the Ultra-Orthodox girls' school, Beis Yaacov, the editor of a local religious newspaper and a popular poet who in both Hebrew and Yiddish recorded the events and emotions of the ghetto years. Atypically, Schneor preached religious socialism and communal property ownership, based on his understanding of *"Love your neighbor as yourself."*

During the seven-day curfew/deportation, the Germans collected all the children, including Schneor's two children, in an old hospital where they lay in a pile, half-conscious, crying out for their mothers. With great effort Schneor got into the children's collection point, located his children, hid them under his long coat, and escaped. However, the Gestapo arrested him and deported his children. By a miracle Schneor was rescued when a Jewish policeman recognized him and smuggled him out of detention.

Despite his terrible pain, Schneor continued to worry about other people's children. Violating the Nazi decrees against Jewish learning, he went from house to house to teach the alphabet to these hidden children for whom he also wrote songs and plays.

On Yom Kippur, after the great curfew/deportation, Alter Schneor led the services on Musaf in his shtiebel (a small local synagogue-cum-study house). Dressed in a white mantle stained with the blood of a victim, he prayed with a torn heart before the God of *Selichot* (Forgiveness), asking for him to pardon Israel's sins and to speed the redemption. The synagogue broke into sobs.

The day arrived for the *Din Torah*, the Divine Lawsuit. The members of the *shtiebl* had fasted and read Psalms all day. At sundown with candles burning, the prosecutor Alter Schneor, wrapped in his tallit, opened the doors of the ark of the Torah. He spoke with a broken heart:

> "Master of the Universe! Parent of your chosen children! We invite you to the *Din Torah*. In what way did we sin before You? In what ways have our infants and our children sinned? Even if we sinned, was the crime so great that our suffering so far has not been enough? You have punished us with more than enough evil decrees. By the authority of the Jewish community that observes Your mitzvot, I tell You that You are forbidden to punish us anymore. Our good deeds are greater than our evil ones. You are forbidden to punish us anymore! No More!"

The community responded, "No more! No more!" and then recited the Kaddish.

---

16. Based on an article that appeared in the newspaper *HaDoar*, #38, 29 Elul 5723 (1963).

BARGAINING WITH GOD: AN UNEQUAL TRADE

The Berditchever called over a tailor and asked him to relate his argument with God on the day before. The tailor said: "I declared to God: You wish me to repent of my sins, but I have committed only minor offenses: I may have kept leftover cloth [which by rights belonged to the client], or I may have eaten in a non-Jewish home, where I worked, without ritually washing my hands before the meal.

"But You, O Lord, have committed grievous sins: You have taken away babies from their mothers, and mothers from their babies. Let us be quits: You forgive me, and I will forgive You."

Said the Berditchever to the tailor: "Why did you let God off so easily? You might have forced Him to redeem all of Israel!"

This well-known story is but one example of the common person's use of the argument motif and of this typically Yiddish ability to use humor to lighten life's loads. (Over a century later, the writer Sholom Aleichem raised this form of holy humor to the literary art of arguing with God, as in the prayer monologues of Tevye the milkman, later immortalized in the musical, *Fiddler on the Roof.*)

Perhaps the most radical form of petition to God is a *Din Torah*, a formal lawsuit with God. This model goes back to the Biblical prophets in which God sends the prophet to arraign Israel and argue God's case. But the

THE
HANUKK
CEREMO

Brach

Song

Maccab
Megilla

Profile

6th Cand
Levi
Yitzcha

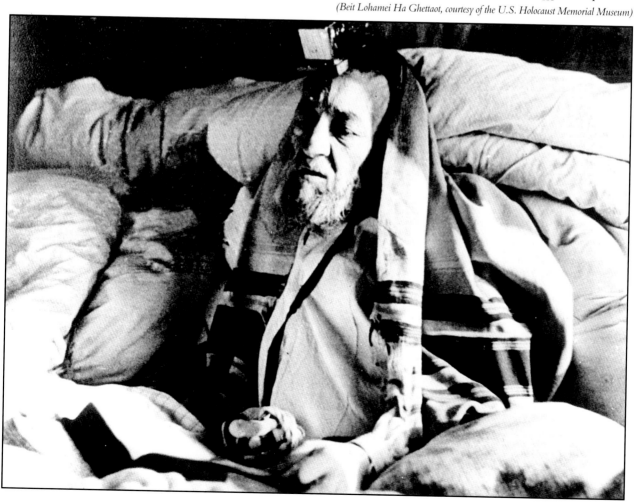

In the Lodz Ghetto in Poland sixty-year-old Shmuel Grossman is praying to God, while ill, lying in his featherbed. The photo was taken by Mendel Grossman, his son, the famous photographer of the ghetto who illegally documented the events on film. His collection was ultimately recovered after the war, but when taken to Israel it was destroyed by the attack of the Egyptian army in 1948.

(Beit Lohamei Ha Ghettaot, courtesy of the U.S. Holocaust Memorial Museum)

Hasidic rebbes, like Levi Yitzchak, reversed the direction of the lawsuit and sought to bring God to trial.

Typical of the stories about Levi Yitzchak is the fact that, his reputation notwithstanding, he was never successful in winning results with his lawsuits on high. The stories about other rabbis' arguments do, on occasion, end with a miraculous reversal of the divine judgment all hoped to see reversed, [as in the next example].

LAWSUIT #4: CHILD SUPPORT FOR YOUR SERVANTS

A terrible famine once occurred in the Ukraine and the poor could buy no bread. Ten rabbis assembled at the home of the "Spoler Grandfather" for a session of the Rabbinical Court. The Spoler said to them:

> "I have a case against the Lord. According to rabbinical law, a master who buys a Jewish slave for a designated time [six years or up to the Jubilee year] must support not only him but also his family. Now the Lord bought us in Egypt as His servants, since He says: *"For to Me are the sons of Israel servants,"*[19] and the prophet Ezekiel declared that even in Exile, Israel is the slave of God. Therefore, O Lord, I ask that You abide by the Law and support Your serfs with their families."

The ten judges rendered judgment in favor of the Spoler Rabbi. In a few days, a large shipment of grain arrived from Siberia, and bread could be bought by the poor. [The Spoler Rebbe felt God had accepted his plea].

THE LAST PETITION: UPON MEETING ONE'S MAKER

[Many rebbes promised their Hasidim that when they were called to their Maker, at the moment of death, they would insist on affirmative answers to their people's long neglected petitions.] Before his own death, Levi Yitzchak, it is said, vowed neither to rest nor to be silent once in Heaven, until God permitted the Messiah to come. But to no avail. His disciples waited in vain.

THE ULTIMATE ULTIMATUM

One Hasidic master, perhaps the most complex and enigmatic, Rabbi Menachem Mendel of Kotzk, argued from a different vantage point, on that narrow ridge between faith and despair. Torn in his life between love of God and rebellion against Him (he remained in seclusion for the last twenty years of his life), the Kotzker Rebbe is said to have once uttered this totally desperate and defiant prayer:

> ADDRESS: Master of the Universe!
>
> PETITION: Send us our Messiah, for we have no more strength to suffer. Show me a sign, O God. Otherwise I rebel against You. **If You do not keep Your Covenant, then neither will I keep the promise, and it is all over: we are through with being Your Chosen People, Your unique treasure.**

---

19. *Leviticus* 25

ARMING A THREATENED NATION

THE HEROIC FUNDRAISER, GOLDA MEIR
(ISRAEL AND U.S.A., 1948)

by Larry Collins and Dominique Lapierre[20]

Golda Meir holding a menorah in the Poalei Zion tableau of "Jewish Rebirth" in Milwaukee, May 18, 1919 — exactly 29 years before the actual birth of the State of Israel on May 14, 1948. (State Historical Society of Wisconsin)

Golda Meir, Israel's first woman Prime Minister (1969-1974), has always been a popular hero due to her down-to-earth, no-nonsense style of leadership. Born in Russia, educated in America, she became a socialist Zionist in Milwaukee, Wisconsin, and made aliya in 1921. By sheer willpower she established herself in Israel in the otherwise male, Russian-Jewish elite of David Ben-Gurion's inner circle.

The heroic moment we have chosen to highlight is the difficult winter of 1947-1948 before the War of Independence began officially on May 15, 1948. During this period of British control and American arms embargo to the region, the civil war with local Arabs had already begun. But the decisive struggle would be the military confrontation with the seven well-armed invading Arab armies. The underground Haganah and the pre-state Jewish Agency had little money to buy arms on the black market of post-World War II and the 600,000 Jews of the Yishuv, the pre-state Jewish community of Palestine, were in mortal danger. The American Jewish community was not yet fully committed to supporting Israel either politically or financially, though it was generous to European Jewish refugees. At this moment Golda stepped in to educate the American Jewish philanthropists to a new sense of responsibility for Jewish military self-defense in the post-Holocaust age.

[In the winter of 1948 there was an enormous] problem preoccupying the leaders of the Jewish Agency in Tel Aviv. One January evening they were summoned to hear a report by Eliezer Kaplan, their treasurer.

---

20. Larry Collins and Dominique Lapierre, *O Jerusalem* (© 1972), reprinted by permission of Simon and Schuster, pp. 162-165.

Kaplan had just returned from a fund-raising trip to the United States with his pockets virtually empty. The American Jewish community was growing weary of the incessant appeals for aid [to Jews from abroad], he reported. The time had come, Kaplan said, to face a bitter reality. In no case could they count on more than five million dollars from America in the critical months ahead.

That figure hit the group gathered around Kaplan like a thunderbolt. One by one, their glances turned toward the stubby man who had followed Kaplan's report with ill-disguised impatience. David Ben-Gurion was better placed than any of them to understand how serious were the consequences of what Kaplan had just said. The rifles and machine guns [which he had already purchased in

---

"What you are doing here I cannot do," Golda Meir told Ben-Gurion. "However, what you propose to do in the United States I can do. You stay here and let me go to the States to raise the money."

Prague on the black market] could hold back the Palestinian Arabs [who had already attacked after November 29, 1947]; but against the tanks, artillery and aircraft of the regular Arab armies [who would invade on May 15, 1948 after the British evacuated and the State of Israel was proclaimed], they would be useless, however courageous the Jewish soldiers might be. Ben-Gurion had drawn up a plan to equip a modern army. To carry it out, he needed at a minimum five, six times the sum mentioned by Kaplan. Springing from his seat, he growled to the men around him, "Kaplan and I must leave for the United States immediately to make the Americans realize how serious the situation is."

At that moment a quiet female voice interrupted him. It belonged to the woman who had found her Zionist faith taking up a collection in Denver, Colorado. "What you are doing here I cannot do," Golda Meir told Ben-Gurion. "However, what you propose to do in the United States I can do. You stay here and let me go to the States to raise the money."

Ben-Gurion reddened. He liked neither interruptions nor contradictions. The matter was so important, he insisted, he and Kaplan should go. The other members of the Agency Executive, however, supported Golda. Two days later, with no more baggage than the thin spring dress she wore and the handbag she clutched in her hand, she arrived in New York on a bitter winter's night. So precipitate had her departure been that she had not had the time to take the convoy up to Jerusalem to fetch a change of clothes. The woman who had come to New York in search of millions of dollars had in her purse that evening exactly one ten-dollar bill. When a puzzled customs agent asked her how she intended to support herself in the United States, she replied simply, "I have family here."

Two days later, trembling on a podium in Chicago, Golda Meir found herself facing a distinguished gathering of the members of that family. They were the leaders of the Council of Jewish Federations, drawn from the forty-eight states of the Union. Their meeting and her arrival in the United States had been a fortuitous coincidence. Before her, in one Chicago hotel room, were most of the financial leaders of the American Jewish community, the very men whose aid she had been sent to seek.

For the carpenter's daughter from the Ukraine [who had grown up in Milwaukee] the task before her was an intimidating challenge. She had not been back to the United States since 1938. On her earlier trips, her associates had been [a very small band of] dedicated Zionists and Socialists like herself. Now she faced the whole enormous spectrum of American Jewish political opinion, much of it indifferent or even hostile to her Zionist ideals.

Golda Meir speaking before the American United Jewish Appeal in New York (1970s)
(Photograph by Dr. Theodore Cohen, Beit Hatefutsot, Photo Archive, Tel Aviv)

THE
HANUKK
CEREMC

Brach

Song

Maccab
Megill

Profil

7th Can
Golda
Meir

announce her name. At the sight of her simple, austere figure moving to the speakers' stand, someone in the crowd murmured, "She looks like the women of the Bible." Then, without a text, the messenger from Jerusalem began to speak:

"You must believe me," she said, "when I tell you that I have not come to the United States solely to prevent six hundred thousand Jews from being wiped off the face of the earth. During these last years, the Jewish people have lost six million of their kind, and it would be presumptuous indeed of us to remind the Jews of the world that six hundred thousand Jews are in danger. That is not the question. If, however, these six hundred thousand Jews survive, then the Jews of the world will survive with them, and their freedom will be forever assured." But if they did not, she said, "then there is little doubt that for centuries there will be no Jewish people, there will be no Jewish nation, and all our hopes will be smashed."

In a few months, she told her audience, "a Jewish state will exist in Palestine. We shall fight for its birth. That is natural. We shall pay for it with our blood. That is normal. The best among us will fall, that is certain. But what is equally certain is that our morale will not waver no matter how numerous our invaders may be."

Yet, she warned, those invaders would come with cannon and armor. Against those weapons "sooner or later our courage will have no meaning, for we will have ceased to exist," she said. She had come, she announced, to ask the Jews of America for twenty-five to thirty million dollars to buy the heavy arms they would need to face the invaders' cannon. "My friends," she said in making her plea, "we live in a very brief present. When I tell you we need this money immediately, it does not mean next month, or in two months. It means right now."

"It is not up to you," she concluded, "to decide whether we shall continue our struggle or not. We shall fight. The Jewish community of Palestine will never hang out

Her friends in New York had urged her to avoid this confrontation. The council's leadership was not Zionist. Its members were already under great pressure for funds for their own American institutions, hospitals, synagogues, and cultural centers. They were weary, as Kaplan had discovered, of appeals from abroad for money.

Yet Golda Meir had insisted. She had telephoned the director of the United Jewish Appeal in Chicago and, despite the fact that the speakers' program of the meeting had been drawn up long in advance, announced that she was on her way. Then, pausing only to buy a coat with which to face the American winter, she had set out for Chicago.

Now Golda Meir heard the toastmaster

the white flag before the Mufti of Jerusalem [Hitler's ally]. But you can decide one thing — whether the victory will be ours or the Mufti's."

A hush had fallen on her audience, and for an instant Golda thought she had failed. Then the entire assembly of men and women rose in a deafening wave of applause. While its echoes still rang through the dining room, the first volunteers scrambled to the platform with their pledges. Before coffee was served Golda had been promised over a million dollars — made available immediately in cash, an act without precedent. Men began to telephone their bankers and secure personal loans against their own names for the sums

---

A hush had fallen on her audience, and for an instant Golda thought she had failed. Then the entire assembly of men and women rose in a deafening wave of applause.

---

they estimated they would be able to raise later in their communities. By the time that incredible afternoon was over, Golda was able to telegraph Ben-Gurion her conviction that she would be able to raise the twenty-five "Stephans" — twenty-five million dollars, in the code they had chosen (using the name of American Zionist leader Rabbi Stephen S. Wise).

Astounded by her Chicago triumph, the American Zionist leadership urged her to set off on a cross-country tour. Accompanied by Henry Morgenthau, Jr., Franklin D. Roosevelt's former Secretary of the Treasury, she set a grueling pace, speaking sometimes three and four times a day. From city to city she moved on her pilgrimage, renewing before each of her audiences her dramatic plea, eliciting from each the same spontaneous, overwhelmingly generous reaction she had produced in Chicago. And from each stop a telegram went back to Tel Aviv tallying the "Stephans" raised during the day. From time to time along the way other

telegrams went out from her hotel room. To Ehud Avriel in Prague, and others seeking to buy equipment for a Jewish army, they brought the most reassuring news those men could hope to receive — the details of the bank transfers which would allow them to go on with their purchases.

Only once in her extraordinary pilgrimage did she falter. It was in Palm Beach, Florida. Looking at the elegance of the dinner crowd before her, their jewels, their furs, the moon playing on the sea beyond the banquet hall's windows, she suddenly thought of her soldiers of the Haganah trembling in the cold of the Judean hills that night. Drinking black coffee on the dais, thinking of the contrast between that scene and the one before her, tears came to her eyes. "These people don't want to hear about fighting and death in Palestine," she thought. But they did, and Golda spoke so movingly that before the evening was over the gathering at Palm Beach had pledged her a million and a half dollars, enough to buy a winter coat for every soldier in the Haganah.

The woman who had arrived in the United States one bitter January night with no winter coat and with ten dollars in her pocketbook would leave with fifty million, ten times the sum Eliezer Kaplan had mentioned, twice the figure set by David Ben-Gurion, three times the entire oil revenues of Saudi Arabia for 1947. Waiting for her airplane at Lydda Airport was David Ben-Gurion, the man who had wanted to go in her place. No one appreciated better than he the magnitude of her accomplishment in the United States or its importance to the Zionist cause. **"The day when history is written,"** he solemnly told her, **"it will be recorded that it was thanks to a Jewish woman that the Jewish state was born."**

A SOCIAL ACTIVIST PURSUES JUSTICE

BELLA ABZUG'S BELLOWING WAYS (1920-1998)

by Blanche Wiesen Cook with selections from Liz Abzug and Mim Kelber[21]

THE HANUKK, CEREMO

Brach

Song

Maccab
Megilla

Profile

8th Cand
Bella
Abzug

> "My mother said I was a feminist from the day I was born."
>
> — BELLA ABZUG

> " 'A woman's place is in the house' — the House of Representatives."
>
> — SLOGAN FOR BELLA ABZUG'S CONGRESSIONAL CAMPAIGN IN 1970

> "Win or lose, Bella Abzug could never be entirely comfortable in a society that did not care enough to yell."
>
> — LIZ ABZUG (HER DAUGHTER)

Bella Abzug is a special brand of American Jewish heroine who grew up in the New York City immigrant community and went on to transform her country's political outlook in the name of civil rights for all, black and white, woman and man, while maintaining her loyalty to Judaism and Israel. Not everyone liked the style and content of her politics, but everyone took notice of her agenda for moral and social reform.

BATTLING BELLA

by Blanche Wiesen Cook

According to her mother, "Battling Bella" was born bellowing, a spirited tomboy with music in her heart and politics in her soul. Born in the Bronx on July 24, 1920, Bella (Savitzky) Abzug predated women's right to vote by one month. A fighter for justice and peace, equal rights, human dignity and environmental integrity, she was elected to Congress and served three very productive terms from 1970 to 1976. She was the first woman in New York State to run for the U.S. Senate in 1976, and the first woman to run in New York City for Mayor in 1977. Continuing to practice law, she lectured

around the U.S. and then finally, during her last 10 years, turned to the international fight for women's rights in the United Nations.

AS A CHILD: PLAYING WITH THE BOYS AND PRAYING WITH THE MEN

A natural leader, although a girl among competitive boys, she delighted in her prowess at marbles, or "immies." When the boys tried to beat her or steal her marbles, Abzug defended herself fiercely with unmatched skill. She also played checkers [and poker,] traded baseball cards, climbed trees, became a graffiti artist, and understood the nuances, corners, and risks of city streets, which were her playground.

Her Hebrew school teacher recruited her to a left-wing labor Zionist group, Hashomer Hatzair. By the time she was eleven, Bella and her gang of socialist Zionists planned to go to Israel together as a kibbutz community. In the meantime, they were inseparable and traveled throughout New York City, hiked in the countryside, danced and sang all night, went to free concerts, museums, the theater, picnics, and meetings. Above all, they raised

21. Blanche Wiesen Cook, *Jewish Women in America,* edited by Paula Hyman and Deborah Dash Moore (copyright by the American Jewish Historical Society, 1998, reprinted by permission of Routledge, Inc., p. 6-9) with a few selections from Liz Abzug [L.A.]. "A Tribute to Bella Abzug at NY State Democratic Convention, May 28, 1998" by permission of the author and Mim Kelber [M.K.]. "Supra-Bella: Her Life and Legacy" from *Bella Abzug* memorial booklet, by permission of WEDO, the Women's Environment and Development Organization.

money for a Jewish homeland — with Abzug in the lead. At subway stops, she gave impassioned speeches, and people tended to give generously to the earnest, well-spoken girl. From her first gang, Bella learned about the power of alliances, unity, and alternative movements.

She worked in her father's butcher shop on 39th Street and 9th Avenue in Manhattan, which he named "The Live and Let Live Market" [in the spirit of Woodrow Wilson's post World War I policy of giving democratic self-determination to all nations]. Then the year Hitler came to power, her father

---

Prohibited by tradition from saying *kaddish* for her father in synagogue, Bella did so anyway.
She just did what she needed to do for her father, who had no son — and learned a lesson for life:
Be bold, be brazen, be true to your heart.

Emanuel died, and Bella emerged as an outspoken thirteen-year-old girl willing to break the rules. Prohibited by tradition from saying *kaddish* [the memorial prayer] for her father in synagogue, Bella did so anyway. Every morning before school for a year, she attended synagogue and davened. The congregants looked askance and never did approve, but nobody ever stopped her. She just did what she needed to do for her father, who had no son — and learned a lesson for life: **Be bold, be brazen, be true to your heart.** She advised others: "People may not like it, but no one will stop you." [Bella told her daughter, Liz, that it was perhaps this early experience of reciting the *kaddish* as a

Boycotting Japanese Silk Stockings in College

In 1940 at Hunter College, Bella was elected President of her class at a time when every girl was expected to wear a pleated skirt and silk stockings. However the silk stockings were purchased from Japan, Hitler's ally, in exchange for scrap iron. So Bella organized a vociferous boycott and the girls wore lumpy cotton stockings instead of silk.

young girl when only boys and men were supposed to do this, that formulated the roots of her later feminism and her battles to achieve equality for women. "I have a funny idea that being sent up to the balcony" — the women's section of the synagogue — "had something to do with the way I turned out to be." — *L.A.*]

BELLA'S HATS AND HOLLYWOOD

Bella's daughter, Liz, reports that: "Early on in her life as a young girl, Bella knew she wanted to become a lawyer, even though she didn't know any lawyers and certainly not any female lawyers. She decided she would apply to the best, most prestigious law school in the country — Harvard Law School. When she was turned down by this, her first choice, because Harvard Law School did not admit women, she instead accepted a scholarship to attend Columbia University Law School."

Immediately after law school, Bella joined a labor law firm that represented local unions. Routinely overlooked when she entered an office to represent the United Auto Workers, or the Mine, Mill and Smelting Workers, or local restaurant workers, she decided to wear hats. Hats made all the difference when it came to recognition and even respect, and they became her trademark. Bella used to say, *"We must each wear the hat of an advocate and pledge to bring passion to our work."*

During the 1950s, Bella Abzug was one of very few independent attorneys willing to take "Communist" cases. She opened her own office, and defended teachers, entertainment, radio, and Hollywood personalities assaulted during the witch-hunt (led by Senator Joe McCarthy in the early 1950's. Bella called herself a "nut" about the First Amendment of the Bill of Rights that protects free speech). [Later, famous Hollywood performers stood by her in all her campaigns and in exchange Bella made a brief appearance as one of Ted Turner's first commentators for a little-known upstart network called CNN and Woody Allen

Bella Abzug (Associated Press Photo by permission)

THE
HANUKK
CEREMO

Brach

Song

Maccab
Megill

Profil

8th Can
Bella
Abzug

agreed. She appealed the case before the Supreme Court and achieved two stays of execution when she argued that "Negroes were systematically excluded from jury service." But she did not achieve a change of venue, and after the third trial and conviction, all appeals were denied.

On her trip south to [segregationist] Jackson for the special hearing board appointed by Mississippi's governor, Abzug never thought much about her personal safety, even though she was [eight months] pregnant at the time. She realized she was in trouble, however, when the hotel room she had booked was denied her and no other room made available. When a taxi driver offered to take her fifteen miles out into the country to find a place to say, she preferred to return to Jackson's bus station and to spend an unsettling night [in a locked bathroom stall to avoid anti-semitic racial bigots who tried to "persuade" her to leave town]. At court the next morning, she argued fervently for six hours on behalf of racial justice, protesting the clear conspiracy to deny Willie McGee's civil rights, as well as the long tradition of race prejudice and unfair discrimination. To cancel his death sentence, she argued in 1950, would restore faith in U.S. democracy throughout the world. Despite worldwide publicity, protest marches, and Abzug's fervent plea to prevent another legal lynching, McGee went to the electric chair. Abzug had a miscarriage, but her dedication to the cause of justice was strengthened by her days in Mississippi.

MS. ABZUG GOES TO WASHINGTON

[In 1961, Bella helped organize the Women's Strike for Peace and led thousands of women, mothers and youngsters on lobbying expeditions to Congress and the White House on behalf of a nuclear test ban. The group gained national stature and influence, and in response President Kennedy, shortly before his assassination, announced his limited test ban treaty — *M.K.*].

featured her in his film *"Manhattan,"* making a political pitch in the garden of the Museum of Modern Art. — *M.K.*].

A TEST OF PHYSICAL COURAGE FOR A PREGNANT LAWYER IN JACKSON MISSISSIPPI, 1950

In an internationally celebrated case, Willie McGee, a black Mississippian, was falsely accused of raping a white woman with whom he had a long-term consensual relationship. [Although this white married woman had often had sexual relations with McGee, she cried "rape" when her husband caught her committing adultery. While other defense lawyers declined to represent McGee], Bella

In 1970, Bella Abzug, a leading reform Democrat, a successful attorney, and a popular grass-roots activist, was urged to run for Congress, which she agreed to do at the age of fifty. Stunning and galvanizing, with her hats and her homilies, she became a household symbol for dramatic change. Representing Greenwich Village, Little Italy, the Lower East Side, the West Side, and Chelsea, she was the first woman elected to Congress on a women's rights/peace platform. One of only 9 women in the 435 seat House of Representatives, Bella was the first Jewish woman in the House. New York agreed, "This woman's place is in the House — the House of Representatives." And so, her daughter Eve proclaimed: "We got her out of our house and into your House." [Her first official act was to introduce a resolution calling on President Nixon to withdraw all U.S. forces from the Vietnam war, then at its height despite mass protests nationwide. In January, 1973, when Nixon was formally inaugurated for his second term, Bella led a counter-inaugural ceremony attended by thousands of protesters at the Washington Monument. She was the first member of Congress to introduce a resolution calling for the impeachment of President Nixon in the wake of the Watergate scandal. — *M.K.*]

She wrote the first law banning discrimination against women in obtaining credit, credit cards, loans, and mortgages, and introduced pioneering bills on comprehensive child care, Social Security for homemakers, family planning, and abortion rights. In 1975, she introduced an amendment to the Civil Rights

On the Courageous of Spirit from Bella Abzug's Speeches[22]

✦ THERE ARE THOSE WHO SAY I'M IMPATIENT, IMPETUOUS, UPPITY, RUDE, PROFANE, BRASH, AND OVERBEARING. Whether I'm any of those things, or all of them, you can decide for yourself. But whatever I am — and this ought to be made very clear at the outset — I am a very serious woman.

✦ WOMEN WILL CHANGE THE NATURE OF POWER, RATHER THAN POWER CHANGING THE NATURE OF WOMEN. Change is not about simply mainstreaming women. It's not about women joining the polluted stream. It's about cleaning the stream, changing stagnant pools into fresh, flowing waters. Our struggle is about resisting the slide into a morass of anarchy, violence, intolerance, inequality and injustice. Our struggle is about reversing the trends of social, economic and ecological crisis. For women in the struggle for equality, there are many paths to the mountain top. **Our struggle is about creating sustainable lives and attainable dreams.** Our struggle is about creating violence-free families. And then, violence-free streets. Then, violence-free borders. In that order. Because the root of the problem is persistent inequalities and growing inequalities. **For us to realize our dreams, we must keep our heads in the clouds and our feet on the ground.**

✦ FIRST THEY GAVE US A DAY FOR WOMEN. THEN THEY GAVE US A YEAR. THEN THEY GAVE US A DECADE. I said then, who knows, maybe if we behave, they'll let us into the whole thing. But we didn't behave. Now we are hoping for a century — and maybe then they'll let us into the whole show. We make it our business to ensure that as we move into the new millenium, there will not only be a women's day or a year, but a women's century.

✦ I URGE YOU, NEVER HESITATE TO TELL THE TRUTH. NEVER GIVE IN AND NEVER GIVE UP.

✦ TOGETHER, WOMEN AND MEN, WE MUST LEARN FROM THE WISDOM THAT SURROUNDS US. When we can truly empathize with the least of us on the planet, we will find our footing. And we will climb together, men and women. And the next millennium will be written as the triumph of the weavers and the dreamers, the poets and musicians, peacemakers and caretakers, **the generous of heart and courageous of spirit.**

22. Reprinted from *Bella Abzug* memorial booklet published by Women's Environment and Development Organization

"Come in, Ms. Abzug!" by Marlette *(Newsday, 1998). Permission requested.*

THE
HANUKK
CEREMO

Brach

Song

Maccab
Megilla

Profile

8th Can
Bella
Abzug

Act to include gay and lesbian rights. As chair of the Subcommittee on Government Information and Individual Rights, she co-authored important pieces of legislation: the Freedom of Information Act and the Right to Privacy Act. Abzug's bills exposed many secret government activities to public scrutiny for the first time.

[In 1978, after Bella had left the House to run unsuccessfully for the Senate, President Carter named Bella co-chair of his National Advisory Committee for Women. When the Committee protested federal budget cuts affecting women, however, the President dismissed Bella, engendering a tidal wave of protests from the Committee (most of whose members resigned) and from the general public. — *M.K.*]

BRAVERY AND BREAST CANCER

[In 1993 she chaired the New York City Commission on the Status of Women, and presided over ground-breaking hearings on links between breast cancer and the environment. Ironically, Bella herself was diagnosed with breast cancer only three months after the first public hearing in 1993, but she recovered quickly. — *M.K.*] Bella used to say, *"In the face of so much pain and my own personal history of breast cancer, I remain an incurable optimist."* **"Whether you are one-breasted, two-breasted, or no-breasted, this is a two-fisted fight against cancer."**

BELLA'S LEGACY: HER LIFE AFTER DEATH

In her last speech, given at the United

Nations on March 3, 1998, the day before she reentered the hospital, Bella pointed out that she had been battling for human rights and women's rights for 65 years. "For all that time," wrote Blanche Wiesen Cook in a personal tribute, **"Bella was a team player. Her understanding that politics cannot be an isolated individualist game, that power requires a gang, a loyal and trusted group of associates who will work and play and fight together, who will laugh and sing and argue together, made her the unique leader and prophet we enjoyed battling beside."**

The long-time Jewish activist and Jewish Renewal Rabbi Arthur Waskow responded to Bella's death in a style she would have appreciated: "[When] I heard of the death of Bella Abzug, I felt as if a hole had suddenly appeared in a piece of the foundation that holds up Reality. She was perhaps the toughest, smartest, bravest Jewish progressive of our generation. I very much doubt that she will want to spend eternity resting in peace. I am sure she has been making fun of the Heavenly Patriarchy, demanding bold and practical reforms on behalf of justice, since 12 minutes after arriving in what the official reports, like all official reports, call Paradise."

> Bella was a team player. Her understanding that politics cannot be an isolated individualist game, that power requires a gang, a loyal and trusted group of associates who will work and play and fight together, who will laugh and sing and argue together, made her the unique leader and prophet we enjoyed battling beside.

Inspirations to Action COLLECTED BY DANNY SIEGEL[22]

The opposite of love is not hate, it's indifference. The opposite of faith is not heresy, it's indifference. And, the opposite of life is not death, it's indifference. Because of indifference one dies before one actually dies.

— ELIE WIESEL,
HOLOCAUST NOVELIST

"A time to embrace." (Ecclesiastes 3:5) If you see a group of Tzaddikim-Good People standing near you, stand up and hug them and kiss them and hug them again.

— ECCLESIASTES RABBA 3:5

Most of the things worth doing in the world had been declared impossible before they were done.

— JUSTICE LOUIS BRANDEIS

To be is to stand for.

— ABRAHAM JOSHUA HESCHEL,
THEOLOGIAN

To be is to do.

— MYRIAM MENDILOW,
FOUNDER OF LIFELINE FOR THE ELDERLY

[God says:] Just as I create worlds and bring the dead back to life, you, human beings, are also capable of doing the same.

— MIDRASH PSALMS 116:8

Shimon [the son of Rabban Gamiliel] says: It is not what one says, but rather what one does, that makes all the difference in the world.

— PIRKE AVOT 1:17

Never doubt that a small group of thoughtful, committed citizens can change the world: indeed, it's the only thing that ever does.

— MARGARET MEAD,
ANTHROPOLOGIST

Charismatic leaders make us think, "Oh, if only I could do that, be like that." True leaders make us think, "If they can do that, then I can too."

— JOHN HOLT, EDUCATOR

We make a living by what we get, but we make a life by what we give.

— WINSTON CHURCHILL,
BRITISH PRIME MINISTER

22. Danny Siegel, *Heroes and Miracle Workers* (1997) by permission of author.

Spiritual Meditations for Personal Rededication and Family Renewal

הַכְנָסַת אוֹרְחִים

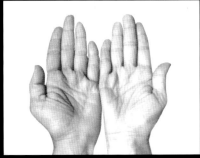

Hospitality

תְּפִלָּה

Prayer

כַּשְׁרוּת

Keeping Kosher

צְדָקָה

Economic Justice

מְנוֹרָה

Menorah

שָׁלוֹם

Peace

לִמּוּד

Study

שְׁלוֹם בַּיִת

Household Harmony

כְּלַל יִשְׂרָאֵל

Jewish Unity

Judaism is in Your Hands

by generous permission of the artist, Rabbi Lawrence Bush

Spiritual Meditations for Personal Rededication and Family Renewal

*A little kibbutznik lights her own homemade menorah created
from bottle caps and white Shabbat candles.*
*(Kibbutz Tzora, November 1959,
Central Zionist Archives, Jerusalem)*

Introduction

SEDER
HANUKKA

Brache

Songs

Maccabe
Megilla

Profile

Spiritua
Meditatio

> "Whoever desires to penetrate the wisdom of holy unification should contemplate the flame ascending from a glowing ember or a burning candle."
>
> — ZOHAR, GENESIS[1]

מְנוֹרָה

Menorah

Lawrence Bush, poster, "Judaism is in Your Hands"[2]

Just as Jewish tradition uses the candle as a metaphor for the human being (*"God's candle is the human soul"*),[3] so the Temple is a metaphor for one's home sanctuary and one's personal inner sanctum. The community's Temple, *Beit HaMikdash* (literally the Home of Holiness where God dwells in the midst of the people) is analogous to the microcosm of one's soul and one's home, a place of sanctity whose table is akin to an altar.

Therefore, we have proposed two new optional spiritual ceremonies. First, a **Kavanot Ceremony** to be read before each candle is lit. We focus our attentions and our spiritual energies on one aspect of the power of personal sanctity (such as the search for purity or the resources of courage). Each day

of Hanukkah and each day of our lives may embody the process of increasing light, just as one more candle is added each night. The Talmud explained this nightly increase of candles, according to Hillel, in terms of the principle of *maalim bakodesh*, ever-rising levels of holiness. One must always try to climb the spiritual ladder. There is a need for ever-increasing levels of personal holiness (*kedusha*). As the oil of the Temple needed to be pure with the seal of the priest, so too, as Hasidic thought emphasizes, the people lighting the candles must try to put themselves through a self-purification process to reach higher levels of sanctity.

In addition, we have proposed a simple **Hanukkat HaBayit** (חֲנֻכַּת הַבַּיִת) ceremony for **Shabbat Hanukkah** for those who want to use Hanukkah as an opportunity to deepen and explore the spiritual dimension of Jewish homelife. It invites one to rededicate one's house to the power of holiness *(kedusha)* and the warmth of family tranquility *(shalom bayit)*. Since Hanukkah has become a home holiday, it is appropriate to celebrate not only the purification and rededication of the ancient Sanctuary in Jerusalem, but also the rededication of the contemporary family hearth in an era of the decline of family unity and home activities.

---

1. translated by Daniel Matt
2. The concept of "Judaism is in Your Hands" derives from *Deuteronomy* 30:11-14, *"Surely the teaching I command you this day is not too baffling for you, nor is it beyond reach. For it is not in heaven . . . neither is it beyond the sea . . . No, this thing is very close to you — to your mouth and to your heart — to observe it."*
   (Poster originally printed in *Reconstructionism Today*, edited by Rabbi Lawrence Bush.)
3. *Proverbs* 20:27

 כַּוָּנוֹת

REDEDICATING OUR INNER SANCTUM
A MEDITATION FOR CANDLE LIGHTING FOR EACH NIGHT

הִנְנִי מוּכָן וּמְזֻמָּן *Hinneni Muchan Um'zuman* / Here I am ready to light the first (second, etc) candle of Hanukkah and here I stand ready to rededicate myself to achieve higher levels of personal holiness and illumination in a world of shadows. Tonight's candle is dedicated to _____. (Name your own value for the whole family or ask each person to dedicate it to their own personal value).

בְּרָכוֹת Now proceed with *brachot* and candle lighting (p. 1) and then read one of the poems below, for the appropriate night from the *Hanukkat Habayit* poem by Chaya Kaplan-Gafni.

כַּוָּנוֹת
Kavanot – Candling the Inner Chambers

by Chaya Kaplan-Gafni

Hanukkah honors the house.
It is the Maccabees' renowned rededication of the House, the House of Holiness, the Beit Hamikdash.
It is the lighting of the fire in the heart, the hearth, the home of a People.

"Hanukkat Habayit" is the celebration of settling into a new home, a housewarming party of a sacred sort. It's as if with every move to a new house we celebrate a miniature Hanukkah. For each home is the manifestation of the Holy Temple in our times, in our own lives. Thus our four walls call for a Hanukkah — a dedication — the lighting of the fire that warms and sanctifies our space.

And Hanukkah's lighting of house is no less than the illumination of the inner Self. For the Self, with her secret stairways, her observing windows, her half-closed doors, is a many storied home, the abode of the soul.

Our task on these eight nights is to rededicate the Temple, in our own times, in our own lives . . . each night illumines a new aspect of self, lighting a new alcove of our inner House of Holies.

AT THE THRESHOLD

Entryway to Our Inner Self

I hesitate at the doorway, anticipating the darkness within.
The nadir of winter having wound itself around the handle, it grows too heavy for my hand.
I think there is little hope for illumination here, a cold house, neglected for years.
My eyes skirt the outer landscape for some welcomed diversion . . .
a restaurant, a neighbor, some simple task for my escape.

But I am bidden to enter. Indeed, the door was made for me alone.
For it is the doorway into my Self . . . dark as she may be, this house is the dwelling of my Soul.
Does she not deserve the illumination of my eyes, inward turned, burning for self-discovery?

I move to enter, and with surprising ease, simply slip through the door . . .
like oil spilling over ancient rock, entering the cracks . . . I have arrived at last.

**THE
HANUKK
CEREMO**

Brach

Song

**Maccab
Megilla**

Profile

**Spiritua
Meditatio**

Kavano

THE FIRST NIGHT

Dedicated to Darkness – the Cellar

Before you light your first candle, stand quietly for a moment in
complete darkness, and let the darkness indeed be complete, with no want
for anything, no need for the distractions of sight . . . simply sense the quiet
Self that sits there patiently waiting for you to take notice, to turn off
the television, to turn off all vision, to be quiet and sense the sanctuary that is the Self.

Standing in the cellar of my self, with an unlit candle in my hand
. . . in the darkness I discover a deeper self than light lets in.

This night I dedicate to inner darkness, to the unknown, unspeakable
seclusions of the soul. It is the darkness that keeps me searching . . . a worthy opponent,
provoking my path to further reaches, my thoughts to further depths. It is the as-of-yet
unillumined, unanswered aspects of an unraveling self, the landscape of dreams and
nightmares, tragic truths and fears.

I dedicate this night to every question I have quested after,
to every confusion that has humbled me,
to every challenge I have mastered,
to the thrill of secrecy.

As this candle casts a shadow, my self in dark outline,
I integrate and dedicate the darkness with the light.
The first night is for the dark cellar of winter,
that which illumines a deeper insight.

Dedicated to Ascension – the Stairway

Standing at the stairs, sights set on ascension.

As you light your candle, envision a stairway rising before you, each step a soul ascension made with a worthy act . . . each good word you have spoken, each good work done by your hands. See how each step leads to the next. Dedicate yourself to singular steps in an upward direction . . . go out of your way to do one new kindness every one of these eight days, for each is a link in the ever increasing chain of compassion that stretches out before you.

This night I dedicate to increase, to the second step of every path.
This is the move towards abundance, to building in increments, an ordered process.
The treasures of the house of Hillel tell of holiness that it should only increase, ever-rise.
Thus it was decreed that we light an additional candle to mark each night . . .
For holiness, like light and all luminescent goodness, should always advance,
like an ascending staircase, ever more inclined, increased, enhanced.

Just as each good act gives forth another, one spark springs forth to a second wick, while a string of candles await.

I stand at the stairway from my depths, ready to rise, to explore.
Having found my foundation in the darkness,
I move with upward momentum, the second night, the second step, the strength to start . . . .

Dedicated to Decisions – the Hallway

Imagine yourself in a hallway, an endless corridor
before you an offering of options, a series of dark wood doors
each opening widens with opportunity, each offers an unknowable path,
letting you choose, demanding you move, challenging you to act

. . . which door do you lunge for?

The hallway is where I will my way through the world.
It is the narrowness that leads to expansion, where one knock determines whole destinies.
This hallway calls for precision, decision, the analysis of options, the care and the courage to choose true, exact, correct. This corridor is the tension before any great act — when the moment calls for a deeper determination to raise it from the vast heap of mundane happenings, to let it become a great occurrence in the course of life.

This night is dedicated to direction, to making decisions in the dark, to taking the leap of faith that leads to miracles. From the narrowness of the Greek domination, the Maccabees chose no less than the doorway to vastest freedom. They did not remain confined, nor walk through assimilation's passive door, but rather lunged for the doorway of self-dominion and independence, fearless of the fight on the other side.

Standing in a hollow hallway, doorways blind my eyes,
I contemplate the path to my future, light three candles as my guide.

Dedicated to the Senses – the Dining Room

See yourself seated at a silvered table, set stately for some feast,
You are guest and host and caterer, called to task, to eat . . .

How full is your plate, how great is your need . . .
Is your spirit nourished as your body feeds?

The fourth night is dedicated to the dining room and her sister space the kitchen. This is the seat of appetite, brimming with all things delightful to the senses. At the center of the table is a fine serving bowl of *shemen*, olive oil, for *shemen* is the sign of the paradox of the sensual, where the sublime and the material meet and dine together, either in harmony or in utter disarray. *Shemen*, the anointing oil of Kings, the markings of Messiah, the essential symbol of Hanukkah, is the dripping robe of Redemption itself.
It is the nourishment for the candle, that upon which the holy flame feeds.
It is the utmost of sublime, but it is also the basest of the mundane. Meaning also "fat" (*shamein*), it signifies all that is thick and physical, the ultimate image of the material world, the mass where spirit resides.

This night is dedicated to delicate balances
where our desires come to dine
offering pleasure in each embellishment
fuel for the fire of life
…..though oil anoints and nourishes
overpour and it will put out the light.

Dedicated to Defiance – the Outer Courtyard and the Inner Will

See yourself standing in a courtyard stained with suffering.
Stationed before you are Hannah and her seven sons.
They stare down Antiochus and a torturous task –
denying their identity or facing their death.

They are a family forced to the edge of existence, given ultimatums they refuse to fulfill.
You are an observer in the outer courtyard, what says your inner will?

The fifth night finds my strength tested.
This night is dedicated to standing strong against external forces, refusing to fold to the host of voices that beckon me away from my core. This is the night of Hannah and her seven sons, caught in an outer courtyard, called upon to convert, to conform to an alien world.
This is a night dedicated to persistence . . . a night not afraid to sacrifice. It is a night of knowing one's identity, of being grounded in an inner courtyard of calm and courage, regardless of the chaos of the world outside.

In the cold of the outer courtyard, crowded with calls to comply,
I call upon the powers of my own inner will, to courageously defy.

The side tab (partially visible):

THE HANUKK CEREMO

Brach

Song

Maccab Megill

Profile

Spiritu Meditati

Kavan

Dedicated to Rebirth – the Bedroom

Your eyes are clouded beneath a canopy,
your limbs lie in linen, in your mouth one last breath . . .
Recall the colors of your days, are you satisfied with the path you have tread . . .
make peace with your person, and resigned to dying, find yourself re-birthed instead . . .

The sixth night leads me to the bedroom, painted with scenes of the Self in her several stages
. . . the same four walls redecorated and redecorated. For one lifetime witnesses many lives,
many bodies worn and shed, personalities developed and discarded, many births and many
deaths. Just as Jerusalem's Temple was lost and won and lost again . . . so too are we forever
falling, and redefining, losing and re-finding, a new beginning born with every end.

Nightly I lay my soul to rest here, my breath slows, the world recedes, I experience the end of all,
only to dream . . . and be reborn, burdenless to the morning. The bed a soft cocoon, a womb, a
tomb . . . a room of rejuvenation. These are the four walls of rebirthing — where the bed of
birth becomes the bed of death — the drive to end yet begin again.

The six flames lift from the ash like a phoenix, reviving life in her circular stride.
Though history be a looping spiral, Redemption lies at the end of the line.

Dedicated to "Advertising the Miracle" – the Light in the Window

As you stand lighting at the window, raise your eyes to look outside,
And behold a face before you, some curious passerby
And then realize it is your reflection, in the window glass, your own eyes
What have you seen in the window's mirror . . . what miracle do you advertise?

The seventh night is dedicated to the window to the world.
This is where the strength and purpose that I have nurtured within
are celebrated in the sight of others.
This is the show of lights that sparkles forth from Self. It is the commandment of Hanukkah
to do *pirsum hanes* — "to advertise the miracle," the miracle that was wrought in history,
that is wrought within me.

May my eyes behold the miracles shining forth from each passing soul . . .
And as I gaze into their windows may my own miracle be beheld as I behold.

Dedicated to Dedication – the Open Door to Redemption

The shamash stands silent at the open door, silhouted before an inner light.
She ushers in a new guest, a new age, as the Messiah steps to her side.
Having journeyed through self to but arrive at the selfless,
the shamash has the final goal of discovery held solid in her outstretched hand.

The eighth night is the night of the shamash, the candle that lights all other lights.
The shamash is the mystical servant, the symbol of service in the world.
I dedicate this night to the self who serves, to the self who has striven for perfection for the sake of the greater whole.

She is the radiant Self of the selfless servant . . . open and extending, sharing light and life, like a flame never diminished with its spreading, giving forth freely of the source that lights us all.

The eighth night is dedicated to dedication, the dedication of the shamash to the service of humankind. She is an open invitation, the current which connects door to neighbor's door — house to neighbor's house, self to community, to nation, world and the utmost of the universe. The shamash, the supreme usher, welcomes us into our own House of Holies . . . and Redemption follows in its wake.

A new immigrant child in Israel blesses the Hanukkah menorah adorned with the priestly benediction, as indicated by the hands with the divided fingers.
(December 1951, Central Zionist Organization, Jerusalem)

To be a Lamplighter

by Menachem Mendel Schneersohn
(The Lubavitcher Rebbe from 1950 to 1994)[2]

The Hasid once asked: "Rebbe, what is a Jew's task in this world?"
The Rebbe answered: "A Jew is a lamp-lighter on the streets of the world.
In olden days, there was a person in every town who would light the gas
street-lamps with a light he carried at the end of a long pole. On the street
corners, the lamps were there in readiness, waiting to be lit; a lamp-lighter has
a pole with a flame supplied by the town. He knows that the fire is not his
own, and he goes around lighting all the lamps on his route."

The Hasid asked: "But what if the lamp is in a desolate wilderness?"
The Rebbe answered: "Then, too, one must light it. Let it be noted that there is
a wilderness, and let the wilderness feel ashamed before the light."

"But what if the lamp is in the midst of a sea?"
"Then one must take off one's clothes, jump into the water and light it there!"
"And that is a Jew's mission?"

The Rebbe thought for a long moment and then said: "Yes, that is a Jew's calling."
The Hasid continued: "Rebbe, I see no lamps!"
The Rebbe answered: "That is because you are not yet a lamp-lighter."

The Hasid asked: "How does one become a lamplighter?"
The Rebbe replied: "One must begin with oneself, cleansing oneself, becoming
more refined, then one sees the other as a source of light, waiting to be ignited. When, Heaven forbid, one is crude, then one sees but crudeness; but
when one is noble, one sees nobility."

Today, the lamps are there, but they need to be lit. It is written, "The soul
of the human is a lamp of God,"[3] and it is also written, "A mitzvah is a lamp
and the Torah is light."[4] A Jew is one who puts personal affairs aside and goes
around lighting up the souls of others with the light of Torah and mitzvot.
Jewish souls are in readiness to be lit. Sometimes they are around the corner.
Sometimes they are in a wilderness or at sea. But there must be someone
who disregards personal comforts and conveniences and goes out to put a
light to these lamps, to ignite these souls. That is the true calling of a Jew —
to be a lamplighter, an igniter of souls.

2. Based on *Sichot HaRebbe* (Talks) from the years 5701, 5700, 5722.
3. *Proverbs* 20:27   4. *Proverbs* 6:23

A PARABLE AND A POEM FOR SPIRITUAL REFLECTION

Those Who Walk in Darkness
by Naomi Shemer [5]

(the contemporary national song writer of Israel, winner of the Israel Prize, who wrote Jerusalem of Gold*)*

THE HANUKK CEREMO

Brach

Song

Maccab Megilla

Profile

Spiritu Meditati

"Those who walk in darkness will see the great light."
Those who yearn for freedom will find a home.
Darkness rules over the lights
and those who stand, still search for miracles.

Who will light a candle for the future?
Who will sing a song?
Who will find in their heart a new bright light?
In yesterday's torch, the fire will still burn.
Sometimes a great miracle occurs.

The candles are lit on my window sill.
There are some who will know how to solve my dream.
It is the same story, the same play
"in those days and at this time."[6]

Don't promise me miracles and wonders.
Even the fog is a sign of the future.
In a stormy season, don't retreat.
On your way you will find hope and light.

"Those who walk in darkness will see the great light."[7]

5. Song reprinted by permission of ACUM.
6. Based on the prophet Isaiah: "The people who walk in darkness have seen a great light, on those who dwell in the land of the shadow of death a light has dawned." (*Isaiah* 9:1)
7. Quoted from the blessing for Hanukkah candles, *Al Hanissim,* "who made miracles possible for our ancestors in those days and at this time."

An old street lamp in Prague

הַכְנָסַת אוֹרְחִים

Hospitality

שְׁלוֹם בַּיִת

Household Harmony

שָׁלוֹם

Peace

כְּלַל יִשְׂרָאֵל

Jewish Unity

Judaism is in Your Hands
by Rabbi Lawrence Bush

חֲנֻכַּת הַבַּיִת

Hanukkat HaBayit Ceremony

REDEDICATING OUR HOME ON SHABBAT HANUKKAH

by Noam Zion

At the conjunction of Shabbat and Hanukkah, when two sets of lights converge, we have an opportunity for increased spiritual awareness of the sanctity of one's home. Shabbat candles celebrate shalom bayit, the peace of one's home, while Hanukkah commemorates the successful thwarting of the threat to our national home, the Temple called the Holy Bayit/Home. Tonight we recall the historical invasion and desecration of the Jerusalem Temple, as well as the subsequent efforts to purify and rededicate our personal temple.

We also wish to acknowledge the contemporary difficulties in keeping our home life pure and strong, a center of joy and of spiritual nourishment. We rededicate ourselves on Shabbat Hanukkah to the life-giving values of a Jewish home, knowing that this process involves serious commitments of time, emotion and energy.

THE BLESSINGS

First we light the Hanukkah candles as usual (page 1). Then we light Shabbat candles (page 2), even before singing the Hanukkah songs. The *shamash* may be used to light the Shabbat candles in order to connect these two holidays — Hanukkah and Shabbat — which intersect and produce a special energy on this night.

The traditional Shabbat meditation for women is appropriate and the blessing for one's children may be used. (see The Passover **Family Participation Haggadah**, *A Different Night*, page 18).

THE CEREMONY

Now begins the special *Hanukkat HaBayit* Ceremomy rededicating our home. We rededicate ourselves to eight values of a Jewish home, one for each night of Hanukkah. Ask each family member, in turn, to read aloud one of the eight selections:

1. הַכְנָסַת אוֹרְחִים *HACHNASAT ORCHIM* / WELCOMING GUESTS AND ACCOMPANYING THEM AS THEY DEPART

No holiday meal is complete without guests, old friends and relatives as well as new acquaintances and travellers. The private space, our home, which we have been able to secure, must remain open and accessible to strangers as Abraham's tent was open in four directions so a guest would not be embarrassed while trying to find a way in. When guests arrived, Abraham and Sarah were quick to run and prepare meat and cakes and make the guests feel at home.

From Abraham we also learn the art of leave taking, how to accompany guests not only to the door but on their way. Jewish law is concerned to make sure that the traveller has a secure way home, since we know the road and its dangers.

2. הַשׁוֹמֵר אָחִי אָנֹכִי *HASHOMER* / "I AM MY BROTHER'S AND SISTER'S KEEPER."

Solidarity within our nuclear family, our Jewish family and our human family is the central tenet of home life. Helping do the collective work, offering support when someone is ill or personally distressed and even giving advice — judiciously phrased and tuned — are concrete expressions of being one another's "keepers." The Rabbis insisted that "All of the people of Israel are guarantors one for the other."

3. וְשִׁנַּנְתָּם לְבָנֶיךָ *TORAH* / "TEACHING YOUR CHILDREN"

As we recall daily in Shma Yisrael, a parent should not neglect any opportunity to discuss a life of values, Torah, with his or her offspring. "When you lie down and when you get up, when you go out and when you sit at home."[6] The secret power of informal education is to turn everyday events into opportunities for learning and teaching. Rabbi Akiba, when he was a student, once "snuck" into his teacher's outhouse at night so he could observe how to conduct himself in intimate issues of personal hygiene. In trying to explain to his teacher the invasion of privacy, Akiba said simply, "This too is a matter of Torah and it must be learned from a master."

6. *Deuteronomy* 6:7

4. וְהִגַּדְתָּ לְבִנְךָ *HAGGADAH* / "TELLING YOUR CHILDREN STORIES"

Not only on Pesach, but on every family occasion family stories need to be told and memories revisited and reinterpreted. The narratives of our Biblical ancestors, our family albums and the report of our daily journeys are the substance of the Jewish cultivation of memory in the home. Cultivating the art of storytelling is the Jew's greatest tool to lead the next generation to connect their lives with their ancestors. Each recipient of a story must make it his or her own, feeling "as if you personally went out from Egypt" and retelling the tale in the first person to one's children and one's students.

THE HANUKK. CEREMO

Brach

Song

Maccab
Megilla

Profile

Spiritu
Meditati

Hanukk
HaBayi

5. קַבָּלַת שַׁבָּת *KABBALAT SHABBAT* / WELCOMING THE SHECHINAH, THE DIVINE PRESENCE

On Shabbat Jews traditionally welcome the spiritual presence of the Divine Shechinah and God's angels by singing Shalom Aleichem / שָׁלוֹם עֲלֵיכֶם. When we visit the Holy Temple or synagogue, we tread gingerly as guests in God's sanctuary, however on Shabbat we become God's hosts inviting the Shechinah into our home, making God feel comfortable among us, making room for spirituality as an active, intimate and familiar presence among us.

6. שָׁלוֹם בַּיִת *SHALOM BAYIT* / DOMESTIC PEACE

At home when powerfully driven individuals retreat into the inner sanctum of the family, the priority should be compromise. Foregoing our will and seeking to harmonize with others is the prerequisite for achieving the tranquility and solidarity of home life. Shalom Bayit involves an effort of mutual reconciliation and the peace of the home is achieved only after that has been attempted.

The Shabbat candles offer the light necessary for socializing around the table. They represent Shalom Bayit and take precedence over Hanukkah candles that symbolize the miraculous battle for dignity and freedom.

7. הִדּוּר מִצְוָה *HIDUR MITZVAH* / BEAUTIFYING YOUR HOME AND YOUR MITZVOT

The Rabbis appreciated the role of aesthetics in human life. As they used to say, "A beautiful house, beautiful utensils and a beautiful spouse expand one's consciousness." Therefore they commended one who spends extra effort and extra funds on beautifying the mitzvot they do, such as buying a particularly nice lulav and etrog on Sukkot, using extra candles and an attractive menorah on Hanukkah and preparing an especially rich meal when the poor are invited to dinner. Our gifts to God and to fellow human beings must be performed not minimally, to do our duty, but with added investment to show our joy in their performance. In this sense beautifying our homes is not a matter of external ostentation but an internal expression of our desire to expand our consciousness and to give pleasure to our Creator and to God's human creatures.

8. מַעֲלִין בַּקּוֹדֶשׁ *KEDUSHA* / CONSTANT GROWTH IN HOLINESS

A home must encourage the individual growth of its members, even though change may be threatening to the family equilibrium. Trusting in one another's power of self transcendence and growth, we allow the individuals and the group to grow constantly in their spirituality just as the Hanukkah candles grow night by night adding more and more light and holiness.

CHAPTER II

Family & Friends, Food & Fun:
Gambling, Gift Giving, Games & Gelt

Postcard by Hermann Junker 1838-1899, Frankfurt (c. 1850), Germany.
(Beit Hatefutsot Photo Archive, Tel Aviv)

Family & Friends, Food & Fun

INTRODUCTION

1. HANUKKAH CELEBRATIONS:
Minimal Guidelines and Maximal Flexibility

Unlike the holy "holi-days" of Pesach, Sukkot and Shavuot, there is no prohibition against working on Hanukkah. In fact, beyond lighting candles and singing Hallel (Psalms) and adding a paragraph about the miracles (*Al HaNissim*) to our usual prayers, there is little or no direction or obligations for how we celebrate this holiday. Unlike Purim (which is also not a holy day on which work is prohibited) there is no explicit obligation to read a Megillah, to drink, to eat, to send food packages to friends (*mishloach manot*) or to donate food and money to the poor so that they too can celebrate. That leaves Hanukkah quite "barren" but also open to innovation.

In this chapter we have devoted the first half to experiencing the holiday with all **our**

A Rabbinic Debate:
For and Against Feasting on Hanukkah

Some medieval rabbis like Maimonides mandated making Hanukkah festive, though no details are given.[1] Other rabbis, like the Rabbi Mordechai Yaffe,[2] maintained that the Talmud intentionally differentiated Purim and Hanukkah precisely on this point of "partying":[3]

On Purim, Haman decreed that the Jews be killed, that is, their bodies were to be destroyed . . . therefore when they were rescued the appropriate commemoration was both through praise and through drink and festivity (eating food, especially meat).

On Hanukkah, on the other hand, Antiochus and the Greeks never decreed that the Jews be killed but only that they change their faith . . . Therefore, when God helped Israel to defeat the Greeks [and save the Jews' souls], the (appropriate) way to commemorate the event was *only* spiritual, through praise and thanks (Hallel) and *not* physical, through drink and festivity. Therefore on Hanukkah (unlike Purim) festive meals are optional, not obligatory.

While Rabbi Mordechai Yaffe prefers that Hanukkah remain a spiritual event, most Jews have followed Maimonides' view that the Festival of Lights must be celebrated in body as well as spirit.

---

1. Maimonides, M.T. Hanukkah 3:3   2. Levush   3. *Shulchan Aruch O.H.* 670:2

senses — taste, sight, hearing and lots of hands-on activities. First there are pictures of the story to help parents retell the story to younger children. In **Telling the Tale in Words and Cartoons** you will find delightful pictures; the children may be invited to color them. Included is a list of recommended children's holiday books, some of which retell the historical tale, as well as a list of quality audio and video tapes.

The sense of taste is addressed in a brief section called **Ethnic Foods: Recipes and their Rationales**, which include latkas as well as hot wine and cheese blintzes. Those latter ideas derive from the Judith story. **Gift and Gelt Giving** proposes an innovative list of eight ideas, one for each night.

However the heart and body of this chapter is doing, not eating or reading. **Games and Activities** provides varied ideas for every age along with amusing cartoon figures. My daughter, Tanya Zion, has created a wide array of games, quizzes, arts and crafts and other popular activities adapted for Hanukkah. Using the flexibility of the eight nights, feel free to pick and choose and vary these pleasurable pastimes.

The second half of this chapter on Hanukkah celebrations offers a series of light but informative and reflective essays ranging from **Christmas and Hanukkah** and their encounter in North America to **Hanukkah Exotica** about the origins of the dreidel and other traditional customs.

This chapter opens with **Parental Guidelines: Hanukkah Hints for Families with Young Children** below. Here we have tried to give parents of young children some helpful guidelines for making this a meaningful family experience.

FAMILY AND FU

Introduc

Cartoo

Food

Game

Gift

Decem Dilem

Exoti

2. PARENTAL GUIDELINES: HANUKKAH HINTS FOR FAMILIES WITH YOUNG CHILDREN

by Noam Zion and Shira Ackerman-Simchovitch

Parents are the "high priests" of informal Jewish family education and their homes are the "temples" for a wealth of learning experiences. With an appropriate vision and plenty of ideas for games and activities, parents and children can create wonderful Jewish memories and personalized family traditions for Hanukkah.

To help develop your family vision for Hanukkah, consider the following six areas:

1. Creating family rituals

2. Retelling Hanukkah stories

3. Mastering basic information

4. Playing games

5. Giving — and not only receiving — gifts

(1) Creating Family Rituals

By involving our children in shaping our family traditions and preparing ritual objects and special foods, we can create family memories that will last a lifetime. Activities like frying latkas or making menorahs will be most effective when seen as part of preparations for a family observance that involves informal occasions for learning and sharing between parent and child. Younger children love to begin to get into the holiday spirit by looking at photo albums of themselves or even their parents as children celebrating Hanukkah. They often ask their parents to recall what they were doing when they were the same age as the child is now. On Hanukkah the children may wish to take a family photo each night, list all the guests who attended, and add these photos to a family **Hanukkah album**. Families who do not have such albums can begin one and add anecdotes told by parents about when they were small.

COOKING TOGETHER

Parents can invite their children to help prepare the special Hanukkah foods. Begin by reviewing recipes from a well-stained Jewish cookbook and perhaps then print out the recipe and begin a family **Hanukkah or holiday cookbook**. The children can illustrate the recipe book. After checking the ingredients, parents can go shopping with the children. After preparing the food, the children can make Hanukkah **place mats** or an illustrated **menu** and set the table for the guests.

Point out the use of oil in these Hanukkah recipes and explain the various kinds of oils we eat. Once at the supermarket, the children can see how many different kinds of oil they can find. Parents can use cooking or olive oil to make a simple oil menorah with a wick. At home the children may make a **display of oils of all sorts** near the Hanukkah menorahs.

MAKING RITUAL OBJECTS

In order to make their own Hanukkah menorah or dreidel, the children can begin by studying picture books of the Temple's seven branched menorah or pictures of Hanukkah menorahs in books on Jewish ritual objects. This can be turned into a game by asking the child to see how many different materials, shapes or decorative motifs can be found. The parent may explain the story of the menorah as well as **display and contrast all sorts of candles** (like candles for Hanukkah, for welcoming Shabbat and for *havdalah* marking the end of Shabbat, for *yahrzeit* marking the memorial of a relative, as well as for birthdays and other occasions).

Generally it is recommended to use **high quality materials** in the children's arts and crafts projects. This will help both the children and the adults to take these art projects more seriously, since children deeply desire to have their work recognized, praised and preserved for the next Hanukkah. Perhaps a special **Hanukkah box** should be prepared and saved from year to year with old decorations, homemade menorahs, etc. These homemade objects become heirlooms, an integral part of the family traditions. Beware of throwing out arts and crafts creations without the child's permission, lest they suspect that you do not really value their

> Educators suggest that narrative drama is the prime way by which children understand the world.

contribution to the holiday. Each child should be able to participate in the actual candle lighting ceremony, although obviously safety comes first when lighting matches. Cleaning up afterwards should also be part of their responsibility.

(2) Retelling Hanukkah Stories

Storytelling is not only a way to convey information about Jewish tradition but a way to engage the child's emotions and imagination. Our national memories become part of the personal inventory of images that remain at the child's disposal for a lifetime.

Educators suggest that **narrative drama** is the prime way by which children understand the world. Even exotic tales which seem far from the child's daily experience are readily comprehended when placed in a storylike form such as the cartoon versions provided below in *Telling the Tale in Words and Cartoons*. The psychologist Bruno Bettelheim assures us that **scary characters** like Antiochus are particularly appropriate for younger children who are trying to work out the good and the bad, the secure and the fearful in their worlds. To read about a formidable enemy who is ultimately defeated provides them with the hope and faith that they will be able to overcome difficult situations in their own lives.

In order for stories to be most thoroughly integrated into the child's world of imagination, they need not only to be heard but retold, to be rehearsed and processed in many ways. This **retelling** might take the form of drawing pictures illustrating a portion of the story after it has been read aloud, of retelling it with hand puppets, of acting it out with dialogue or of recreating the scene in Lego or clay. A parent may wish to stop reading in the middle of the story and ask the children what ending each might add or what would happen if something different had occurred than what historians tell us actually happened. A child might even write a letter or record on tape an oral telephone call to one of the characters in the Hanukkah story. Some suggestions on creative story telling can be found below in the section called *Games and Activities*.

BUILDING A HOME LIBRARY FOR JEWISH HOLIDAYS

Parents may decide to create a **Jewish holiday bookshelf** beginning with Hanukkah. Decide on a sum or number of books to be purchased before each holiday and work with your children and their grandparents, uncles and aunts to build up a prominently displayed collection. Prepare a list and perhaps distribute it to relatives who wish to bring a gift for Hanukkah. *(See the suggested Hanukkah Book and Resource List below, page 127.)* During Hanukkah the books may be displayed on a little table just as they are in a bookstore or a library before a holiday.

Another suggestion is to have an outing with your children and their friends to a big

---

Playing with Fire: Attractions and Hazards

For young children as well as adults there is an intrinsic attraction to the fire so central to the observance of Hanukkah. Therefore, parents must find a way to allow children's fascination to express itself and yet to guarantee their safety. This begins with choosing menorahs of non-flammable materials — beware of wood and plastic — and preparing a secure table, perhaps covered in aluminum foil, at a safe distance from curtains and books. Establish rules about long loose hair near a flame and about lighting multiple menorahs when several people with a burning *shamash* may be anxiously reaching over one another and over already lit candles in order to reach their candles. Some of the arts and crafts and cooking projects suggested also require parental supervision due to sharp instruments or frying pans of oil. Each family will need to find its own balance between the pleasures of "playing with fire" and the obligation to preserve life and limb.

comfortable bookstore where you can get a cup of coffee and cookies, read a few stories and maybe purchase a book for your collection.

(3) Mastering Basic Information

Mastering the facts and the rituals gives children a tremendous feeling of power in the best sense. Their broad and sometimes confusing world becomes more ordered and subject to their control when they understand how and why. Perhaps this explains the desire of school age children to be quizzed and to

---

Children must be givers as well as receivers of gifts. Gifts should include not only store-bought items but also handmade products and gifts of the heart.

---

quiz others. Many of the information games provided in the *Games and Activities* section contribute to that sense of ownership, success and recognition which children often crave. An outing to the local Jewish museum can provide an enjoyable visual survey of the holiday's traditions and ritual objects.

(4) Playing Competitive Games

Though we sometimes are disturbed with our children's competitiveness, it is an important part of their sense of self. In playing games they learn to lose as well as to win, to follow rules and to negotiate arguments over the application of the rules. Traditionally the gambling aspect of dreidel games has been a central social activity for adults and children. However dreidel playing involves mere **luck**, while some of the games we have suggested below involve **skill** development such as a complex game of strategy like Stratego or Risk. These are appropriate ways to celebrate the Maccabean tactics used in defeating the Greek empire.

Children can deal with occasional losses but they must be protected from a sense of

total failure. By playing multiple games and allowing a different child to pick his or her favorite game on different nights, everyone can play what s/he feels most comfortable with. If gambling with candles or chocolates or coins reinforces the sensitivity of the losers, then perhaps the winnings can actually be given to the needy rather than to the lucky winner. One way or another **everyone needs to be a winner at some point in playing Hanukkah's competitive games**.

(5) Giving — and Not Only Receiving — Gifts

In the American culture of holiday gift giving it has become customary to give children gifts, sometimes even every night. Given this reality, there is much room for involving the child in the whole process, from discovering what people in the family really want, to purchasing gifts for others, to preparing gift wrapping and cards with Hanukkah motifs, to creating a ritual order in the distribution and opening of the gifts. **Children must be givers as well as receivers of gifts** and gifts should include not only store-bought items but also handmade products and gifts of the heart.

Some people have suggested creatively that each night be designated with its own unique gift giving protocol: grandparents night, giving to the needy, giving nonmaterial gifts and so on. Each family can create its own traditions of giving, of receiving and of saying thank you. *(see Gelt and Gift Giving below page 155)*

We hope this brief review of our vision of Jewish family education on Hanukkah will make it easier to use the many concrete ideas for activities presented in this chapter.

TELLING THE TALE IN WORDS AND IN CARTOONS

by Tanya Zion

A HANUKKAH + 2 + n...

©TZ

featuring:

humor, trickery, war and much more!

JEWS

IDOLS

ELEPHANTS THE DEADLY PET

JASON THE TRAITOR PRIEST

ANTIOCHUS THE MAD KING

AFTER BEFORE

JUDITH THE BRAVE HEROINE

THE GREEK SOLDIERS

MACCABEES THE FIGHTER FAMILY

OIL CRUSE THE MIRACLE

HOLOFERNES THE HEADLESS GENERAL

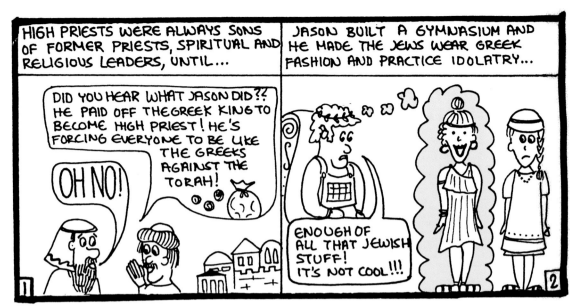

Cartoons

THE GREEKS PUT IDOLS IN THE TEMPLE AND HELD PARTIES THERE EATING + DOING FORBIDDEN THINGS!

"NO MORE **BRIT MILA** CIRCUMCISION FOR JEWISH BOYS!" ORDERED KING ANTIOCHUS. 6

"NO MORE SHABBAT!" SAID THE KING... 8

THE KING ORDERED ALL TORAH SCROLLS HE FOUND — TO BE BURNED! ANTIOCHUS KILLED ANYONE WHO DISOBEYED HIM... 10

ON THE KING'S BIRTHDAY, HE FORCED THE JEWS TO EAT THE MEAT SACRIFICED TO ZEUS, THE GREEK GOD, AND MADE THEM MARCH IN HIS HONOR... 9

OFF WITH THEIR HEADS!

12 SOME PEOPLE SAID THAT KING ANTIOCHUS WAS CRAZY...

FOOLISH...

MEAN AND WICKED...

WANT TO SEE AN EXAMPLE? ➝

11 SOME JEWS RAN AWAY TO THE MOUNTAINS AND HID IN CAVES... THERE THEY SECRETLY LIT CANDLES FOR SHABBAT AND ALSO CONTINUED TO TEACH + LEARN TORAH...

KING ANTIOCHUS USED TO SWITCH HIS ROYAL ROBES FOR A COMMON PEOPLE'S TOGA AND WALK THE STREETS DISGUISED AS A COMMONER...

THE KING WOULD THEN SUDDENLY DECIDE TO GIVE PEOPLE GIFTS! ...YOU NEVER KNEW WHAT YOU MIGHT GET...

GOLD! I'M RICH!

?! A CHICKEN?!!

A ROCK?

13

ONCE HE WALKED INTO A PUBLIC BATH-HOUSE WITH A VESSEL FULL OF EXPENSIVE OIL + PERFUME! SOMEONE WANTED TO SMELL IT...

14

HEY! WHAT'S GOING ON???

WANT SOME? HERE...

HA! HA! HA!

SO HE POURED IT ALL ON HIS HEAD!

15

HEY!

OOOW!

OUCH!

GIMME SOME!

BUT BECAUSE THE PERFUMED OIL WAS SO EXPENSIVE AND SPECIAL, EVERYONE WANTED SOME... AND SO...

ANTIOCHUS THE KING JUST DID EVERYTHING TO THE

EXTREME

HE JUST LAUGHED WHILE OTHERS SUFFERED...
HE DIDN'T REALLY CARE ABOUT ANYONE EXCEPT HIMSELF!
AND THE JEWS FOUGHT TO SURVIVE AND STAY INDEPENDENT, NEVER KNOWING WHAT TO EXPECT NEXT...

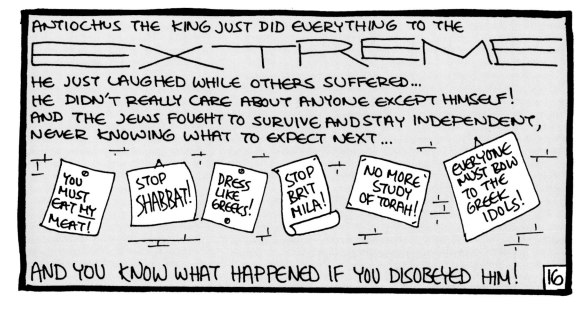

YOU MUST EAT MY MEAT!

STOP SHABBAT!

DRESS LIKE GREEKS!

STOP BRIT MILA!

NO MORE STUDY OF TORAH!

EVERYONE MUST BOW TO THE GREEK IDOLS!

AND YOU KNOW WHAT HAPPENED IF YOU DISOBEYED HIM!

16

ALTHOUGH SOME OF THE JEWS TRIED TO BECOME LIKE THE GREEKS, MOST JEWS DIDN'T WANT TO LEAVE THE SPECIAL WAYS OF THE TORAH...

A PRIEST NAMED MATTATHIAS FROM THE TOWN OF MODI'IN SAW HOW MANY JEWS WERE FORCED TO GO AGAINST THEIR TRADITION.

WHEN THE GREEKS ORDERED MATTATHIAS TO SERVE AS AN EXAMPLE TO OTHER JEWS BY BOWING DOWN TO IDOLS + OFFERING SACRIFICES TO THE GREEK GODS...

HE REFUSED! MATTATHIAS CALLED ON OTHER JEWS TO JOIN HIM...

MATTATHIAS AND HIS 5 SONS GATHERED AN ARMY OF JEWS...

2

Jonathan
Elazar
Mattathias
Simon
John
Judah the Maccabee

THE FEW JEWS PREPARED TO FIGHT THE MANY GREEKS...

3

SURPRISINGLY ENOUGH, THE JEWS BEAT THE GREEK ARMY IN MANY BATTLES!

IN ONE BATTLE THOUGH, THE GREEKS NOT ONLY OUTNUMBERED THE JEWS, BUT FOUGHT WITH MORE + BETTER WEAPONS AND...

RODE ON ELEPHANTS !!!

4

ELAZAR THOUGHT HE SAW THE GREEK GENERAL BECAUSE ONE OF THE ELEPHANTS WAS DECORATED ...

WITHOUT A 2nd THOUGHT, ELAZAR CHARGED TOWARDS IT!

5

ELAZAR TOPPLED THE ELEPHANT OVER, KILLING SOME GREEK SOLDIERS

BUT ELAZAR HIMSELF WAS CRUSHED TO DEATH...

6

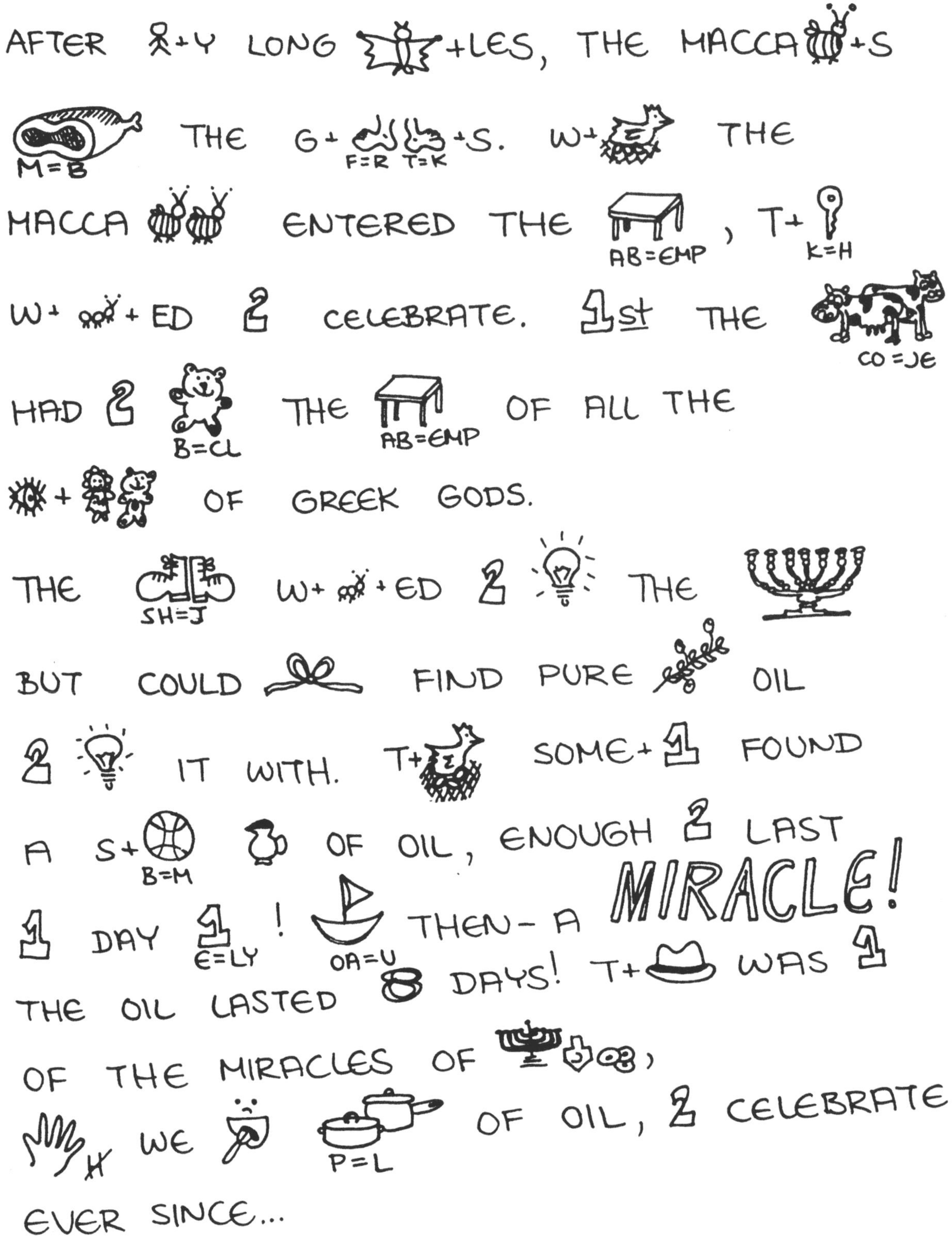

AFTER ☧+Y LONG +LES, THE MACCA +S

THE G+ +S. W+ THE
M=B F=R T=K

MACCA ENTERED THE , T+
AB=EMP K=H

W+ +ED ♫ CELEBRATE. 1st THE
CO=JE

HAD ♫ THE OF ALL THE
B=CL AB=EMP

+ OF GREEK GODS.

THE W+ +ED ♫ THE
SH=J

BUT COULD FIND PURE OIL

♫ IT WITH. T+ SOME+1 FOUND

A S+ OF OIL, ENOUGH ♫ LAST
B=M

1 DAY 1 ! THEN - A *MIRACLE!*
E=LY OA=U

THE OIL LASTED 8 DAYS! T+ WAS 1

OF THE MIRACLES OF ,

WE OF OIL, ♫ CELEBRATE
H P=L

EVER SINCE...

SELECTED HANUKKAH BOOK, MUSIC AND RESOURCE LIST

[☆ = Editors' family favorites]

YOUNGER CHILDREN (AGED 4-10)

David Adler, *Chanukah in Chelm; One Yellow Daffodil*

Jane Breskin Zalben, *Papa's Latkas; Beni's First Chanukah; Pearl's Eight days of Chanukah*

Aliana Brodman, *The Gift*

Chaya Burstein, *Hanukkah Cat*

Janice Cohn, *The Christmas Menorahs: How a Town Fought Hate (Billings, Montana)*

Barbara Diamond Goldin, *Just Enough is Plenty; A Hanukkah Tale; While the Candles Burn: Eight Stories for Hanukkah*

Malka Drucker, *Grandma's Latkas*

Marilyn Hirsh, *Potato Pancakes All Around*

Eric Kimmel, *Hershel and the Hannukah Goblins; The Chanukah Guest;* and many more

Arthur Levine, *All the Lights in the Night*

Fran Manushkin, *Latkas and Applesauce*

Margaret Moorman, *Light the Lights: A Story about Celebrating Chanukah and Christmas*

Malka Penn, *The Miracle of Potato Latkas*

Mark Podwal, *The Menorah Story*

Joanne Rocklin, *The Very Best Hanukkah Gift*

Peninah Schram and Steven Rosman, *Eight Tales for Eight Nights*

Isaac Bashevis Singer, *Zlateh the Goat*

Yehuda and Sarah Wurtzel, *Lights: A Fable about Hanukkah*

Marci Stillerman, *Nine Spoons*

Sadie Rose Weilerstein, *K'tonton in the Circus: A Hanukkah Adventure*

Harriet Ziefert, *Eight Days of Hanukkah*

Ray Zwerin, *Like A Maccabee*

MIDDLE SCHOOL CHILDREN

Sholem Aleichem, *Hanukkah Money*

Barbara Cohen, *The Christmas Revolution*

Howard Fast, *My Glorious Brothers*

Lynn Kositsky, *Candles*

Amy Koss Goldman, *How I Saved Hanukkah*

Malka Penn, *The Hanukkah Ghosts*

Michael Rosen, *Elijah's Angel*

Isaac Bashevis Singer, *The Power of Light*

☆ Ephraim Sidon, *The Animated Menorah: Travels on a Space Ship*

Susan Sussman, *There's No Such Thing As A Chanukah Bush*

HANUKKAH HISTORY RETOLD FOR YOUNGER CHILDREN

Marilyn Burns, *The Hanukkah Book*

Miriam Chaikin, *Light Another Candle*

Malka Drucker, *Hanukkah: Eight Nights, Eight Lights*

Harriet Feder, *Judah Who Always Said "No!"*

Jerry Koralek, *Hanukkah: The Festival of Lights*

Karla Kuskin, *A Great Miracle Happened There*

Marilyn Hirsh, *The Hanukkah Story*

Roni Schotter, *Hannukah*

Maida Silverman, *Festival of Lights*

Nina Jaffe, *In the Month of Kislev*

Deborah Uchill Miller and Karen Ostrove, *Modiin Motel: An Idol Tale*

ACTIVITY BOOKS

☆ Chaim Mazo, *The Energizing Hannukah* (Pitspopany Press)

Tali Marcus Minelli, *Chanukah Fun*

Madeline Wicker and Judyth Groner, *Miracle Meals: Eight Nights of Food and Fun*

MUSIC CD'S

Theodore Bikel, *A Taste of Chanukah*

Theodore Bikel, *To Life: Channukah and Other Jewish Celebrations*

Debbie Friedman, *Not by Might, Not by Power*

Paul Zim, *The Magic of Chanukah* (Simcha)

VIDEOS

☆ Yehuda and Sara Wurtzel, *Lights: The Miracle of Hannukah* (Sisu Home Entertainment)

Chanukah: Shalom Sesame

AUDIO TAPES

Cherie Karo Schwartz, *Stories of Hanukkah* (Kar Ben Copies)

CD ROM

Who Stole Hanukkah? Mystery Game (JEMM)

PARENT-CHILD GUIDE BOOKS

☆ Joel Lurie Grishaver, *Building Jewish Life: Hanukkah* (Torah Aura)

Vicky Kelman, *Together: A Child-Parent Kit, Hanukkah*

Mae Shafter Rockland, *The Hanukkah Book*

Cartoons

ETHNIC FOODS

RECIPES AND THEIR RATIONALE

from Annette's Kitchen in Talpiot, Jerusalem

The rationale for Hanukkah recipes is neither deep nor ancient. What is universal in medieval and modern recipes is the ingredient of oil which is obviously connected to the miracle of the cruse of oil that burned for eight days. Cheese dishes are customary because Judith used milk products to fill the Greek General Holofernes up with a heavy meal that would make him sleep deeply. She also used wine to cause him to doze off before he could molest her and to enable her to remove his head without resistance. Therefore we have included a hot wine recipe. Potatoes have no special significance but they have become traditional in eastern European homes and so potato chips — also made with lots of oil — are perhaps a modern equivalent. For health reasons, many will prefer low fat oils. Enjoy.

EASTERN EUROPEAN POTATO LATKAS

3 cups of grated potatoes in long strips, drained by placing them in a strainer with a heavy object on top to press out the excess liquid (if you're in a hurry, just grab handfuls and squish the liquid out).

1 cup of grated carrots, if you like

2 eggs, beaten

½ onion, grated, drained

salt and pepper

3 T. of flour, corn flour, or matza meal

oil for frying

PUT IT ALL TOGETHER making sure it is not too liquidy and there is enough egg to bind the ingredients together. Drop by tablespoons into deep hot oil and fry on each side until golden. Drain excess oil on brown paper bags or paper towels. The result should be about 24 crispy latkas.

Serve with applesauce and sour cream, or jam.

LATKA HINTS

Reduce calories by using a non-stick pan and make sure the oil is very hot; otherwise latkas absorb oil and get soggy. Keep first batches warm (and away from your family) in 200° F. oven until ready to serve.

MOROCCAN LATKAS

4 large potatoes, boiled and mashed

2-3 eggs

¼ lb. grated parmesan or cheddar cheese

1-2 T. flour

2 T. chopped parsley

salt and pepper to taste

(breadcrumbs or flour for frying)

PUT ALL INGREDIENTS in large mixing bowl; knead slightly until mixture is pasty.

TAKE ONE TABLESPOON of mixture at a time and pat into round flat shapes. Dip in breadcrumbs or flour and fry until golden.

Yields about 2 dozen delicious latkas.

HERBED LATKAS

3 cups grated potatoes (4 large), not drained

2 eggs

⅓ cup grated onion

3 T. flour

1 t. salt

½ t. parsley flakes

½ t. rosemary leaves, crushed

¼ t. sage

¼ t. pepper

flour

baking power

salt and pepper

BEAT EGGS till light. Stir in onions, flour, salt, herbs, pepper. Peel potatoes & grate to make 3 cups; mix everything together. Fry till browned on both sides.

— *Julie Auerbach, Cleveland*

HOT SPICY WINE

Serves 6-8

One bottle of sweet Kiddush wine

One bottle grape juice or sparkling wine

2-4 cups of water

A drop of brandy (optional)

Two oranges

Two apples (green or red)

One banana

2 cinnamon sticks or a dash of cinnamon

5-6 whole cloves or a dash of cloves (powder)

Dash of nutmeg

2 teaspoons of honey or brown sugar

PUT LIQUIDS IN POT. Slice the oranges with the rind into wheels (quarters), cut the unpeeled apples into small pieces and put into a pot.

ADD SPICES.

SIMMER over a low flame.

ADD MORE OR LESS WATER, according to the taste (and age) of the company, and finally slice a banana into the pot.

SERVE THE WINE AND FRUIT HOT in decorative glasses, add a small spoon for each person.

— The traditional Zion family beverage during candle lighting

BLINTZES

BATTER:

3 eggs

½ cup of water

½ cup of milk

¾ cup flour

2 T. melted butter, margarine, or oil

COMBINE ALL TOGETHER AND REFRIGERATE for at least 2 hours. Heat frying pan and grease slightly. Put in 3 T. of batter and tilt the pan so it is covered with a thin layer of batter. Let brown and carefully turn it over for a few seconds on the other side. Remove onto a plate. Makes about 20 pancakes.

FILLING:

1 lb. cottage cheese, farmers cheese or cream cheese

1 egg + 1 egg yolk

sugar (from 2 tablespoons upwards depending on how sweet you like them)

lemon peel

(raisins)

COMBINE ALL.

SPREAD THE FILLING in the pancake (about 2 tablespoons). Fold in the sides and roll up. Fry in butter or bake in oven in greased pan 425 degrees Fahrenheit until brown. Serve with sour cream.

You can fill them also with vegetables, blueberries, etc.

SUGAR COOKIES

1 cup butter or margarine

1 cup sugar

BEAT TOGETHER. ADD:

1 egg

1 teaspoon of vanilla

GRADUALLY ADD:

2 cups of flour (have another ½ cup handy)

DIVIDE INTO 4 PARTS. Refrigerate 2 hours minimum. Roll out and use Hanukkah cookie cutters in the shape of candles, dreidels and menorahs.

PLACE ON AN UNGREASED COOKIE SHEET. Bake 350 degrees for about 8 minutes. Cool.

YOU CAN PAINT THE COOKIES with a mixture of food coloring and water and use cotton swabs as paint brushes. Decorate with miniature chocolate chips, candies, Cheerios, cornflakes, raisins, snipped dried fruit, coconuts, etc.

PERSIAN POTATO OMELETTE

2 medium size potatoes, boiled, drained, and mashed until very smooth

2-3 T. butter or margarine

6 eggs

4-5 scallions or chives, chopped

2 T. chopped parsley

½ t. turmeric or saffron

1 T. lemon juice

salt and pepper to taste

MIX ALL INGREDIENTS in large bowl till smooth. Pour mixture into greased casserole.

BAKE AT 325° F. for about ¾ hour or until set and browned.

Remove onto serving dish, slice in wedges and serve the omelette cold or warm.

Optional: add cooked peas, carrots or spinach to the mixture. The omelette becomes a main dish for your Hanukkah meal.

FAMILY AND FU

Introduc

Cartoo

Food

Game

Gifts

Decemb
Dilemm

Exotic

Hanukkah Snacks

Besides latkas or blintzes, you may put out olives of all sorts or multiple types of potato chips (invented by an American Indian chef in a restaurant in Saratoga, N.Y., in 1853). This goes with Hanukkah candies such as chocolate coins for snacks. Make sure to have chocolate chips on hand to use for gambling with the dreidel, so people can bet freely and nosh at the same time.

GAMES AND ACTIVITIES FOR ALL AGES

by Tanya Zion

F.C. Kirchner, Nurnberg, 1734. From "Ceremonies of the Jews"
(Jewish National and University Library, Jerusalem,
courtesy of Beit Hatefutsot, Photo Archive, Tel Aviv).

Hanukkah is a classic time for home activities with friends and family of all ages playing together. With the variety of people and the number of nights available it is best to have a broad repertoire of games and projects from which to choose. Some of these require advanced preparations and some can be played on the spur of the moment. For the word games, for example, it is recommended to copy the relevant page in advance so several people can fill in the answers simultaneously. Perhaps a set of activities can be reproduced and made into a little Hanukkah booklet for one evening's entertainment. Try to peruse the options before candle lighting.

Table of Contents

1. PLAYING WITH FIRE AND LIGHT

Making a Peanut Menorah

The fuel of Hanukkah candles, whether of wax or of oil, is simply an organic material produced from the sun's light through photosynthesis. In burning organic materials the process is reversed and the light and heat of the sun are released. Many of the foods we eat, such as latkas fried in oil, are burned up in our stomachs. To get an idea about the tremendous amount of chemical energy found in our food, take an ordinary peanut and conduct the following experiment: make your own peanut menorah. (For more scientific aspects of combustion see the article on "The Chemical History of the Candle" in Chapter V in the companion volume, *The Big Book of Hanukkah*.)

What do I need?

- a piece of cardboard
- 8 straight pins
- a fireproof surface (e.g., a kitchen tile)
- 8 peanuts (removed from their shells)
- matches

NOTE: The Fire Power of the Peanut Menorah
by Dr. Sherman Rosenfeld

How long does it take for the peanut menorah to burn?

Of course it depends. The time it takes a peanut to burn would vary, depending on the wind in the room, the size of the flame, and other factors. But under the same conditions, the same weight of a peanut would burn much longer than the same weight of a piece of bread, because it contains so many more calories.

How do we count calories especially on Hanukkah when we eat so many oily foods?

A calorie (with a lower c) is defined as the heat flow needed to raise the temperature of one gram of water by one degree Celsius. A Calorie (with a capital C, called a kilocalorie by physicists) is 1000 time larger than a calorie. This means that if you burn a peanut, the heat flow from that peanut will raise the temperature of a certain amount of water a certain number of degrees Celsius; from this, one can conclude how many Calories a peanut has. It turns out that an average peanut contains about 6.5 Calories (which is equal to 6500 calories). This is a lot of Calories for a little bit of food. The reason: a peanut is 48% fat, 26% protein and only 16% digestible carbohydrates. All carbohydrates and proteins contain about 4.2 Calories per gram, but fats contain more than double the Calories! (9.3 Calories per gram)

What is the "fire power" of a peanut?

Consider this: Say we took 80 grams of water (about 80 ml) and placed a burning peanut beneath it (in a well-insulated set-up, to prevent heat loss). If the water started at room temperature (about 20 degrees Celsius), the burning would cause the water to reach boiling (100 degrees Celsius, 212 Fahrenheit). Since the temperature increase is 80 degrees Celsius, it required 6400 calories of heat flow (80 degrees x 80 grams water), which equals 6.4 Calories. Another way of putting it is to say that 3 average-sized peanuts could boil a cup of coffee.

What do I do?

(1) Stick the pins completely through the cardboard. Set the cardboard on the fireproof surface, so the ends of the pins point into the air.

(2) Carefully stick the peanuts onto the ends of the pins, then guess how long they will burn and write down the guesses.

(3) Carefully light the match. Place the top of the flame under the peanut until the peanut ignites.

(4) Time how long the peanut burns. Whose guess was closest?

The Spectrum of Light

The white light of the Hanukkah candles sends forth a rainbow of light. Take a prism or a defraction gradient and you can see for yourself how white light is made up of many different colors. Flash a light through a prism or purchase a defraction gradient from the local science museum and hold it up to a Hanukkah candle, a fluorescent light, or a light bulb and see the difference in the colors of the spectrum. Notice that the candle will emit a "continuous" spectrum of red, orange, yellow, green, blue, indigo, violet with a bright red area indicating heat. A fluorescent lamp will show vertical lines in the spectrum. Each source of light has its own "spectrum fingerprint."

Playing with Fire

Fun but hazardous, beware!

In a safe place with proper supervision line up two to four contestants behind a starting line. Then give them a signal to run to a station, pick up a box of matches, a box of Hanukkah candles and a simple menorah. Who can insert and ignite all nine candles in the proper order first. Make sure each contestant has plenty of room and that the area is safe and does not create a fire hazard.

FAMILY
AND FUN

Introduct

Cartoo

Foods

Games

Gifts

Decembe
Dilemm

Exotica

2. WORD GAMES

For this as well as most of the word games, you will need pens (or better, pencils) for everyone as well as multiple copies of these worksheets.

Word Search   BY EDEN AND YEDIDYA ZION

```
L E L L A H W A N O I T A C I D E D E R
A L H A N I S S I M T E A S A P J O T G
S A R E G F D E L D N A C O T L Y T R L
O Z O H H Y C Y H A K U N N A H H H S I
L A O H N B V C A T J Q W E R A G J H G
S R U T P U J H R H Y U A B U N K G A H
I O I S Y U H N N I O P L I K A F N A B
C B R T T H G I E Y U I P O T H B M S A
E M W N A E N O M S A H A B O H I O H D
E I V E L S I K B B M M O E P V J P I F
G R Y S U H C O I T N A T S S A K T A L
E A E E B A C C A M D E O D L T I K G A
L C R R O M N L I O I L I M O D I I N S
T L T P P A L I O I Y E N T Y K G M J S
F E T N H I U R L L N P A M P J H U H S
B G L P O O W U R E U H G M S L D A H V
T L E G E A W R Y N K A F N G A M A Y A
G L G E Y Y V B M H J N U N H A M F I O
E O S D G W O D N I W T S P S A R C W T
```

Kislev, Oil, Hasmonean, Antiochus, Window, Maccabee, Elephant, Miracle, Solstice, Presents, Shamash, Latkas, Modiin, Elazar, Eight, Doorway, Judith, Sufganiot, Gelt, Rededication, Hallel, Candle, Al Hanissim, Hannukah, Hannah, Light, Menorah, Judah.

Scrambled Messages

What does it really say???

Pretend you are part of the intelligence (spy) unit of the Judean army. Your fellow Maccabees sent you this secret message and you need to decipher it. Unscramble as many words as you can in up to eight minutes and then prepare your own coded message for the other players. *(Hint: all the messages are Hanukkah related.)*

1. Yphap hkaanuhk!
2. Ew thilg itheg snelacd ni het hanemor
3. Saitamttah asw eth gihh stripe
4. Het csamecabe eld eht hiwsej torevl
5. No nakhhuka, ew fireupid eth pelemt

Hidden Words

The goal of the game is to find as many words as possible that are hidden in a phrase! The rules are: you may switch around the order of the letters to create as many words as you like, you don't have to use all the letters but remember — you may not reuse (or "double") letters unless they appear more than once in the phrase. Before you begin, each contestant should take a sheet of paper and pen/pencil and write the phrase at the top of the page. (Make sure everyone spells the words correctly!) If you'd like, set up a time limit for the game and appoint a time keeper. You may set a limit of about 2 or 3 minutes. After the time is up, have each contestant read out his words. If someone else has found your word too, you get 5 points. If no one else found that word, you get 10 points! Any word that has more than 4 letters gets an extra 2 points.

Get pencils or pens for everyone and a timer for the judge. Ready? Set, Go!

Lighting the Menorah
Judith killed Holofernes
Festival of Lights
Judah the Maccabee
Playing Dreidel
Singing Maoz Tzur
Eight days of Hanukkah
Antiochus Epiphanes
Greeks fought Jews
Maccabees from Modiin

Spelling Game

How many different ways can you spell the name of this holiday?

Word Origins: A Multiple Choice Quiz for Adults and Teenagers

Many English words and phrases are related to candle lighting or other Hanukkah activities. You use these words many times but do you really know what they mean and where they come from? Here is a chance to find out.

There are 4 optional answers but there is *only one* correct answer. *(See the answers at the end of this section.)*

1. The word "**match**" comes from:
   A. The Latin word "*maxa*" which means "suddenly, in an instant," because of the way the match flares up
   B. The fact that when the match was invented, the newspaper ad said, "there's no match for this!"
   C. The Latin word "*myxa*" which means "wick" — a lamp nozzle
   D. Match is the shortened version of the original Greek word "matcha-aliverus" that means light of the gods, or fire

2. The word "**wax**" comes from:
   A. "wax" — to grow and increase
   B. "wax" — the Old English word for "weave," from beeswax which is produced in a honeycomb
   C. "wax" — to change shape, because it is pliable
   D. "wax" — the Roman term for a hard material that softens in heat

3. The word "**lamp**":
   A. means shine, give light
   B. means hold light, contain light
   C. comes from the words light + amplitude (lamp)
   D. means white in Latin

4. The word "**light**":
   A. means not-heavy
   B. means natural fire
   C. means not tangible, spiritual
   D. means white

5. The word "**candle**":
   A. means to flow
   B. means to grow
   C. means to show
   D. means to glow

6. The word "**oil**":
   A. oil is short for the Latin term "oiliva terumsa"
   B. oil comes from the word "olive"
   C. oil was first produced in China and was originally named "Oy-Li" in Chinese
   D. "oil" derives from a mistranslation of the Hebrew "*shemen*" and means "fat"

7. The word "**potato**" originally meant:
   A. sweet potato
   B. apple (Hebrew term for potato is "*tapuach adama*" = ground apple)
   C. potato as we know it today
   D. radish

8. What did Shakespeare mean when he wrote *"let the sky rain potatoes"* in his play "Merry Wives of Windsor"?
   A. may we never be hungry again
   B. may God strike my enemies on the head
   C. may we be aroused to love
   D. may the ground be plentiful for our potato harvest

9. *"Hide your light under a bushel"* means:
   A. to be especially modest
   B. spirituality can be found in nature
   C. to have bad-eye sight in the dark
   D. a military code for a blackout in wartime

10. About whom was it said *"be a light for the nations"*?
   A. people who work in lighthouses
   B. the United Nations (U.N.)
   C. the Jewish people
   D. people who sell light fixtures

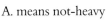

Hidden Hanukkah Messages

1. *Take out every Y and M and see what you spell:*

   HYANYMUMKKAYHYIYSMMYAMLYYSYMOMM
   CYALYLMEMMDYMTYHMEYYFMEYYSYTMIMV
   AYLMYOMMFYYLMIYGYYHMTMSY.

2. *Take out every B and C and find the names of two important Hanukkah heroes:*

   BCBJBUCCDBCABBHCBCABBNCDBCJCCUC
   DBIBCTBCHB

3. *What does this message say? Find out by reading every other letter, starting with the first letter — A:*

   AHNSTVICOTCBHNUMSETSHOEYGIREEPESK
   DKBINNMGEFROCRXBFAHDKETJAEKWPSRTC
   OWOQBNSDEVRCVNETSEHGACBMBSAITU

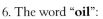

Games

Word Games

Hanukkah Ad Lib

Only one player should read the categories of words needed to fill in the blanks, while the others are requested only to suggest appropriate words that are missing, without knowing the context. For example: "name a noun, verb and adjective." Whatever words are chosen are then written in place of the blank spaces in the story. When you have completed all the missing words, read the story out loud, and see what happens. It will probably be a whole new kind of Hanukkah tale!

There are many _____(adjective) **stories about Hanukkah. My favorite is about** _____(male name), **who was the son of** _____(name). **He was a(n)** _____(adjective) **fighter, who always** _____(verb in past tense) **for the Jewish** _____(plural noun). **One day he** _____(verb, past) **to fight the** _____ (adjective) **Greeks, and saw they had many** _____(plural noun) **and about** _____(number and plural noun)! **But he was not** _____ (adjective)!

When he saw one _____(noun) **that was especially** _____ (adjective), **he thought the** _____(profession) **must be on that one! So he** _____(verb, past) **quickly and decided to** _____(verb) **the** _____(animal). **He rushed towards it, taking his** _____ (noun) **in his** _____(body part) **and suddenly all he could** _____(verb) **was** _____(color), **and everything around him felt** _____(adjective). **He had been** _____(verb, past) **under a(n)** _____ (noun)! **People never forgot his** _____ _____(adjective and verb), **and they will always consider him "the** _____ (adjective) **warrior who** _____(verb, past) **his life for his** _____(noun).

Write Your Name in Greek and Hebrew

Try writing your name in Greek and Hebrew letters. The table on the right shows you which letter to use for each sound in English. Some English letters are missing. You can see which letters to use instead below:

c use κ   j use ι   q use κ

v use φ   w use ου

My name in Hebrew is _____

My name in Greek is _____

THE GREEK AND HEBREW ALPHABETS				
CAPITAL LETTER	SMALL LETTER	LETTER NAME	SOUND	HEBREW LETTER
A	α	alpha	a	א
B	β	beta	b	ב
Γ	γ	gamma	g	ג
Δ	δ	delta	d	ד
E	ε	epsilon	e	א
Z	ζ	zeta	z	ז
H	η	eta	e or ay	ה
Θ	θ	theta	th	ת
I	ι	iota	i	
K	κ	kappa	k	ק
Λ	λ	lambda	l	ל
M	μ	mu	m	מ
N	ν	nu	n	נ
Ξ	ξ	xi	x or ks	ח
O	o	omicron	o	ו
Π	π	pi	p	פ
P	ρ	rho	r	ר
Σ	σς	sigma	s	ס
T	τ	tau	t	ט
Y	υ	upsilon	u or oo	ו
Φ	φ	phi	f or ph	פ
X	χ	chi	ch	כ
Ψ	ψ	psi	ps	
Ω	ω	omega	oh	ו

3. Games of Sight & Memory

Sight Games

Hanukkah, as you already know by now, is the holiday of LIGHT. We can see light using one of our senses — sight. Have you ever considered how it feels not to be able to see? How much do we depend on our sight without even noticing it?

Here are a few suggestions for sight-games that you can play anytime and anywhere!

Seeing and Remembering

1. This can be played with a friend or on your own. First choose your setting — inside or outside — try playing it both in places with which you are familiar (or think you are!) and in strange new places.

2. Take turns — one of you takes a few minutes to look around really well and try to remember as much as you can. (For example: if you're outside, do you see any cars? Where? Parked or driving? What color? Are there any people? Trees? Houses? etc.) Try to remember what you see, where these things are and as many details about them as you can.

3. When your time is up, cover your eyes (you can use your hand or a scarf). Describe to your friend everything you remember seeing. If you can't remember, have the friend help you out by asking questions or giving hints.

4. You can evaluate each other — decide on a rating system — for example: 1 point for each object, 1 point for knowing where it is and ½ a point for every detail you remember about it (color, shape, position etc.).

5. When you think you've said it all, open your eyes and look around. How well did you do? Doesn't everything look a little different now?

(If you play this on your own, you can turn around instead of covering your eyes and write down everything you remember and later check yourself!)

The Blind Person and the Guide

This game can be played with 2 players or more (even numbers only), either inside or outside. Take turns being the "blind" person and the seeing guide. The "blind" person's eyes should be closed and covered with a scarf or cloth. This game can be played at different levels of difficulty and trust. Since the game requires a lot of trust, we suggest you start with the easiest level and work your way up slowly. Just remember! Players switch roles, so remember what the great rabbi, Hillel, said, "Don't do to your friend what you wouldn't want done to you!"

Level 1 : Physical Contact:

'Blind' and 'Guide' should hold onto each other — by holding hands, or placing your hands on your partner's shoulders. The seeing guide should lead the 'blind' person around, don't forget to walk slowly, to give out directions ("Careful! There's a step, pick up your foot!"). Do your best not to bump the

'blind' person into anything! Once this gets too easy, try just holding one hand.

Level 2 : Verbal Contact:

Now that you've established some trust, let go. On this round, don't touch each other (unless your partner is going to fall). The seeing partner may only guide using vocal instructions. You'll probably find that you have to say more than you did before (more detailed and frequent directions).

Level 3: An Obstacle Course

If you are really ready for some fun and both partners agree to be adventurous — you can direct your partner into, above, under and through different obstacles!

Afterthoughts:

Notice how much of your self-confidence relies on being able to see? What did you notice about the trust in the relationship between "guide" and "blind?" Which role did you like more? When did it stop being scary and start being fun? Did any other sense get stronger because you couldn't see — your hearing abilities for example?

Picture Games

Here are some possible activities based on the 2 pictures at left:

1. Look carefully! What's the difference between these two seemingly identical pictures? (Hint: there are at least 8).

2. Choose one of the pictures and look at it for a few moments. Try to memorize as many details as possible, then cover up the picture and describe it to a friend. When you're done, check and see how many details you remembered!

3. Now you may color the in.

Kosher Menorah

What is wrong with this Menorah and the way it was lit?

What's Missing?

Set out eight different colored candles in a row.

1. Look at them for a few moments and then cover your eyes or turn away.

2. Have someone take one of the candles away.

3. When you look again you must try to guess — what color is the missing candle? You only get at most two guesses a round.

4. For a bonus, look and then turn away and name all the colors in order.

4. QUIZZES AND GUESSING GAMES

Hanukkah Trivia

Here is an array of games aimed to quiz yourself!

The Chai (18) Matching Game

Match the items from the right column to those in the left column. There is only one correct match per item.

Date of the Hebrew month when Hanukkah begins	**1**	**A**	5
The year BCE of the Rededication of the Temple	**2**	**B**	Jerusalem
Latkas	**3**	**C**	Service candle
Number of sons of Mattathias the Maccabee	**4**	**D**	Greek general Holofernes
Dreidel	**5**	**E**	Maccabeus
Number of days of Hanukkah	**6**	**F**	36
Number of blessings said on the first night of Hanukkah	**7**	**G**	165
Number of candles needed for eight nights of Hanukkah (*not* including the *shamash*)	**8**	**H**	Levivot
		I	Sevivon
Number of letters on a dreidel	**9**	**J**	4
Number of Hannah's sons killed	**10**	**K**	Greek elephant
Judith's enemy	**11**	**L**	King Antiochus IV
Mattathias's rival	**12**	**M**	25
Capital of Greek Syria	**13**	**N**	Antioch
Judah's Greek nickname	**14**	**O**	7
Shamash	**15**	**P**	8
Elazar's (Judah's brother) enemy	**16**	**Q**	3
Capital of Judea	**17**		
Murderer of Hannah and her seven sons	**18**	**R**	Jason the Greek-appointed High Priest

Fill In The Blanks

Fill in the missing words:
(if you'd like, you may use the words in the treasure box below)

1. Hanukkah starts on the 25th of _____.

2. Mattathias was the leader of the _____; he had _____ sons.

3. Hanukkah is also called the "festival of _____."

4. Maccabeus in Greek means _____.

5. Antiochus was the king of the _____ empire.

6. Jews were forbidden to perform commandments (mitzvot) like _____ and _____.

7. The Greeks filled the Temple (Beit haMikdash) with _____.

8. Only one jug of _____ was found.

9. It took 8 days to produce enough pure _____ oil to light the menorah in the Temple.

Idols of Zeus • Kislev • five • hammer • circumcision • Greek-Syrian • olive • Shabbat • lights • oil • Maccabees

Jeopardy

As in the famous television game show, the contestants choose a category and a value (the higher the sum, the more difficult). The game host then reads out an ***answer***. Contestants must then define the question to which this answer is given, in the form of "who is . . . ?" or "what is . . . ?" For example, choose the category "Jewish Holidays" for $200 and the answer is "Festival of Lights," the correct answer (meaning the question) is "What is Hanukkah?"

The categories in this game are: "Heroes/Villains," "Customs" and "Hebrew."

Note: Do not show the answers to the contestants until they pick a category and an amount! You can easily create the game board on a piece of paper as explained below, showing only the categories and values. The game host should hold the book and read the answers out loud as they are chosen. Optional — you can keep score and even secretly choose one of the boxes to be "double jeopardy." What we have suggested is only the beginning — we invite you to add categories and answers and play a few rounds of the game!

The "Feely" Box

The "feely" box is an interactive quiz game for small children.

Prepare a small carton box (such as a shoe box) and create an opening just big enough for one's hand, not allowing one to see the contents of the box. Choose a few Hanukkah related objects (such as a dreidel, candle or potato) and place them in the box. Now direct the child to put their hand in the box and try to guess what the object is, based only on touch.

	Heroes/Villains	Customs	Hebrew
$100	Mattathias	Window	*Shamash*
$200	Hannah	Half an hour	*Hanukkiya*
$300	Elephant	44	*Kad shemen*
$400	Jason	Right to left	*Pirsum hanes*
$500	Holofernes	Left to Right	*Al hanissim*

138

5. NUMBER GAMES

8 Boom!

This is a great game for kids and/or adults — just remember — it's not as simple as it looks!

Sit in a circle and decide who begins. Now, in clockwise direction, every participant says a number starting from 1 (for example: 1-2-3-4 . . . 9-10-11 . . . etc.). BUT since it's Hanukkah tonight, every time a number is a multiple of the magical number 8 (for example: 8, 16, 24, 32 . . . etc.) you skip that number and go to the next (for example: 5-6-7-9-10 . . .).

Counting must be done relatively quickly, no time to think!

If it was your turn to skip but you got mixed up and said the 8 number, you're out of the game — unless no one noticed your mistake on time and the next person continued counting as usual, in which case you are safe. If someone did notice your mistake, he must yell out "BOOM!" and then you're out of the game for that round. The winner of the game is the last one left . . . Good luck!

If you would like to make the game more complicated, prohibit the saying not only of multiples of 8 like 8, 16, 24, but also numbers which include the numeral 8 like 18, 28, 38 even if they are not multiples of 8.

Chai (18) Candles

On the last night of Hanukkah we use 9 candles — one *shamash* and eight Hanukkah candles. Two players need 18 candles — *chai*, the Hebrew letters for "life" (*chet* = 8 ; *yod* = 10), as in the toast, *L'chaim*.

There are two ways of playing the game: using 18 real candles set out in a row before the players or by drawing 18 candles on paper. You can play this game many times, each time resetting the 18 candles or drawing an additional row.

Players take turns, each time "removing" one, two, or three candles from the row working one's way from either side of the row (by picking up the candles or crossing them out). The player to be left with the last candle loses.

Warning! This game is not as easy as it seems so while you play the game, try to think ahead. Try to plan the moves so as to leave the last candle for your opponent, and not get stuck with it yourself! Sometimes it is better to remove only one candle and other times you may win by removing more.

Hanukkah *Gelt*: Spend Exactly $10.00 on Celebrating Hanukkah

You have received a gift of Hanukkah *gelt* (= "money" in Yiddish) of exactly $10. You may spend it in the store as you wish (buying any items you want, buying an item as many times as you want, and there is no need to buy all the items) as long as you spend no more or less than $10. Happy shopping! See all items available and their prices below:

Menorah **$3.50**

Dreidel **.25** each

Story book **$1.75**

Hanukkah candles **$1.40**

Sack filled with candy and chocolate coins **$2.20**

6. Arts and Crafts Projects and Drama

Potato Heads

Warning: This activity involves using a knife, so parental supervision is advised for very young children. Otherwise it is appropriate for all ages, any number of participants and can be done again and again! This activity might get a little messy, so it is best done in the kitchen. This is all about creativity so — enjoy!!!

(We suggest being ecologically useful by recycling and using these potatoes later for cooking purposes or even as fancy decorations for the food served).

What do I need?

- Potatoes (at least one per person)

- Regular kitchen knife, peeler, scissors

- Stuff — anything you can think of! Collect different things you can find around the house. Here are some suggestions: raisins, beads, buttons, carrots, string, doll clothing, color crayons, pieces of colorful paper, cloth, noodles, spaghetti, matches, straws, apples, toothpicks, pipe-cleaners, beads, etc., and glue.

What do I do?

That's really simple — and it's up to you! Choose your potato (small, big) and set all the materials out in front of you. Now let's get to work!

   A potato head needs eyes, a nose, a mouth . . . maybe even ears, hair, glasses, clothes (like a tie or hat) . . . .

Remember — you can either carve the shapes into the potato, stick other objects into it, or draw on it! (Note: sometimes it's easier to stick things into the potato if you first cut into the potato and then wedge the object in that space.)

Just an example: use raisins for eyes, twisted noodles for curly hair, a pipe-cleaner for glasses, a carrot tip for a nose, matches for arms and carve in the smiling mouth (maybe even a few teeth . . .).

Additional ideas:

- Hold a competition — "most attractive potato," "most original," "scariest," "tastiest" . . . etc.

- Try making potato heads that resemble people — famous figures, family members, Hanukkah characters (like the Greeks or Maccabees or even Elazar's elephant)!

- Use the potato figures you made to put in a home theater version of the Hanukkah story.

- Looking for more ideas? Older children might want to create other shapes out of their potatoes. For example: animals, objects, or just neat designs and shapes! Create your own art gallery or zoo!

Potato Stamps

- Cut a potato in half.

- On the inside face of the potato, carve out a Hanukkah shape (like a dreidel, candle, etc.).

- Paint the raised part of the potato or stamp it on an ink pad.

- Now stamp the wet paint/ink onto white paper. That way you can create your own Hanukkah cards.

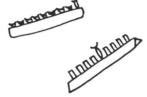

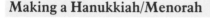

Making a Hanukkiah/Menorah

Advice: Before you begin this activity, you should spend some time reading about the laws of what makes a "kosher" menorah, found in the appendix of this book, ***"How to Light Right"*** (page 236).

Here are some basic reminders of the rules:

- All 8 candles (except the *shamash*) should be on the same level (equally high).

- The *shamash* should be visibly different than the other candles — either higher/lower or set further away from the others.

Like many activities in this book, here are just a few basic ideas and examples — any other creative ideas you can think of yourself are great!

Warning! If you're planning to use this menorah, please remember NOT to use anything flammable like paper, thin plastic, etc. near the candles.

What do I need? And what do I do?

1. First of all we will need something for the base (bottom) of the menorah, like: a piece of glass, metal, empty yogurt containers, strong plastic, wood, clay, fimo, etc. If you'd like, you can use egg cartons or thick cardboard as long as you cover it with aluminum foil so it can't burn! The size of the menorah will depend on whether it is for large or small candles, for wax or oil.

2. Next, we will need something to hold the candles:

Once again — anything will do such as metal / plastic caps of bottles. (Note: if you use an aluminum-covered egg carton, you already have the candle holders right there! egg cartons can be used both ways — either the open side up, putting the candle inside or upside down, opening down, sticking the candles on top . . . .)

3. Now, we will need glue — choose the strength of the glue depending on your materials.

4. And now — just anything for decoration!

Color it with pens, colors and crayons. Put glue on the menorah wherever you want, then stick on it sand, beads, cellophane, glitter and pieces of colorful paper.

Additional ideas:

- You might want to write something on the menorah — like the blessing said over the lighting of the candles or a line from your favorite Hanukkah song. Don't forget to leave the artist's signature and date! (It might be worth millions some day!)

- Save your menorah from year to year and create a collection.

- Choose a theme and make your menorah in that theme — for example: nature (draw flowers, glue leaves on to it), or the story of Hanukkah having each candle holder representing a different character.

- Try to make your own copy of an interesting menorah you have seen in a book.

Make a Dreidel

What do I need?

- A piece of cardboard, or heavy-duty paper
- A sharpened pencil or match will serve as the spinner.
- Scissors
- A cup
- Pencil/pen
- Colors/markers/crayons to decorate as you wish.

What do I do?

For Round Dreidels:

1. Put the cup on the cardboard (opening down) and using the pen or pencil, trace around it in the shape of a circle.

2. Now, carefully cut the circle out (if the paper is very thick, you might want to use a knife instead of scissors — with adult supervision only!)

3. Decorate both the circle and the pencil/match/stick you're going to use. (Ideas: Besides coloring it, you might want to try wrapping string or ribbon around it, or gluing pieces of colorful paper on it). Just remember not to overdo the decoration, since it is important the dreidel stays as balanced as possible. Draw lines dividing the dreidel surface into 4 equal quarters with one of the 4 Hebrew dreidel letters in each quarter.

4. Careful! (This step should be done carefully and with adult supervision!) Using a sharpened pencil, scissors' tip or a nail's tip, or even a wide-needle, create a hole in the center of the circle. Note! Try to make the hole in the exact center of the circle. Try to create a hole only as big as is necessary to insert your spinner, so it won't just slip through. Tip: make the hole slightly smaller than necessary and widen it, by pushing the middle piece through, so that it's an exact fit!

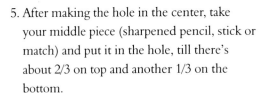

5. After making the hole in the center, take your middle piece (sharpened pencil, stick or match) and put it in the hole, till there's about 2/3 on top and another 1/3 on the bottom.

6. All that's left is to play! Good luck.

For Square Dreidels:

Steps 1, 2 are replaced by cutting a square out of cardboard. Step 3 — add the letters to the sides of the dreidel: נ ג ה ש/פ. All other steps are the same.

Additional ideas:

- Experiment with dreidels in different shapes (for example: try creating a pentagon, hexagon etc. . . .) and sizes, using different materials as "middle pieces" on which the dreidel turns. Check out which one of your dreidels can spin the longest.

The Hanukkah Bubble Bottle

Since this is holiday of oil, here is a great science project using oil.

Note! This might get a little messy, best done in the kitchen!

What do I need?

1. A glass/plastic bottle or container with a hermetically sealed top. (It must be made of a clear material).
2. Water (regular tap water, room temperature)
3. Oil (any regular cooking oil)
4. Food coloring (any color!)

What do I do?

1. Pour water into the container, about 3/4 full. Add a few drops of food coloring into the water. Mix until the water is all evenly colored.

2. Pour a little oil into the water so it creates some bubbles, but not too much.

3. Close the top of the container well!

4. Now slowly turn the container upside-down (make sure you do this over a surface that can get a little wet — in case the top isn't entirely sealed).

Cool, huh? See how the oil bubbles float up through the water? Do you know why? You can carefully keep turning the container and watch the bubbles move. Don't worry — no matter how much you try to shake and move, the oil and water will never mix!

(Additional idea: try shining a flashlight through the bottle in a darkened room).

A Matchbook Story

What do I need?

Paper, scissors, pens/markers/crayons, empty matchbox, glue

What do I do?

1. Cut a piece of paper into a long strip (as long as you want, but only as wide as the matchbox).

2. Fold it (back and forth, like an accordion), each fold slightly less wide than the matchbox.

3. Write a short story about Hanukkah with pictures, or draw a picture-story (like a cartoon, break the story and pictures up into a few scenes). Note: you can use the *Maccabees' Megillah* story from this book to help you, or tell your own Hanukkah story based on your family experiences.

4. On each side of the folded paper, write, draw and color a piece of the story you prepared, accompanied by small drawings.

   Tip: first count how many folds you have in the paper so you know how to "break up" your story into sections. You can decide if you want to use both sides of the paper or not. Note! Don't forget to leave the end of the paper empty — so you can later glue this side into the box!

5. Glue one end of the story (the side of paper you left empty) into the matchbox. (Note: it's not necessary to glue it in, you can also just store the story in the box).

6. Using the remainder of the paper, cut out a square of paper (the size of the matchbox). Glue this square of paper on the outside cover of the matchbox.

   Tip: you can use the matchbox to trace its shape and size on the paper.

7. On the outside cover of the box: write the title of your story, your name (author and illustrator!) and color or draw on it, as you wish.

8. Now carefully fold the story into the box and slide it into the cover. This makes a great present!!!

Additional ideas:

- Create a whole series of these matchbox-stories.
- You can also put riddles or comic-strips in the matchbox.

Salt Dough Recipe

What do I need?

¾ cup (180 ml) white flour

3 Tablespoons (45 ml) salt

⅓ cup (80 ml) water

1 teaspoon (5 ml) cooking oil

What do I do?

1. Mix salt, flour and cooking oil. Add water gradually while stirring.

2. Use rolling pin to roll dough out to desired thickness

3. Make something — you can choose from the activities suggested above or think up your own!

4. Place on greased baking tray, bake preheated 250 F. (120 C.) till firm — about 2 hrs.

Cool and paint with food coloring.

Medallions

Since the Maccabees expressed their political independence from the Greeks by issuing coins of their own, you too may try your hand at designing and producing coin-like medallions.

What do I need?

Make salt dough *(above)*.

What do I do?

After you've completed the first 2 stages of making the salt dough:

1. Using cookie cutters, fingers, knives, forks, spoons, pencil tips, paper clips and anything else you can think of, cut the dough into the desired shape and create a design on it . . .

   Note: If you wish to hang the medallions on a string, don't forget to create a hole (using a pencil) in the top, large enough for a string or ribbon to go through.

2. Place on greased baking tray, bake preheated 250 F. (120 C.) till firm — about 2 hrs.

3. Cool and paint.

These medallions can serve as great Hanukkah gifts, as medals for the game winners or as portraits of Hanukkah heroes for dramatizing the Hanukkah story.

Playing With Light and Shadow

As you know, Hanukkah is the festival of lights . . . so keeping with this theme of dark and light, here are some shadow ideas. Instead of being afraid of shadows, we're going to play with them! There are many possibilities to do so, here are just a few . . . .

Note: these activities should be done together with someone else and maybe even invite an audience!

"It's Me!"

What do I need?

- 3 or more people
- A flashlight
- A large white sheet of paper. We recommend one large sheet of paper per participant.
- A marker, pen or pencil (it's good if it's thick so you can see it)
- Scotch Tape

What do I do?

1. Use a piece of paper the size of your body (if you don't have paper large enough, tape a few white sheets together). Find an empty wall, door or closet, and tape the paper to it. (The height of the paper should be about as tall as you are).
2. Turn off the lights, and have one person shine the flashlight directly onto the paper (don't stand too close!)
3. The second person should stand in between the flashlight and the paper. By doing this, you are actually creating your shadow (silhouette) on the paper. (Try moving the flashlight's position till you get the shadow you want).
4. The third person should take the marker/pen and carefully trace the shadow created onto the paper.
5. Take turns having your shadow drawn! When you take each sheet of paper off the wall, remember to sign your name so you know who's shadow it is! You can even color it in!

Additional ideas: Try making different silhouettes by standing in profile, or making a shadow of different parts of your body and so on.

Shadow Theatre: Two Options

Shadow Theater One

What do I need?

- A flashlight, maybe even two.
- Straws, Popsicle sticks, or sticks from the garden
- Something to hide behind (like a couch, a bed or row of chairs)
- Several sheets of paper or cardboard, any color (It's dark anyway!)
- Scissors
- Scotch tape
- Any kind of marker
- Optional — musical instruments or a "sound effect" person

What do I do?

1. Trace any kind of shape you want onto the paper (it can be animal shapes, people, objects, masks, etc. . . .). There's no need to color it in. You might decide to make certain shapes depending on what play you put on!
2. Cut the shapes out.
3. Using the sticks or straws, tape one to each shape — as a handle. Make sure it can be held easily. These are your characters in the play!

continued on next page

4. Now set up your theatre: there should be a hiding place for the actors like a couch or a row of chairs. This is the "back-stage" area where you should store all your characters. Behind the back-stage should be the stage — an empty wall (if you need to, ask adults to help you remove objects from the wall). The "lighting assistant," with the flashlight, should be in front of the "back-stage" and with a clear view of the stage (see illustration). If you have an audience, don't forget to set up seats for them too!

5. Before you invite the audience in, you should write the play! It doesn't all have to be written down, you might want to just decide on the basic plot and assign roles (decide who is in charge of moving the different characters, and who is in charge of each of the voices and sound effects). Remember: it's Hanukkah! Why not act out one of the Hanukkah stories? You might want to rehearse a few times to get used to working in the dark with shadow-characters . . . .

6. Lights! (turn off the lights) Camera! (turn on the flashlight) Action! (enjoy!)

Note: This is just the beginning! You can use the characters you made for many different plays, and you can always make new characters!

Shadow Theater Two

What do I need?

- A flashlight, maybe even two.
- A white bed sheet
- Optional — musical instruments or a "sound effect" person

What do I do?

1. Find a way to hang the bed sheet up (leaving enough space on both sides of it, not directly on a wall; for example: hang the sheet from the top bunk bed, over the bottom one leaving the actors space on the lower bed). If you can't hang it up, try finding volunteers to hold up the sheet (they should be tall).

2. Place the flashlight (or appoint someone to hold it) behind the sheet, but shining onto it.

3. The actors (you!) should also be behind the sheet, between the light and the sheet so that from the other side of the sheet the audience can see your shadows!

4. Write the play! (see section 5 of "Shadow Theatre" above).

5. Lights off and flashlight on! Action!

Additional ideas:

1 — We didn't even mention the basic idea of shining a flashlight onto an empty wall and using your hands to make different shapes!

2 — Or just turn off most of the lights in the room, leaving a flash-light, candle or the door open just a crack… now look around you at all the different shadows created on the wall, what do you see? Try to imagine different shapes and images! (Do you notice the difference between shadows made by a flashlight and a candle?)

A Jewish Piggy Bank for Hanukkah Gelt

It's traditional to give money as presents on the nights of Hanukkah. But where are you going to keep all that money? A Gelt Box!

What do I need?

- A cardboard box, perhaps from a small used milk carton
- Pieces of cloth or colored construction paper (choose any color and pattern you like!)
- Scissors
- Pen/pencil
- Pins

Optional: To color and decorate, you can use glitter, markers or beads that can be glued onto the box.

What do I do?

1. First you should decide on the material and patterns of the cloth or paper you use to cover the box.

2. Put a slit in the top of the box big enough for coins. Enjoy, and remember what the Rabbis said, "Who is really rich? The person who is happy with what s/he has!"

Costumes for Your Hanukkah Theatre Productions

The *Greek Clothes* worn by Greek citizens of the Empire and by the Jewish Hellenists who wanted to be like the Greeks, were relatively simple. Both men and women wore a basic piece of clothing called a chiton — a rectangle of cloth with holes for the head and arms. They would tie it around the waist with string and use pins to hold it up above one shoulder. Young men and children wore the chiton at knee length while older men and women wore it to the ankles or even to the ground. You can use a white sheet for your *chiton* and a string or belt to tie around the waist.

The Greeks would either walk barefooted or with sandals or shoes. Everyone wore a hat or bonnet during the summer to protect themselves against the scorching sun. Did you know that in those days a suntan was not at all fashionable?! Wealthy people had jewelry — necklaces, bracelets, earrings or ornaments for their hair. It was fashionable for the rich men to curl their hair.

Hanukkah crowns — Cut a strip of sturdy paper a little longer than the circumference of your head. Then cut out a shape you wish to have on your crown — dreidel, menorah, image of a Hanukkah character, candle. When you have decorated both pieces of paper, glue or staple the shape to the middle of the strip and have someone staple the strip to fit the size of your head. Now you are equipped with a suitable costume for your Hanukkah plays!

Armor and weapons for soldiers — Create a helmet, sword and shield using things you have at home. For example: a sword from construction toys or Lego or a large wooden spoon or a paper towel tube, a shield from a round piece of cardboard with a strip of cardboard stapled on to it on both ends, so you can hold on or a pot as a helmet and its top as a shield. Aluminum foil will come in very handy to wrap the armor.

Paper Hanukkah Lanterns

What do I need?

• 9 x 12 inches (23 x 30.5 cm) construction paper
• scissors
• ruler
• glue stick
• glitter and/or crayons
• tape
• yarn or string

What do I do?

1. Fold paper in half, long sides together.

2. Cut four slits evenly spaced along the fold, leaving about an inch of paper uncut on the side opposite the folded side.

3. Open paper with folded edge face up and lay paper flat.

4. Decorate the paper by coloring or spreading glue and then sprinkling glitter on it. Use Hanukkah patterns like a dreidel, if possible.

5. Bring short edges of the paper together and secure with staples at each end. The strips should bend out.

6. Set the lantern on the table or hang by using yarn taped on the inside of the top rim.

Hanukkah Gift-Giving: Gift Wrapping and Cards

Spend some time and effort preparing your own wrapping paper and ribbons as well as writing nice greeting cards. You can very easily use computer-generated pictures and fonts or get ideas from books about gift-wrapping.

7. GAMBLING AND SPINNING DREIDELS

The Traditional Dreidel or *Sevivon* Game

The Hebrew word for dreidel is *sevivon* which, as in Yiddish, means to turn around. Dreidels have four letters on them, they stand for the saying *"Nes Gadol Haya Sham"* meaning "A great miracle occurred there." In Israel, instead of the fourth letter *"shin"* there is a *"peh"* because the saying is *"Nes Gadol Haya Po"* — "A great miracle occurred here." Playing with the dreidel is a traditional Hanukkah game played in Jewish homes all over the world and rules may vary. Here's how to play the basic dreidel game:

1. Any number of people can take part in this great game.

2. Each player begins the game with an equal number (about 10-15) game pieces, such as pennies, nuts, chocolate chips, raisins, matchsticks etc.

3. At the beginning of each round, every participant puts one game piece into the center "pot." In addition, every time the pot is empty or has only one game piece left, every player should put one in the pot.

4. Every time it's your turn, spin the dreidel once. Depending on the outcome, you "give or get" game-pieces from the pot:

   a. **נ** — means *"nisht"* or "nothing." The player does nothing.

   b. **ג** — means *"gantz"* or "everything." The player gets everything in the pot.

   c. **ה** — means *"halb"* or half. The player gets half of the pot. (If there is an odd number of pieces in the pot, the player takes half of the total plus one).

   d. **ש** (outside of Israel) — means *"shtel"* or "put in"/**פ** (in Israel) — means "pay." The player adds a game piece to the pot.

5. If you find that you have no game-pieces left, you are either "out" or may ask a fellow player for a "loan."

6. When one person has won everything, that round of the game is over!

7. We suggest that if you use money to play the game, ask players to donate part or all of their winnings to tzedaka (charity). You can ask parents to match these contributions. This way everyone wins and you can share the Hanukkah gifts with those in need!

Variations on the Traditional Dreidel Game[4]

(1) Dreidel Gamble Race

This game is appropriate for 2-4 players. Draw a scoreboard — a table with the 4 letters of the dreidel (at the top of each column), each with 5 empty spaces (in a row beneath the letter), one per spin in a round. Each player chooses a different letter of the dreidel. Every time the dreidel is spun, whoever bet on the correct letter, advances on the scoreboard. After 5 spins — the end of the round, check which player advanced the furthest in the race! If you'd like, new bets can be taken at the end of every round, so that a player may choose to switch the gamble to a different letter, hoping for better luck! (★If there are less than 4 players, players can choose two letters to bet on rather than one, or certain letter outcomes can be meaningless.)

(2) The Perfect Score

In this game, as in "blackjack," every player's aim is to reach 21 or as close as possible to that sum without scoring more than 21. To each of the 4 letters of the dreidel, assign a new value which is a number of Jewish importance — such as 1 (one God), 5 (five books of Moses), 4 (matriarchs), 8 (eight nights of Hanukkah), 10 (ten command-ments). Every player is required to spin the dreidel twice and add the sum of the score received. After that first round, each player may decide if they wish to spin again, an unlimited number of times, trying to reach

---

4. Games 1, 2, 4, and 7 were adapted with permission from Larry Bush and Susan Griss, *Reconstructionism Today*, Winter 1966.

the sum of 21 without surpassing that score. In case of a tie, play till the score of 36 or 44 (the number of candles used on Hanukkah — with or without the shamash).

(3) Two Spinning Contests

This contest demands skill in the art of dreidel spinning. It's all in the wrist! What do I need? A dreidel, a stop-watch or digital wrist-watch. Each player spins the dreidel once, and the length of the spinning-time is recorded. Since it takes a little practice and "warming up," each player has three chances to spin the dreidel and may choose the best score of three. The winner of the contest is the player with the longest spinning record.

Beat the dreidel: your dreidel may know how to spin, but do you? Each player competes against their own dreidel spin. As soon as you've spun the dreidel you begin spinning yourself — whoever falls first has lost. Remember — the more rounds you play, the tougher it becomes to keep your balance and win!

(4) Stack the Latkas

This is the Hanukkah version of musical chairs. Set out a row of chairs, one less than the total number of players. One person does not play the game but is responsible for the important, skillful task of spinning the dreidel. Players must move and circle the chairs as long as the dreidel spins. When the dreidel stops, everyone must find a seat (in a chair or someone's lap). After each round, one chair is removed. No one is ever "out" since you may always sit on someone's lap. The game continues until everyone is piled up like a stack of latkas!

(5) Hot Latka

Players sit in a circle passing the dreidel from hand to hand. One player sits in the middle of the circle spinning another dreidel or singing a Hanukkah song. The passing stops when the song/spin ends and whomever was caught holding the dreidel, replaces the player in the center.

(6) Dreidel Thief

Players (at least two on each team) sit side by side across from the opposing team. The teams take turns being team "A" or "B." Team A passes the dreidel behind their backs back and forth until team B says "stop." Team A pulls out their hands from behind their backs, all clenched in a fist. Team B proceeds to guess in which hand the dreidel is hiding, and whatever hand they point to must be opened. If they find the dreidel, they win a point. Whoever has eight points, wins the round.

(7) Dreidel Baseball

Call a letter out loud, then take three "swings" (spins). If the letter appears once out of three, it's a single! Twice — double! All three times — triple! After a triple or a double, you receive an extra turn to spin one more time. Guess the outcome exactly and get a home run!

8. SPORTS: THE OLYMPIC GAMES/MACCABIAH

The Olympic motto is *Citius, Altius, Fortius* — Faster, Higher, Stronger. For explanations about the background of the Olympic games and the Maccabiah see page 19. Here are some suggestions of games you can play to create your own Olympics/Maccabiah!

Menorah Relay Race

Note: Not appropriate for young children, minimum 4 contestants.

Set up 2 menorahs, with all 8 candles in them, a box of matches and a lit shamash which can be moved. Divide the contestants into two teams. Each team should stand in line in front of a menorah (Hanukkiah), then take an equal amount of steps backwards. This game is similar to a relay race. The goal is to light your menorah before the other team does. The first runner goes up to the menorah and lights the shamash then brings the lit shamash back to the team, the next runner takes the shamash and goes (as quickly as possible without letting the flame blow out) to the menorah and lights one candle. Then the shamash is returned to the team and the next runner goes… until the whole menorah is lit. Note: If a candle that has been lit has blown out, it must be lit again by the following runner on the team! If you'd like to play again, just blow out all the candles and start again!

Potato Peeling Contest

This can be a great game to play in the kitchen and it is useful for making latkas too! Set up each contestant (or team) with a pile of potatoes, a peeler and a trash can or bowl for the peels. Prepare a big bowl for the peeled potatoes and put it in the middle. Now on your marks, get set, start peeling! Whoever finishes peeling their pile of potatoes first, wins and gets the first latkas when they are ready!

Balls of 8

This can be a contest against yourself or against a friend. Using a ball (about the size of a tennis ball), throw it up in the air once and catch. Then throw it up again and before you catch it, clap you hands once. On the next throw clap twice, then three times, etc. till you reach — that's right! The magical number 8! Once you've reached 8, continue playing, this time counting back down (8, 7, 6 . . .) and so on . . . . If you don't catch the ball or don't clap the right amount of times, you lose your turn and the other contestant gets a try. When it's your turn again, start from the number you left off at. Good luck!

Obstacle Course

You might be a Greek athlete in the big Olympic games or you might be a Jew training to fight the Greeks, but in order to get in shape and train your mind for difficult challenges, you must pass through an obstacle course — successfully and quickly!

Set up an obstacle course around the room — find things to climb over, run around and crawl under… Find activities that demand your coordination and quick thought. Use everything possible — chairs, pillows etc. Taking into account the ages of the participants, you can make a beginner's route and an advanced route. Here are some ideas: roll on a mattress; jump over a pile of books; put down a pile of clothes like a coat, hat and some kind of "weapon," the contestant must put all these things on in 10 seconds; crawl under a low rope; pick up something heavy; run around a chair 5 times and so on.

Note: This might make somewhat of a mess so it's better done in a bedroom or den than living room. And remember — safety is always an important rule!

Potato in a Spoon Race

This is a great but simple race. Every contestant gets a big spoon or ladle and a potato (more or less the size of the spoon). Placing the potato in the spoon in your hand, your goal is to go as fast as you can to the other side without letting the potato drop and without using your hands! On your marks, ready — set — go!

9. IDENTIFYING MENORAH LOGOS[5]

In Israel the national emblem is the seven-branched menorah used in the Temple. Therefore many organizations use it in their logo. Examine the menorah logo and the name of the organization and match the logo to the appropriate organization. Check your answers against the list on page 154. Now try to design your own menorah logo to fit your hobbies or your family.

L

I

F

H

A

C

1. The Histadrut National Labor Union
2. The Religious Sports Federation
3. The Israeli Olympic Committee
4. The Israeli Medical Association
5. The Center for the Blind in Israel
6. Israel Fashion Medallion
7. The Society for the Rebuilding of the Jewish Quarter in Jerusalem
8. Productive Zionism Poster
9. The Botanical Gardens of Jerusalem
10. Diamond Polishing Factory
11. Israeli Travel Agents' Service
12. Israeli Philharmonic

E

D

J

K

G

B

---

5. Some of these designs are reprinted by generous permission of Dan Reisinger, graphic artist, Tel Aviv.

10. GAMES OF SKILL AND CHANCE

GAMES OF SKILL —
How good are your aim, coordination and sight?

Candle in the Bottle

What do I need? A bottle or carton of milk or juice (the narrower the opening of the container, the more difficult the game) and a box of Hanukkah candles.

What do I do? Stand over the bottle and hold the candle at waist height and drop it in the bottle. The winner gets the best score from 18 candles dropped.

Lighting the Menorah, or Pin the Flame on the Candles

1. Draw a menorah on a large poster-board or sheet of paper. Draw candles in the menorah but don't "light" them! Hang the menorah on a wall.

2. Using a separate sheet of paper, cut out 8 flame shapes.

3. On the back of each flame put some glue or scotch tape.

4. All contestants should stand in line in front of the menorah, a few steps away. Each contestant holding a flame.

5. Blindfold the first contestant and spin him or her around a few times — just to get them confused. The goal is to light the menorah — or — "pin the flame on the candles" . . . .

Note: Coloring the picture and flames is optional but extra fun!

Antiochus Says

We are all familiar with the game "Simon says." Although Simon is also a character relevant to Hanukkah, a Maccabee leader, brother of Judah, we've chosen to adapt this game into "Antiochus says." Knowing who Antiochus was will help you play the game! Antiochus IV was the Greek king who decreed that Jews must stop their religious customs and become like the Greeks, worship idols etc.

There are 3 levels of difficulty in this game. When you become experts at the first level, move on to the next:

Level 1 — Greeks: All contestants are Greeks. Therefore, when the leader says "Antiochus says . . . " before giving an instruction (for example: raise your hands, dance around, touch your toes . . .) you must follow the order. But if there is just an instruction without first saying "Antiochus says" then you do nothing. If you get mixed up and do it wrong — you're out for that round of the game. (Confused? So far level 1 is precisely like the original "Simon says" game).

Level 2 — Jews: Can you guess how Jews will react to orders given by Antiochus? That's right! If the leader gives a plain instruction they will obey but if he first says "Antiochus says . . . " then they must not obey or else they will be out of that round of the game.

Level 3: If you've mastered the game, get ready for this! Just like in the Maccabean reality, there were both Jews and Greeks. This time contestants have a mixed identity: half are Jewish the other half are Greek. Just to keep you confused, don't stand with your fellow Jews/Greeks — you must stand next to someone of the other identity!

Just as in the previous levels — the Greeks obey only if the instruction comes from King Antiochus, the Jews obey only if it doesn't come from Antiochus. Good luck!

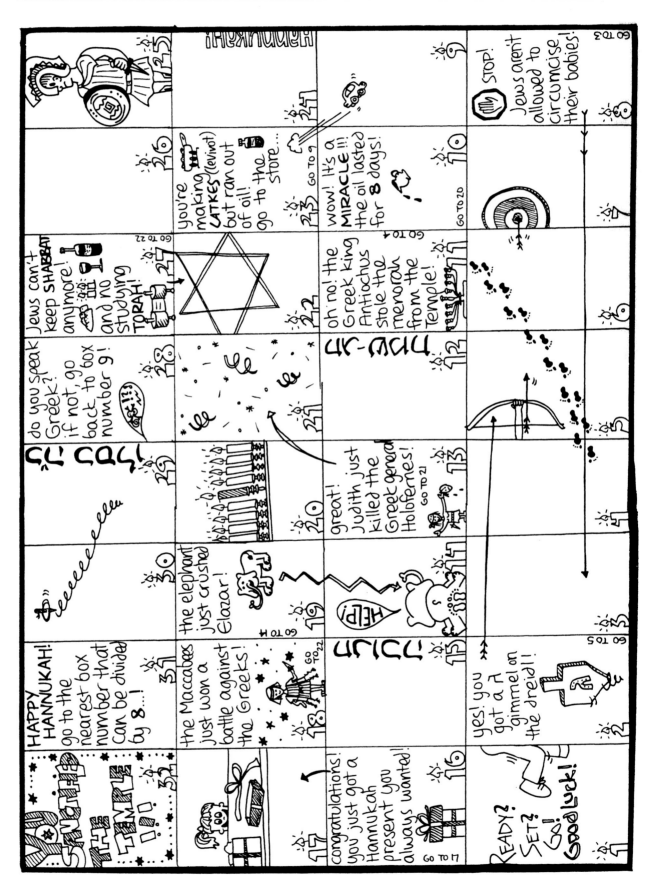

Maccabees' Chutes and Ladders

What do I need? The attached board game (left), one die, and one playing "soldier" per contestant. Advance on your turn according to the number on the dice you threw. If you reach a ladder, good for you! Climb up it and jump forward, but if you reach a chute, unfortunately you must slide down and fall back.

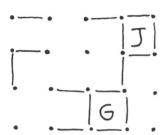

Conquer the Temple

On a sheet of paper, draw dots as shown below, about 10 x 10. This game is played one on one — Greek vs. Jew. As in the 165 BCE, the Maccabees are fighting the Greek soldiers for control of the Temple in Jerusalem. On every turn, each contestant may draw a single line, connecting any two adjacent dots, horizontally or vertically. Your aim — to create a box of conquered land. Whoever completes the box by drawing the final fourth line, can claim that land as his own by writing the letter "G" or "J" in it. As the game continues try to strategize and make sure you are the one closing as many boxes as you can till the whole Temple ground is covered. Count all the boxes and see who has gained the most ground and conquered the Temple!

This game can be played again and again by simply drawing dots on a sheet of paper as shown above. In addition, we recommend a big family game of "Maccabean" military strategy like Stratego or Risk.

Gelt in Bowl

Place a bottle or bowl on the floor and line up the contestants a few steps back from it. Each contestant receives a number of coins. Take turns throwing the coins into the container at varying distances. Make it harder by throwing with the left hand or while standing on one foot.

GAMES OF CHANCE — How Good is Your Luck?

There are many games based on chance. We suggest card games in keeping with the Hanukkah theme, "War" and "Crazy Eights;" spinning the dreidel (see "Gambling" section); and the board game, "Chutes and Ladders," on page 152.

Answer Pages

Spelling Game (p. 132)

Hanuka

Hannuka

Hanukkah

Hannukah

Chanuka

Channuka

Chanukah

Channukah

That's right! 8!

Scrambled Messages (p. 132)

1. Happy Hanukkah!
2. We light eight candles in the menorah
3. Mattathias was the high priest
4. The Maccabees led the Jewish revolt
5. On Hanukkah, we purified the temple

The Chai (18) Matching Game (p. 137)

1 = M; 2 = G ; 3 = H; 4 = A; 5 = I; 6 = P;
7 = Q; 8 = F; 9 = J; 10 = O; 11 = D;
12 =R; 13 = N; 14 =E; 15 = C; 16 = K;
17 = B; 18 = L

Hidden Hanukkah Messages (p. 133)

1. HANUKKAH IS ALSO CALLED THE FESTIVAL OF LIGHTS
2. JUDAH AND JUDITH
3. ANTIOCHUS THE GREEK KING FORBADE JEWS TO OBSERVE SHABBAT

Word Origin (p. 133)

1. correct answer: **(C)** — The word match originally meant "wick," from the Latin "*myxa*," a lamp nozzle. Only in 1831 does it become an "ignitable stick" also called a "lucifer" from the word "*lux*" (light).

2. correct answer: **(B)** — The word wax originates with bees' wax from the word "weave" in Old English, since beehives appear to be woven together in combs.

3. correct answer: **(A)** — The word "lamp" means shine, give light, from the Greek word for torch or oil lamp.

4. correct answer: **(D)** — The word "light" derives from the Greek "*leukos*" (white) hence the word "leukemia" and the Latin "*lux*" (light) or "*lumen*" as in lucid, lucifer (match), illustrate, lunar (moon), lustre, illuminate.

5. correct answer: **(D)** — The word "candle" comes from Latin, it means to be white, to glow. Hence the word "in-candescent" which means glowing. The ancient Christian holiday of church candles is called Candelmas (Feb. 2).

6. correct answer: **(B)** — The word "oil" derives from the Greek and Latin term for olive since the chief oil of the Mediterranean is olive oil. Only in the 19th century did we begin to use the term "oil" (from olives) for alternative organic oils from sunflowers, peanuts, corn or for petroleum oil (originally from organic materials).

7. correct answer: **(A)** — Potato was originally the English name for the "sweet potato" from the Spanish term "*patata*." The Spaniards learned of sweet potatoes from Haiti where it was called "*batata*" in the Tainu language. Today's use of "potato" begins only in the late 16th century when Europe began to eat white potatoes. In modern Hebrew the potato is called *tapuach adama* — an earth apple.

8. correct answer: **(C)** — In Shakespeare's day the sweet potato was supposedly an aphrodisiac that aroused one to love, so Falstaff in "Merry Wives of Windsor" (1598) wished "let the sky rain potatoes."

9. correct answer: **(A)** — "Hide your light under a bushel" means displaying excessive modesty about one's abilities. A bushel is a wooden basket used to measure grain or fruits. The phrase comes from the New Testament (*Matthew* 5:14-15) where after Jesus urges his disciples "to be the light of the world," he adds: "The city that is set on a hill cannot be hidden. Neither do people light a candle and put it under a bushel, but on a candelabrum."

10. correct answer: **(C)** — The Jews — in the prophet Isaiah's words in the Bible.

Jeopardy (p. 138)

(note: contestants' answers may vary a little and still be OK)

Heroes/Villains:

$100 — Who is the Maccabean leader, father of Judah?

$200 — Who is the Jewess whose 7 sons were killed because they wouldn't bow to idols?

$300 — Who killed Elazar?

$400 — Who is the High Priest appointed and supported by the Greeks?

$500 — Who is the Greek general beheaded by Judith?

Customs:

$100 — Where do you place the menorah?

$200 — What is the minimum time for Hanukkah candles to stay lit?

$300 — How many candles are used during 8 nights of Hanukkah (including the *shamash*)?

$400 — What is the order of adding candles to the menorah every night?

$500 — What is the order of lighting the candles in the menorah (from new to old)?

Hebrew:

$100 — What is the "service candle," used to light all others?

$200 — What is the Hebrew term for menorah, holder of 8 candles?

$300 — What is a "flask of oil," as in the legend of the oil that lasted for 8 days?

$400 — What is "advertising of the miracle" — the aim of lighting the menorah for everyone to see?

$500 — What is the special prayer added on the days of Hanukkah to the blessing after meals and *Amidah* prayer?

Kosher Menorah (p. 136)

According to Hillel, candles must be added to the menorah nightly from right to left and lit from left to right. All the candles, except for the *shamash*, should be on the same level.

Israeli Menorah Logos and Organizations Match (p. 150)

1 = B; 2 = D; 3= H; 4 = G; 5 = L; 6 = K

7 = A; 8 = C; 9 = F; 10 = J; 11 = E; 12 = I

D.

GELT AND GIFT GIVING

1. GELT AND GIFT GIVING IDEAS

*I*n the mid-twentieth century in North America, Christmas and then Hanukkah became more commercialized with an inordinate emphasis on shopping and elaborate gift giving. Some Jewish families have tried to "go one better" on Christmas, by giving children an added gift every night. However, we might really "go one better" by improving the quality and variety of giving and by making sure everyone who receives is also giving something. We can vary the identity of the giver, the type of gift and the designated recipient for each night.

Scholars have pointed out that there is no Biblical or Rabbinic recommendation for giving Gelt (Yiddish for money) or gifts on Hanukkah. Gelt was distributed informally in Eastern Europe and it was expanded to actual gifts only in America, while in other countries Jews do not give gifts at all on Hanukkah. However, Jewish law does require the head of the household to give pleasure-inducing gifts on the other two week-long holidays — Pesach and Sukkot.

The 12th century philosopher and legalist Maimonides sums up the obligation to make everyone happy on these holidays by purchasing wine for the men, fashionable clothes for the women and candies and nuts for the children. Gift giving priorities may have changed but the principle remains that even though holidays may celebrate great historical events, it is important to involve everyone in the celebration by giving them ***personalized gifts***. Today, Sukkot and Pesach are no longer honored in that way but Hanukkah has certainly taken up the slack. In fact, many scholars maintain that Hanukkah is based on Sukkot so the parallels may well justify the current gift giving craze — at least ex post facto.

On the next page you will find many options for personalizing and varying Gelt or gift giving on Hanukkah. They have been organized as eight options for eight different nights. In fact, each family needs to develop its own traditions regarding gift giving. Perhaps this list will enrich your family customs.

A Thumbnail History of Gelt: The Origin of Coins

9000 BCE — The earliest currency were cattle, called *pecus* in Latin, from which we derive the term pecuniary meaning pertaining to monetary interests. Bartering goods is still practiced among children today.

2000 BCE — Bronze ingots (metal bars often in the shape of cattle) were used for exchange.

1000 BCE — Silver and gold replaced bronze and the Egyptian money was in the shape of heads of cats, a sacred animal. The value of gold and silver was measured by weight, hence the ancient Hebrew *shekel*, a term derived from the verb to weigh.

640 BCE — The Lydians of Anatolia (Turkey) invented the first real coins whose value was stamped on them with a wedge or *cuneus* (as in cuneiform, the wedge-made alphabet). Here is the origin of the term coin.

The great advantage of coins was that they could be *counted* rather than *weighed*, hence the term "counter" or "teller." On the coins were imprinted heads of state like Antiochus IV, whose likeness we have from his coins. Gold or silver coins were minted with a fixed weight but thieves quickly learned to counterfeit them from lesser metals, to shave edges or to shake them against one another in a bag until a significant amount of gold dust was left in the bag to be sold.

16th-17th century CE — Serrated edges stopped coin shaving from precious coins. Curiously, the English term "**dollar**" harks back to the German 16th century mines in *Joachimstaler* (Czechoslovakia), that is, Joachim's "Tal" (valley, dell or dale) where they minted a large silver coin called the "taler" or "doler." Today's coins are made from nonprecious metals.

1ST NIGHT

Everyone gives/receives from everyone else (including guests, children and adults)

In our family of eight (including parents, grandparents and children), for example, each member is assigned a different night and must prepare a round of gifts for everyone on that night. Of course, not everyone is home every night of Hanukkah but the principle is that everyone gives to everyone else at one's own level. In other families there is a pre-assigned Grandparents,' Parents' and Children's night when all the gifts come from those designated givers. **Don't forget to prepare extra gifts for guests.**

2ND NIGHT

Homemade Gifts

Rather than "the best money can buy," try a night of homemade and handmade presents whether they are art, jewelry, place mats, bookmarks or sweaters. Even if you cannot make your own, you might buy handmade gifts like a personalized wooden dreidel for each person.

3RD NIGHT

"Secret Admirer" Gifts

This custom comes from the Israeli Scouts: Before Hanukkah or on the first night prepare a bag with all the names of the participants for a later night. Ask everyone to pick one name but keep it secret. Then each one prepares a gift for up to a specified amount and wraps it nicely with the name of the recipient but not the name of the donor. On a later night of Hanukkah everyone finds a personal gift from a secret admirer who will remain nameless. Enjoy the mystery and the surprise.

4TH NIGHT

Gelt Giving and Gambling as well as Tzedakah

Here is an original idea: David and Sheila Wiener, who helped spark the idea for this book, give everyone cash (*Gelt*) but they make each recipient an intriguing offer: "whatever portion of your gift you wish to donate to a tzedakah of your choice will be matched (and maybe doubled or tripled) by us." This applies to donations made by the children as well as by the guests (up to a certain amount).

Alternatively everyone can be asked to bring cash to be used in a tzedakah "gambling" game of dreidel or cards. The winner chooses the beneficiary of the tzedakah.

5TH NIGHT

Grab Bag

Ask everyone to buy one or two gifts that are each less than $5 and wrap them without names. Place them in a bag and then take turns reaching in and removing one gift at a time.

6TH NIGHT

"Quality Time" Gifts

Often after a wonderful holiday celebration we wonder why we don't spend more time together with friends and relatives. So this Hanukkah give each other a promise of quality time spent together. Prepare a nice greeting card with homemade coupons or certificates that promise such things as a long distance call, a night at the movies, a game of Monopoly, a walk on the beach or a weekend skiing, and so. The gift of quality time helps create family memories which are themselves the greatest gifts.

7TH NIGHT

Edible Gifts and Canned Goods for the Homeless

Make it a night to bring something tasty whether it is homemade or not (sugar cookies in Hanukkah shapes, Barton's or Elite's chocolate candy coins, and so on). But also bring canned goods that are easily transported to shelters for the hungry or make a donation to *Mazon*, the Jewish fund for the hungry of the world.

8TH NIGHT

Give of Yourself: Coupons to be Redeemed Later

On this evening all gifts must involve a promise of some future personal service. For example, "I promise to give my mother an hour of housecleaning without complaint" or "to give my brother a home-cooked meal" or "to read my child a whole book" or "to teach my friend to play guitar."

The Origin of Hanukkah Gelt

The medieval custom of giving children Hanukkah gelt has no explicit significance religiously or historically. However coins do play an important role in the Maccabean history. As Maimonides notes,[7] the Greeks not only desecrated the Temple but they also "fleeced" the Judeans of their money. In fact, the initial raids on the Temple were motivated by the desire to plunder the gold in the Temple treasury. Later when the Hasmonean state was recognized as fully independent, its right to mint its own coins was acknowledged. Coins have long been symbols of sovereignty and in England they were even called "gold sovereigns." These Hasmonean coins show the likeness of their kings and some display the earliest image preserved of the Temple's seven-branched candelabrum.

---

7. *Mishne Torah*, Laws of Hanukkah 3

2. GIFTS THAT CREATE COMMUNITY

by Lewis Hyde[6]

Since gift giving has become more widespread on Hanukkah, let us look more deeply at the spirit of gift giving and its potential for helping people to bond together. Below are selections from Lewis Hyde's The Gift, *that illuminate not merely the culture of material exchanges of objects, but the supreme gift, the willingness of people like the Maccabees to give their lives for a cause.*

Gifts in Motion: "The Indian Giver"

When the Puritans first landed in Massachusetts, they discovered a thing so curious about the Indians' feelings for property that they felt called upon to give it a name. In 1764, when Thomas Hutchinson wrote his history of the colony, the term was already an old saying: "An Indian gift," he told his readers, "is a proverbial expression signifying a present for which an equivalent return is expected." We still use this, of course, and in an even broader sense, calling that friend an Indian giver who is so uncivilized as to ask us to return a gift he has given.

Imagine a scene. An Englishman comes into an Indian lodge, and his hosts, wishing to make their guest feel welcome, ask him to share a pipe of tobacco. Carved from a soft red stone, the pipe itself is a peace offering that has traditionally circulated among the local tribes, staying in each lodge for a time

---

6. *The Gift* by Lewis Hyde, Vintage Books–Random House ©1979, 1980, 1983, pp. 3, 4, 19, 21, 22, 41, 43, 44, 95, 97-99. Reprinted by permission of Random House.

Gifts

but always given away again sooner or later. And so the Indians, as is only polite among their people, give the pipe to their guest when he leaves. The Englishman is tickled pink. What a nice thing to send back to the British Museum! He takes it home and sets it on the mantelpiece. A time passes and the leaders of a neighboring tribe come to visit the colonist's home. To his surprise he finds his guests have some expectation in regard to his pipe, and his translator finally explains to him that if he wishes to show his goodwill he should offer them a smoke and give them the pipe. In consternation the Englishman invents a phrase to describe these people with such a limited sense of private property — "Indian givers."… The opposite of "Indian giver" would be something like "white man keeper" (or maybe "capitalist"), that is, a person whose instinct is to remove property from circulation, to put it in a warehouse or museum (or, more to the point for capitalism, to lay it aside to be used for production).

The Indian giver (or the original one, at any rate) understood **a cardinal property of the gift: whatever we have been given is supposed to be given away again, not kept.** Or, if it is kept, something of similar value should move on in its stead, the way a billiard ball may stop when it sends another scurrying across the felt, its momentum transferred. You may keep your Christmas [or Hanukkah] present, but it ceases to be a gift in the true sense unless you have given something else away. As it is passed along, the gift may be given back to the original donor, but this is not essential. In fact, it is better if the gift is not returned but is given instead to some new, third party. The only essential is this: *the gift must always move.* There are other forms of property that stand still, that mark a boundary or resist momentum, but the gift keeps going.

In the Pentateuch the first fruits always belong to the Lord. In Exodus the Lord tells

Moses: *"Consecrate to me all the first-born; whatever is the first to open the womb among the people of Israel, both of human and of beast, is mine."* The Lord gives the tribe its wealth, and the germ of that wealth is then given back to the Lord. Fertility is a gift from God, and in order for it to continue, its first fruits are returned to him as a return gift.

Now that we have seen the figure of the circle we can understand what seems at first to be a paradox of gift exchange: when the gift is used, it is not used up. Quite the opposite, in fact: the gift that is not used will be lost, while the one that is passed along remains abundant.

In E.M. Forster's novel *A Passage to India*, Dr. Aziz, the Moslem, and Fielding, the Englishman, have a brief dialogue, a typical debate between gift and commodity:

> Dr. Aziz says, "If money goes, money comes. If money stays, death comes. Did you ever hear that useful Urdu proverb?" and Fielding replies, "My proverbs are: A penny saved is a penny earned; A stitch in time saves nine; Look before you leap; and the British Empire rests on them." He's right. An empire needs its clerks with their ledgers and their clocks saving pennies in time. The problem is that wealth ceases to move freely when all things are counted and priced. It may accumulate in great heaps, but fewer and fewer people can afford to enjoy it.

Gifts versus Commodities

It is the cardinal difference between gift and commodity exchange that a gift establishes a feeling-bond between two people, while the sale of a commodity leaves no necessary connection. I go into a hardware store, pay the man for a hacksaw blade and walk out. I may never see him again. The disconnectedness is, in fact, a virtue of the commodity mode. We don't want to be bothered. If the clerk always wants to chat about the family, I'll shop elsewhere. I just want a hacksaw blade.

But **a gift makes a connection.** To take the simplest of examples, the French anthropologist Claude Levi-Strauss tells of a seemingly trivial ceremony he has often seen accompany a meal in cheap restaurants in the South of France. The patrons sit at a long, communal table, and each finds before his plate a modest bottle of wine. Before the meal begins, a man will pour his wine *not* into his own glass but into his neighbor's. And his neighbor will return the gesture, filling the first man's empty glass. In an economic sense nothing has happened. No one has any more wine than he did to begin with. But society has appeared where there was none before. The French customarily tend to ignore people whom they do not know, but in these little restaurants, strangers find themselves placed in close relationship for an hour or more.

Threshold Gifts

[At life cycle events, when people pass from one stage to another, or at holiday times that mark changing seasons, **gifts create bonds between generations**.]

Woody Allen used to tell a joke: "My watch is an old family heirloom . . . My grandfather sold it to me on his deathbed."

Threshold gifts may be the most common form of gift we have, so well known as to need little elaboration here. They attend times of passage or moments of great change. They are with us at every station of life, from the shower for the coming baby to the birthday parties of youth, from graduation gifts (and the social puberty rites of earlier times) to marriage gifts, from the food offered newcomers and the sick to the flowers placed upon the coffin. Once in my reading I came across an obscure society that even gave gifts to celebrate the arrival of a child's second teeth — only to realize later that of course the writer meant the tooth fairy!

Threshold gifts mark the time of, or act as the actual agents of, individual transformation. In some way the fluidity of gift exchange assures the successful metamorphosis. Woody Allen used to tell a joke at the end of his stand-up routine: he would take a watch from his pocket, check the time, and then say, "It's an old family heirloom. [Pause] My grandfather sold it to me on his deathbed." The joke works because market exchange will always seem inappropriate on the threshold. A man who would buy and sell at a moment of change is one who cannot or will not give up, and if the passage is inevitable, he will be torn apart. He will become one of the done-for dead who truly die. Threshold gifts protect us from such death.

There is a story in the Babylonian Talmud of a man whose astrologers told him that his daughter would not survive her marriage. She would, they prophesied, be bitten by a snake and die on her wedding day. As the story goes, on the night before her wedding the girl happened to hang her brooch up by sticking its pin into a hole in the wall where it pierced the eye of a serpent. When she took the brooch down in the morning, the snake came trailing after it. Her father asked if any act of hers could account for her having so luckily avoided her fate. "A poor man came to our door yesterday evening," she replied. "Everybody was busy at the banquet, and there was none to attend to him. So I took the portion that was given to me and gave it to him." "You have done a good deed," her father said, and he went about thereafter lecturing that "charity delivereth from death." And, the Talmud adds, "not merely from an unnatural death, but from death itself."

The astrologers had predicted that the daughter would not survive the passage from maiden to wife, but she does survive through an act of spontaneous generosity; she has the right spirit on the day of her wedding . . . A moment of change is guarded by the giving of gifts.

[When parents give their children significant gifts] a **transformation of a person** occurs as artifacts are detached from others and invested in ego. This means that there are two sides to each exchange and to each transformation: on the one hand, **the person approaching a new station in life is invested with gifts that carry the new identity**; on the other hand, some older person — **the donor who is leaving that stage of life — dis-invests himself of an old identity by bestowing these same gifts upon the young**.

Giving One's Life

Not only do most cultures classify human life as a gift, but they take in particular the life of a newborn child to be a gift that has been bestowed upon its parents. (Bestowed by whom? By the gods, by the earth, by the spirits of the recently dead, by the tree near the water hole which is known to make women pregnant — however the local story has it.) The recipients of this gift are its custodians so long as the child is dependent upon them, and they may, under special circumstances, exercise their right of bestowal. The child whose body organs are given away when it dies is one instance, albeit an unusual one; the young woman whose father gives her in marriage is a second.

In the modern world the rights that adults have in their children — male or female — normally pass slowly from parent to child during adolescence and become fully vested in the child when he or she is ready to leave home.

If our lives are gifts to begin with, however, in some sense they are not "ours" even when we become adults. Or perhaps they are, but only until such time as we find a way to bestow them. The belief that life is a gift carries with it the corollary feeling that the gift should not be hoarded. As we mature, and particularly as we come into the isolation of being "on our own," we begin to feel the desire to give ourselves away — in love, in marriage, to our work, to the gods, to politics, to our children. And adolescence is marked by that restless, erotic, disturbing inquisition: Is this person, this nation, this work, worthy of the life I have to give?

While no gift ceremony accompanies enlistment (no sergeant says, "Who giveth this man?"), in our popular mythology it is the mother (or the wife, if the man is married) who gives a man to the army. When a man actually dies fighting for the state, the [American] newspapers all say the mother "gave her son," and she is the one who receives the flag of her country handed across the coffin.

We may apply Lewis Hyde's insight to the story of Hanukkah — both its religious martyrs and its fighting Maccabees. Here we meet individuals who have found an answer to the question: what is a worthy cause for which to give my life? The point is not the death but the dedication of the giver. One can give one's life to a cause, in the sense of dedicating oneself to live, as well as to die, by its principles.

The Gift of Life: Blood Donations and Organ Donors

Though it is certainly not a traditional practice, it might be appropriate to add to Hanukkah giving a willingness to donate blood or to sign up family and friends as potential organ donors, as is often done when renewing a driver's license.

CHRISTMAS AND HANUKKAH

AMERICAN DILEMMAS AND ENCOUNTERS

SEASON'S GREETINGS!

FAMILY AND FU

Introduc

Cartoo

Foods

Game

Gifts

Decemb
Dilemm

Exotic

1. "MERRY CHANUKA": THE CHANGING HOLIDAY PRACTICES OF AMERICAN JEWS, 1880-1950

by Jenna Weissman Joselit[8]

"In our town," noted suburban parent Grace Goldin in 1950, "Hanukkah is no longer a Jewish holiday; it's a major competitive winter sport." Recast as the functional equivalent of Christmas, the Maccabean festival enjoyed a decided measure of revival during the post-World War II era. At a time when the number of American Jews who observed kashrut and the traditional Sabbath fell off markedly, Hanukkah was one of the few Jewish ritual practices actually to grow in popularity. "It is the good fortune of Hanukkah," explained the author of a 1951 article entitled *More About Hanukkah in the Home*, "to become **the first [Jewish holiday] to revive in an American setting**."

Several factors help to explain Hanukkah's latter-day appeal. An example of Jewish cultural adaptation at the grass roots level, it brought together in one formidably effective entity the shared concerns and interests of the postwar "baby boom" generation: the renascence of Jewish cultural identity engendered by the rise of the State of Israel in 1948 on the one hand and the intense child-centeredness of postwar suburban society on the other. Then again, the growing ecumenism of postwar society, captured vividly in Will Herberg's analysis of America as a tripartite culture (Protestant, Catholic and Jew), gave parity to Hanukkah, making room for that holiday within America's civic religion.

Though it reached its apogee in the 1950s, the revival of Hanukkah capped a long process of reinterpretation and reevaluation, a

---

8. Reprinted by permission from the *Uses of Tradition*, edited by Jack Wertheimer, (p. 303-322), copyright by the Jewish Theological Seminary of America.

process whose origins date back some eighty years earlier, to the 1880s, and whose development owes much to the American celebration of Christmas. At that time, significant numbers of American Jews, many of them German in origin, marked the advent of the winter season by celebrating some form of Christmas.

In the years following the Civil War, the American Christmas began to change from a restrained, religious occasion into a veritable "festival of consumption" by lending itself to the "quickening and fertilizing influence" of commercialization. During the 1870s and 1880s, a period when the exchange of Christmas greeting cards and the custom of decorating one's home with a Christmas tree became normative and widespread, department stores like Macy's pioneered the display of "Christmas windows" while Woolworth's, the national chain of five and dime stores, first introduced consumers to its mass-produced selection of Christmas tree decorations. By the early years of the twentieth century, Christmas became, in the words of historian Daniel Boorstin, "overwhelmingly a season of shopping." Given these developments, it was no wonder that American Jews were beguiled by the holiday. As one American Jew of that era explained, "no one who has an eye for beauty and sweetness can withstand the marvelous charm exercised over young and old by the advent of [Christmas] night."

It was not just the inherent attractiveness of the American Christmas that drew American Jews to the holiday; it was also the perceived absence of such qualities, the "lack of romance" in the Jewish festival. When compared to the charms of Christmas, those of Hanukkah paled in comparison. "How humble and insignificant does the one appear by the side of the other," declared Dr. Kaufmann Kohler, a leading Reform rabbi, at once capturing and promoting **the image of Hanukkah as pallid, enervated, and even meek**. With its exuberance and profound family spirit, Santa Claus, and Christmas tree,

Christmas "gives a zest to life that all the Hanukkah hymns in the world, backed by all the Sunday-school teaching and half-hearted ministerial chiding, must forever fail to give," [reported a contemporary writer]...

However liberal the Reform rabbis might have been in other matters, they drew the line at the notion of Christmas trees in Jewish homes and construed the practice as a supreme act of disloyalty to the tenets of Judaism. "How can the Jew, without losing self-respect, partake in the joy and festive mirth of Christmas? Can he without self-surrender, without entailing insult and disgrace upon his faith and race, plant the Christmas tree in his household?" Dr. Kohler asked rhetorically, resorting to uncharacteristically fierce language.

In the 1950's Rabbi Albert observed: "Hanukkah is only one of our festivals, and a minor one at that; but we exalt it above all our holidays." A writer in *The Reconstructionist* in 1948, added, "We magnify it beyond all reason, and establish it as a major holiday in our children's minds." Sociologist Marshall Sklare, studying Jewish communal life on the "suburban frontier," confirmed these trends: **"Hanukkah, in short, becomes for some the Jewish Christmas,"** he stated unequivocally.

Admittedly, many American Jews continued to celebrate some form of Christmas, sharing in what one observer called the "loveliness of the day." And yet, the confluence of market and social forces ensured that Hanukkah could indeed serve as a powerful "antidote" to Christmas. "A Yuletide spirit," observed one student of postwar contemporary Jewish life, has "infused into [sic] the Hanukkah greeting cards, the exchange of gifts in Hanukkah wrapping, complete with colorfully decorated Hanukkah ribbons." Thanks to these developments, the modern American Jew, it seemed, no longer had cause to dread the "cruel month" of December: Hanukkah with its range of "better facilities," from Jewish storybooks to decorative napkins, could now serve as a fulfilling and viable cultural substitute.

Interestingly enough, the outside world in the years following World War II came increasingly to share that assessment, not only freighting Hanukkah with the same cultural and social significance as Christmas but yoking the two together in demonstration of America's "cultural oneness." Joint Christmas-Hanukkah observances in the public schools were the most apparent, and far-reaching, examples of the growing parity

---

However liberal the Reform rabbis might have been in other matters, they drew the line at the notion of Christmas trees in Jewish homes and construed the practice as a supreme act of disloyalty to the tenets of Judaism.

---

between the two holidays . . . As a case in point, public school educators developed the strategy of convening a "holiday" assembly on a "compromise date" in December that not only featured both a Christmas tree and a "Menorah candle" but also the singing of Hanukkah hymns and Christmas carols. The same prevailing spirit of postwar ecumenism and neighborliness even affected the new medium of television: special holiday broadcasts.

Despite the pressures of conformity, American Jews in search of a more authentically Jewish rationale for and expression of Hanukkah did not have to look too far afield: they could draw on Zionism to legitimate the Hanukkah experience and to provide a more positive, less compensatory, role for that holiday. **The establishment of the State of Israel in 1948 heightened the cultural importance and relevance of the Hanukkah story**, leading American Jews to identify the soldiers and citizenry of Israel, those "modern brave warriors," with the ancient Maccabees and to reinterpret their ancient triumph as a "vehicle for secular nationalist sentiment." "Hanukkah 5703

Finds the Maccabean Spirit Alive Again in Palestine," triumphantly reported the *Hadassah Newsletter* in 1942.

The relationship between the embryonic state and the increasingly popular celebration of Hanukkah was not only spiritual and cultural but also graphic and material. Throughout this period, the wholesale introduction into the American Jewish mass market of mass-produced Palestinian and then Israeli menorahs made of the characteristic patinated bronze ("greenware"), or bearing the iconic symbols of the new state, underscored the association between the two. In fact, the popularity of Israeli-made menorahs and of Israeli products in general fueled and in a real sense legitimated the transformation of Hanukkah into a gift-giving holiday.

Kosher chocolate manufacturers also indulged the American Jewish public's fascination with Israel by producing a line of overtly nationalistic games to accompany their Hanukkah candies. Lofts Chocolates, for example, introduced a spinwheel game entitled "Valor against Oppression" which featured contemporary Israeli heroes like Moshe Dayan and Yigal Yadin. Barton's, in turn, introduced the "Barton's Race Dredel [sic]," an Israelified version of Monopoly whose board featured a map of Israel, miniature Israeli flags, menorahs, and the following text: "Every Jewish boy and girl thrills to the heroic story of the Maccabees . . . We light the candles every night, . . . recite the blessings, sing the songs, play chess, go to parties and dance the *hora*."

December Dilemma

2. The December Dilemma

by Charles Silberman[9]

The principal cause of the flight from Jewishness by earlier generations has been removed. Having gained the acceptance that earlier generations craved, contemporary Jews are comfortable enough with their Jewishness to express it publicly through literature, music, dance, theater, and a variety of other art forms.

The growth in public expressions of Jewishness has its counterparts in the private sphere, and for the same reasons. Consider, for example, the profound change in the attitudes of American Jews today towards Christmas and Hanukkah. **For American Jews, Christmas used to be the most awkward season of the year.** From January until Thanksgiving, Jews might have been able to persuade themselves that they were just like everyone else, except that they observed (or more often did *not* observe) the Sabbath on Saturday instead of on Sunday; but from Thanksgiving until New Year's Day the pretense fell apart, for the world suddenly became Christian. The omnipresence of Christmas trees and decorations in homes and public places; the ubiquitous Santa Clauses in department stores and on street corners; the public school pageants and carol recitals; the manger scenes in front of churches and, often, City Hall; the genuine warmth that normally reticent people displayed; and, most of all, the kindly strangers asking young children what they hoped Santa would bring them — all these normal manifestations of the Christmas spirit served to remind Jews of how different they really were.

In an age in which to be different was to feel inferior, Christmas came to be seen as a Jewish problem as well as a Christian holiday . . . Such were the complexities, in fact, that Jewish families did not merely see Christmas as a problem; they felt the need to have a policy toward it. For example:

- Should children sing religious Christmas carols in school? Should they pretend to sing? Or should their parents ask that the youngsters be excused from participating?

- Should Jewish families acknowledge Christmas in some form — say, by sending Christmas cards — or should they try to ignore it? If they send Christmas cards, should the cards go to Gentile friends only or to Jewish friends as well?

- Should the family go beyond acknowledgement and actually *celebrate* Christmas, and if so, how? Should family members exchange gifts, and if so, what kind? Should the children be permitted (encouraged?) to hang Christmas stockings? And what about Santa Claus: should children's gifts be attributed to him or should they come directly from parents and grandparents?

- These questions were resolved relatively easily, compared to the great symbolic issue of the Christmas tree. Families had to decide whether or not to have a tree, and if so, how large it should be and how it should be decorated — specifically, whether it should have a star on top, and if so, what kind — the conventional five-pointed star or a six-pointed Jewish star?

- [For intermarried families the issue was compounded: How do I respect my non-Jewish spouse's desire for a religious tradition and a love for his/her non-Jewish family, while teaching our children to choose Judaism?]

For all the variations in the Christmas "policies" Jews adopted, they tended to fall into one of three groups. Among Orthodox Jews, insulated against the larger society, Hanukkah remained what it had always been — a minor festival in the Jewish calendar. (Unlike the major holidays, work is not prohibited on the first or last days of Hanukkah, nor is there an elaborate synagogue liturgy.) A much larger group, eager to acculturate without becoming fully assimilated, tried to hold their children's allegiance to Judaism by turning Hanukkah into a major holiday. Hanukkah was "better than Christmas," children were told, because they received eight gifts — one on each of the eight nights of the festival — instead of only one. But parents who made this argument usually did so without conviction and without persuading their children. The pull of Jewish tradition was sufficiently strong, in any case, so that Hanukkah never really became a major holiday — certainly not an occasion on which the extended family gathered, as was

9. *A Certain People*, by Charles Silberman, ©1985, p. 231-234, including quotes from Anne Roiphe, *Generation Without Memory: A Jewish Journey in Christian America,* ©1981 by Anne Roiphe, reprinted by permission of Simon and Schuster.

The Menorah or the Tree?
The Religious Significance of Christmas Decorations

by Rabbi Roland B. Gittelsohn[10]

One of the most pathetic spectacles in American Jewish life is the Jew who justifies his observance of Christmas on the ground that is a secular, national holiday, with no religious significance. Though it is in a sense cruel to deprive such a person of his reassuring rationalizations, both honesty and Jewish self-respect require that we face Christmas honestly for what it really is. What, then, is the real significance of those seemingly innocent Christmas customs with which so many of our people delight to adorn their homes?

Like many other ceremonies and symbols of both Judaism and Christianity, the Christmas tree may have originated in pagan life. It was soon given deeply religious significance, however, by Christianity. Its early Christian use was based on a legend that the night Jesus was born all the trees of the forest bloomed and bore fruit despite the snow and ice which covered them. By more thoughtful and theologically-minded Christians, the **tree** is still meant today to symbolize the resurrection and immortality of Jesus, as well as the wood used for the cross of crucifixion. Grim irony indeed that Jews, so many of whose ancestors were persecuted and perished because of their alleged complicity in the crucifixion of Jesus, should now embrace a symbol of that very event!

One Christian authority summarized the significance of the Christmas **tree** in these words: "In quieter moments its real significance may be hinted: For it is a symbol of Christ, as the Tree of Life who offers freely to all his gifts of light and life and wisdom."

Of what religious significance are the decorations used on the Christmas tree?

One explanation [of the **star** on top of the tree] goes back to Martin Luther, whom the stars in the sky reminded one Christmas Eve of "him who for us men and for our salvation came from heaven."

The **tinsel** seen on Christmas trees is known as "angel's hair." It is meant to recall the heavenly hosts who are supposed to have attended the miraculous birth of the Christian Savior.

The **apples** which were once part of the tree's adornment, and the simulated apples more commonly used today, are supposed to remind us of the apple which tempted Adam and Eve in Eden. Christian doctrine teaches that from the seeds of that very apple grew the tree used for the cross on which Jesus met his death.

Surely the inhibition-removing **mistletoe** at least is devoid of religious significance? Must we be deprived of this too? I'm afraid we must. No better description of the place of mistletoe in the Christian scheme of things can be found than in the words of a popular Christmas hymn:

> The mistletoe bow at our Christmas board,
> Shall hang to the honor of Christ our Lord:
> For he is the evergreen Tree of Life.

10. From Bernard Postal and David White, editors of *The Best Ten Years in The Jewish Digest* (D.H. White Co., 1965, p. 201ff) reprinted from *The Hanukkah Anthology* by permission of the Jewish Publication Society.

December Dilemma

the case with Passover; but the pull of Christmas was so strong that many families continued to be ambivalent about their choice.

For a significant number of Jews, however, substituting Christmas for Hanukkah was an important step on the road to becoming fully American; most members of "Our Crowd" [both old Sephardic and German Jewish immigrants of the early 19th century] adopted Christmas as their holiday early in the century. Christmas played an important symbolic role for upwardly mobile Eastern European Jews as well; as Anne Roiphe has put it, "**Christmas is a kind of checking point where one can stop and view oneself on the assimilation route.**" Roiphe's mother, whose Polish-born father had founded the firm that manufactures Van Heusen shirts, had been eager to have a Christmas tree during her own childhood. She "described to me how at Christmas time she would stare at all the store windows on upper Broadway, at the gentle, glowing lights of the Christmas tree, and how she wanted that tree in her home, bright and covered with tinsel and sparkling cotton at the base," Roiphe has written. But her mother's parents, who remained moderately observant Jews despite their wealth, would not consider it. When she was first married, therefore, Roiphe's mother had trouble deciding what her "Christmas policy" should be.

The question was resolved by Roiphe's German governess when Roiphe was born on December 25; it became customary for the entire extended family to gather for a combined Christmas-birthday dinner. "We exchanged presents under the tree, extra ones

---

The most popular rituals were those that met five criteria: they can be redefined in contemporary terms; they do not require social isolation or a distinctive lifestyle; they provide a Jewish alternative to a widely observed Christian holiday; they do not have to be performed with great frequency; and they are centered on the children.

---

for me because it was my birthday," Roiphe recalls. "My birthday cake was always decorated with red and green. My mother, who may have experienced some guilt over the first tree, threw herself into the Christmas spirit with all her unused energy. On the dining table we had wreaths and reindeer pulling little carts. We had ice cream molds in the shape of Santa Claus and Christmas bells. We had holly on the mantel and mistletoe hung from the chandelier . . . ." **We [are] American,"** her mother explained when family members objected, **"and Christmas . . . is an American holiday!"**

Until a few years ago that was how Anne Roiphe and her family saw it too. In fact, in 1978, Roiphe wrote an article for *The New York Times Magazine* entitled "Christmas Comes to a Jewish Home," in which she

described the Roiphe family's observance of Christmas. The article was greeted by an avalanche of angry, often hostile, letters from Jewish readers. The mail came from close friends as well as from strangers; almost everyone who wrote was enraged that Roiphe appeared to be recommending her assimilated life style to others.

It is a sign of the times, and of the changing attitudes of American Jews toward "the assimilation parade," that the Roiphe family now celebrates Hanukkah with an elaborate party and exchange of gifts, lighting candles on a beautiful menorah that Anne Roiphe's children helped her select. The change had its origin in her 1978 article. Taken aback by the reaction, Roiphe spent the next few years exploring Judaism and her attitudes and relationship to it.

It was a profitable exploration. Roiphe discovered that there was considerably more to Judaism than "the thin, watered-down Jewishness" she had experienced as a child. To her surprise she found that she felt a close connection, even attachment, to Jewish tradition, and she came to see her Thanksgiving and Christmas celebrations as "eclectic, thin, without magic or the density of time." Roiphe's attachment is cultural, not religious; there is much about Judaism that she finds hard to accept and some things she rejects outright. But the attachment is real, and her searching goes on, guided by "a renewed or new connection to Jewishness, an amazed connection that supersedes all my ambivalences and doubts." "Taken all together," she has written, "the nationhood is a landscape of incredible grandeur, and the culture itself, the more one knows of it, well, the more it shines with radiance."

Anne Roiphe's experience is worth recounting because it exemplifies an important trend, in which lighting Hanukkah candles increases, generation by generation, among secular as well as religious Jews. [For example,] a distinguished publisher grew up in a completely assimilated home in which Christmas rather than Hanukkah was celebrated. As is customary in this heavily Jewish industry, he used to give an annual Christmas party for literary agents, authors, and other publishers. He still gives the party, but since 1979 or 1980 it has been a Hanukkah party, with a menorah on the mantel and potato latkas (pancakes), the traditional Hanukkah food, among the *hors d'oeuvres*. A small change, perhaps, but one with important symbolic overtones.

This kind of change first became evident in the 1950s when . . . Jews who had left their "urban *shtetls*" for predominantly Gentile suburbs began to worry about whether their children would remain Jews. Studying the relatively assimilated Jews of "Lakeville" in 1957-58, Marshall Sklare discovered to his surprise that lighting **Hanukkah candles — a ceremony that occupies a fairly low place in the hierarchy of religious obligations — had become the single most widely observed ritual**. Two Jews in three lit Hanukkah candles; the only other ritual observed by a majority of Lakeville residents — three in five — was attending a Passover seder. Comparing Lakeville Jews' ritual observances with those of their parents, Sklare found an increase from one generation to the next in the proportion lighting

Hanukkah candles and only a slight decline in the number attending a seder; with every other ritual — observing the dietary laws, lighting Sabbath candles, fasting on Yom Kippur, and so on — the pattern was the reverse — there were precipitous declines from the parental to the next generation.

Although this pattern of observance was hard to understand from a traditional religious standpoint, Sklare pointed out, it made perfect sense from a sociological perspective. The decisions of Lakeville Jews concerning which rituals to observe were the result of two quite contrary pulls: their desire to remain Jews and their desire to be at home in American culture. Thus the most popular rituals, Sklare suggested, were those that met **five criteria**: they can be redefined in contemporary terms; they do not require social isolation or a distinctive lifestyle; they provide a Jewish alternative to a widely observed Christian holiday; they do not have to be performed with great frequency; and they are centered on the children.

Hanukkah and Passover meet these criteria perfectly. They are child-centered festivals — Passover intrinsically so and Hanukkah through a long process of adaptation to American life. Unlike the Sabbath, moreover, Passover and Hanukkah need to be observed only once a year instead of once a week; and unlike the dietary laws, they do not require a distinctive lifestyle, nor do they impose any barriers to easy social relations with non-Jews. On the contrary, acculturated Jews increasingly invite Gentile friends to their seder services, and an interfaith seder the Sunday before Passover has become commonplace in many communities. By downplaying the traditional emphasis on God's benevolence and miraculous intervention and emphasizing instead the struggle for religious and political freedom, **American Jews have turned Hanukkah and Passover into holidays that subtly underscore their Americanness as well as their Jewishness**.

[For example,] the racks of Hanukkah cards one now sees in greeting-card stores in

The Lights of Kwanza: African Americans Invent Their Own Hanukkah

In 1966 Dr. Karenga decided to invent an original Afro-American holiday to express and to promote Black unity. Using ancient African tribal traditions he set Dec.26th as the opening night of a seven-day holiday centered on candle lighting. Originally based on an African harvest festival, it is designed to reinforce teamwork and uses the symbol of an ear of corn for each child. Often the tribal saying is repeated, "It takes a village to raise a child." The seven candles include a black one lit first in the center and three red and three green on either side lit from left to right. As each candle is lit in the candelabrum called *kinara* (Swahili for candleholder), one of seven principles is symbolized: unity, self-determination, collective work and responsibility, cooperative economics, purpose, creativity, and faith. The word pronounced in unison by those celebrating is the Swahili term *Harambee* for "Let's pull together."

December Dilemma

The December Dilemma:
"To One of My Best Friends — A Jew"

Dear Friends:

At this darkest season of the year, there is often confusion over bright lights and holiday gifts. A number of years ago, a Religious School teacher told me of her dismay. In a discussion with her students on the meaning of Hanukkah, she was shocked to discover the number of Jewish families who have Christmas trees in their homes or who exchange Christmas gifts.

Hanukkah's deepest meaning lies in its affirmation of the freedom to be different, to maintain our distinctive religious practices even though we are a small minority in American society. This is precisely the meaning of the Maccabean revolution. Hanukkah commemorates those who proclaimed their own special identity and destiny which they were unwilling to give up even at the cost of their lives, much less for the comfort of being different. They knew who they were. So must we!

The following letter drives home the most significant point of the "December Dilemma" and helps us understand who we are.

Dear Jewish Friend,

You showed me the Christmas tree you placed in your home. You thought I would be flattered and pleased. It is a beautiful tree, carefully set up and painstakingly decorated, but I am neither flattered nor pleased.

To me, a Christian, the tree is a symbol of my most sacred religious holiday. It has become, in our home, the mark of our Christianity during the season of the year when we celebrate the birth of Christ.

I ask myself what meaning the tree has for you. It cannot be a Christian religious symbol, since you have told me often that as a Jew you do not accept Christ. For you, it must then be no more than a pretty decoration. How can I help feeling resentful when you take my sacred religious symbol and make it a mere decoration? And when I hear you refer to it jokingly as a "Hanukkah Bush," I am ashamed for you.

But most of all I'm sorry. Sorry for you. You mentioned "Hanukkah." I see some of my Jewish neighbors decorate their homes so beautifully in its honor. I hear their children sing pretty songs and tell the exciting and significant story. I am sorry that all this is so strange and foreign to you, that you do not give your children an opportunity to partake of its joy and share its celebration.

Many thanks for wishing me a Merry Christmas. As a really good friend, one of your best, I wish you a Happy Hanukkah.

Your Christian Neighbor

Truly, I hope that you and your family celebrated Hanukkah with song, with joy, and with overwhelming pride in being what you are.

In friendship and faith, I am,
Rabbi David J. Gelfand

most large cities provide clear evidence of how American that holiday has become. "You know it's Hanukkah," Snoopy says on the cover of one popular card, "when the 'Fiddler on the Roof' comes down your chimney." We would have flinched at such a card when I was young — if, indeed, we could have conceived of venturing into a store to buy a Hanukkah card at all; it was not until after World War II that manufacturers saw a potential market and began turning out Hanukkah cards in sizable numbers. Now one can even buy a "Hanukkah stocking" — a blue-and-white sock sprinkled with six-pointed stars.

Hanukkah has become more popular, interestingly enough, despite a small increase in the number of Jews who celebrate Christmas. For some American Jews, it would appear, having a tree is no longer a mark of detachment from Jewish life. Witness the fact that 12 percent of the Jewish communal leaders surveyed in 1983 — board members of the United Jewish Appeal, B'nai B'rith, American Jewish Committee, Anti-Defamation League, and American Jewish Congress — have Christmas trees. Younger Jews are more likely to have trees than their elders, a difference attributable to their higher rate of intermarriage. It is not surprising that this should be so; for born Christians, after all, Christmas is filled with childhood memories and inextricably tied to present as well as past relations with parents, grandparents, and siblings.

3. THE CHRISTIAN MENORAHS: HOW BILLINGS, MONTANA, DEFENDED HANUKKAH (1993)[11]

In 1993 Billings, Montana, suffered a wave of hate crimes by the Ku Klux Klan and the white supremacist Aryan Nations. These included marching into an Afro American church, spray painting swastikas on the home of a Native American, overturning tombstones in the Jewish cemetery and finally throwing rocks through windows displaying a Hanukkah menorah. The turning point was the town's decision to fight back and the symbol of the struggle for religious, racial and ethnic freedom was appropriately, the display of a menorah by over 10,000 non-Jewish residents among 85,000 citizens. Let us focus on the trigger that began the turn-about as the passive majority stood up to the violent minority. Below we will retell the story in a dramatic way, by creating fictional but appropriate dialogue.

In December 1993 Isaac Schnitzer, a six year old Jewish boy (whose father was a Jewish doctor and his mother a devoted convert to Judaism) decorated his window with a colorful paper Hanukkah menorah.

The next day a rock came flying through that window, leaving broken glass across Isaac's bed. Luckily Isaac was not in his room. Who could have done this, wondered Isaac? His parents comforted him: This is another hate crime. People hate minorities including Jews. Isaac replied, you mean someone threw a rock at my window because I am Jewish? The police assured the Schnitzers that they would do their best to protect them but perhaps they should remove their menorah from the window in order not to invite further vandalism. However Isaac's mother refused to "lower her profile," to hide her Judaism. She told her son: we will keep up our Hanukkah decorations and we will not hide. Then she called the press and asked them: "Please make this front page news because I want people to understand what it's like to be Jewish."

The Schnitzers discovered that there had been many more hate crimes and that many in the community would be supportive of its minorities. When the African-American church was harassed, tens of people came to the church to show their support. The Reverend reported, "they rallied round and let them (the bigots) know, 'Hey if you bite one, you bite us all,' and that was a very good feeling we had." When a Native American's home was spray painted with a swastika, thirty painters from the local union turned out to repaint it. One painter lamented, "we can paint the house over, but what do you do with those [Native American] children's memories? They're scarred." The head of the local human rights organization said, "If they want me to be silent, then that's just not going to happen."

When Isaac's room had been vandalized, his five year old non Jewish neighbor came over with a hand made Hanukkah decoration to put up in his room. When the activists met to decide how to respond, someone recalled the legend of the Danish King during the Nazi occupation of Denmark. The story goes that when the Nazis required every Danish Jew to wear a yellow star, the king chose to wear one as well. Christian and Jewish citizens would not be forcibly distinguished and their solidarity undermined. (Later on Rosh Hashana as the Nazis planned their surprise arrest and deportation of Danish Jews, the Danish underground preempted them by spiriting away thousands across the sea to neutral Sweden). The Holocaust story reminded the people about the danger of silently giving in to violent prejudice.

Soon the campaign began to put a menorah or a picture of one in every window in

---

11. For educational resources on this story see *The Christmas Menorahs* by Janice Cohn, Albert Whitman Co., 1995, and the video "Not in Our Town" with the Teacher's guide by the California Working Group (Wedothework @igc.apc.org)

Discussion Questions with your Children

✦ How did Isaac and his mother feel?

✦ What would you have done if you were Isaac? his parents? the next door neighbor?

✦ Do you think this could happen in your neighborhood?

✦ What is similar or different in the story of the Maccabees?

✦ Have you seen an act of courage like the ones done by the Schnitzers' neighbors? Describe it.

✦ Why do you think the massive display of Menorahs helped decrease the hate crimes?

Citizens Protesting Anti-Semitic Acts, Billings, Montana, 1994.

Billings. That was a small act of courage but a big expression of brotherhood. The hate organizations threw bricks through more of the newly decorated Hanukkah windows such as the one in the Methodist church. Nevertheless 10,000 residents put up menorahs and the hate crimes decreased markedly, because "ordinary citizens put themselves on the front line against hate and intolerance." Hanukkah really did become a celebration of freedom because people expressed their convictions publicly in the window, even if it meant receiving a brick through the glass.

Watchwords for Freedom[12]

"The only thing necessary for the triumph of evil is for good men to do nothing."

— EDMUND BURKE
ENGLISH POLITICAL THINKER

"The opposite of hate is not love, it is indifference."

— ELIE WIESEL, NOBEL LAUREATE
AND HOLOCAUST NOVELIST

"The test of courage comes when we are in the minority; the test of tolerance comes when we are in the majority."

— RALPH W. SOCKMAN

12. These quotes were collected by the California Work Group in their viewing guide to *"Not in Our Town."*

Jews/America/A Representation, © 1996 Frederic Brenner. Reprinted by generous permission of the photographer.

Watchwords for a Festival of Freedom

"In Germany they came first for the Communists, and I didn't speak up because I wasn't a Communist. Then, they came for the Jews and I didn't speak up because I wasn't a Jew. Then they came for the trade unionists, and I didn't speak up because I wasn't a trade unionist. Then they came for the Catholics and I didn't speak up because I was a Protestant. Then they came for me, and by that time no one was left to speak up."

— **Pastor Martin Niemoller**
  German opponent of Naziism

The Nazis in the Dachau Concentration Camp used variations on the triangle to create a Mark of Cain to categorize inmates according to religion, ideology, sexual orientation and race.

Yellow on yellow Star of David . . . . Jew
Black on yellow. . . . . Jew, anti-social, or insane
Red . . . . Left-wing German political prisoner
Brown . . . . Gypsy
Black. . . . . Anti-social, lesbian
Red with black circle below . . . . Jehovah's Witness
Pink . . . . Homosexual

December Dilemma

4. THE MENSCH WHO SAVED CHRISTMAS: AARON FEUERSTEIN (METHUEN, MA, 1995)

by Jon Auerbach and Jon Milne, Boston Globe[13]

In Billings, Montana, Christians helped save Hanukkah from the anti-semites. In Methuen, Massachusetts, when a big textile factory burned down two weeks before Christmas, the Jewish owner helped save Christmas for his employees who were threatened by an economic tragedy.

Samuel Feuerstein, who died in 1983, left his son, Aaron, a twofold legacy: responsibility for an Orthodox synagogue that had grown to be the largest in New England, and for a textiles operation that had remained in the region long after others had moved south. (Malden Mills makes synthetic fleece for L.L. Bean outdoor clothes). Both had been built by the Feuersteins and had come to define the family: The synagogue represented their unbending spirituality, the mill their unbending work ethic.

In the last two years, both temple and mill have burned down. For Aaron Feuerstein, the president and owner of Malden Mills, both tragedies have only strengthened the resolve of a man whom friends and family call one of the most driven human beings they've ever encountered. "He is unstoppable when he wants something," said his daughter, Joyce Feuerstein.

"When all is moral chaos, this is the time for you to be a mensch."

Yesterday, Feuerstein sat in a makeshift office, still wearing the same brown-checked suit he was wearing at his birthday party when the blaze broke out Monday night, and once again vowed to rebuild. In the days since the fire, he has repeated that pledge many times. He has already made sure his 2500 employees were paid on time. He has given them **Christmas bonuses** and promised them another month's pay as well as 3 months of health insurance payments. He has told customers that partial production should resume within a month.

Feuerstein said it was a 2500-year-old quote from the Jewish tradition that has kept him strong in recent days. **"When all is moral chaos, this is the time for you to be a mensch."** [Hillel's original formulation was: *"Where there is no one to be a mensch, a responsible leader, then you be one."*] In Yiddish, the word *"mensch"* means more than just a man. It carries a sense of righteousness that friends, family and co-workers say has been the driving force in Feuerstein's life. [Some call him the *"Mensch* of Malden Mills."]

Chuck Henderson, recalls how Malden Mills extended generous credit when his own outdoor equipment company was foundering a few years ago. The credit line saved his company, he said. "That's the kind of guy Aaron is," Henderson said. "If he's got half a loaf of bread, he's going to share it around."

Former Mayor LeFebre recalls the first time he met Feuerstein, in 1979. Feuerstein was wearing an elegant suit and a pair of Converse sneakers, then still being manufactured in Lawrence. LeFebre thought at first this was some sort of symbolism. "I found out it wasn't. It was about his wanting to get up and walk around the plant at any time to know what his people needed."

From that visit grew Feuerstein's participation in the first federally sponsored job-training programs in the Merrimack Valley, helping to organize English classes for immigrants and special skills classes for textile workers.

Ronald Alman, head of the textile workers union in New England, said of Feuerstein: "He believes in the process of collective bargaining and he believes that if you pay people a fair amount of money, and give them good benefits to take care of their families, they will produce for you." Alman also gave Feuerstein high marks for steadfastly remaining in Massachusetts. "He had every opportunity to move down South. I mean, they opened up gates for him. But he refuses to do it," Alman said.

Family, friends and co-workers say much of this resolve stems from Feuerstein's dedication to his father. Said Rabbi Gershon

---

13. Boston Globe, Dec 15, 1995 Metro Section page 1, "Methuen's Unstoppable Hero." By permission.

Gewirtz, of the Young Israel of Brookline synagogue: "Aaron often told me, 'I know what my father would have wanted,' and that's what he did."

Feuerstein approaches everything he does with an often relentless intensity. He has given up reading once-loved spy novels to spend his evenings memorizing Shakespeare and the Talmud, and leaves his office door open to allow an endless flow of factory workers access.

Speaking yesterday of his charred factory, Feuerstein said he expects the new mill to be up and running in time for the High Holy Days next fall. The desire to rebuild as quickly as possible, he said, is as much about looking after his employees as it is about profits. "They've been with me for a long time," he said yesterday. "We've been good to each other, and there's a deep realization of that, that is not always expressed, except at times of sorrow."

5. A Reform Rabbi's "Crusade" against the Jewish Christmas (Atlanta, 1958)

by Melissa Fay Greene[14]

Rabbi Jack Rothschild, a great civil rights activist of the 1950's in Atlanta, was also a leading force in the transformation of the Reform movement's attitudes to Jews celebrating Christmas, especially German Jews in the Old South. Melissa Greene retells his story and his congregation's ambivalences with historical depth and with a humorist's wit. The generational conflict between the Rabbi (emeritus) Marx and the young upstart Rabbi Rothschild is particularly intriguing. The two represented opposed attitudes to the kind of accommodation needed in Western society. Marx represented the Pittsburgh Platform of 1885 and Rothschild stood for the Columbus Platform of 1937, two opposed versions of Reform Judaism.

"Classical Reform" Reformed

The nineteenth and early-twentieth-century German-Jewish Reform rabbis yearned to be modern, to be shorn of the locks of medieval mysticism, to read from left to right, to lose [the image of] Shylock . . . "Today we accept as binding only the moral laws . . . but reject all such as are not adapted to the views and habits of modern civilization," said the Reform movement's **Pittsburgh Platform of 1885** that came to be known as "Classical Reform" and that swept the southern congregations. In the Pittsburgh Platform, Judaism was a religion, not a people, and ceremonies and rituals were not necessary in the modern era: ". . . their observance in our days is apt rather to obstruct than to further modern spiritual elevation." The Pittsburgh Platform made reference to the "God-idea." Dr. Marx was educated and ordained in, and was one of the outstanding exponents of, the Pittsburgh Platform, "Classical Reform." By 1860, most of the synagogues in the South were Reform, and they became practitioners of Classical Reform Judaism.

Congregations in Sunday dress faced forward quietly in pews. Rabbis appeared in business suits and did not insist on adherence to arcane rules extending into the privacy of people's everyday lives. The religion offered was somewhat generic: English hymns to a Supreme Being; an organ producing solemn bass notes during moments of private reflection; an English prayerbook containing words like *Thy, Thou, loving kindness* and *supplication*; a sermon advocating moral reform — and the whole contained within ninety minutes.

The Temple members followed Dr. Marx in order to sail with him upon the western tide of Reform. "They wanted to be members of the business community without any special tag . . . They wanted to be Rotarians. They wanted their religious activities to be closely related to those of their Christian neighbors. The longer the German

Decembe
Dilemma

14. M.F. Greene, *The Temple Bombing* (Random House, p. 54-60, 102-105), by generous permission of the author.

Jews had been here, the more they wanted that kind of identification. They didn't want to say: 'I'm not Jewish,' but: 'I'm Jewish, but it's not so different.' Marx wanted as much conformity as possible with, I guess, Episcopalian. He didn't want Catholic and he didn't know what the Church of England was, but he thought High Church Episcopalian was a pretty good model."

For Marx, the expression and practice of a man's religion properly belonged within the private sphere of the home. As a rabbi, he addressed himself chiefly to a more fitting public question: How may I speed the acceptance of my Temple members by the white Christian majority on terms of absolute equality?

In search of this acceptance, he had steered the Temple farther and farther from its traditional moorings. His reading of the situation had taught him that if strangers and exotics were despised in the South, then Jews

---

Simply, quietly, in a world ruled by Anglo-Saxon Protestants, southern Jews had laid aside their yarmulkes; forgotten their Hebrew letters; cultivated a taste for shellfish, baked ham, and pork roast; and celebrated Christmas and Easter with their children.

---

must be neither. He would recast these bearded sons of peddlers . . . .

In 1937, the official body of Reform rabbis replaced the Pittsburgh Platform with the **Columbus Platform**: Jews *were* a people, the rabbis now held; rituals and ceremonies *should* be included in the liturgy; Zion was the center of Jewish spiritual life; and the supreme being was "God." Jacob Rothschild was ordained in the principles of the Columbus Platform.

The Columbus revisions were adopted by most Reform congregations in America outside the South. In the South they were largely ignored. Thus, when Rabbi Rothschild arrived from Pittsburgh and met Dr. Marx in Atlanta, it was the Son of the Columbus Platform (Rothschild) meets the Son of the Pittsburgh Platform (Marx). Of his two Pittsburgh imports — the Platform and Rothschild — Marx, and many others of his generation, decidedly fancied the former.

The Rabbi/Reverend Emeritus Marx

Marx had been furious when he was "promoted" to emeritus status in preparation for the hiring of a new rabbi and compelled to sit through a flowery musical program of commemoration and tribute. Without his approval, the Temple board — eager to move into modern times a little less encumbered by their tireless septuagenarian — interviewed and hired Rothschild. As Marx had made perfectly clear for many years, he was not in need of assistance and was not planning to retire.

Toward the end of that first summer under one roof, Rothschild was obliged to approach Marx to plan his upcoming installation. "What installation?" snapped Marx. A ceremony was scheduled for September. Rothschild needed to know which parts of the service Marx wanted to perform. Marx pulled a sheet of paper from his desk and waved it at Rothschild. "This resolution says I shall be the rabbi of the congregation until my successor has been duly chosen and qualified. Young man, you may have been chosen, but you will *never qualify*."

"Soon after Jack came, the everlasting light in the Temple went out," remembers [a congregant]. "The story is that Jack called Dr. Marx and said, 'Dr. Marx, what shall I do? The everlasting light has gone out.' And Dr. Marx said: 'Why are you asking me? It never *went* out while *I* was rabbi.'"

From a religious point of view, Rothschild disagreed about the eternal light. Although it had never failed during Marx's tenure, much else that Rothschild saw as quintessentially Jewish had flickered. Simply, quietly, in a world ruled by Anglo-Saxon Protestants, southern Jews had laid aside their yarmulkes; forgotten their Hebrew letters; cultivated a taste for shellfish, baked ham, and pork roast; and celebrated **Christmas** and Easter with their children. Many of the age-old traditions of Judaism had become virtually indecipherable to them.

Marx was an adherent of the concept that there was such a thing as "**too Jewish**." His eradication of the "too Jewish" elements from the lives of the Temple Jews meant, in essence: "We all must live in society. We, as Jews of the American South, must make a home for ourselves here, in one of the Diaspora's hinterlands. Let us not, therefore, go out of our way to cling to religious anachronisms, thereby making ourselves strange to our neighbors. Let us release our grip on Judaic antiquities, while preserving in our lives, and for our children, the distilled and relevant core of the Jewish faith. Let us make of religion a private matter, and adapt our public personae to the demands of our region and country."

He himself explained in 1909, reflecting upon the superiority of the Reform service over the traditional one: "Our services are cast on a high place of sanity, which, while recognizing the importance of sentiment, does not generate into hysteria so prejudicial to the intellectual side of man's religious nature." The title *Rabbi*, for example, was too Jewish: *Reverend* or *Doctor* frequently was preferable. Prayer shawls and head coverings were too Jewish. Bar mitzvahs were eliminated in 1898 as "inexpedient," as were candlelightings, wine, the holy language of Hebrew, and the *bris*, or religious circumcision ceremony. The Sabbath service was abbreviated, Anglicized, and made generally more efficient. The shofar, or curved ram's horn, sounded in soul-rattling blasts at the conclusion of the holy fast day of Yom Kippur, was replaced by a mellower-sounding trumpet; and the fast itself gave way as many people dashed out to a nearby drugstore during a break in the prayer service. Marx himself disregarded the Jewish

dietary laws. He also preached virulent anti-Zionism up to and through 1948, out of fear that support of a Jewish State might expose American Jews to charges of dual loyalty.

An organ and choir enhanced the Temple's worship services. In 1906, the Temple became one of eighteen Reform temples in America to offer Sunday morning worship. This particular innovation failed, however, when the choir members protested: all were Christians, and they needed the day off to attend their own church services. "We had beautiful music in the Temple," said Janice Rothschild. "We had the best voices in town. We really had fabulous music. It wasn't particularly *Jewish* music, but it was beautiful." "At the dedication of the new Temple in 1902, Massenet's 'The Last Sleep of the Virgin' was performed, and apparently no eyebrows were raised."

Rabbi Jack Rothschild: "Why can't we have Christmas?"

[Rabbi Jack Rothschild tried to change the orientation of the congregation]. "Why can't we have Christmas?" he rhetorically asked in a sermon entitled *"What Can We Tell Our Children?"* and quietly, as if to children, he explained: "It is a religious holiday, of *Christians*. We are *Jews*.

"[Some of you may say,] 'I want a Christmas tree.' [But I answer,] it is a symbol of the birth of Jesus, and the crowned star of Messiah-ship . . . [Others may say,] 'What about Santa Claus?' [But] I've never been able to understanding the feeling that Jewish parents have to do their part to keep alive the myth of Santa Claus. *Tell our children the truth.*"

And when he finished and looked smilingly down on his congregation, he saw they slouched beneath glumly, like children just told that Santa Claus is a fake.

Rothschild felt impeded, sidetracked, by the congregation's ceaseless snack-like appetite for the superficial and the inappropriate; whereas within him there yawned a hunger, a starvation, for matters of fundamental importance.

He wanted to think, with them, about ethics, about how a person ought to live who has one eye on his neighbor and the other on the cosmos. He wanted to perfect, with them, a clear new Jewish voice, the timbre of which would be compelling, due in part to a grasp of modern life and in part to the inheritance of ancient wisdom. He wanted what every rabbi since the dawn of the rabbinate has wanted: for his congregation to see the holy Jewish texts as a moral blueprint for their lives.

But in 1946 and for much of the next twenty years, the congregation greeted Rothschild's innovations not with laughter but with, in effect, a collective gasp, followed by the southern admonition of *"Whoa, boy."*

They did not accept his basic premise — so antithetical to the lifework of Dr. Marx — that Judaism ought to be somehow more to them than a religion, that Jews were a "people." Ethnicity was not so in vogue in the 1950s. So thrilled were they to be Americans (in such a century!) they naturally shied from anything that would seem to add an asterisk, a hyphen, a foot-note to their full and normal citizenship. They rained personal letters upon Rothschild, as correctives.

The Temple in Atlanta

One prominent congregant, a pharmacist, wrote in 1952:

> We shall continue to shout from the housetops, "THERE IS NO SUCH THING AS A JEWISH PEOPLE. WE ARE AMERICANS OF THE JEWISH FAITH."

> I agree to teaching the children Jewish history. I like the idea of books relating to Jewish stories and plays, but I certainly do not subscribe to the idea of laying stress *only* on One Country, to wit: ISRAEL, and having the children work out puzzles which when pieced together show a map of Israel, the wonders of Israel, or the face of Ben Gurion.

The Congregation's Point of View: The Blue and White Christmas Tree

When, in the 1960s, they celebrated Jack Rothschild's twentieth anniversary as rabbi of the Temple, the congregation would lampoon its initial feelings of dismay and panic. They would recall, in a song composed by a congregant and sung by pant-suited, laughing Sisterhood members, what they had been thinking during Rothschild's early years:

> *Rothschild! What a lovely name,*
> *And what a lovely family tree.*
> *He's probably a nephew of that charming Baron Guy!*
> *But this Rothschild hit Atlanta like a Jewish General Sherman.*
>
> *He wasn't related to Baron Guy.*
> *He wasn't even German!*
> *He's so Yankee! He's so cranky!*
> *When we're here — twice a year — hear him fuss!*
> *He's Reform all right, but to him that means Reforming us!*
>
> ***Why should he object to a Christmas tree***
> ***When it's such a beautiful sight?***
> ***How mean can he be? Maybe he'll agree***
> ***If we keep the tree BLUE and WHITE!***

HANUKKAH EXOTICA:

ON THE ORIGIN AND DEVELOPMENT OF SOME HANUKKAH CUSTOMS

by David Golinkin[15]

In memory of Ro'i Shukrun on his second yahrzeit; a Maccabee of our time who was killed in action in Lebanon on 25 Av 5757.

Most of the laws of Hanukkah are related to the lighting of the menorah or *chanukiya*;[16] however, in this article we shall describe some of the customs of Hanukkah. The main difference between laws and customs is that laws stem from rabbinic interpretations of the Torah and Talmud which then filter down to the Jewish people, while customs usually start with the people and filter up to the rabbis. Through customs, the Jewish people have shown their love for God and tradition and immeasurably enriched all aspects of Jewish observance.

We shall begin with one well-known Hanukkah custom — the **dreidl** — and then proceed to describe the origin and some of the historical permutations of lesser known customs: **solving *katovess* (riddles); card playing; eating cheese dishes; and reading from the medieval Scroll of Antiochus**.

1. Dreidl[17]

The dreidl or *sevivon* is perhaps the most famous custom associated with Hanukkah. Indeed, various rabbis have tried to find an integral connection between the dreidl and the Hanukkah story. The standard explanation is that the letters נ ג ה ש which appear on the dreidl in the Diaspora stand for נס גדול היה שם "a great miracle happened *there*," while in Israel the dreidl says נ ג ה פ which means "a great miracle happened *here*." One nineteenth century rabbi maintained that Jews played with the dreidl in order to fool the Greeks if they were caught studying Torah which had been outlawed. Others figured out elaborate gematriot[18] and word plays for the letters נ ג ה ש. For example, נ ג ה ש in gematria equals 358 which is also the numerical equivalent of משיח or Messiah! Finally, the letters נ ג ה ש are supposed to represent the four kingdoms which tried to destroy us:

N = Nebuchadnetzar = Babylon;

H = Haman = Persia = Madai;

G = Gog = Greece; and **S** = Seir = Rome.

As a matter of fact, all of these elaborate explanations were invented after the fact. The dreidl game originally had nothing to do with Hanukkah; it has been played by various people in various languages for many centuries *(see the chart on next page)*. In England and Ireland there is a game called *totum* or *teetotum* which is especially popular at Christmas time. In English, this game is first mentioned as "*totum*" ca. 1500-1520. The name comes from the Latin "*totum*" which means "all." By 1720, the game was called *T-totum* or *teetotum* and by 1801 the four letters

(see the chart on next page)

---

15. Rabbi David Golinkin is President and Associate Professor of Jewish Law at the Schechter Institute of Jewish Studies of the Masorti (Conservative) Movement in Jerusalem. His latest book is the *Responsa of the Va'ad Halakhah*, Volume 6 (5755-5758). This essay is an abbreviation of a scholarly article which will appear later in full with all the necessary footnotes.

16. In the Diaspora, the Hanukkah lamp is called a *menorah*; in modern Israel it's called a *chanukiya*. Technically speaking, the menorah is the seven branched candelabrum which was used in the Tabernacle and in the Temple in ancient times (*Exodus* 37:17-24; *Numbers* 8:1-4) and should not be used to describe a Hanukkah lamp.

17. Based on Israel Abrahams in Emily Solis-Cohen, ed., *Hanukkah: The Feast of Lights*, Philadelphia, 1937, pp. 105-106; Y. Rivkind, *Der Kampf Kegn Azartspielen bei Yidn*, N.Y., 1946, pp. 49-54; Yom Tov Levinsky, ed., *Sefer Hamo'adim*,Vol. 5, Tel Aviv, 5714, pp. 225-226; Akiva Ben Ezra, *Minhagey Hagim*, Jerusalem and Tel Aviv, 5723, pp. 138-139; Sidney Hoenig in Philip Goodman, ed., *The Hanukkah Anthology*, Philadelphia, 1976, pp. 265-266; and Uri Sela, *Yediot Aharonot*, 27 Heshvan 5748.

18. A *gematria* is an explanation based on the fact that every Hebrew letter has a numerical value, so if word x = 100 and word y = 100, this can become the basis for a homiletical explanation connecting the two words.

FAMILY AND FUN

Introduction

Cartoons

Foods

Games

Gifts

December Dilemma

Exotica

COUNTRY	NAME OF THE GAME	TAKE ALL	TAKE HALF	PIT IN MORE	DO NOTHING
England, Ireland c. 1500 CE	Totum *(in Latin)*	T = Totum	A = Aufer	D = Depone	N = Nihil
England 1801	T-totum	T = Take	H = Half	P = Put down	N = Nothing
France 1611	Toton	T = Toton	A = Accipe	D = Da	R = Rien
Sardinia, Italy	Tutte	T = Tutte	M = Mesu	P = Pone	N = Nuda
Germany	Torrel, Trundel	G = Ganz	H = Halb	S = Stell ein	N = Nichts
Hebrew or Yiddish	Dreidl	G ג = Gadol	H ח = Haya	Sh ש = Sham P פ = Po	N נ = Nes

already represented four words in English: **T** = Take all; **H** = Half; **P** = Put down; and **N** = Nothing.

Our Eastern European game of dreidl (including the letters נ ג ה ש) is directly based on the German equivalent of the game: **N** = Nichts = nothing; **G** = Ganz = all; **H** = Halb = half; and **S** = Stell ein = put in. In German, the spinning top was called a "torrel" or "trundl" and in Yiddish it was called a "dreidl," a "fargl," a "varfl" [= something thrown], "shtel ein" [= put in], and "gor, gorin" [= all]. When Hebrew was revived as a spoken language, the dreidl was called, among other names, a *sevivon* סביבון — which is the one that caught on.

Thus the dreidl game represents an irony of Jewish history. In order to celebrate the holiday of Hanukkah which celebrates our victory over cultural assimilation, we play the dreidl game which is an excellent example of cultural assimilation! Of course, there is a world of difference between imitating non-Jewish games and worshipping idols, but the irony remains nonetheless.

2. *Katovess*:[19] **Hanukkah Riddles**

The custom of Hanukkah *katovess* is first attributed to Rabbi Israel Isserlein (Austria, 1390-1460), after which the word is used frequently in Hebrew and Yiddish until the twentieth century. Unfortunately, neither the etymology nor the pronunciation of the word are clear. Hanukkah *katovess* were word games and riddles which were especially popular at the festive meals of Hanukkah and they were frequently connected to the Hanukkah candles. The following examples are taken from Leket Yosher in which R. Yosef (Yozl) Ben Moshe of Hoechstaedt describes the customs of his beloved teacher R. Israel Isserlein:[20]

A) "Remove my cloak (בגד) from me, then you will find my number." Yozl (יוזל) in gematria is 53; בגד in gematria is 9. If you remove 9 from 53 you get 44 which is the number of candles needed for the eight nights of Hanukkah including the *shamash*!

B) "If the servant falls you must attend to him; but if the master falls, no one comes to set him up." This riddle refers to the laws of the Hanukkah candles. If the *shamash* or "servant" goes out you must relight it. This is because you are not allowed to derive benefit from the Hanukkah candles, so if you inadvertently use the light you are, so to speak, using the *shamash*. But

---

19. For the sources and etymology of this word, see my Hebrew article in *Sinai* 106 (5750), pp. 175-183 along with the additions by H. Guggenheimer, ibid., 108 (5751), pp. 175-176.
20. *Leket Yosher*, ed. J. Freimann, Berlin, 5663, section Orah Hayyim, p. 153.

if the "master" or Hanukkah candle goes out you don't have to relight it because once you lit it, you have fulfilled the mitzvah.[21]

C) **"ושר שמריה יהי רם שרשו"** was written by Shmerel or Shmaryah and it means "Shmaryah sang, may his root (or origin) be elevated" which sounds like nonsense. But Shmerel was really quite clever since this *katovess* is a palindrome which reads the same in both directions!

Hanukkah *katovess* are no longer in vogue, but it would be good to revive this beautiful custom which flourished in Germany and Eastern Europe for at least four hundred years.

3. Card-Playing on Hanukkah:[22] Jewish "Black Jack"

The Ashkenazi custom of playing cards on Hanukkah is first mentioned as a permitted activity in the responsa of R. Jacob Weil[23] (d. before 1456). R. Israel Isserlein (1390-1460) was opposed to the custom because the children used to play cards by the light of the Hanukkah candles and it is forbidden to derive benefit from the Hanukkah candles as explained above.

Rabbi Yair Chaim Bachrach (1638-1702) of Worms describes the efforts of his father Rabbi Moshe Shimshon Bachrach (1607-1670) to abolish card-playing on Hanukkah:

And it annoyed my pious father that the

miraculous days [of Hanukkah] which were established to thank and praise God should be designated for card-playing and frivolity. And he tried to forbid it and move it to the eight days of their festival [= between Christmas and New Year] which would not entail canceling commercial transactions because people stay at home [in any case], but he did not succeed because they would not agree to change the custom.[24]

Indeed, R. Yosef Yuzpe Kashman Segal of Frankfurt reports in 1718 that "in all the communities they decreed not to play cards all year long except for Hanukkah and Purim when they allowed it."[25]

Rabbi Moshe Shimshon Bachrach was not the only rabbi opposed to card-playing on Hanukkah. Rabbi Yechiel Michal Epstein (1829-1908) of Navarodok, Russia vented his spleen against this custom in the *Arukh Hashulhan*,[26] which is now one of the standard codes of Jewish law:

But those who play cards [on Hanukkah] their punishment is great, and due to our many sins this leprosy has spread among the house of Israel!

An almost contemporaneous account of card-playing on Hanukkah can be found in Herman Leder's Yiddish memoir *Reisher Yidn* which describes the Jews of Reishe (Rzeszow) in Galicia ca. 1900:

We were far removed from mischief and foolishness. We did not devote ourselves to such things, not even to idle talk, except for Hanukkah when we stopped learning for several hours a day and played cards or watched as others played. I was one of the

---

21. See *Shulhan Arukh Orah Hayyim* 673:1-2.
22. This section is based on Yitzhak Rivkind, *Hadoar* 5/7 (1 Tevet 5686), pp. 101-102 and 5/9 (22 Tevet 5686), pp. 133-134; Rivkind, *Der Kampf*, pp. 48-49; *Sefer Hamo'adim*, pp. 229-230; and Akiva Ben Ezra, pp. 136-138.
23. *Responsa of R. Ya'akov Weil*, Jerusalem, 5748, No. 135.
24. *Responsa Havot Yair*, Jerusalem, 5757, No. 126
25. *Noheg Katzon Yosef*, second edition, Tel Aviv, 5729, p. 188, par. 12.
26. *Orah Hayyim* 670:9

These cards were usually hand-painted by the teacher or the children in heder and the card game played was very similar to black jack.

latter because I never had any money, and without money, one cannot play cards. So I stood around and *kibbitzed*. Frequently, the one I was standing next to and at whose cards I was looking, lost every round. Suddenly, he woke up, so to speak, from his sleep, turned around to me, and said in a loud voice: "Get away from here you jinx! You are unlucky! I am losing because of you!" So I immediately went away; after that, not one of the players wanted me to stand near him.[27]

Finally, a word must be said about the cards themselves. In Yiddish, they were called *kvitlech* which means little notes or *klein shass* which means a small Talmud (sic!) or *tilliml* which means a small book of Psalms (sic!) or *lamed alefniks* which means "31ers" (the deck had 31 cards, one for each of the 31 kings of Canaan mentioned in Joshua, Chapter 12). These cards were usually hand-painted by the teacher or the children in heder and the card game played was very similar to black jack.

4. Cheese on Hanukkah

In his glosses to the *Shulhan Arukh*[28] Rabbi Moshe Isserles (Cracow, 1525-1572) relates:

It is customary to recite songs and praises [to God] at the festive meals which are common [on Hanukkah] and then the meal becomes a mitzvah meal. Some say that one should eat cheese on Hanukkah because the miracle occurred through milk which Judith fed the enemy.[29]

The Kol Bo (14th century France) says that the daughter of Yohanan the High Priest fed the Greek King *"a cheese dish in order that he become thirsty and drink a lot and get drunk and lie down and fall asleep."* That is what transpired; she then cut off his head and brought it to Jerusalem and when his army saw that their

hero had died, they fled "and that is why it is the custom to cook a cheese dish on Hanukkah."[30]

The question, of course, is where did the Kol Bo find this story? It sounds like the story of Judith and Holofernes as found in the Apocryphal Book of Judith. Indeed, cheese is mentioned in some ancient versions of Judith 10:5 which lists the foods that Judith took with her when she left the besieged city to visit Holofernes. Nevertheless, Judith 12:17-20 which describes the way in which Judith got Holofernes to go sleep says explicitly that Judith gave him wine to drink and not a cheese dish! In any case, the Book of Judith seems to have been written in Hebrew but has only reached us in Greek translation and was unknown to medieval Jews. They, however, knew the story of Judith from medieval Hebrew sagas called "The Story of Judith" and the like. Some eighteen versions of the medieval story have been published until now and most of those versions, like the Book of Judith itself, say that Judith gave Holofernes wine to drink, but two of the versions do indeed mention milk or cheese.

The medieval midrash *Ma'aseh Yehudit* says that Judith *"opened the milk flask and drank and also gave the king to drink, and he rejoiced with her greatly and he drank very much wine, more than he had drunk in his entire life."*[31] In other words, Judith gave Holofernes both milk and wine.[32]

Megillat Yehudit relates that after fasting, Judith asked her maidservant to make her two *levivot* [= pancakes or fried cakes]. The servant made the *levivot* very salty and added slices of cheese. Judith fed Holofernes the

27. Herman Leder, *Reisher Yidn*, Washington, D.C., 1953, p. 186.

28. *Orah Hayyim* 670:2

29. *Kol Bo* and *R'an* are quoted in Moshe Isserles (O.H. 670:2)

30. *Kol Bo*, ed. Lemberg, 5620, parag. 44, fol. 3c.

31. This midrash was reprinted by A. Jellinek, *Bet Hamidrash*, Part 2, Leipzig, 5613, p. 19 and by J. D. Eisenstein, *Otzar Midrashim*, Vol. 1, New York, 5675, p. 207.

32. [It is clear that the author was influenced by the story of Yael and Sisera in the *Book of Judges* because the phraseology was borrowed from *Judges* 4:19.]

levivot and the slices of cheese *"and he drank [wine] and his heart became very merry and he got drunk and he uncovered himself within his tent and he lay down and fell asleep."*[33]

5. The Scroll of Antiochus[34]

There is one custom which we would expect to find on Hanukkah which is missing — the reading of a scroll in public. After all, on Purim we read the Scroll of Esther every year in order to publicize the miracle. Why don't we read a scroll on Hanukkah in order to publicize the miracles which God wrought for our ancestors in the days of Mattathias and his sons? The result is that most Jews only know the legend about the miracle of the cruse of oil[35] and not about the actual military victories of the Maccabees.

The answer is that, in truth, there is such a scroll which was read in private or in public between the ninth and twentieth centuries. It is called "The Scroll of Antiochus" and many other names and it was written in Aramaic during the Talmudic period and subsequently translated into Hebrew, Arabic and other languages. The book describes the Maccabean victories on the basis of a few stories from the *Books of the Maccabees* and *Shabbat 21b* with the addition of a number of legends without any historic basis whatsoever. The scroll is first mentioned by *Halakhot Gedolot* which was written by Shimon Kayara in Babylon ca. 825 C.E.: "The elders of Bet Shammai and Bet Hillel wrote *Megillat Bet Hashmonay* [=the scroll of the Hasmonean House] . . . ."[36]

---

33. A.M. Haberman, *Hadashim Gam Yeshanim*, Jerusalem, 1975, p.45.
34. See *EJ*, Vol. 14, cols. 1045-1047.
35. *Talmud Shabbat 21b*
36. *Halakhot Gedolot*, ed. Venice, 5308 [=Warsaw, 5635], fol. 141d.

Sephardic Customs for a Woman's, a Teacher's and a Child's Delights

Sephardic observances expand the repertoire of popular customs which we might adapt and revive today. In Syria, for example, the synagogue *shamash* (servant or caretaker) used to send a gift of a decorative tapered candle to each family to use as their *shamash* (service candle for use with the menorah). In Damascus, the children would collect food or money during the week and on the last day of Hanukkah they would prepare **three meals — one for their teachers, one for the poor, and one for themselves.** After Hanukkah is over, a *taanit dibur* is observed, that is, one **"fasts" for a full day from conversation**. This was designed to curb one's tendency to *lashon hara* — malicious gossip — especially during social occasions such as on holidays.

In Kurdistan, in Iraq, children used to prepare an **effigy of Antiochus**. The stuffed doll used was nicknamed "Hanukkah" and children collected donations of flour and oil to make pancakes, while singing Hanukkah songs and carrying the effigy from place to place. On the last day of the holiday the effigy was thrown into a bonfire.

In Bukhara, southern Russia, **parents baked cakes for their children's teachers with gold and silver coins wrapped in the dough**, while Eastern European children collected their Hanukkah *gelt* in a **decorative box** and used the money to purchase study texts. Since Antiochus ordered that Jewish books be destroyed, the reinforcement of Jewish learning was felt to be a particularly appropriate activity for Hanukkah.

In some North African communities **the seventh night of Hanukkah is dedicated to heroines like Judith and Hannah**. Women would gather in the synagogue, take out the Torah and receive a blessing from the rabbi in the name of the matriarchs. The women ate cheese and dairy products that recalled Judith's device for overcoming Holofernes. In Salonika, Greece, the **female solidarity** engendered by the Hanukkah heroines lead the girls who were angry with one another to become reconciled, just as is customary on the eve of Yom Kippur. Generally, women refrain from all household tasks while the candles are burning, and some take a vacation from these chores for the whole eight days. As the Rabbis taught, women have a special place in the miracle of Hanukkah and therefore in its celebration.

Exotica

Furthermore, we know that this scroll was read in public at different times and places. Rabbi Isaiah of Trani (Italy, ca. 1200-1260) says that "in a place where they are accustomed to read *Megillat Antiochus* [=The Scroll of Antiochus] on Hanukkah, it is not proper to recite the blessings [for reading a scroll] because it is not required at all."[37]

But Rabbi Amram Zabban of G'ardaya in the Sahara Dessert viewed this reading as a requirement. In his *Sefer Hasdey Avot* published in 1926 he states:

> *Megillat Antiochus* according to the custom of the holy city of G'ardaya, may God protect her. The cantor should read it in public in the synagogue after the Torah reading on the Shabbat during Hanukkah. And he reads it in Arabic translation so that the entire congregation should understand [in order to] publicize the miracle which was done to our holy ancestors, may their merit protect us . . . .

The Jews of Kurdistan,[38] on the other hand, used to read the Scroll of Antiochus at home during Hanukkah.

It would seem that there is no point in reviving the specific custom of reading the Scroll of Antiochus in public because that work is legendary in nature and not a reliable source for the events of Hanukkah. But we do possess such a source for those events — the *First Book of Maccabees*, which was written in Hebrew in the Land of Israel by an eyewitness to the events described therein.

Therefore, we should thank Rabbi Arthur Chiel who published the *First Book of Maccabees*, Chapters 1-4 as a separate booklet twenty years ago under the title "The Scroll of Hanukkah."[39] It is intended for reading in public or in private during the holiday. We should adopt this beautiful custom and begin to read those chapters in public every year on the Shabbat of Hanukkah after the haftarah. By so doing, we will be reviving the custom of reading a "scroll" on Hanukkah but, more importantly, we will thereby disseminate the oldest surviving account of the "miracles and triumphs" which God performed for the Jewish People "in those days at this season."

There are many other Hanukkah customs worth investigating, but these examples will suffice to show how the Jewish people have enriched and enhanced the Festival of Lights.

---

37. *Tosfot R"id* to *Sukkah 44b* catchword *Havit*, Lemberg, 5629, fol. 31b.
38. Erich Brauer, *Yehudey Kurdistan*, Jerusalem, 5708, p. 273.
39. Rabbi Arthur Chiel, *Megillat Hanukkah*, New York, 1980, 61pp.

[Editor's note: In *A Different Light* we have created a *Maccabees' Megillah* from the *First and Second Books of the Maccabees* in order to encourage home retelling of the historical story as recommended here by Rabbi Golinkin].

Gallery: The Art of Hanukkah

Zechariah's Messianic Menorah by Yosef HaTzorfati

The seven-branched golden Menorah is surrounded by two olive trees, representing the High Priest Yehoshua and the political leader Zerubbavel. These two leaders were involved in the restoration of the Temple in 516 BCE after the return from the Babylonian exile. The olive trees provide the Menorah with a continuous supply of fuel. The description of the Menorah from Zechariah is read in the Haftorah for the first Shabbat of Hanukkah, and concludes with a messianic vision of peace, "Not by Might, and Not by Power, but by my Spirit." (Zechariah 2:14 ff.) (The Cervera Bible, Spain circa 1300)

Chair Menorah and Dreidels from Eastern Europe

The chairs are made of lead, usually by children, and often melted down after use because lead has a low melting point.
(Courtesy of Henry and Bella Muller)

The Statue of Liberty and American Flag Hanukkah Menorah, by Mae Shafter Rockland

This unique Menorah synthesizes modern American and ancient Jewish symbols of freedom. The Statue of Liberty, donated by the Republic of France in honor of its sister Republic, is adorned with a quote from the Jewish poet Emma Lazarus which appears on this menorah as well: "Give me your tired, your poor, your huddled masses, yearning to breathe free." (Art Resource/Jewish Museum of New York. Princeton, NJ, 1974. Wood covered in fabric with molded plastic figures)

The Israeli-American
Hanukkah Stamp
by Hannah Smotrich

The joint issue of U.S.A. and Israel, 1996
(Courtesy of the Israeli Philatelic Service)

Lubavitch Mitzva Mobiles Visit an Israeli Army Camp on Hanukkah

*Prime
Minister
Yitzchak
Rabin Lights
a Thirteen
Candle Bar
Mitzvah
Menorah*

*(Government Press
Office, Israel, c. 1994)*

la louenge de dieu tout
puissant me createur
et redempteur qui par
sa sainte misericorde
voult en ce mortel mode
naistre homme de mere vierge et souffrir
mort et passion par les mains des
Juifz pour nous tous racheter denfer

au quel par le pechie du premier homme
nous feusmes soubzmis et obligiez
Et pour auoir entendement par
langage francois de listoire de la
destruction des Juifz et de la cite de
iherlm ensemble de toute la tir diceulx
Juifz ce que plusieurs appellent la
vengence de la mort et passion de nre

King Antiochus IV and the Maccabean Revolt

Josephus Flavius, History of the Jewish War *(France, last quarter 15th century; Musee Conde, Chantilly, France. Giraudon/Art Resource, NY)*

Maccabean Battle Scenes: Medieval and Modern

Hanukkah by David Sharir   *Mattathias and his five sons battle the Greeks and their war elephants*

(Courtesy of the Safrai Gallery, 19 King David Street, Jerusalem 94101, Fax: 972-2-624-0387; serigraph 225; A225 E.A. 50; 1981)

Judith, The Maiden of Peace
by Sandro Botticelli (Italy, 1445-151

This Renaissance image still embodies the medieu
identification of Judith with Fortitude, Chastity,
Temperance, Wisdom, Humility and Justice. Ju
represented not only the ideal woman — a parag
of chastity who slays the sexually aroused aggress
with his own phallic sword — but also the mode
a wise and just Christian prince. Her perfection
allows for no defects or complexity, even though
other artists may consider her a seductive betraye

Judith uses her fortitude to lead Israel in battle
against its impious enemy. She is portrayed wit
her maid running quickly from the camp of the
Assyrians with the battle raging in the backgrou
Even though Judith carries in one hand the bloo
sword of Holofernes whose head she has remove
she is portrayed as a pastoral maiden of peace. S
holds in her other hand an olive branch since her
heroic act has brought peace to her people. Judith
transcendent beauty — truly Divinely given as
Book of Judith emphasizes — partakes in no w
earthly sexuality or seduction. (based on Margari
Stocker, Judith: The Sexual Warrior, p. 24-25)

Judith: Images of a Heroine/Villainess

Judith, My Murdering Mistress and Her Mother by Cristoforo Allori (Italy, 1577-1621)

Judith the upper class widow is draped in magnificent tapestries, yet she has found the inner strength to kill and to display the head of her people's would-be destroyer. This might be a viewer's first reading of the picture. However, art historians add that Allori had a personal grudge to bear in this portrait. Instead of an embodiment of all Christian virtues, Judith, the heroine-cum-femme fatale, has been chosen to express his ambivalence toward an entrancingly beautiful yet cold, cruel woman. Judith is portrayed with the face and figure of Allori's mistress who has just abandoned him — figuratively slain him. The severed head of the love-struck Holofernes is a self-portrait of the artist himself. The accomplice of this remorseless betrayal is the maid, bearing the face of the mistress' own mother. Judith's beauty explains to all the fatal attraction of this heartless, homicidal heroine. (based on Margarita Stocker, Judith: The Sexual Warrior, *p. 27)*

Uri-On: The Israeli-Jewish Superman

Michael Netzer, Jonathan Deutsch, and Yossi Halper created the first Israeli comic book (Israel Comics Ltd.) in 1987. The story sought to give an Israeli-Jewish content to an American Superman who was defending his ancient homeland against invasion of extraterrestrials. Israelis on the religious right wing as well as those on the secular left responded positively to the comic book. The hero is called Uri-On meaning "Light and Power" — and his emblem is the Menorah, the Israeli national symbol. (Courtesy of Michael Netzer)

CHAPTER III

Hanukkah Today:
Contemporary Jewish Thinkers Reflect on the Relevance of Hanukkah

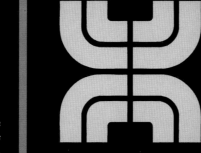

Dan Reisinger's Contemporary Menorah Logos for Modern Israeli Institutions

(by generous permission of the graphic artist)

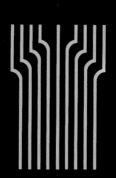

Hanukkah Today:

Contemporary Jewish Thinkers Reflect on the Relevance of Hanukkah

Introduction

"Text and experience are mutually enlightening," said the scholar of midrash, Judah Goldin, about the Jewish art of interpretation. When Jews reread the Torah annually, they not only reinterpret the ancient text in the light of contemporary experience, but they also let the text speak to them from other worlds, with perspectives very different than the contemporary one. This two-sided dialogue of past and present is the key to the vitality of Jewish tradition in general.

In the modern era, Jewish thinkers (such as S.R. Hirsch, Franz Rosenzweig, Herman Cohen, Eliezer Schwied, Irving Greenberg, and the editors' teacher, David Hartman) have identified a "new" Jewish text, a new Torah, to be interpreted every year — the **Jewish holiday cycle**. The customs, laws, and stories of each festival are not merely law or folklore but a Jewish philosophy of life embodied in a people's pattern of celebration.

In this sense, the Hanukkah candles, for example, are not merely a reminder of the historic restoration of the ancient Temple, but they are also a spiritual message about the perennial struggle between the forces of darkness and of light in our personal, communal and cosmic lives. Putting the candles in our window is a proclamation of faith, the taking of a stand in favor a particular way of life, just as one might put up a political message in a big banner on one's front yard. It is not sufficient to light the candle at the proper time or to read a summary of the historical event. **One needs to make public a thoughtful message about what this holiday means personally.** Therefore we believe it necessary to add a section on Jewish thinkers who have tried to give Hanukkah such a contemporary spiritual message.

The thinkers collected below represent some of the best of Jewish thought in the last 50 or so years. Each brings his or her own intellectual prism to bear on the Festival of Lights. For some, it is a psychological standpoint, for others it is gender or politics or spirituality or the dynamics of Jewish identity. All of these thinkers, like many of our readers, are Western educated Jews seeking to maintain loyal and yet critical commitment to both Jewish and Western tradition.

Both Rabbis David Hartman and Irving ("Yitz") Greenberg are students of the great modern Orthodox Talmudist and philosopher, Rabbi Joseph Dov Baer Soloveitchik, and both have created institutions to promote the pluralist study of Torah for scholars, rabbis, educators and Jewish leaders of all backgrounds. Both Daniel Gordis and Harold Schulweis are leading Conservative rabbis.

David Hartman, in his first essay, reinterprets the supernatural miracle of the long-burning vessel of oil in a psychological way. The "miracle" resides not so much in how long the oil actually burned but in the initial faith of those human beings who lit so little oil yet trusted that somehow it would last. Analogously, the Jews knew "realistically" that they did not have sufficient resources to see through the project of rekindling the menorah and rededicating the Temple since they were confronting powerful Greek aggression. Yet they began the revolt and saw it through to the end. In his second essay Hartman asks what new message the Jews can proclaim in a democratic world in which, for the most part, there is no persecution like that of Antiochus. How does the shift from the closed world of the ghetto to Western pluralism transform the meaning of the holiday?

Daniel Gordis, like David Hartman, attempts to redefine "miracle" in a way acceptable to contemporary, scientifically sophisticated Jews. He takes the miracle of the long-lasting cruse of oil to be a metaphor for the durability of the Jewish people in history, and tries to identify a contemporary Jewish mission worthy of our continuing to survive.

Harold Schulweis, one of the great congregational leaders in the Conservative movement, has done much to transform the synagogue framework into a more personal place for spiritual pursuits in smaller communities, chavurot. His reflections on Hanukkah give priority to the everyday miracles of making "something out of something" rather than the miracles of producing "something from nothing."

Irving Greenberg focuses on a different issue — the "wars of the Jews" among themselves, then and now. He finds historic analogies to the contemporary struggle of Ultra-Orthodox, Zionist secularists and liberal religious Jews. For him Hanukkah commemorates an ancient civil war between traditionalists, assimilationists and moderates and it teaches us that the current "civil war" can be resolved through pluralist coalition building.

Professor Judith Kates and Rabbi Mordechai Gafni interpret Hanukkah in terms made very popular in the 1990's. **Judith Kates** takes a feminist perspective and asks why the Rabbis chose to emphasize the role of women heroines in the context of the holiday. She analyzes the story of Judith as an analogue to the Greek threat to penetrate and desecrate the inner sanctum of the Temple. In response the Jewish woman *par excellence*, Judith whose name means "the Jewish woman," turns the tables on the Greek king and penetrates his bedroom and desecrates his body and thereby becomes a female savior of her people. **Mordechai Gafni** treats Hanukkah as a repository of personal wisdom for spiritual growth. In an intentional analogy to the eight ways of spiritual illumination in the Far Eastern Tao tradition of wisdom, he constructs eight ways to Jewish spiritual enlightenment derived chiefly from Hasidic sources.

Herman Wouk (1959), the Orthodox novelist, Rabbi Mordecai Kaplan (1937), the founder of Reconstructionism, and Professor Theodore Gaster (1950), the secularist academic historian of religion, all use the Hanukkah story to address the dilemma of the American-born Jews of the mid-century who wanted desperately to be accepted by the WASP majority culture of that period. None of these three reject the positive values of America or call for a withdrawl from the corrupting influence of modernity on Judaism. Yet each sought to counterbalance, in different ways, the sociological pressure on Jews to conform.

Herman Wouk describes in sympathetic ways the prominence of the "December dilemma" during the 1950's, in which the subtle "pressure to emulate one's neighbors" proves more effective than any political or physical coercion has been in undermining Jewish identification. He uses gentle irony to describe the exaggeration of the celebration of the minor observance of Hanukkah due to its competition with the Christmas spirit of gift giving. Yet he calls for a stubborn response of non-conformism by the Jewish minority. Like the Maccabees who defied the all-conquering Greek Empire and its culture, the Jewish people can preserve its identity both when faced by Soviet-style coercion and by American-style conformism.

Mordecai Kaplan was the son of an Eastern European rabbi who became a leading Conservative rabbi and helped found the Reconstructionist Movement. He set himself a more difficult and controversial task than Gaster or Wouk. Gaster and Wouk spoke to the fast-assimilating American Jews of the 1950's about the spirit of non-conformism embodied in the Maccabees and about the mistaken tendency to ape anything Western. Yet Kaplan understood that the Jews, both in the eras of Hellenism and of Americanism, were attracted to assimilation by truly positive values which they found lacking in traditional Judaism. Therefore he believed that the ability to positively assimilate Western American values into Judaism was essential for Jewish survival. He distinguished between **passive** and **active assimilation**, between mindless imitation and thoughtful borrowing. Judaism needs to "reconstruct" itself in the light of modern science, ethics and aesthetics. That is the unexpected message that he discovers in the holiday of the reconstruction, cleansing and rededication of the Temple.

Theodore Herzl Gaster, whose father was an early supporter of secular Zionism, is himself an early promoter of multi-culturalism. In an era when the ideal of the American melting pot was the catechism of the children of Jewish immigrants seeking entrance into suburban life, Gaster argued that the message of Hanukkah is ethnic particularity. As a historian of religion he retells the political history of the Maccabees to show that they were fighting not merely for religious freedom but for the right to their own national culture. While many 20th century Jews were seeking to overcome the barriers of social anti-semitism by acting like everyone else, Gaster claimed that "the real issue at stake was not the right of Jews to be like everyone else but rather the right to be different."

Trusting in a New Beginning

Lighting the Surviving Cruse of Oil

The primary reason offered by the Talmud for the celebration of Hanukkah is the miraculous burning of the single remaining pure cruse of oil which enabled Jews to rededicate the Temple and to commence rebuilding the community's spiritual life. Contrary to normal expectations, the flame continued to burn for eight days. The Talmud explains the holiday of Hanukkah as follows:

What is (the reason for) Hanukkah?

Our Rabbis taught:

On the twenty-fifth of Kislev commence the days of Hanukkah, — eight days on which lamentation for the dead and fasting are forbidden. For when the Greeks entered the Temple, they defiled all the oils therein, and when the Hasmonean dynasty prevailed against and defeated them, they searched and found only one cruse of oil with the seal of the High Priest, but it contained sufficient oil for one day's lighting only. Yet a miracle occurred and they lit the lamp that burned for eight days.[2]

Although there may have been sufficient oil in the cruses of oil, which had been ritually defiled, **Jews insisted on using only pure oil even though the quantity found appeared to be insufficient. The willingness to rely on one small but pure cruse of oil symbolized the reluctance to compromise their standards of excellence and moral ideals.** Uncompromising commitment to purity and trust in the eternal regenerative power of personal integrity were concretely expressed in the symbol of the cruse of oil chosen to light the first Hanukkah lamp.

Jews throughout history loved to retell the story of the tiny cruse of oil, which refused to burn out. In recounting this tale, they indicated their deep hope that the small community of Israel could survive and generate light irrespective of its size and power. Israel's fervent commitment to and trust in its way of life were sufficient reasons to retain hope in the community's future regardless of the empirical conditions of history.

In considering the miracle of the cruse of oil, our Rabbis asked why the holiday of Hanukkah was celebrated for eight days rather than for seven days. Since there was, by all accounts, sufficient oil for one day, only seven of the eight days of burning may be designated as miraculous days. Though several ingenious explanations were offered, what strikes me as being the miraculous feature of the initial day was the community's willingness to light the lamp in spite of the fact that its anticipated period of burning was short-lived. **The miracle of the first day was expressed in the community's willingness to light a small cruse of oil without reasonable assurance that their efforts would be sufficient to complete the rededication of the Temple.** Hanukkah celebrates the miracle expressed by those who lit the lamp and not only the miracle of the lamp's continued burning for eight days.

The "miracle" of Jewish spiritual survival throughout its history of

---

1. Rabbi David Hartman is a liberal orthodox Jewish philosopher who moved from North America to Jerusalem where he built a pluralist center for advanced Jewish study, the Shalom Hartman Institute.
2. *T.B. Shabbat 21*

The willingness to rely on one small but pure cruse of oil symbolized the reluctance to compromise their standards of excellence and moral ideals.

wandering and oppression may best be described by our people's strength to live without guarantees of success and to focus on how to begin a process without knowledge of how it would end. Uncertainty of success often paralyzes one's initiative to act. It is not uncommon for people to refuse to study Torah because of their belief that they lack sufficient time and will power to become accomplished scholars. Human initiative is undermined by the rationalization that since completion of the task in question is not assured, there is no point making the required effort to begin.

The 'miracle' of Jewish spiritual survival may best be described by our people's strength to live without guarantees of success.

The Hanukkah lights encourage one to trust human beginnings and to focus one's passions and efforts on whatever opportunities are available at the present moment. One ought to pour infinite yearnings even into small vessels. The strength to continue and to persevere grows by virtue of the courage to initiate a process by lighting the first flame. Only lamps which are lit may continue to burn beyond their anticipated life span. Only he who devotes even fifteen minutes a day to learning will discover his latent powers to study and concentrate. Only he who breaks the chains of moral complacency by giving a minimal amount of *tzedakah* (charity) will discover greater capacities to respond to those in need.

One brings children into the world without knowing whether one will be able to love and provide for their needs throughout a lifetime. Only in actually caring for one's children does one discover and expand one's capacity for love and concern. Human capacities and achievements grow as a result of action and not as a result of noble ideals and well-meaning intentions. The Hanukkah lamp burned for eight days because of those who were prepared to have it burn for only one day.

The eight days of Hanukkah incorporate the miracle of the first day, which signifies the miracle of human courage to begin to build within imperfect human situations. There were undoubtedly many people who were skeptical of the decision to light the Temple lamp with a single cruse of oil. "Why light a flame which is bound to burn out before the Temple is completely rededicated? Let the Temple remain ritually defiled until we are certain that we have enough oil to light the lamp for a long period. Why initiate a process which we cannot complete? Wait until the conditions are ripe!" Those who went ahead and kindled the lamp ignored such "voices of reason" and they availed themselves of the precious opportunities at hand. And the miracle of Hanukkah occurred.

Those who decided to proclaim the establishment of the State of Israel in the twentieth century were Jews who had learnt the message of Hanukkah as well. There were many "reasonable" voices that counseled cautious waiting for the right moment. "Be cautious! Wait until your army is stronger. Wait until the vast majority of world Jewry will actively support the Zionist ideal and will choose to participate in the national-political rebirth of the Jewish people." Despite its detractors, a minority of the Jewish people went ahead and proclaimed the rebirth of the State of Israel.

The powerful flame of Israel was ignited in 1948 by a small component of the Jewish people. Today few would deny that history has shown that those who had the courage to light the flame were correct. World Jewry realizes that the Jewish soul must be kindled by the flame whose source is in Jerusalem. It is no accident that the symbol of the State of Israel is the menorah. The flame, which burns in the hearts of Jews throughout the world, was initially kindled by a small flame, ignited by those who heroically proclaimed: "We are reborn!"

THE COURAGE TO PUT OUR JEWISH LIGHTS IN THE FRONT WINDOW

On Hanukkah the Jew demonstrates his love for his particular tradition without fear and hesitation. In order to publicly demonstrate the Jew's loyalty to his particular tradition and to openly affirm the miracle of Hanukkah, the Jew is required to place the Hanukkah lamp where it will best be noticed from outside.

> *Our Rabbis taught: It is incumbent to place the Hanukkah lamp by the door of one's house on the outside. If one dwells in an upper chamber, one places it at the window closest to the public domain. However, in time of danger, one places it on the table in the privacy of one's home and that is adequate.*[3]

In lighting the Hanukkah lamp, the Jew announces to the outside world: "This is my flame. Gaze on this light and know that from this home a Jewish light burns. If you accept me in these terms, I am prepared to share my light with you and to be an active member within a shared universe of experience. If, however, you seek to extinguish my flame, then I shall remove my lamp from the windowsill and place it on my private table to be viewed by my family alone."

The challenge facing Judaism today is not only whether we can withstand our enemies but also whether the light visible in the marketplace radiates a profound and compelling message.

In times of danger and persecution, the Jew may withdraw into the privacy of his particular framework of experience. He must not succumb to the standards of the marketplace, which denigrate the value of his unique identity and particular way of life. In the face of hostility and oppression, the Jew lit the menorah for the members of his family so that the flame of Judaism would be internalized in their souls. The marketplaces of his-

tory led one to believe that Judaism had died and had become a lifeless fossil. Yet in the private corners of Jewish homes families gathered together, told the story of Hanukkah, recited the blessings over the kindling of the candles and sang a song in celebration of their people's courage to remain loyal to Torah despite oppression and public derision. Although for Jews the streets of Western civilization were often dark and bleak, the soul of the Jew was aflame.

Today, because of the rebirth of the State of Israel, Jews can place their menorahs on the windowsills of history. We need not speak among ourselves only; we may share our flame with the outside world. Judaism is visible in the marketplace of history because of the courage of those modern Maccabees who set into motion the process of rebuilding our people in its ancient homeland.

The challenge facing Judaism today is not only whether we can withstand our enemies but also whether the light visible in the marketplace radiates a profound and compelling message. Now that the menorah has been taken off our private tables and placed in the window for all to see, we must examine whether the light itself is beautiful and inspiring.

Many traditional Jews believe that Jewish particularity is incompatible with modern mass culture and that the Judaic bonds holding together the community cannot bear the stress caused by exposure to the cultural rhythms of the larger non-Jewish society. According to this school of thought, Hanukkah celebrates the Maccabees' courageous repudiation of the world culture of their time, Hellenism. "Hellenistic" and "Hellenization" have become derisive terms,

---

3. *Babylonian Talmud Shabbat* 21b

which connote the assimilating Jew, the cultural opportunist without deep roots in his community's value system. Those who accept this assessment of Judaism in the modern world turn to social and cultural separation in order to secure Judaism's survival.

There are others who are skeptical as to whether this ghettoization can succeed. Modern communication makes it impossible to escape acculturation to modern "Hellenism." It is, in their opinion, futile to resist. We should accept our fate and accommodate ourselves to the inevitability of our eventual assimilation.

A third option rejects the defeatism of the latter point of view and also the separatism of the former. We question the belief that Judaism has always survived because of its radical separation from the surrounding culture. Hanukkah does not commemorate a total rejection of Hellenism but, as the historian Elias Bickerman shows in *From Ezra to the Last of the Maccabees*, the revolt focused specifically on those aspects of foreign rule, which expressly aimed at weakening loyalty to the God of Israel.

The major question, which we must ponder on Hanukkah, is whether the Jewish people can develop an identity that will enable it to meet the outside world without feeling threatened or intimidated. The choice, hopefully, need not be ghettoization or assimilation.

We can absorb from others without being smothered. We can appreciate and assimilate that which derives from "foreign" sources and at the same time feel firmly anchored to our particular frame of reference. That, however, requires that we gain an intelligent appreciation of the basic values of our tradition. Learning was not essential for our grandfathers because they were insulated by their cultural and physical Jewish ghetto. In order for the Jew to leave the protective framework of that ghetto it is necessary for him to have a personal sense of Jewish self-worth and dignity.

Jewish self-enlightenment is a prerequisite for opening our windows to the marketplace. Then we can absorb as well as propagate light.

> Jewish self-enlightenment is a prerequisite for opening our windows to the marketplace. Then we can absorb as well as propagate light.

---

2. DANIEL GORDIS

THE MIRACLE OF JEWISH SURVIVAL[4]

Hanukkah candles have to be situated in a place where they can be seen from the outside. Jewish tradition calls this dimension of the ritual *pirsuma de-nissa*, "the proclamation of the miracle." [But what's the miracle and is it one we still wish to proclaim? To whom is this message directed?]

It is ironic: at times, the non-Jewish world seems to understand this message better than the Jews themselves. **Blaise Pascal** (1623-1662), a Catholic Frenchman, both physicist and theologian, said of the Jews:

> This people is not eminent solely by its antiquity, but is also singular by its **duration**, which has always continued from its origin till now. For whereas the nations of Greece and of . . . Rome and others who came long after, have

4. Daniel Gordis, *Does the World Need the Jews?* (Simon and Schuster/Scribner, 1997, by permission from pages 110-111, 119, 122, 129-132). Gordis, the founder of the California Conservative Seminary, is now Director of the Jerusalem Fellows for prominent Jewish educators.

long since perished, [the Jewish people] ever remains — in spite of the endeavors of many powerful kings who have a hundred times tried to destroy it.

Similarly, when the eighteenth-century French writer — and notorious anti-Semite — **Voltaire** (1694-1778) discussed the possibility of miracles with the Prussian king Fredrick the Great, the king challenged him to point to one authentic example of a miracle. "Sire," Voltaire is reputed to have replied, "the Jews."

Jews have often said the same of themselves. When the biblical prophet Malachi, speaking several hundred years before the Common Era, seeks to remind the Jews of God's power, he points to the fact that they had not disappeared in the face of adversity. In the midst of chastising them for their

---

Hanukkah became a holiday about survival, about the spirit overpowering the sword, about good overcoming evil, and about the few — if their cause is just — ultimately vanquishing the many.

---

lapsed faith, he reminds them of miracles they do not appreciate: *"For I am the Lord — I have not changed; and you are the children of Jacob — you have not ceased to be."*[5] The mere fact that the Jews have not "ceased to be" strikes both Voltaire and the prophet Malachi as virtually miraculous.

Mark Twain was also impressed by the **Jews' secret of immortality**. He wrote in his article *"Concerning the Jews"*:

[The Jew] has made a marvelous fight in this world, in all the ages; and has done it with his hands tied behind him. He could be vain of himself, and be excused for it. The Egyptian, the Babylonian, and the Persian rose, filled the planet with sound and splendor, then faded to dream-stuff and passed away. The Greek and the Roman followed, and

made a vast noise, and they are gone; other peoples have sprung up and held their torch high for a time, but it burned out, and they sit in twilight now, or have vanished. The Jew saw them all, beat them all, and is now what he always was, exhibiting no decadence, no infirmities of age, no weakening of his parts, no slowing of his energies, no dulling of his alert and aggressive mind. All things are mortal but the Jew; all other forces pass, but he remains. What is the secret of his immortality?

Hyperbolic, to be sure. But as Jews search for an authentic and compelling identity in modernity, as we seek our authentic voice once again, Twain reminds us of an obvious but forgotten truth: **our very survival is part of our message**. Hanukkah is about the tenacity of the Jews, but more broadly, it is about the persistence of good, the endurance of the weak. Hanukkah thus urges modern Jews to reflect on their survival, to wonder how we have persevered beyond all expectation, how it is that in spite of all the obstacles thrown our way, our history still inspired Voltaire — who hated Jews — to speak of us as a miracle.

For the rabbis, Hanukkah was not just a celebration of military victory. Nor was it simply about the miracle of the cruse of oil, as important as that was to their conception of the festival. Rather, Hanukkah became a holiday about survival, about the spirit overpowering the sword, about goodness overcoming evil, and about the few — if their cause is just — ultimately vanquishing the many.

[The way the Rabbis, Hillel in particular, shaped the candle lighting ceremony involves an ever increasing number of lights each night.] As they increase in number each evening, the flames are meant to reassure other peoples who worry that their own blazes will die out. The ritual responds by assuring them that the power of their community, their people, their culture and their tradition will not decrease, but will actually increase. The growing number of

---

5. *Malachi 3:6*

To be a Jew
is a matter of
making a
statement,
of reminding
the world of
the possibility
of survival for
those who
would seem to
have no hope.

candles is the ritual's way of saying, "you will not dwindle, but rather, you will grow."

As each evening of Hanukkah comes, Jews around their Hanukkiot (the plural of Hanukkiah) are treated to a sort of ritual dance. It is not a dance of people, but a dance of flames and wicks. As the candles burn low, or as the oil in the Hanukkiah gradually runs out, the fires do not simply disappear. For the last few moments of their burning, they flicker, seemingly ready to be extinguished, when suddenly they leap back to life. Just when it seems that the flame is gone, it suddenly revives. One moment there is darkness, and next, light is reborn and renewed. There is a beauty, an almost magical quality, to this display. It is a quasi-desperate exhibition, a suggestion that the fire does not want to die. It struggles desperately to live. Though the flame will eventually die out, our response is to light the flames again the next evening, adding an additional candle or wick to the collection, making our point that we simply will not allow the lights to go out.

That is the point of Hanukkah. It is about lights, but not only the lights of the candles. Hanukkah proclaims and insists that the downtrodden, the powerless, the dispossessed and the all but vanquished are these flames.

"We have survived, apparently against all odds," we say to the world, "and we believe that you can — and will — as well."

By making the Hanukkah lights a public ritual, noticeable by all, Jewish tradition reminds us that Hanukkah is not about us alone, but about peoples and nations everywhere. That is why we do not allow the lights to go out; and that is why we place them in a public place. The ritualized dance of the frail and fragile flames is a tenacious struggle the entire world needs to witness.

To be a Jew thus becomes a matter of making a statement, of reminding the world of the possibility of survival for those who would seem to have no hope, of speaking with an authentic and distinct historical voice that has something of value to say to human beings wherever they may languish. That is a dimension of Judaism that is unique; it is authentically Jewish. And it does not make Jews out to be better or innately superior. It is a distinctly Jewish role, for it emerges out of an engagement with Jewish tradition and Jewish texts. And today more than ever, it is a role that matters, that can make a difference. That is the point of *pirsuma de-nissa*, "the proclamation of the miracle."

Harold M. Schulweis

LIGHTING THAT FIRST CANDLE
TO MAKE A SOMETHING OUT OF SOMETHING

The second blessing over the Hanukkah lights praises God for performing miracles "in those days at this season." A rabbinic observation questions the propriety of this benediction for the *first* evening. For if the miracle refers to the small amount of oil in the sanctuary lamp that lasted seven days beyond its normal capacity, why speak of miracles on the first night? After all, on the first night there was sufficient oil present, and its burning was natural enough. That part of the blessing on the first evening appears superfluous. The benediction for miracles, then, should only be recited on the second night.

One commentator explains that the reason we recite the blessing for miracles even on the first night is because there are all kinds of miracles in the world. Creation, for example, is a miracle in which something is created out of nothing. Theologians call such an act "*creatio ex nihilo*" or in Hebrew *yesh me-ayin*. But there are other miracles that refer to acts that create something out of something (*yesh me-yesh*). The first night's blessing over the oil that was present illustrates the second type of miracle, one that makes something out of something; something sacred out of some ordinary material already existing. Those kinds of miracles require human initiative and activity. Humans do not create the world out of nothing. The world is given to us. But humans can change the world, shape it according to whatever image is in our heart and mind. And when the transformation is done for the sake of God and goodness it is miraculous.

On the first evening of Hanukkah, before the match is struck to light the candle, we are literally in the dark. We cannot make out faces or things in the unlit room. There are obstacles all about us, partitions, walls, pieces

---

Miracles are experienced through the capacity of human beings to turn the real into the ideal. Miracles create something out of something, something transcendent out of something ordinary.

---

of furniture. When the candle is lit we see that nothing in the room has changed. Things are as they were in the dark. But with that instant illumination we experience a revelation. In the flash of that momentary light we know where things are, what obstacles are to be avoided. In that moment we are oriented to the world about us. Nothing new had been created except our awareness of the environment that gives us greater opportunity to choose, to know where to stand and where to move. We can make something out of something. Our capacity to discover wonders and signs is a gift for which we offer thanks thrice daily, evening, morn, and noon: "You grace the human being with knowledge and give him the power to understand."

In many cultures miracles signify strange, mysterious, unnatural events like a man walking on water or flying in the air. But in

the language of our tradition, Hebrew, the word for miracle is *nes*. It means "sign," from whose root the term "significance" is derived. To witness the miraculous is to observe in an ordinary event extraordinary significance, an event so important that it cries to be raised up and celebrated. The victory in the second century over the Greek-Syrian forces that sought to extinguish Jewish freedom is a *nes*, a signpost in our history that points to the direction of our lives. Hanukkah is the celebrated significance of the Jewish ideal of religious freedom.

The world in which we live is real. The swords and spears and elephants of the Greek-Syrians were real, as were the strengths of the Maccabeans. Miracles are experienced through the capacity of human beings to turn the real into the ideal. Miracles create something out of something, something transcendent out of something ordinary. The paragraph added to the *Amidah* and to the grace after meals during the eight days of Hanukkah celebrates the significance of transformation, "for You have delivered the strong into the hands of the weak, the many into the hands of the few."

The sense of sign-significance applies to our daily lives. We cannot often create or alter the given, change the diseases, accidents, misfortunes dealt out to us. We can, more often than we expect, make something out of them, create something out of something. Negative experiences can be converted into affirmations of life. Adversity may be used to refine the human spirit, to bring forth courage and compassion never suspected. The triumph of the human spirit over tragedy is a divine-human encounter, a creation of something of transcendent meaning formed out of something common.

What happened on the fifth day of Iyar in our time — the day of Israel's independence — reaffirms the miracle, *nes*, that took place on the twenty-fifth of Kislev over two thousand years ago. The Hanukkah lights remind us that miracles are as real as the transforming power of ideals.

TWO KINDS OF HERO FROM THE MACCABEAN ERA
THE HASIDIC MARTYR VERSUS THE INNOVATIVE ZEALOT[6]

The battle against the Syrian Greeks and their representatives, the radical Jewish Hellenizers was fought by a coalition of traditionalists and moderates. The traditionalists were called Pietists (Hasidim) and they constituted the first religious group in history to voluntarily choose martyrdom over religious assimilation. Later, the Hasmonean family of Mattathias the priest and Judah the Maccabee his son began the activist military revolt against Hellenist tyranny. The success of the revolt depended on the ability to enlist both the Pietists and the moderate Jews who had found ways to accommodate Judaism and Hellenism. This model of coalition building has important implications for a contemporary strategy for Jewish survival in the West.

Rabbi Irving (Yitz) Greenberg reviews the historic "political" parties of the Maccabean revolt and draws out the implications of this model. Rabbi Greenberg, a liberal Orthodox rabbi, created CLAL — an organization dedicated to intrafaith dialogue, coalition building and Torah study for Jewish leaders of all denominations.

The Pietists (Hasidim) —
The First Martyrs in History.

Throughout Judea there were groups of pious Jews — called Pietists (Hasidim) — who were most unhappy with the Hellenizing pressures of the Greek King Antiochus and of the followers of Jason and Menelaus [radical Hellenizers who bought the office of High Priest-cum-Governor of Judea by bribing Antiochus IV]. The Hasidim believed, however, that they were bound by the Torah not to revolt against any foreign king who ruled over them. The foreign king was the "rod of God's anger," and Jews must accept their fate. If they repented, God would redeem them. If the king exceeded his role and harmed Jews excessively, God alone could and would punish him.

[Then a money-starved Antiochus sent his army to plunder the gold utensils of the Temple]. The sack of the Temple stunned the Hasidim. The First Temple was destroyed at God's will because of Jewish sinfulness. This second sack could only mean that the Lord was angered at Jewish Hellenizing apostasy and at the failure of pious Jews to do something about it. Some of the Pietists began to attack and harass the "wicked Antiochenes" (Jewish Hellenists) in Jerusalem.

To Antiochus, the turmoil in Jerusalem brought a long-standing concern to a head. He was seeking to unify the world. Yet here were the stubborn, rebellious Jews refusing to worship with the citizens of the empire and harassing those Jews who were responsive to the new universal dispensation. Antiochus decided that the obstreperous fanatics must go; Judaism must be "purified" to be a conforming citizen religion of the great Greek Syrian Seleucid Empire. And so he issued a series of edicts. On penalty of death, all Jews must cease observing the Torah; instead they must follow an imposed, "purified" Judaism. An Athenian expert was sent in to direct the practices of the "purified," that is, universalized Judaism. Monthly sacrifices to the gods were begun. Sacred prostitution was set up in the Temple. A statue of Zeus was erected, and Zeus' name was associated with the Temple. The offering included the sacrifice of pigs on the altar. The laws of purity of the Temple were systematically violated.

It should be noted that Antiochus was not imposing his own faith in these decrees. He seems to have concluded that this is what pure Judaism would have been, had it been truly a religion with decent respect for the opinion of mankind. It was neither the first nor the last time in Jewish history that a "universalist," determined to straighten out the Jews and/or

6. Irving Greenberg, *The Jewish Way: Living the Holidays*, pp. 260-265, 278-280, reprinted by permission of Simon and Schuster, copyright 1988 by Irving Greenberg.

Judaism, showed gross ignorance of the faith, condition, and integrity of the Jews.

Had these "recalcitrant" traditional Jews been prone to philosophize, they might have argued that it was important for Judaism not to disappear, but since they were untutored city folk and farmers, they could not articulate a philosophic defense of their position. They only knew the old ways and clung to them passionately, outragedly, doggedly. The Hellenists smiled condescendingly.

Backed by the power of the king and the growing religious indifference of the elite, the rituals of Zeus worship and pig sacrifice were extended widely and successfully throughout Judea. Hellenization seemed unstoppable. The few who resisted were arrested, punished, and slain. The king's order proscribing the Torah was enforced with a vengeance. Sabbath observers and those who practiced circumcision were condemned to death.

In their simple faith, the Pietists believed that as long as Jews were faithful to God they were under divine protection, yet obedience to God's commandments had become a crime punishable by extreme severity. They also

---

Yet martyrdom alone could not have stopped the massed power of the Seleucids and Hellenizers. In Hasidic reasoning, apocalypse was the only hope left.

---

believed that it was sinful to revolt against the king. As more and more innocents were put to death, a significant fraction of the Hasidim concluded that the only resistance possible was to remain faithful and die for God's commandments. And so the concept of **martyrdom** developed into an ideal. The stature of the prophet and the martyr became merged into one: the highest stage of serving God.

The willingness to make this greatest of sacrifices, to die rather than to deny the Lord, became central in Jewish (and later Christian)

testimony in the following centuries. Immortality and resurrection — ideas that heretofore had hardly played a role in Judaism — became central in Hasidic thinking. The promise of eternal life and rebirth undergirded the strength of Hasidic faith. This devotion should have warned the Syrians and their Hellenizing collaborators of stiffening resistance.

Yet martyrdom alone could not have stopped the massed power of the Seleucids and Hellenizers. In Hasidic reasoning, **apocalypse** was the only hope left. Indeed, had the Hasidism survived the persecution and won out within the Jewish community, the religion would have been decisively turned onto a path of pacifism, apocalyptic expectation, and denigration of secular life and human activity. The classic dialectic that moored Judaism in daily life would have been decisively broken.

The Maccabees — From Martyrdom to Revolt

In 167 BCE, in the town of Modiin, the new sacrificial cult was introduced. The resentment at the forced paganization and the desecration of the altar with the unclean pig boiled over in an act of rebellion. Mattathias, a priest of Modiin, stabbed a Jew who sacrificed in the new cult, killed the king's agent, and pulled down the sacrilegious altar.

Mattathias' social position made him the natural person to lead a revolt. He was a priest of a small town — not Jerusalem. He combined in himself enough aristocratic status and exposure to Hellenism to be a leader. At the same time he was a "country" man who shared the conservative party's position and was detached enough and rival enough to fight the Jerusalem priests and their policies.

Elias Bickerman, a noted scholar, has pointed out that Mattathias did not demand the right of freedom of religion, nor did he fight for individual conscience. **This was "a conflict between earthly power and the**

law of the state of God" — opposition to a King's order that was at variance with the commandments of God.

Mattathias shared the Pietists' faithfulness to Judaism. Where, then, did he find sanction to revolt against the king in defiance of what appeared to be the prophets' repeated strictures that the children of Israel not revolt against kings "whom the Lord had placed over them." Mattathias justified his act by analogy with the **act of zealotry** of the Biblical priest Pinchas in the desert, striking down Zimri, [for his attempt to lead Jews to pagan worship]. That act — unjustified by law and in contradiction to the priestly role — was validated after the fact by God's blessing.[7] Mattathias dared to assert that a king who commanded the violation of the Torah could not rule Jews by divine right. In effect, Mattathias was operating out of a covenantal model in which humans could not "leave it all to God" but had to initiate some action to save the Torah and the Jews. In some

Hasidim's conception, God did everything; humans only observed, repented, persisted, and waited on the Lord for deliverance. Significant numbers of Hasidim were highly critical of Mattathias' action as impious.

This split is not a simple case of **Maccabees versus Hasidim**. The controversy between Mattathias and the main wing of the Pietists was over how to properly apply their shared values. Mattathias and his men were saying that God had given a significant role to humans, including the authority to apply the principles of the tradition creatively. As for the passive, passionate Pietists, theirs was not to question why, theirs was but to do or die.

Mattathias and his five sons fled to the mountains to escape the government's punishment for their act of political terrorism. They were joined by other Jews, among whom were militant Hasidim who came over to Mattathias' view of the right to fight.

---

7. *Numbers* 25:6-13

Irving Greenberg

COALITION BUILDING IN THE DAYS OF THE MACCABEES AND TODAY:

IN PRAISE OF ZEALOUS TRADITIONALISTS AND MODERATE MODERNISTS

In Praise of Stubborn Pietists (the Hasidic Martyrs)

Those stubborn Hasidim raised a subtle issue of political existence and religious truth that is only coming into its own in the twentieth century. Ultimately, the touchstone of human survival will be the ability of people with passionately held beliefs and absolute commitments to allow for pluralism. National peace will turn on the capacity of groups organized around values to allow the inherent dignity of the other into their own structures. How to achieve this respect without surrendering to indifference or group selfishness is the great challenge. On

Hanukkah, Jews celebrate that challenge and affirm the Jewish determination never again to let universal rhetoric ("to make the world safe for . . . ") cripple the Jews' right to defend themselves. On Hanukkah, Jews urge humankind to take responsibility for the varieties and multiforms of human life. Hanukkah is also a profoundly Zionist holiday, for it asserts the right of politically self-determined existence for each group.

Hanukkah is a paradigm of the relationship

What model of Hanukkah can speak to our generation? [Hanukkah is about] the clash of the universal with the particular. Hellenism saw itself as the universal human culture, open to all. [Maccabean Judaism saw itself as a defense of a particular religious way of life.] Mattathias, Judah Maccabee, and the brave people who saved Judaism were not fighting for a pluralist Judea. They were fighting against the state's enforcement of Hellenist worship because they believed it was a betrayal of Israel's covenant with God. When, after decades of fighting, they liberated Jerusalem and purified the Temple, they established a state in which Jews could worship God in the right way — not in just any way. Hanukkah is not a model for total separation of church and state.

The Maccabee victory saved particularist Judaism. It preserved the stubborn **Jewish insistence on "doing their own thing" religiously**; never mind the claims of universalism that only if all are citizens of one world and one faith will there truly be one humanity. By not disappearing, Jews have continued to force the world — down to this day — to accept the limits of centralization. Jewish existence has been a continued stumbling block to whatever political philosophy, religion, or economic system has claimed the right to abolish all distinctions for "the higher good of humanity." Since the centralizing forces often turned oppressive or obliterated local cultures and dignity, **this Jewish resistance to homogenization has been a blessing to humanity and a continuing source of religious pluralism for everybody, not just the Jews**.

In this time, too, many universal cultures — Marxism and Communism, triumphalist Christianity, certain forms of liberalism and radicalism, fascism, even monolithic Americanism — have demanded that Jews dissolve and become part of humankind. All these philosophies have claimed that Jews can depend on their principles and structures to provide for Jewish rights. The Maccabee revolution made clear that a universalism that denies the rights of the particular to exist is inherently totalitarian and will end up oppressing people in the name of one humanity. Universalism must surrender its overweening demands and accept the **universalism of pluralism**. Only when the world admits that oneness comes out of particular existences, linked through overarching unities, will it escape the inner dynamics of conformity that lead to repression and cruelty.

between acculturation and assimilation. The final victory of Hanukkah was set in motion by the resistance of the most traditional elements — many of them "square" country folk — to the growing encroachment of Hellenistic values. In many ways, the rebels were in greater conflict with their fellow Hellenizing Jews than with the Hellenes. The arrogant universalism in Hellenism demanded that Jews give up their distinctive religious ways for the greater good. Many Jews agreed, but the Pietists did not.

Hanukkah dramatizes the positive strength of Pietism, of Hasidism's unquestioning loyalty to Judaism. It challenges modern Jews to review their own easy acceptance of cosmopolitanism and sophisticated culture as superior to the sentiment and tribal feeling of being Jews. It asks whether, consciously or unconsciously, modern Jews share part of the Hellenizing, assimilating majority. Like the crisis of the Holocaust and threats to Israel, it forces people to face up to the issues: Are they ultimately Jews? In an ultimate crisis of loyalties, would one choose Jewish survival?

People who would never consider a Hebrew day school for their child, because what is American comes first, are making Judaism a secondary loyalty. People who would be more upset if their child married an Orthodox Jew than if their child married a Gentile have really made a determination of primary loyalty. The lesson of Hanukkah is that a strong priority to being Jewish is the key to right choices in Jewish history. Sometimes one should not reason. There has to be a primordial will to Jewishness first or to Israel's survival first. The reasoning and the willingness to negotiate some issues come second.

In Praise of Dynamic Moderates (the Maccabean Rebels) and Coalition Building

At the same time, it is not enough to be stubborn or to ignore the surrounding culture. This tactic works only when Jews are isolated. It was not working in the big cities of Judea in the second century BCE, and it will not likely work well in the highly magnetic culture/society of today.

The Hasidim of those days could not have won the battle alone. In the conflict, many Hellenizing Jews decided to stand by their fellow Jews rather than by the Greeks. **A coalition won the victory of Hanukkah — the traditionalists united with acculturating Jews who decided to come down on the Jewish side.**

The entire process [of resisting Hellenist religious coercion] forced a choice on many Jews who had been drifting into Hellenism. In the crunch, seeing their Jewish brothers defending their home soil, seeing the destruction of local Jewish populations to advance the interests of Syrians, made many people decide that they were primordially Jews, not Hellenists. Judah and his band might never have succeeded but for the shift of moderate Hellenizers to the side of the revolt. Thus, what started as a revolt of the fundamentalists became a viable coalition of simple traditionalism and moderate Hellenization.

The Hasidim's simple faith was their great strength, but their non-analytic obedience to the law made them vulnerable. The *First*

Without fundamentalism there would have been no Maccabean revolt. Without moderate Hellenization the revolt would not have succeeded.

Book of Maccabees tells how a band of Hasidim was trapped in a cave on the Sabbath by a Syrian/Hellenizer army. The Jews, refusing to fight or even to wall up the caves on the holy day, were killed without offering resistance.

Mattathias and his band, however, resolved to defend themselves if attacked on the Sabbath. The Rabbis formulated this principle. "*You shall observe my statutes and laws that a man shall do and live by them* — and not die by them . . . From this we learn that life saving overrides the Sabbath." Ultimately,

this principle was generalized in the ruling that every commandment of Torah except three — idolatry, murder, and certain sexual immoralities — can be overridden to save life.

Unlike the Hasidim, who left everything to God, the Maccabees drew upon the covenantal model in which humans were called to take action and to make judgments about the appropriateness of that action. It is not that the Hasmoneans did not believe in the divinity of the commandments; it is that they were able to ask different questions of the Torah: Is there a goal to be reached? Is there a priority when principles conflict? Is there a role for human judgment and action in executing the covenant?

The development by the Maccabees of a hierarchy of value — which in this case expressed itself in priority for life — reflects a philosophical influence. The concept of a fundamental principle that expresses itself in all commandments, and that guides the resolution of conflicts of values, draws upon philosophic, literary, and rhetorical analysis of texts and their relationships. Exposure to Hellenist modes of thinking and philosophy evoked greater depth and sensitivity to such thinking in the Maccabean and later leadership — just as contact with more developed literary and philosophic models enriched traditional rabbis' capacity for halachic and narrative thinking in the past two centuries. Such thinking became a hallmark of the Maccabees and the later rabbis. They responded respectfully to Hellenism's ideas and methods, but only where they could enrich and be assimilated compatibly with the tradition.

In short, **without fundamentalism there would have been no Maccabean revolt; without moderate Hellenization the revolt would not have succeeded**. The differences between these allies led to significant splits later on and to errors on both sides. Yet, without the coalition, the Maccabean Jews very likely would have been destroyed.[8]

---

8. *The Jewish Way*, p. 264-265.

Finding the Middle Way: Acculturation without Assimilation.

The Rabbis deepened Judaism to cope with a dynamic civilization, one with more highly developed cultural models. In that response, Judaism rose to new heights of competence and developed the ability to swim in the sea of Hellenism. The present host culture of Jewry is even more developed, magnetic, and challenging. Jews and Judaism will have to master the field. **Properly done, acculturation (modernizing) is an alternative to assimilation.** Since no one group can offer all the answers for all the life situations or cope with all the options in society, it becomes very important to form coalitions to cover the field, to correct one another, to give Jewry the strength of variety and numbers.

The further lesson of Hanukkah is not to write off assimilating Jews. In a showdown (as in 1967 and 1973), many more Jews will be with the cause of Jewish survival than appears on the surface. A coalition of traditional, acculturating, and assimilating Jews pulled off the Maccabee miracle. What is needed is a coalition and symbiosis of traditional Jews, modernizing Jews, and those assimilating Jews who can still be reached. The real task is to begin the "guerrilla warfare" that weans people from their excessive absorption in the status quo and liberates them for authentic Jewish existence.

4. JUDITH A. KATES

JUDITH, THE HIDDEN HEROINE OF HANUKKAH
FROM VIRGIN VICTIM TO SEDUCTIVE SAVIOR

Judith Kates, a professor of Jewish literature,[9] stands in the forefront of Jewish women reclaiming and reshaping their Jewish literary heritage. She finds an interpretative key to understanding the invasion and desecration of the Temple by the Greeks in the ancient historical romance about her namesake Judith. Though this story has no explicit connection to the Maccabees, Jewish tradition has always associated it with Hanukkah and Judith Kates offers a deeper reading of Judith that shows why.[10]

The Sacred Enclosure Threatened

The *Book of Judith* presents us with a stark, yet stirring, image of the land and people of Israel under threat. At its narrative core, an enormous battering ram of an invading army, significantly numbered as 120,000 infantry and 12,000 cavalry, is arrayed against the mere "12" — the symbolic total of the tribes of Israel, reduced further in this story to two individuals — and women at that! With this vast force poised to invade the literal and figurative central space of the Jewish people, the text draws our attention to Jerusalem and the Temple at its center. *"When the Israelites who lived in Judea heard of all that had been done to the nations by Holofernes . . . and how he had plundered and totally destroyed all their temples, they were terrified at his approach. They were in great*

9. Dr. Judith A. Kates is Professor of Jewish Women's Studies at Hebrew College, Brookline, MA and co-editor, with Gail Twersky Reimer, of *Beginning Anew: A Woman's Companion to the High Holy Days* (1997) and *Reading Ruth: Contemporary Women Reclaim a Sacred Story* (1994).

10. Quotations from *Judith* are based on *The New English Bible*; quotations from the Hebrew Bible are from *JPS Hebrew-English Tanakh* (Jewish Publication Society, 1999). My translation-paraphrase of the midrash is based on a text in A. Jellinek, *Beit HaMidrash,* vol. 1. My thinking on the Temple as inner space analogous to the female body has been influenced by Bonna Devora Haberman, "The Yom Kippur Avoda within the Female Enclosure" in *Beginning Anew: A Woman's Companion to the High Holy Days* and on Judith as representative of the Jewish community by Amy-Jill Levine, "Sacrifice and Salvation: Otherness and Domestication in the Book of Judith" in *A Feminist Companion to Esther, Judith and Susanna.*

alarm for Jerusalem and for the Temple of the Lord their God." The geographical setting of our story, the town of Bethulia, is chosen because its inhabitants can *"occupy the passes into the hill-country, because they controlled access to Judea, and it was easy to hold up an advancing army, for the approach was only wide enough for two men."*[11] The "high priest in Jerusalem at that time" looks to the men to hold tight, like the Greek heroes at Thermopylae, to this narrow entrance to the open, vulnerable and infinitely precious space occupied by the Temple.

As in later rabbinic texts in which the word *"bayit"* (house or home) is understood to refer to the woman whose place it is, here the *bayit* of the Jewish people is personified as a virgin threatened with violent penetration.

Throughout the narrative, we are reminded of this **sacred enclosure** as the symbolic goal and motivation for action. The heroine and chief actor in this story initiates her action with prayer, *"at the time when the evening incense was being offered in the Temple in Jerusalem,"*[12] and as her final deed, leads her people to Jerusalem where they engage in the quintessential rituals of Temple worship — *"As soon as the people were purified, they offered their burnt-offerings, freewill offerings and gifts."* Judith herself dedicates to God *"all Holofernes' possessions"* including the bed net, symbol of the sexually charged strategy of her triumph, which she transforms into *"a votive offering."*

The Temple, *Beit Hamikdash*, (literally "house" or "home of the holy place") figures as both symbol and microcosm of the homeland, the household of the people. It creates a tangible place where human connection to God, the source of physical and spiritual life, is made manifest and secured. Its spatial configuration draws our awareness inward toward increasingly private spaces of intensifying divine energy and presence,

spaces both precious and dangerous. In the symbolic field of the Temple, moving inside means going both higher and deeper, closer to the divine and to the source of all energy, all life. Penetration of this sacred enclosure requires awe, careful preparation, respect for boundaries, and is limited to legitimate "members of the household." Yet this very space, in the *Book of Judith*, is the goal of an invading force which has already violated the outer circle surrounding it, the homeland, Eretz Yisrael. In telling its story of an "Assyrian" general who seeks to destroy the Temple and to require that *"Nebuchadnezzar alone should be worshipped by every nation,"*[13] this text parallels the Hanukkah narrative of Antiochus. The story of Hanukkah becomes, through this parallel, the trauma of the invaded sacred enclosure, the *Beit Hamikdash* and the larger *bayit*, the homeland that surrounds it.

The language of the *Book of Judith* invites us to perceive this sacred inner space not only as geographical location, but also as the human core of the Jewish people. As in later rabbinic texts in which the word *"bayit"* (house or home) is understood to refer to the woman whose place it is, here **the *bayit* of the Jewish people is personified as a virgin threatened with violent penetration**. Invasion of the land, destruction of the Temple, is a rape. The town on the hill passes, chosen to defend the narrow, tightly closed access to that vulnerable inner space, is called Bethulia, which resonates with the Hebrew *"betulah"* — virgin. The land overrun by a huge invading army, the besieged city whose people are so tormented that they are on the verge of opening their gates to penetration, and most especially the Temple, a place whose innermost space is its most lifegiving, are the precious and beautiful woman, the *"enclosed garden"*[14] violated. Land, people and Temple, the heart of both, figure here as the infinitely vulnerable, virginal female body, with its fragile, narrow opening guarded by increasingly feeble defenses against the overwhelming thrust of the aggressor.

---

11. *Judith 4*   12. *Judith 9*   13. *Judith 3*   14. *Song of Songs* 4:12

"The Jewish Woman" as Rescued or as Rescuer?

What astonishes us in *Judith* is the persona of the rescuer. Salvation for the threatened virgin in this narrative comes not through a Maccabee-like warrior, but through a woman. Even more surprisingly, her tools of rescue are not only her faith, brilliant intellect and eloquent speech, but also the femaleness of her body, that very sexuality apparently mobilized in the text to represent vulnerability and victimization. The text, with consummate literary artistry, weaves a tapestry out of allusions to earlier narratives found in the Hebrew Bible to create a character who will both echo and transform representations of women as saviors of the Jewish people.

Her name itself, Judith, as many scholars have suggested, seems designed to point to her role as epitome of the nation —- *Yehudit* in Hebrew and *ioudeit* in Greek — meaning "the Jewish woman." But this representative function is complicated by apparent contradictions from our first introduction to her. Later Biblical, as well as much Second Temple period literature, frequently personifies the community, *knesset yisrael*, as a woman, either powerless, suffering victim in need of protection and rescue or faithless wife, straying after other loves. Conventional connotations would suggest that Judith, who is not only woman but widow, constantly in mourning, represents the community through the figure commonly invoked in the Torah for the most vulnerable and needy of humans. In the context of this narrative, we might perceive widowhood at its most extreme, the woman/community bereft and abandoned, about to fall before a ruthless predator.

The Zionist "Judith:" The Victim Turned Avenger[15]

In 1965 "Judith" in Daniel Mann's movie is played by Sophia Loren who portrays a Jewish Holocaust survivor who had been married to a Nazi officer now hidden in Syria (the original home of the Biblical Holofernes the Assyrian). He is helping the Arab armies with the tactics necessary to exterminate the new Jewish state. Judith/Sophia Loren joins forces with the Israeli Mossad to assassinate her husband.

The movie echoes both the murder of the Assyrian General Holofernes by his bedmate, the enemy Jewess, and the contemporary struggle of post Holocaust Israel to create a self-reliant militarily independent nation by overcoming its previous passivity during the Holocaust. The movie rests on the factual basis that German scientists did work for the Arabs and that Adolph Eichmann, the Nazi arch-exterminator, who fled to Argentina, was eventually hunted down by the Israeli Mossad with the help of his discarded mistress who "betrayed" him. But equally it builds on the romantic image of the Israeli woman soldier who fought "like a man" in the War of Independence in 1948. In a sense the Jewish people's former passivity was identified with "feminine weakness" but now the woman had turned the table on the nation that had raped her.

The psychologist and concentration camp inmate Bruno Bettelheim recalls that in the camps most people were deprived of the ability to regard themselves as autonomous beings. The capacity to resist was the sure way to restore their self-image as human beings. Once a woman prisoner, who may have been sexually abused, grabbed the gun of a Nazi officer and shot him to death [as Judith had taken Holofernes' sword to decapitate him].

But this widow is given an enormously long genealogy, connecting her back through names associated with the tribe of Shimon (Salamiel-Shelumiel, Sarasadae, Zurishaddai) all the way to Israel-Jacob. She is described as wealthy, beautiful (using the same Greek phrases that are used for the beauty of Rachel and Esther in the Greek translation of the Bible), extraordinarily pious and respected. She is introduced at a moment of communal crisis, when the city has been under siege for 34 days and its leaders have given God 5 more days to "show his mercy" before surrendering on what would be the 40th day of the siege. She herself has lived secluded as a widow for 3 years and 4 months — that is for 40 months, the confluence of communal and personal units of 40 suggesting the significant spans of time in which crucial leaders have transformed the history of the people of Israel

15. Editor's summary based on Margarita Stocker, *Judith: The Sexual Warrior*, p.200-203.

Under the watchful censorship of the church, wealthy Renaissance patrons' desire for sexually alluring pin-up girls for their mistresses' bedroom or bathroom could be satisfied best by painting the chaste but seductive Biblical Judith with Holofernes her lover. Sometimes these Biblical heroines decorated the anterooms of a high class brothel in which local prostitutes served as models for the artists who specialized in this field of commercial portraiture, especially in Rembrandt's Netherlands.

Even the darker side of the painting of Judith who betrayed her would-be male lover and slit his throat without remorse could appeal to masculine fantasies of sado-masochistic sex. In fact, the inventor of this term and this genre, the Polish anti-semite Leopold Sacher-Masoch (1870) portrays his novel's hero as idolizing Holofernes: "I envied the hero Holofernes because of the regal woman who cut off his head with a sword and because of his beautiful sanguinary end." Thus one could "love" Judith knowing and desiring to be dominated and emasculated by her betrayal.

---

16. Editor's summary based on Margarita Stocker, *Judith: The Sexual Warrior*, p. 28-30, 38, 176-177).

(Moses, Joshua, Deborah). We see her summoning the leaders of Bethulia (including the chief magistrate, also from the tribe of Shimon but the antithesis of his ancestor in activism) to teach them the deficiencies in their theology and to re-interpret the meaning of this historical crisis. Most crucially, she declares that her action on behalf of the community will not simply be prayer, as conventional expectations of the role of pious widow (and the male leader) suggest, but that she herself will take on the role of protector — rescuer and "go out" to save the people.[17]

The constant reiteration of Judith (and her female servant) going out (from Bethulia and then, back and forth from the enemy camp), highlights the pattern of reversals through the entire second half of the book. In Tanach the phrase that designates a military leader is one who "goes out before the people." Here male warriors wait helplessly inside the walls, while the "weak" woman goes outside the walls to the open space of danger. The enemy "lord" who expects to "achieve his ends" is defeated by another "lord," the God he has held in contempt.[18] The "head" of the vast army literally and figuratively loses his head to a mere woman. Judith may, like Yael,[19] kill the enemy general in a tent, but in this story it is his tent, his "inside," while she comes from "outside." **She invades the space of the invaders.**

Judith Redeems
the Good Name of Dinah;
The Victor Replaces the Victim

The leitmotif of "going out" not only initiates a narrative pattern of ironic reversals that recalls the similar structures of reversal in the *Book of Esther*. It also deliberately evokes a narrative that occupies the background of our consciousness as soon as we hear the name Shimon, and is explicitly brought into the foreground in Judith's prayer: *"O Lord, the God of my ancestor Shimon! You took in hand a sword to take vengeance on those foreigners who had stripped off a virgin's veil to defile her, uncovered her thighs to shame her, and polluted her womb to dishonor her. You said, 'It shall not be done'; yet they did it. So You handed over their rulers to be slain, and their bed, which blushed due to their treachery, to be stained with blood."*[20] Judith evokes the story of Dinah[21] who "went out" and was violated by the "foreign" ruler, interpreting the revenge of her ancestor Shimon as, in reality, the instrument of God's

---

17. *Judith* 8   18. *Judith* 11:6   19. *Judges* 4-5
20. *Judith* 9:2-3   21. *Genesis* 34

vengeance on the polluters of the inner space of the virgin's womb. But *Judith* **stands the Dinah story on its head**. The one who goes out may look like the unprotected female about to be raped. She is, in fact, the rescuer and avenger. While the foreign rulers see her as juicy prey for their lust *("Go to the Hebrew woman and persuade her to join us . . . It would be a disgrace if we let such a woman go without enjoying her company — literally, 'without having her'"),*[22] she uses Holofernes' predatory desires as the fulcrum in her strategy. The image of the bed polluted by Dinah's violated nakedness becomes the focus of Judith's aggression and its coverings the symbol of her victory, turned into a "votive offering" in the pristine, unviolated Temple, protected by "a woman's hand."

Most strikingly, the devastating silence of Dinah's voice in the *Genesis* narrative is transformed into Judith's masterful action and the rhetorical fullness of her voice. *"O God, You are my God, hear now a widow's prayer. . . they have planned to desecrate your sanctuary, to pollute the dwelling-place of your glorious name, and to strike down the horns of your altar with the sword. Mark their arrogance, pour out your wrath on their heads, and give to me, widow as I am, the strength to achieve my end. Use the deceit upon my lips to strike them dead . . . shatter their pride by a*

> Most strikingly, the devastating silence of Dinah's voice in the *Genesis* narrative is transformed into Judith's masterful action and the rhetorical fullness of her voice.

---

woman's hand. For your might lies not in numbers nor your sovereign power in strong men; but You are the God of the humble, the help of the poor, the support of the weak, the protector of the desperate, the deliverer of the hopeless . . . You and You alone are Israel's shield."[23] In her language, Judith fuses the purity of the woman and the sanctuary. To protect it, she designates herself as the new Shimon.[24]

Judith also expresses a prophetic humility, an awareness of human action as mere instrument of the God who protects the desperate, very much in the mode of the chapter from Zechariah chosen by the Rabbis as a Hanukkah reading *("Not by might, nor by power, but by My spirit — said the Lord of Hosts").*[25] We may see her as another Esther, taking off her clothes of mourning and dressing *"so as to catch the eye of any man who might see her,"*[26] just as Esther puts on *"malchut"* — royal garments or "royalty"[27] to stand up to Ahasuerus. But Judith is even more like the young David, so boyish and beautiful (feminine) that he arouses the scorn of the enormous enemy, Goliath. Yet he confidently declares himself the instrument of the Lord of Hosts: *"For the battle is the Lord's and He will deliver you into our hands."*[28]

The Primal Crime: Violating the Inner Sanctum

The ambiguities created by these subversions of conventional gender expectations pervade later midrashim more explicitly connected to the Maccabees' struggle, some of which include pieces of the story of Judith. In one medieval midrashic tradition, [reprinted in abbreviated form above under the title *Hannah, Daughter of Mattathias*, page 42] the rebellion against the "Greek" oppressors is precipitated by the foreigners' violation of the privacy of Jewish homes and the sexual integrity of Jewish women. They make a decree that anyone who affixes a door bolt to his house will be killed. The ability to close one's door, to make an inviolate private space, becomes a symbol of autonomy (integrity of self) and identity. Because of this attempt to destroy Israel's honor *(kavod)* and internal integrity *(tzni'ut)*, the Jews get rid of their doors altogether, leaving their houses open and eliminating the space of their eating, drinking, conjugal relations and even sleep, the

---

22. *Judith* 12:12   23. *Judith* 9
24. *"The deceit upon my lips"* is like the *mirmah*, the "deceit" of Dinah's brothers in *Genesis* 34:13.
25. *Zech.* 4:6   26. *Judith* 10:4
27. *Esther* 5   28. *I Samuel* 17

necessities of daily life. The next decree forbids women to immerse themselves in the ritual bath on pain of death, causing the men to give up sexual relations with their wives. The third and climactic oppression comes in the form of *ius primae noctis* (first night privileges) — every young bride must go from her chuppah to a night of sexual submission to the governor *(hegemon)*. The Jews suffered this decree for 3 years and 8 months until **Hannah, the daughter of Mattathias the high priest**, married a Hasmonean named Elazar. At her wedding feast, she tore her clothing and stood exposed to all. When her father and brothers wanted to kill her for shaming them, she called them to account — *"Do you consider yourselves shamed because I stand naked in front of these righteous ones, but not when you deliver me to the uncircumcised one to violate me? Learn from Shimon and Levi, the brothers of Dinah, who were only two. You are five brothers, besides more than two hundred of the flower of the priesthood."* This, according

The Reformation's Judith:
The Freedom Fighting *Femmes Fortes*[30]

"**S**trong women" fit the ideal of the Protestants of France, Germany, Britain and the Netherlands who fought for religious and political liberty from Pope and Catholic tyrants alike. Judith was both religiously and politically motivated to be violent in the name of God. Her revolt against Holofernes the corrupt boastful general and against the capitulation to Assyria of the weak king of Judea, Uzziah, served to justify Protestant political rebellion against "rightful" yet not religiously righteous Catholic rulers. German potters supplied the Calvinists in the war-torn Netherlands with both expensive and simple cups and dishes ornamented by Judith's figure, the patron of religious resistance against corrupt rulers. In particular, embattled Protestant queens identified explicitly with Judith. Jeanne, Queen of Navarre in France, led the French Protestants, the Huguenots, in a bloody civil war and so she naturally commissioned the great poet Du Bartas to write an epic poem entitled *"Judit"* (1574) that praises, dangerously, the heroism of a tyrannicide.

to the midrash, roused up the men of the Hasmonean family to begin the great rebellion that culminated in the victory we celebrate at Hanukkah.

In this and similar midrashim, the themes of sexual violation and integrity provide the fundamental imagery for the struggle between Jews and "Greeks." Here too **violation of women and invasion of inner space express the emotional, as well as the conceptual meanings inherent in pollution of the sacred enclosure of the Temple**. The female protagonist, as in Judith, displays more clarity of mind and firmness of purpose than the men of the story, and provides the impetus for courageous action. But the woman remains "inside," while the men, the true activists, "go out" to defend the faith.

What remains unique in the literary masterpiece, the *Book of Judith*, is the extra-ordinary transformation of the expectations aroused by conventional notions of gender, as well as by the texture of allusions to Biblical narratives. The use of a female character as both symbol and literal embodiment of the community of Israel has a long history in Jewish texts by the time of the *Book of Judith*. But **the transformation of that female body from victim to rescuer** suggests a more radical message. The female body, for centuries the symbol of the community as victim of oppression, becomes the means of rescue. Judith prays that God's power (*yad chazakah* — literally strong hand) manifest itself through "a woman's hand" (*"shatter their pride by a woman's hand"*).[29] Standing "outside" holding the enemy's head in her distinctively female hand, she symbolizes a human community, which can mold its vulnerability and apparent powerlessness, its "femininity," into resources of strength. Perhaps her presence, in particular, brightens the Hanukkah lamp we place in our homes at the meeting point of inside and outside.

---

29. *Judith* 9:10

---

30. Editor's summary based on Margarita Stocker, *Judith: The Sexual Warrior*, p. 54-57, 61.

THE EIGHT-FOLD PATH TO SPIRITUAL ILLUMINATION

Hanukkah is a spiritual Journey. It is a quest for illumination and enlightenment — what the mystics referred to as "ha'arah" deriving from the Hebrew word **"or"** — light. The eight-fold path of Jewish consciousness is unfolded in each of the lights of Hanukkah. Each light captures in its glow a particular understanding of the spiritual path that we all must walk in our quest for higher ways of being in the world.

✸ The First Illumination: The Path of Soul Print[31]

We begin at the beginning with the source of the light. Zohar teaches that the source of Hanukkah light is from the *Or HaGanuz* — "the hidden light." In the Hasidic unpacking of this mystical tradition, the hidden light refers to an interior place in every human being. The beginning of spiritual work is to acknowledge the existence of such a place. The essence of who I am is, in mystical terms, my *Or HaGanuz*, my hidden light. Every person has a public persona and a more internal, psychological profile. The hidden light, however, refers to neither. It is deeper, infinitely more complex, grand, beautiful and mysterious. It is what drives me to greatness and to pathology, it is what moves me to choose one partner or a particular life path over another. **It is the DNA of my soul. It is my soul print.** The infinite value and dignity of every human being comes from the radical uniqueness of every person on the face of the earth. No two fingerprints and no two soul prints are ever the same. I begin my spiritual journey by attempting to make first contact with my soul print — my hidden light.

There is a Hasidic tradition to gaze into the flame of the candles for as long as they continue to burn. Mystically the meditation on the hidden light of the candles has within it the power to open a window to the hidden light of my own unique soul. Thus we begin our eight-fold journey on Hanukkah with a trip inward to our own unique source of illumination. It is only after we have come to identify our spiritual signature, our soul print, that we can begin to wend our very special way towards increasing illumination and joy.

✸ The Second Illumination: The Path of Receiving

Real spiritual work is always about connection to the other as well as to the highest part of my self. The inability to form that connection is what the mystical masters refer to as "exile," what we moderns would call loneliness and alienation. Not to be connected to other and self is to be lonely. Loneliness is not a social ill or a psychological issue, it is a malaise of the soul.

In biblical consciousness the goal of living is the good. The entire first chapter of Genesis proclaims grandly after each stage of creation unfolds, *"God saw that it was good."* "Good," explains the Italian kabbalist Luzatto, is the fundamental goal of the world. But goodness resides not only in aesthetic order but in human connectedness. God declares, *"It is not good for the human to be alone."*[32] All the good of creation, "God saw that it was good," is undermined by the experience of loneliness.

Loneliness is the inability to share the essence of who I am with an other. There are two major causes for the experience of loneliness. The first stems from my failure to acknowledge that I am unique and special — that I have a soul print. What I have not found in myself I cannot share with other. The second cause stems — even after having claimed my uniqueness — from not having found a person to receive my soul print.

---

31. This selection is derived from *Soul Print*, a forthcoming book by Mordechai Gafni (Curtis Brown Publisher). Gafni, an Orthodox rabbi, uses his rabbinic and academic training to teach a personal, spiritual Torah to the seeker generation in Israel both via television and in popular lectures and books.
32. *Genesis* 2:18

Loneliness is Not to be Seen as I Am

A story: My son was eight years old. I was on my way to the United States for a lecture tour. My son gave me a shoe box of his things to take with me. I was saying goodbye to him when he gave it to me and didn't pay much attention. When I returned to Israel the first thing he said to me was — "Abba, what did you think of my box?" Now truth be told, I had not really looked at it carefully — it had been an intense trip with enormous physical and emotional demands and the box had somehow slipped my mind. Although I did not say any of this to my son — instead offering some lame comment on his box, he understood. He took the box from my suitcase and very quietly took his things out and put them on the bed: a rock of strange dimensions, a spoon, a picture of me, a particularly rare baseball card and the like. He looked at me, a tear rolling down his cheek, and said, "Abba, I gave you my box. In it were all the things I love. These are my things and you didn't receive them." At that moment I felt his pain and understood what loneliness really means. Loneliness is when I feel like I am not being seen for who I am. Loneliness is not to be received — not in my public or psychological self — but in my secret self.

The Hasidic Rebbe Tzaddok Hacohen from Lublin writes that the ultimate esoteric knowledge is the knowing of another human's soul. It is secret knowledge not because it is forbidden to transmit it to others, but because it is so difficult to share it with others. Paradoxically — as long as I have not received myself, I am unable to fully receive the other. This is so because I need other to fill my emptiness — to provide me with the self-definition and identity that I have not claimed for myself. To receive others is to be fully focused on listening to their music, to their soul print, without trying to rewrite it in the image of my hidden needs. It is only then that the dance of giving and receiving — which are really one — can begin. Kabbalah, the name for Jewish mysticism, means to receive. **To be a Kabbalist, an illuminated one, is to know and practice the art of receiving.**

The ultimate esoteric knowledge is the knowing of another human's soul.

✴ The Third Illumination: The Path of Shadows

As the Hanukkah candle sheds light, it also reveals shadows beyond its reach. To touch our soul print we must first enter and embrace our shadow. Here is a story by the mystical master, Rebbe Nachman of Bratzlav, which we tell after the lighting of candles:

A son leaves his home and travels for many years in distant lands. Upon his return he tells his father that he has become a master craftsman. In particular he has learned the art of making a menorah, a candelabrum, which is essential to being a spiritual teacher. His proud father, wanting to demonstrate his wisdom and craft to the community, invited all the master craftsmen to see his son's menorah. The craftsmen however all quietly told his father that they thought his son's work to be lacking; indeed each pointed out a different deficiency in the menorah. His father being both hurt and disturbed confronted his son with the poor reviews of his work. To which his son replied; "You will notice, father, that each of the criticisms addresses a different part of the menorah. In fact, the deficiency that each person saw was a reflection not of the menorah but of themselves, of their own particular emptiness. **Identifying one's unique deficiency,**" said the son, "**is the gate to the true illumination that the menorah can provide.**"

To see the light shed by one's own peculiar deficiencies is to undergo spiritual transformation, what classic sources call *teshuva* — repentance or return. Ironically, sin begins with our longing to be ourselves fully. Pathology is the distorted expression of the soul reaching for itself. The self, the soul, is at the same time divine and includes our human darkness, our shadow. The shadow, in both Hasidic teachings and modern psychology, represents the rages, anxieties and jealousies that lurk beneath the thin veneer of our consciousness. Those dimensions of our

Jacob Reclaims his Shadow Self

To return from sin, according to contemporary Talmudist and philosopher Rabbi Joseph Soloveitchik, is to "engage in self-creation." This requires us not to deny our existing self, but to reclaim it and give it new form. The biblical figure of Jacob is the model for this idea. All his life he denies his shadow. His name, Jacob, comes from the Hebrew word *akov* — "crooked" or "tricky" — a shadow quality. When young Jacob goes to his father for a blessing, Isaac asks: "What is your name?" Jacob lies and gives his brother's name. His deceit comes from his unwillingness to own his Jacob-ness, his true self.

Only when he reaches middle age is Jacob willing to face the traumas of his youth and meet Esau, the brother he had cheated; he is finally able to confront his own darkness. When the angel that Jacob wrestled asks him: "What is your name?" the reader hears the echo of the same question put to him by his father years before. But by now Jacob has faced his shadow, has embraced his whole self — including the deceit and the lies and their meaning — and has emerged stronger. "My name is Jacob," he responds. The angel then blesses him with the name *Yisra-el* — which poetically plays on the word Yashar, meaning straightness or integrity. Jacob the crooked becomes Yisrael, the Straight One of God. We can only rise to integrity by tracing internal crookedness to its root and reshaping it.

soul that we deny, will express themselves, nonetheless, in pathology and darkness. As Carl Jung wrote: "The psychological rule says that when an inner situation is not made conscious it happens on the outside, as fate." For example, a wealthy person shoplifts, seemingly without need. One's peculiar style of sin expresses an unclaimed part of the self. It will not be silenced; it will act in the world to heal its pain.

Mordechai Lanier, the Hasidic Rebbe of Ishbitz, taught that **every person reaches God through one's "hisaron," his "deficiency," through one's own shadow**. Our uniqueness, our creative power, our potential point of intersection with the Divine is concealed within the shadow. The archetype of artistic creativity in Jewish tradition is Bezalel, who built the Tabernacle in the desert, where humans meet the Divine. The literal meaning of the name "*Bezal-el*" is no less than "in the shadow is God."

The Robber-turned-Rabbi and the Energy of Sin

While the classic image for evaluating human beings is the scale (sins on the one side, merits on the other), the story of the Talmudic robber-turned-rabbi, Reish Lakish, offers us a new way of seeing one's self. By working through our darkness to its source we are able to transform sins into merits. The scale becomes irrelevant. We become new, unified, with only merits to our name. The Talmud says, "Repentance is so great that through its power, intentional sins become merits." This is, however, a troubling statement. We understand that divine grace allows repentance to erase our sins, but how can sin become its antithesis?

Reish Lakish led a band of highway robbers; he was moved to return to Judaism by an encounter with Rabbi Yochanan. "Your strength should be for Torah," Rabbi Yochanan told him. From this Reish Lakish understood that precisely through his unique passion and energy — which until then had been expressed destructively — would he find his way to God.

Schneur Zalman of Liadi, the founder of the Habad Hasidic dynasty, explains that Reish Lakish's statement refers to the inner force/impulse of the sin. By acting altruistically, using the very passion that propelled the vice, the sin is transformed, it becomes a merit. Nietzsche expressed this point provocatively, the good can never gain the upper hand unless it is "infused with energy generated by murder." He writes in *Thus Spake Zarathustra*: "Of all evil I deem you capable: therefore I want the good from you; verily I have often laughed at the weaklings who thought themselves good because they had no claws."

We can go further, and understand Reish Lakish's words as referring not only to the energy of the sin, but to the story behind it, the reason the sin came about. This is the secret of spiritual growth which flickers in the light and the shadow thrown by the Hanukkah candles.

✵ The Fourth Illumination:
The Path of Rock-Climbing

The decision needed to be made. As the Maccabees prepared to rededicate the Temple, so recently desecrated by the Greeks, they discovered only one flask of oil — enough to burn in the Temple menorah for one day. Why start the project if we cannot finish, they thought. We might raise the people's hopes and then dash them again. Better to wait till we have enough oil. Others argued against these wise words of caution. They felt this was an opportunity that may not repeat itself. Who knows what the future holds? *Carpe Diem* — we need to risk, to seize the day.

Candles cannot be lit and enlightenment cannot be attained without risk. The menorah is supposed to be lit on the "*petach*" — at the gateway of the house or at least at the window, at the border of the inside and the outside — a place of risk and opening.

R. Nachman of Bratzlav used to tell a mystical Kafkaesque tale before lighting the Hanukkah candles. Here is a small extract.

"There was a man who was visited by a guest. They began to talk until by and by the talk turned to the deep matters of the soul. 'I want to study with you,' said the man to the guest. 'But I cannot study with you now,' replied the guest, 'but follow me beyond the *petach* and I will teach you.' Suddenly the man was not sure who the guest was — human or demon — from the good side or the other side. 'If I wanted to harm you,' said the guest, 'I could have done so while in your house.' And so the man followed him beyond the *petach*, and immediately they were flying . . . and then once again he was in his house engaged in normal conversation . . . and then again he was flying . . . and then again in his house . . . and then again flying."

This is a story about risk, the constant need to move beyond the *petach*, the doorway, in order to fly, while always returning to the house, to the stable roots of normalcy before flying again.

This willingness to go beyond one's limited world can be understood in terms of Rabbi Nachman's idea that there are two kinds of knowledge: *makkif* and *penimi*. Knowledge I have not yet acquired, literally "that which surrounds," is *makkif*. *Penimi* is the internal knowledge that is already mine, "that which is inside." According to Rabbi Nachman, learning is a process of transforming *makkif* into *penimi*. How do I bring that which is beyond, to the inside of me? How do I transform *makkif* into *penimi*? I must let go of what I already know. Herein lies the risk. Nachman teaches, I must let go of my comfortable certainty, in order to open myself up to a new, higher level of knowledge.

Two applications of this idea come readily to mind. In the realm of belief I often need to give up a primitive belief in order to come to a deeper understanding. If I tended to view God as only a kindly old grandfather in heaven and then I read a profound work of mysticism or philosophy that challenged that belief in God what am I to do? The answer is: **if I am committed to growth and truth, I need to let go of my old conception in order to be open to a new and higher understanding**. However, there is that moment when I am dangling over the abyss with no belief. I have advanced sufficiently not to be able to retain my old picture but am not yet able to truly understand the picture that is offered in its stead. This is the most dangerous place of all.

Organized religion has historically hidden teachings which would challenge our standard, if somewhat primitive, understandings, preferring them to the risk of getting caught dangling over the abyss, not for a moment but a lifetime. This is why mystical teaching was esoteric. Organized religion preferred a

---

All growth entails an element of risk. Learning is not a gradual, safe ascent, like climbing a ladder or a flight of stairs.

dogmatist to a skeptic. And all too often the attempt to move from a dogmatist to a mystic failed, with the person stalled for life in the place of the skeptic. Today however we have no choice — the call of the climb echoing from our souls is too powerful to mute. Today, without reaching for our mystical self, the skeptic will surely take over. The old dogmas can no longer hold us.

The second application that comes to mind is in relation to my own self-understanding. If I have always understood myself in a particular way — and that understanding has been my navigational compass in the world

---

While ultimate learning may take place through rock climbing , sidewalks are generally safer modes of mobility in daily life.

---

and it is not easy to challenge. Often when our self-understanding is challenged in therapy or in a consciousness-raising weekend, we succeed in destroying our old sense of self; however, we have not had time to build anything new in its place. Again we are left dangling over the abyss without the lifeline of a clear identity — a dangerous place indeed. And yet grow we must, for stagnation is impurity and death.

Rabbi Nachman's lesson is plain: **all growth entails an element of risk**. Learning is not a gradual, safe ascent, like climbing a ladder or a flight of stairs. Rabbi Nachman believes in **rock climbing**. Any rock climber will tell you that one does not climb rock faces like Spiderman. Human hands are not suckers, which provide a certain grip while you reach for the next rock. Quite often in order to reach the next hold I must let go of all my previous holds. I see above me a hold for my right hand. If I push up with my right leg, if I give a 'spring,' I will be able to reach the hold for my right hand. But to do so I must let go of my left hand and remove my left foot from where it is resting. In making the 'spring,' pushing up with my right foot, there is a split-second when that

right foot is the only thing connecting me to the rock face. My left foot, my left hand, and my right hand, are in the air. If I catch the hold with my right hand a split-second later, I am safe. But if I miss — I fall. It is the brief heart-catching moment of the 'spring,' the leap into *makkif*, having let go of *penimi*, that R. Nachman sees as the ultimate learning: **learning through uncertainty**.

It is important to point out here that while ultimate learning may take place through rock climbing , sidewalks are generally safer modes of mobility in daily life. Rock climbing is an expedition we plan for from the sidewalks of our lives. But once on the face of the cliff, some novice rock-climbers freeze, paralyzed by the fear of uncertainty. Others deny they have further to climb, making a house on the side of the rock. The great enemy of the seeker of truth, according to Reb Nachman, is smugness and self-satisfaction. It is crucial that I do not fool myself into thinking that I have "arrived." This will only result in stagnation. We need to be especially discerning to know the difference between stagnation and core certainty. They can look remarkably similar on the outside.

The fourth path of illumination, rock climbing, requires that we follow the light of the candle out the window, across the doorway, out into a world not yet our own but waiting to be illuminated and to illuminate us in return, if we are willing to take risks.[33]

✺ The Fifth Illumination: The Dancing Path of the Dreidel

The fifth movement in the spiritual Journey of Hanukkah is imaged in the dance of the flickering candle and in the whirl of the dreidel. The dreidel dances gracefully on the table before us, transfixing our gaze, awing us with its elegant and choreographed

---

33. See Mordechai Gafni's forthcoming book, *The Dance of Uncertainty*, especially the chapters on "R. Nachman and the Void" and "Rock-climbing" (published by Jason Aronson).

movements. The goal of the spiritual novice in watching the dreidel is no less than to become the dreidel, to learn to live in dance.

In dance, I allow myself to be carried by the essential rhythms of the music. Dance is at its core an act of trust. I trust the music. I trust my body. I trust that though I will always fall, I will always land in the right position. Without the trust that the universe is such that I can land on my feet, I could never live and certainly never dance. I dance only when I hear the music and let it guide me. I live my highest story only when I trust my music and let it guide me. Often, I will fall in ways that I never dreamt possible. Dance teaches me how to transform the fall into dance.

The Faith to Fall — into God's Arms

Faith, says the Rebbe of Ishbitz, is the belief that whenever I fall, I fall into God's hands. How many of us can fall back into the arms of a friend without trying to desperately break the fall at the last second? Faith is to know that God is my dance partner whom I can trust.

A friend of mine, a prominent scholar in medieval philosophy and mystical thought, once traveled from New York to visit Reb Menashe, a Jerusalem mystic. I accompanied him. "What does *emunah*, faith, mean to you?" Reb Menashe asked the scholar.

The scholar reviewed various positions on the matter of faith, from medieval to Hasidic. Reb Menashe listened patiently and then responded: "It is so much simpler than that," he said, "*Emunah* is the feeling that the baby has that its mother will not drop him."

A child wrapped in the cradling arms of his or her mother conveys the most powerful yet gentle image of certainty. The mother, merely by being present, confers unconditional love to the child. The nursing mother, in Hebrew called the *omen*, gives the child a sense of safety and clarity. As Reb Menashe was aware, the word *emunah — faith —* plays on the word *omen — nursing mother*.

When we get older, we can achieve a higher level of faith — one that incorporates yet moves beyond our beginnings. When we learn how to walk and then to run on our own, we understand that God is not only our mother, but God is also our lover and dance partner. Beyond the autonomy of walking on our own two feet is the trust achieved in dancing now on one foot and now on the other with our partner. God as our dance partner needs to anticipate our falls. "Seven times does the spiritually developed person fall," says the Talmud, "and seven times does he rise again." Similarly the mystical notion of "descending in order to rise" captures most beautifully the dances of our lives that allows us to trust enough to descend, to fall, to lose our balance, in order to spin and whirl through existence.

Anyone who has ever seen Greek folk dancing can associate the idea to a visual image. When Zorba the Greek dances, first he dips very low. To the untrained observer he appears to be falling. However the downward fall motion is transformed into a dance step. In Hasidism the verse, "*you transformed my mourning into dance,*"[34] is understood in precisely this way. **The art of living is to know how to transform the inevitable falls into the dance of life.** The dreidel spins beautifully and yet every spin, no matter how exquisite, ends in a fall. We pick up the dreidel and spin again and again. To dance is an act of trust that the world has rhythm. To dance is to connect with the energy flow of the universe in the most primal way.

The Hebrew word for dance is "*Mechol*." Literally the word includes among its meanings both dance and forgiveness. For we may transform our falls into glorious dance movements, if we are but willing to forgive ourselves. That essential flexibility of dance is essential for any and all spiritual growth.

From the dance of subatomic particles in the Tao of physics to the dance of the reed gently bending in the wind, the structures and free forms of dance are, according to Tzadok Hacohen from Lublin, the core stuff of the universe. As we spin the dreidel and ponder the flickering flame we discover the illumination of the dance of life.

---

34. *Psalm 30*

✺ The Sixth Illumination:
The Path of Conversation

The candles partake, the mystics teach, in the **Light of the Messiah**. Rebbe Nachum of Chernobyl, mystic and philosopher, points out that the Hebrew word for messiah, *"Mashiach,"* can be understood as the Hebrew word *Ma-siach* — meaning dialogue or conversation. The radical implication of his assertion is that the messiah is potentially present in every human conversation. In a word, sacred conversation is the vessel which receives the Light of the Messiah.

As one Rabbinic midrash suggests, to bring the redemption we need only respond to the voice of God calling us to sanctity from Sinai. A voice goes forth every day from Sinai saying, "I am the Lord your God." We heard the voice originally that day at Sinai not merely because God spoke to us but because we listened. Not only we human beings but the whole world. On the day of revelation a bird did not chirp, the angels did not sing, an ox did not bellow, and the sea did not rage — the entire world fell silent and therefore the voice that came out of Sinai could be heard. The voice can be heard only from the silence. In the prophetic account of the descent of the Divine chariot so beloved of Jewish mystics, the biblical prophet Ezekiel envisions

---

The word "vocation" derives from the Latin *vocare*, voice. We are called by the God-voice within us.

---

something he calls *chashmal*, a unique word, explained by the mystics as the "color of speaking silence." *Chash* means silence and *mal* means speech, hence *chashmal* is speaking silence. Our silence enables the opening revelation of Divine speech. This is the secret of the *Chashmal*.

That revelation was heard long ago when God spoke to human beings, a once in the life of the universe event, says the book of Deuteronomy, *"a great voice which was never repeated."* But the Rabbis and mystics insist that the voice of Sinai is accessible even after the echoes of the original revelation are long

since lost in the wind. It is, as understood by an alternate understanding of the same biblical phrase, *"a great voice which does not cease."* Where, however, is that voice to be found?

Perhaps in the voice of the human being. When we listen on the deepest level, we are really uncovering the God voice within us. To have a voice is to be called. The word "vocation" derives from the Latin *vocare*, voice. We are called by the God-voice within us. The third book of the Torah begins with the words, *"God called to Moses."* The Zohar in a different context writes, "when Moses came, the Voice came." It was the voice of Moses which allowed the voice of Sinai to become audible. The human voice and the divine voice are not identical, however God speaks through human beings. The messiah will come, suggests the Talmud, "when you listen to his voice," which requires listening both to the voice from within and the voice of fellow human beings. When human beings live a life of vocation, they are giving voice to the image of God within. Our deepest voice — that which emerges out of recesses of our soul when we are able to get truly quiet and listen to our self and that of the other — is an echo of God's voice.

The Hasidic master Kalonymous Kalman Epstein in his seminal work *Meor VaShemesh, The Light of the Sun,* explains that the demarcating characteristic of messianic times is that every person will be their own spiritual master. This is his radical reading of the prophetic vision "and no man will anymore learn from his fellow to know God, for everyone will know from the wise to the simple." Every person will find voice and that voice will be their spiritual guide. When we discover the light of the messiah conversing with us from within, then we have discovered another path to illumination.

✸ The Seventh Illumination:
The Path of Finitude

If I hold onto an image of perfection too closely then no partner can ever satisfy me. Perfection becomes my greatest enemy. It is only when I let go of my need to realize my fantasy of infinity that I can create relationship with a real person. Herein lies the beauty and the paradox. By letting go of infinity and embracing the finite I open up the window of return to infinity. It is only through a complex imperfect relationship with a particular person that I can touch the infinite beauty of love. The universal is always mediated by the particular.

Two spiritual assumptions underlie this path:

1) In every person is a touch of divinity, through feeling that touch I can grasp the all. For, like a holograph, the all inheres in every part. The moment of divinity, which resides in the frail vulnerable human being, is no less than the portal to eternity.

2) I can only hold what I am able to give up. By giving up the image of the ultimate, I am able to find the ultimate, the sublime, in the imperfection of one limited person or moment.

This perspective, the ability to find the whole within the partial, intimations of the infinite in the finite, may help us appreciate the spiritual path of the Maccabees. When the Maccabees reclaimed the Temple from Greek Syrian domination only three years after the hostilities began, they wanted to re-light the menorah, the symbol of religious renewal. But all of the oil had been defiled by the Greeks, except for one pure cruse with only enough oil for one day of light. Yet they began the Hanukkah, the Rededication, and celebrated for eight days during which the oil in the Temple menorah never gave out.

The ability to be so joyous for eight days was an act of hope, not acknowledgement of a new reality of victory. The Maccabees knew their battle for independence was far from over. The Greeks had not yet sent their professional armies. In fact, the Hanukkah holiday was but a lull in a long protracted war that took 25 years. In the ensuing battles after the first Hanukkah, Judah and all his brothers

except Simon are killed. On that first Hanukkah, the brothers knew when they entered the Temple that they were still in the middle of the story. They realized that they may not survive future battles. Their victory was partial at best. Moreover, the symbol of the incompleteness of their victory was the fact that they had only one cruse of oil. It would take time to produce sufficient oil to keep the menorah lit and of course to reach the strength necessary to withstand the Greek Empire's counterattack. Why then should they light the menorah? Why celebrate a mere fragile beginning to their revolt?

Despite it all they decided to light the menorah. In doing so **the Maccabees affirmed their ability to rejoice in a partial fulfillment, to experience blessing even as the contingency and fragility of reality threatens at every moment to undermine the Joy. That then is the miracle of the first day; that despite it all, they had the wisdom and courage to light the menorah, in a world where fulfillment is at best tenuous.**

Philosopher David Hartman in his book, *A Living Covenant*, beautifully unpacks this idea. He writes that the ability of the Jew to recite a blessing of thanksgiving applies even after eating merely an olive's worth of food, even though the biblical requirement for blessing is only when one eats sufficient food to be fully satiated. We understand however that if we wait to be "ful-filled" entirely we will never experience blessings. Therefore, we affirm the surfeit of blessing contained even in an olive's worth of food. This is the defining characteristic of Rabbinic spirituality, in every partial fulfillment, there is a taste of the whole.

Now we see why each night of Hanukkah has its own illumination to be cherished. There is no need, nor is it possible to light all eight candles every night. Rather we need to experience the whole in the light of each individual candle and to bless it and the light it brings into our lives.

Mother Teresa:
Every Moment is a Holograph

Every fleeting moment in which I experience fulfillment or meaning is indeed all of fulfillment and all of meaning. Every moment is a holograph, meaning the all is present in every part. Any moment of the divine contains the entire divine, even if experienced in the depths of despair.

A reporter is finally given the opportunity to interview Mother Teresa. Ushered into her simple room the reporter bursts out, "Don't you think it is terrible, Mother Teresa, there are ten thousand refugees pouring into Calcutta every day from besieged Bangladesh and there is no food or housing for them!"

"No," replied Mother Teresa, "It is wonderful. See, this starving little boy just took food . . . ." The reporter's attention is drawn to the shriveled youngster on her arm who has just taken a spoonful of milk.

It is the mark of spiritual depth to be able to live fully in the miracle of that isolated moment of beauty. Mother Teresa understood that in one moment of human value and human meaning I can experience the love of God and the core certainty of the cosmos.

Mother Teresa's words echo the *Dayyenu* song of the Passover Haggadah. "If God had only done this one thing for us, it would have been enough for us — *dayyenu!* If God had only split the sea and done nothing else for us, it would have been enough!" Even more

startling — "If God had brought us to Mount Sinai and not given us the Torah, it would have been enough!"

These are surely a series of highly questionable statements. What good is standing at Mount Sinai without receiving the Torah? What is the point of traveling to the mountain at which the Biblical text says the divine revelation took place — if the revelation does not take place? How could this have been enough for us? How could we have sung *dayyenu* if we had never received the Torah?

The song is teaching us that any moment of divinity contains within it all of divinity. I can come to all of God, truth, beauty or goodness, through any one moment of encounter with them. This is the profound human implication of the metaphysical teaching that divinity is indivisible and infinite. The core of this attitude is the interconnectedness of the all. Every particle is an expression of the one. Every moment, place and person is full and thus offers fulfillment. Further, every particle connects us to and contains within it the whole. This means that through one moment of core certainty — in which the world was for a few moments fully real and meaningful — I can connect to all the meaning, certainty, truth, beauty and goodness in the cosmos. That means that in every present encounter all of the past and future is folded into the moment. All of the person's memories and dreams are at play in the encounter which takes place in the now. That is holiness — *'Kadosh.'*

Rabbi Nachman's "Fractals":
Within Every Part Dwells the Whole

Rabbi Nachman of Bratzlav suggests that I can find core certainty of being through locating any one act, moment or character trait of goodness in my life. For mystical master Rabbi Nachman this is not only a psychological exercise to hold certainty amidst the confusion. It is an essential cosmic principle, and corresponds to the popular modern scientific theory of "fractals" which posits that within every part exists the whole. Therefore, if I can experience my core certainty of being in any part, then in that part I can experience the whole. R. Nachman teaches that if I can only touch a fleeting moment of my goodness and nothing

more, if there is only one point in my life story where I experienced certainty about my value and dignity, that is enough — *dayyenu*. For in that singular moment of certainty, all of the value, dignity and core certainty of my essential worth sings to the skies. In this sense the ten sefirot, which collectively and singly each contain the entirety of God's presence, are not simply numbers or even jewels: they are our life stories. In all the beauty and the pain, the laughter and the tears of our life's story, we need find only one quiet moment of goodness, however fleeting, to fill our souls with the music of eternity.

✸ The Eighth Illumination:
   The Path of Eros

The lighting of the candles is, in essence, a re-enactment of the rededication of the Temple by the Maccabees. In the re-enactment we are trying to re-connect with Temple energy. Why is it so vital to us that we longingly mourn the destruction of the Jerusalem Temple and yearn for its rebuilding?

What is it that we are meant to yearn for? Surely another building on the bitterly contested Temple mount holds no inherent redemptive promise. Further, would it not seem that mystic, vegetarian Chief Rabbi of Eretz Yisrael, Abraham Kook, was right, when he said that the animal sacrifices, which characterized the ancient Temple, hold little attraction for spiritually evolved moderns? Without answering this question a large portion of Jewish ritual and consciousness is rendered at best unintelligible.

Three Talmudic texts and an ancient esoteric mystical tradition need to guide us in our search for understanding. The first text, by its very strangeness, jolts us to the realization that our intuitive impressions of the holy may need fundamental re-orienting. Said R. Isaac, "From the day the Temple was

---

What is this strange and holy tale trying to teach us? That the seat of Eros and the seat of holiness are one.

---

destroyed, the taste of sex was taken away, and given to the sinners i.e. those engaged in illicit sex . . . as the verse says in Proverbs, '*Stolen waters are sweet.*'" In the context of this passage illicit sex refers specifically to adultery; while the taste of sex is an idiom meant to refer to the ultimate sexual experience. According to this eyebrow-raising passage, the difference between Temple and post-Temple spirituality is that after the destruction, the fullest erotic joy of sex was very difficult to access with our lawful partners. The yearning for the Temple is in effect understood as a yearning for Eros of the most intense kind.

The second rather shocking text is a description of the innermost sanctum of the Temple. **In the Holy of Holies, relates the Talmud, were two angelic cherubs locked in embrace, erotically intertwined.** Furthermore, according to the first book of Kings, the walls of the first Temple were covered with erotic pictures of these sexually intertwined cherubs. This is our first indication of a close association between holiness and Eros. **The primary image in the Holy of Holies, the innermost precinct of holiness in the Temple, is a symbol of Eros.**

The final source to examine is the Talmud's description of a mythic dialogue between the Rabbis and God attributed to the Second Temple era. The Rabbis are concerned lest Jews be tempted to engage in pagan worship as they did in the era of the First Temple and thus bring about the destruction of the Second Temple as well. The Rabbis entreat God to nullify the power of the drive towards idolatry. God grants their wish allowing them to slay the inclination for idolatry. But where might they find this unholy drive? Immediately a fiery lion emerges from . . . the holy of holies, the innermost sanctum of the Temple. This lion who resides in the innermost sanctum of the Temple is identified by the prophet as the primal urge toward idolatry and slain.

The Rabbis, apparently feeling that it was a moment of grace, entreat again. Allow us, they say, to slay the drive for sexuality as well. God grants their wish and again a fiery lion emerges from the Holy of Holies, this second lion is understood to be the primal sexual drive. When they attempt to slay this lion however the world simply stops functioning. Chickens don't lay eggs, people don't go to work, the desire to get married is suspended and all productivity and, according to the Hasidic reading of the text, all spiritual work, grinds to a standstill. The Rabbis understand that they have gone too far and retract their request. At most they can blind and weaken this instinctual drive but it may not be eradicated.

What is this strange and holy mythic tale trying to teach us? The underlying teaching would seem to be that the seat of Eros and the seat of holiness are one. The first lion to emerge from the Holy of Holies personifies the drive for idolatry, the second the sexual drive. Both however are but expressions of common underlying reality — that of Eros. The seat of Eros is none other than the Holy of Holies in the Temple

Idolatry at its core is not primitive fetishism. It is rather a burning lust for the holy. Under every tree, in every brook, courses primal divinity. The idolater, like the prophet, experiences the world as an erotic manifestation of the God force. It is therefore only the prophet who is able to identify the lion as the drive for idolatry. One nineteenth-century kabbalistic writer suggests that this passage is about the end of the prophetic period and that the idolater and prophet were in fact flip sides of the same coin. True, the Rabbis of the Second Temple eliminated the Jewish attraction to paganism but it also crippled the spiritual ecstasy necessary for prophecy and the Second Temple no longer knew prophetic visions. The symbolism of the lions emerging from the Holy of Holies is the Rabbis' way of teaching that Eros is Holiness.

Eros in this understanding includes sexuality as a primary manifestation but it is clearly not limited to sex. It rather refers to the primal energy of the universe. Eros is where essence and existence meet. Eros is to taste essence in every moment of existence. As this third passage indicates, the drive to uncover the divine sensuality of the world is not without its dangers. The erotic may overwhelm us to the point that our ethical sensitivities are swept away and our sacred boundaries overrun. And yet the need to experience the world in all of its divine Eros remains a primal human need and according to this text the Temple of Jerusalem was organized in response to that need.

The Talmud relates that at the time of the destruction, fruits lost their taste. Laughter vanished in the life of the polis, and the vitality of sexuality, teaches R. Isaac, was reserved for those seeking illicit adulterous thrill. When fruits lose their full erotic taste, when laughter becomes mechanical and only in response to sexual humor, then true Eros, the Temple, has been destroyed. It is therefore not surprising to experience love's displacement into the illicit sexuality.

The passionate yearning for rebuilding the Temple is the longing to redeem Eros from its distortions. We need to move from the Eros of longing, which symbolized the exile, to an Eros of fulfillment. We need to experience the full intensity of erotic relationship with partners to whom we are committed. Put succinctly, rebuilding the Temple requires the channeling of our corrupted passion for illicit sexuality back into the holy and ethical context of my relationship with my spouse. Reclaiming the sacredness of Eros is the path to the restoration of the Temple experience in our lives.

Rabbi Akiva:
The Holy of Holies is a Love Song

After the destruction of the Temple, Rabbi Akiva, the mystic Rabbi and the subject of the most romantic love story of the Talmud, taught that "all the Biblical books are holy but **the Song of Songs is the Holy of Holies**." Akiva is doing more than extolling the virtue of the God-Israel relationship allegorized in King Solomon's Song of Songs in terms of passion and sensuality. Akiva is elevating **the experience of passion and sensuality to the guiding force in all of our relationships with the world, with our partners and with the divine. In a post-Temple reality, the primary site of Divine revelation is in Eros.**

The passionate yearning for rebuilding the Temple is the longing to redeem Eros from its distortions.

---

6. Herman Wouk

HANUKKAH TODAY (1959)[35]

In a thousand years of national existence on the soil of Palestine the Holy land, the Jews over and over drove out oppressors and regained independence, but the Maccabean war, a battle for religious liberty, alone found a place in the rites of our faith. It stood out. It was the Jews' first full-scale encounter with the question that was to haunt them in the next two thousand years: namely, can a small people, dwelling in a triumphant major culture, take part in the general life and yet hold to its identity, or must it be absorbed into the ranks and the ways of the majority? In the two great worlds of current affairs — the Communist empire, which so much resembles an ancient military dictatorship, and the tolerant, skeptical free West — they face the question again.

---

35. Herman Wouk, the American novelist, describes his view of Hanukkah in *This is My God*, p. 81-85, copyright 1988 by the Abe Wouk Foundation.

Hanukkah:
The Last and the Least of the Minor Holidays

A casual question about Hanukkah occasioned the writing of my book, *[This is My God]*. Yet there is nothing really accidental, in the United States in 1959, in starting an inquiry into Judaism with a question about Hanukkah, the last and least of the minor holidays; last in time or origin, least in prescribed observances.

It is the one holy day not rooted in Bible narrative; the one day that celebrates a military event; the day, in short, that comes closest to being a bridge between ancient Judaism and our modern world, and that lies farthest from the Mosaic revelation. Adventuring back in time toward Sinai, we encounter Hanukkah first among the calendar milestones. The observance is nearest to us not only in time, but in the nature of the crisis that gave rise to it.

Hanukkah celebrates the successful revolt of the Jews, in the days of the Second Temple, against the Seleucid Greeks, inheritors of the Syrian chunk of Alexander the Great's collapsed empire. The eighth in the line of Seleucid kings, Antiochus Epiphanes, undertook to force the Greek religion on Judea, on the old but evergreen theory that religious non-conformists were a threat to the state. He so far succeeded that in 168 B.C. his armed forces installed an idol in the Temple in Jerusalem and appointed Jewish apostate priests to sacrifice swine to the Greek god in the courts of Solomon.

Antiochus made it a capital crime throughout Palestine to teach the Bible or to circumcise boys. His army went through the country, installing idols and apostate priests in every village, unopposed at first by the stunned and cowed populace. The break came when one old man, Mattathias of the priestly Hasmonean family, refused to sacrifice to the fetish set up in his town of Modiin, and killed with his own hand the man who stepped up to slaughter the swine in his place. His five sons rescued him from the army, took to the hills, and organized a rebellion, which in three years swept the Greeks from all Judea. Thus the act of one resolute old man changed an evil tide of events. The entire future of Judaism may well have turned on the blow Mattathias struck.

On the twenty-fifth of Kislev, 165 B.C., the loyalists led by Judah Maccabee, the warrior son of Mattathias, recaptured the Temple and began eight days of purifying and rededicating ceremonies. Hanukkah means Dedication. The festival marks these eight days when the Temple was restored to the worship of God. The service continued thereafter for over two centuries, until the Romans overthrew Jerusalem in the year 70 and destroyed the House of the Lord, which has yet to be rebuilt.

I have here summarized the Hanukkah story because it is not, like the Bible narratives, part of common Western culture.

The Communist position on the Jews is generally, though with less crudity, that of Antiochus. Our religion the Soviets consider a barbarous relic, superseded in wisdom and soundness by Marxism. The training of children in this exploded Semitic superstition goes against good sense and the interests of the state. So the police discourage such teaching, in ways sometimes oblique and sometimes forcible. For Greek religion substitute Marxism, and the Russian Jews are back where their fathers were in 168 B.C. — with whatever differences one may find in the relative truth and beauty of the Greek and Communist cultures.

The challenge of the West is different, though just as serious. The proposition is the old one: that the Jews are confronted with a better way of life and should give up their religion for it. Forces that are not coercive, and therefore do not call forth the human impulse to fight them, urge Jews along this path. The position of the government, and indeed the deep conviction of most American leaders, is that the Jewish community has the right to hold fast to the faith of its fathers and ought to do so. What contradicts them is the

Can a small people, dwelling in a triumphant major culture, take part in the general life and yet hold to its identity, or must it be absorbed into the ranks and the ways of the majority?

tidal force that Tocqueville long ago marked as the great weakness of a democracy in his unforgettable phrase, "the tyranny of the majority." The pressure to emulate neighbors, the urge to conform to popular views and manners, the deep fear of being different — these, in the United States, are the forces of Antiochus. Where the power of the sword long ago failed, the power of suggestion has recently been doing rather better.

It would be pleasant to believe that the stabbing relevance of Hanukkah to Jewish life

in America has occasioned the swell of interest in the holiday. But a different and perfectly obvious cause is at work. By a total accident of timing, this minor Hebrew celebration falls close in the calendar year to a great holy day of the Christian faith. This coincidence has all but created a new Hanukkah.

The old Hanukkah was a shadowy half-holiday of midwinter, a time of early night and late morning, of snow and slush, of days filled with blue-gray gloom only half dispersed by feeble yellow street lamps. It hardly seemed a holiday at all. Fathers left for business in the morning in work clothes. Children trudged off to school by day and scrawled homework at night. There was no celebration in the synagogue, no scroll to read, no colorful customs, no Bible story. For eight nights running one's father, when he came home from work, gathered the family, chanted a melody heard only at this time — so that it came for ever to recall the sadness of winter twilight, the feel of cold wet wind on chapped hands, the hiss of steam radiators, and the smell of falling snow — and he lit candles in an eight-branched menorah on the window sill: one the first night, two the second, and so forth, until on the last night eight candles flared in a row. But even then the menorah made but a quiet little blaze. The candles, like the holiday, were slender and unpretentious; pale orange, inclined to bend and wilt, and quickly burned out; not at all like the stout Sabbath candles that flamed half the night.

The first evening of Hanukkah had the most life, because then the parents and grandparents gave the children Hanukkah money, a quarter or a half dollar; riches indeed, if a careful mother did not at once produce the steel savings bank and force the children to feed the coins into that horrible thin black maw which consumed half the joy of childhood. And on that night there was a novelty of the latkas, the cakes of potato batter fried in deep fat, which only the calorie-thirsty engine of a child could properly digest and be thankful for.

At Hebrew school there was a sort of temperate quasi-Purim; perhaps the acting out of battles between Jews and Greeks, with cardboard helmets, shields, and swords. The teachers told the Maccabean tale and added a legend of a lamp miraculously burning eight days in the Temple. It all seemed of small account because it wasn't in the Bible and because nothing was made of it in the synagogue beyond a few added prayers.

The colossal jamboree of the department-store Christmas, of course, overwhelmed Hanukkah like a tidal wave.

Sometimes the children were given nuts, raisins, and hard candies; and also strange little gambling tops, dreidls, with which one could quickly triple one's hoard of sweets or lose it all. That, more or less, was the old Hanukkah; vivid and recognizable enough, from year to year, but frail compared to Sukkos and Passover or the weekly Sabbath. The colossal jamboree of the department-store Christmas, of course, overwhelmed it like a tidal wave

It was entirely natural for a new Jewish generation growing up in the United States to feel each December like children in the dark outside a house where there was a gay party, pressing their noses wistfully against the windows. That Judaism had its own rich and varied occasions of gaiety (as perhaps we have seen) was beside the point. Most second-generation Jews were but poorly trained in their own faith; and anyway the Christians had a brilliant mid-winter feast, and the Jews did not. Some families solved the problem in the simplest way by introducing Christmas trees, Christmas presents, and Christmas carols into their homes. They argued that it was harmful for their children to feel underprivileged, and that the Christmas tree was a mere pleasant ornament of the season without religious content.

Meantime in schools where there were large numbers of Jewish children a dual celebration of Christmas and Hanukkah sprang up, as an official symbol of mutual courtesy and tolerance. This in turn generated a new Jewish interest in Hanukkah. Even those Jews who were celebrating Christmas in their homes — tree, holly, "Born is the King of Israel," and all — began to find it seemly to add an electric menorah for their windows, and perhaps even to light the candles. This apparently solved the problem by giving the children the best of both worlds.

Of course all rabbis, even of the most extreme Reform tendency, inveighed against this institutional hodge-podge, on the grounds that it could do nothing in the long run but muddle the children. But pulpit words in such a situation are handfuls of sand against a rising river. I once knew a gifted and most liberal-minded Reform rabbi in the suburbs who preached against Christmas trees in Jewish homes. He was called on the carpet by his board of trustees and sternly warned to confine his remarks to religion and leave people's private lives alone.

The interesting point here, and the only one worth making, is the way the pressure of the majority can persuade one that its demands are one's own spontaneous desires. A Jew who feels large chunks of his heritage slipping away from him, and observes himself behaving more and more like the massive majority, should make very sure that this is a result he truly wants, and that he is not being stamped willy-nilly by the die-press into a standard exchangeable part.

The aggrandizement of Hanukkah itself is a fortunate accident. The level of knowledge of all Judaism must rise when any part of it happens, for whatever reason, to gain attention. The son of my skeptical friend is not likely to stop after learning about Hanukkah. A lack of clear and satisfying religious identity hurts American Jews most in December. That is why the apparently trifling issue of the Christmas tree generates such obduracy and such resentment. It rasps an exposed nerve. It is a good thing that Hanukkah is then at hand. If the old custom of Hanukkah money has become the new custom of Hanukkah gifts, that is a minor shift in manners. The tale of the Feast of Lights, with its all-too-sharp comment on our life nowadays, is very colorful. It is of the greatest use in giving the young a quick grasp of the Jewish historic situation. The gifts win their attention. The little candles stimulate their questions. The observance seems tooled to the needs of self-discovery.

The Hanukkah candles by law burn in the window so that the passer-by can see them. The sages called this "proclaiming the miracle." The legend runs that the Maccabees found in the recaptured Temple only one flask of oil still intact under the high priest's seal, and therefore usable in the golden candelabra. It was a single day's supply. They knew that it would require at least eight days to get more ritually pure oil, but they went ahead anyway and lit the great Temple menorah. The oil burned, the legend says, for eight days.

This Midrash is an epitome of the story of the Jews. Our whole history is a fantastic legend of a single day's supply of oil lasting eight days; of a flaming bush that is not consumed; of a national life that in the logic of events should have flickered and gone out long ago, still burning on. That is the tale we tell our children in the long nights of December when we kindle the little lights, while the great Christian feast blazes around us with its jewelled trees and familiar music.

The two festivals have one real point of contact. Had Antiochus succeeded in obliterating Jewry a century and a half before the birth of Jesus, there would have been no Christmas. The feast of the Nativity rests on the victory of Hanukkah.

7. Mordecai Kaplan

IN PRAISE OF ACTIVE ASSIMILATION
"CLEANSING" THE "TEMPLE OF OUR FAITH"[36]

Two Kinds of Assimilation: Egypt and Judea

When the conquests of Alexander the Great brought the Jewish people under Greek domination, they came for the first time into contact with a civilization which, like their own, had created human values of universal significance. Judaism was faced with the challenge of Hellenism on two fronts, as it were, the one in **Egypt**, the other in **Palestine**. The reaction of the Jews to the impact of Hellenism on these two fronts differed, but their experience on both fronts is of great significance to us.

A process of assimilation was inevitable. But "assimilation" is an ambiguous term. It may be used in an active sense and in a passive sense; it may mean assimilating, and it may mean being assimilated. A minority group may appropriate elements of the culture of the majority and so relate them to its own sancta that they stimulate the creativity and will to live of the minority. That is **active assimilation**. On the other hand, it may be so overawed by the achievements and prestige of the majority civilization as to accept the standards of the latter uncritically, lose its own self-respect and abandon its national sancta altogether. In that

36. *Reconstructionism Today*, (Winter, 1996, p. 4-7) excerpted these selections from *The Meaning of God in Modern Jewish Religion* by Mordecai Kaplan, 1937. Rabbi Mordecai Kaplan, born into an Orthodox rabbinic family, became a seminal thinker in the Conservative Movement and ultimately founded the Reconstructionist Movement. These excerpts are reprinted by permission of the Jewish Reconstructionist Federation.

case, it is doomed to extinction.

For several hundred years the dominant reaction of the Jews of **Egypt** was that of active rather than passive assimilation. The Neo-Platonic philosophy which was then current impressed the Jews profoundly and set them to studying anew their own national writings to convince themselves that the Torah had anticipated the wisdom of the Greek philosophers. Their contact with Greek thought did not therefore result in an abject subservience to Greek standards, but led them to seek new meanings in the traditional culture and institutions of Judaism. In Alexandria their interest in Jewish scriptures was such that it led to the first translation of the Bible into a foreign tongue, the Septuagint, and the first Jewish philosopher, Philo.

What can the Jews learn from their past experience with challenging civilizations?

In **Judea**, the impact of Hellenism upon Judaism had different consequences. Judea was never a seat of Greek culture at its highest. The superficial qualities of a civilization are much more communicable than its deeper and loftier values. The Hellenistic movement in Judea was not inaugurated by a group of idealists. It originated with a little clique of Jews who acted as tax farmers. Serving as intermediaries between the main body of the Jews and the foreign rulers, they found it to their advantage to flatter their masters and play the sedulous ape. This imitation fortified their economic position, and enabled them to maintain authority over the rest of the Jews. The Jewish Hellenists believed that the possession of wealth and power established the superiority of the Greek civilization over the Judaic one. They were enamored of the militarist spirit of the Greek civilization and of the voluptuousness which it had assimilated from the oriental kingdoms it had

conquered, and not of the "sweetness and light" of Greek culture.

The peasants and artisans who constituted the bulk of the Jewish population only learned to associate Hellenism with the oppressive regime and the social arrogance of the politically favored. If that was Grecian civilization, their own tradition stood on a much higher ethical plane. They therefore resented with vehement protest any expression of irreverence on the part of the Hellenists for the Temple, the priesthood, or other *sancta* of Jewish religion. When the Hellenists fell back upon the intervention in their behalf of the Grecian king, Antiochus, a revolutionary situation was created, and the Hasmoneans became the champions of the revolutionary cause.

Lessons for Survival

What can the Jews learn from their past experience with challenging civilizations? In the first place, it is important that Jews avoid the mistake of those Judean Hellenists who indiscriminately aped everything that was characteristic of the dominant alien civilization, without any regard for the *sancta* of their own Jewish civilization. We have the modern equivalent of these Jewish Hellenists in the Jew who is willing to identify with the worst features of our western civilization, with its deification of mammon, its worship of success, its glorification of mere bigness, its apotheosis of power. Social climbing undermines the entire order of the spiritual values. It places a premium upon success, regardless of the methods whereby that success is attained.

But if an indiscriminate acceptance by Jews of all the elements of the dominant western civilization would be fatal to the survival of Judaism, an indiscriminate rejection of all it stands for, even if possible, would only be ruinous. [Jews must] react to the modern situation as the Jews of Alexandria met the challenge of Hellenism. Jews must discover what there is in western civilization that has universal import, must relate these aspects of it to the traditional *sancta* of Judaism, and thus integrate them in the very fabric of Jewish civilization. Such a course is bound to stimulate the spiritual creativity of the Jewish

---

Paradoxical as it may seem, if a nation wishes to survive, it must not make survival itself its supreme objective, but rather aim at the achievement of good. That alone makes national survival important to its individual members.

---

people and issue in the production of new cultural and social values that are distinctively Jewish because they are born of the collective experience of the Jewish people. Paradoxical as it may seem, if a nation wishes to survive, it must not make survival itself its supreme objective, but rather aim at the achievement of the highest intellectual, aesthetic and social good that alone makes national survival important to its individual members

The advocates of a secular nationalism often err in assuming that by giving emphasis to the content of Jewish civilization, to such component elements as land, language and communal organization, we insure the nation's survival. But this is not enough. Only when these component elements are given **religious significance** of universal import can they be depended upon for survival value. Only by fostering such a religious orientation to life as will issue in the affirmation of the holiness or supreme worth of life, can any nation generate a national will to live adequate to its survival, in the face of challenge or persecution.

Reconstructing Judaism

But if the Jewish religion is to save Jewish life in our day, it must be **reconstructed**. The Jewish religion must be brought into rapport with the best achievements of modern civilization and rendered expressive of the most universal human values. It must

be made rational, ethical, and aesthetically creative.

(1) The Jewish religion must be made to conform to the demands of **rationality**. If Jewish religion should ever be generally identified with superstition, its doom would be sealed.

(2) Jewish religion must be made to harmonize with our highest **ethical** demands. The main significance of the democratic movements of modern times must be sought in the ethical implication of democracy that every person has a share of responsibility, and hence should be given a corresponding measure of power for determining the social order of which he [or she] is a part. The religious tradition of Judaism, like that of other religious civilizations, is still couched in terms of conformity to a revealed law, and still tends to put on a super-natural intervention the responsibility for social change. Jewish religion must identify God as the spirit that, immanent in human nature, urges [people] by means of their **ethical** insights to fulfill the destiny of the human race. It must not justify any social injustices, even if they conform to the traditional law. It dare not, for example, withhold from woman equal status with man as responsible ethical personalities, merely because the traditional codes, which are supposed to be revealed, accord her an inferior status.

(3) Finally, Jewish religion must be reconstructed **aesthetically**.

To produce art is to be creative, to give new meaning to reality. Since the experience of value in life constitutes our knowledge of God, all sincere art is sacred. In the past, religion emphasized "the beauty of holiness"; modern religion must also emphasize the holiness of beauty. If Jewish religion deliberately cultivated the aesthetic powers of the Jewish people, it would bind them to it with ties of gratitude and reverence that would go far to insure every necessary effort on their part to perpetuate Jewish life.

> The challenge of our modern Occidental civilization to Judaism could be converted from a menace to Jewish survival into a positive aid to Jewish survival.

These are some of the ways through which the challenge of our modern Occidental civilization to Judaism could be converted from a menace to Jewish survival into a positive aid to Jewish survival. Such a way of meeting the challenge would be utilizing the traditional method through which Judaism survived the impact of Hellenism. If the observance of Hanukkah can awaken in us the determination to reconstruct Jewish life, by informing it with a religious spirit characterized by absolute intellectual integrity, unqualified acceptance of ethical responsibility and the highest degree of aesthetic creativity, it will indeed be a **Festival of Dedication**. It will mean **a cleansing of the temple of our faith** to render it again fit as a habitat for communion with God. So long as the Jewish people is thus linked in communion with the Eternal, it can look forward to an eternal life for itself.

8. Theodore Herzl Gaster

THE ORIGINAL MESSAGE OF HANUKKAH
THE INALIENABLE RIGHT TO BE DIFFERENT[37]

Hanukkah, the Jewish Feast of Dedication, ostensibly commemorates a historical event — the rededication of the Temple at Jerusalem in the year 165 BCE. But many of the religious festivals of the world which come to us as commemorations of historical events are really expressions of basic human emotions which those events happen to have evoked and focused.

Back of that narrative, however, and back of the annual festival lies the recognition of something deeper — something, which was indeed expressed in that particular event but which itself transcends it. What **Hanukkah celebrates** is the **inalienable right of human beings to their own character and identity**; and, in commemorating the way in which that right was once defended, the festival reasserts it from year to year. For that reason, Hanukkah is no mere antiquarian relic, but an occasion of ever-living, contemporary significance.

It is important, however, that the message of Hanukkah be understood correctly. Hanukkah is not — as is so often supposed — a festival of independence; it is a **festival of dedication**. And the difference is crucial. What it asserts is not the right of every man to "be himself" and do as he pleases but to be a servant of God and in that service to defy princes. Moreover, the only God whom a man is required to serve is the God revealed to him in the history and experience of his people, not the idol imposed from without. **The condition of independence is consecration, and its hallmark is devotion.**

Another thing that the festival teaches is the **value of the few against the many**, of the weak against the strong, of passion against

---

37. Theodore Herzl Gaster (whose first name reflects his father's involvement with the early Zionist congresses headed by Dr. Theodore Herzl) is a famous scholar of ancient religions and their rituals. This selection comes from *Hanukkah and Tradition: Feast of Lights* p. 85ff, (Henry Schuman Publisher, 1950).

indifference, of the single unpopular voice against the thunder of public opinion. The struggle which it commemorates was the struggle of a small band, not of a whole people; and it was a struggle not only against oppression from without but equally against corruption and complacence within. It was a struggle fought in the wilderness and in the hills; and its symbol is appropriately a small light kindled when the shadows fall.

Antiochus — Father of the Melting Pot

In 168 BCE, Rome had managed successfully to block the plans of the Greek Syrian king, Antiochus IV, who was seeking desperately to annex the land of Egypt to the Seleucid empire. To meet the threat, the king needed desperately to rally all of his subjects. But this was an exceptionally difficult task, because those subjects were of disparate races and cultures, and many of them had been mutual enemies before being bowed beneath the common yoke. The danger of disunity on one hand and of a possible switch to Rome on the other was accordingly ever present; and Antiochus was consequently obliged to accomplish by coercion what he could scarcely hope to do by persuasion or by reliance on any intrinsic loyalty: all of the peoples of his empire were to be welded together by *executive decree* into a solid cultural front.

On a winter's day in 167 BCE, the full force of this policy fell upon the Jews. The king issued a formal edict requiring that the Temple of God in Jerusalem be turned over to the worship of his own national god and ordering the Jews, on pain of death, to abrogate their own laws and ceremonies and to participate in the national cult. This was not — as is too often supposed — a mere act of anti-Semitism, and it was not motivated by any doctrinal opposition to the Jewish religion. Rather was it part and parcel of a

Before there was Separation of Church and State

The separation of church and state is an axiom of modern democracy, and we have become so accustomed to it that it is difficult for us to appreciate the other side of the picture. We think of religion as something concerned with the destiny of man and with his relation to God, and we think of the state as the political organism of society. The province of one, we hold, in no way impinges on that of the other, except insofar as religious doctrines may influence social conduct; and it is accordingly quite intelligible for a man to say that he is a citizen of his country and a Christian or Jew.

In ancient times, however, such a dichotomy would have had no meaning; for religion was not a personal faith or individual persuasion but rather, in a very real sense, the total organization of society. The god was not a theological abstraction or a mere metaphysical concept; he was the actual spirit of the community personified — a symbolic being like Uncle Sam or John Bull. His house was not merely an abode of divinity or a place of worship; it was also a city hall, a center of the social administration. His ministers were not merely priests or hierophants; they were also civil servants — magistrates, physicians, and sanitary inspectors. The animals presented to him in expiation of sin were the counterpart of fines which might today be paid into court as penalties for breaches of the law; and the seasonal festivals which were held in his honor were primarily functional procedures designed to replenish the communal vitality at regular intervals. There was no distinction between community and congregation; a nation was the people of its god, and its territory was his estate. When it was attacked, it was its god that was being attacked; and when it went to war, it was as the army of its god, under his banner and command, that it sallied forth to battle.

It was on this basis that the ancient people of Israel founded its existence. If the whole of the cult were ever to cease, or if all of the statutes of God were to be discarded, Israel automatically would be at an end, inasmuch as it would have lost its distinctiveness and its *raison d'etre*.

political program the purpose of which was to break down the divisiveness of separate religious communions by forcing them all into **a single national "church."** The god of this "church" was to be the Greek Zeus; all local shrines were henceforth to be dedicated to him and to serve exclusively as centers of his cult. In order to emphasize the fact that the "church" was an organ and expression of the state, Antiochus himself assumed the role of god incarnate, arrogating to himself the title of *Epiphanes*, or "[God] Manifest." The Temple of the Jews in Jerusalem was by no means the only house of worship to be forcibly accommodated to the new order; the sanctuary of the Samaritans on Mount Gerizim was likewise transformed into a shrine of Zeus, and at Daphne even the Greek Apollo was obliged to yield place to the national god.

For the Jews, the new edict was the bitter end; for what was now threatened was not merely their political autonomy but their very identity. Yet Hellenization had by this time penetrated so deeply and made such inroads upon their traditional loyalties that few indeed were alive to the peril or even recognized it as such. The upper classes were "Hellenes of the Mosaic persuasion"[38] and had long since surrendered any claims to cultural distinctiveness or national independence. The authorities were quislings[39] almost to a man. The resistance (was it ever different?) came from a small, unofficial minority; and it was touched off by a purely local incident.

The First Hanukkah: Defeating Dionysus in December

The Festival which Judah and his followers observed on those memorable December days was *not* as is so often supposed, a *festival of victory and liberation*; for they were not so naive as to imagine that a few successes in guerrilla warfare, however sensational and spectacular they may have been, had automatically restored the independence of the Jews or finally decided the political issues at stake. The purpose of their celebration was simply and solely to rededicate the House of God.

In order to dramatize the occasion and to invest it with a becoming measure of dignity, they made a point of repeating exactly the same ceremonies as had marked its original dedication in the time of Nehemiah [after the rebuilding of the Second Temple three hundred years earlier]. That event had taken place on Sukkot.[40] Accordingly, although Sukkot actually fell nearly three months earlier in September, its traditional ritual was adopted as a precedent. The ceremonies were made to last eight days, corresponding to the seven days of Sukkot and the succeeding Shemini Atzeret; and, inappropriate though it was to the season of the year, throughout that period a steady stream of "pilgrims" wound its way to the shrine bearing the wreathed wands and palm branches *(lulavs)* characteristic of Sukkot and intoning psalms *(Hallel)* customarily recited on that occasion. So effectively was the parallel drawn that, almost half a century later, when the Jews of Jerusalem exhorted their brethren in Egypt to adopt the annual celebration of Hanukkah, they could find no more suitable way of describing it than as the **December version of Sukkot**.[41] As a matter of fact, the association of the ceremony with the ritual of Sukkot could invoke an even higher and more venerable authority; for Solomon's Temple, too, had been dedicated at that very same season.[42]

December was the time of year in which the great **festival of Dionysus** — the so-called "Rural Dionysia" — was celebrated in the countryside; and the ancient chronicler informs us expressly that, by decree of the king, the Jews were compelled to take part in it, "wearing the wreaths of ivy and joining the sacred processions."[43] The festival took the

---

38. Gaster is punning on the self-designation of assimilated German Reform Jews in the 19th C. who called themselves "Germans of the Mosaic Persuasion" to emphasize that being Jewish was a religious, not a national identity.

39. *Quisling* refers to a traitor to one's people who collaborates with the enemy occupation. In World War II the Norwegian traitor Vidkun Quisling was the puppet political leader appointed by the Nazis during the occupation.

40. *Nehemiah* 8:13-18   41. *II Maccabees* 1:9

42. cf. *I Kings* 8:2, 65   43. *II Maccabees* 6:7

form of an orgiastic revel. After a preliminary period of "purification," the participants, now regarded as in a state of holy enthusiasm, clothed themselves in the skins of fawns or foxes, crowned their heads with ivy leaves, carried in their hands wands wreathed with green leaves and topped with pine cones, and repaired to the hills and mountains, where, in the light of torches, they spent the night in wild dances, rending the air with piercing shrieks of excitement and the equivalent of ecstatic hallelujahs to their god. As part of the ceremonies, the torches were dipped again and again into water or wine so that they might sizzle for a moment and flare with a brighter blaze, thus symbolizing the fiery nature of Dionysus and the "new light" which was thought to burst upon the world whenever he made his appearance among men.

When this picture is kept in mind, the full significance of Judah's ceremony becomes apparent. Although designed first and foremost as a ritual for the rededication of the Temple, it served at the same time as a pointed and *stinging satire* upon the contemporaneous pagan festivities. Every detail of the Dionysian ritual was therein parodied and ridiculed. The preliminary purifications found their counterpart in the cleansing and purifying of the House of God from the contamination of the pagans themselves; in the festal parade, in the procession of pilgrims around the altar; in the carrying of wreathed wands, in the bearing of the lulav; in the wild shouts, in the chanting of psalms; in the blazing torches, in the relumed candelabrum.

Thus, the first Hanukkah stands out in a clear light; it was at once a proud reassertion of the Jewish faith and a ringing protest against the ways of the heathen.[44]

The Message of Hanukkah for the Modern Jew[45]

[In conclusion], Hanukkah commemorates and celebrates the first serious attempt in history to proclaim and champion the **principle of religio-cultural diversity in the nation**. The primary aim of the Maccabees was to preserve their own Jewish identity and to safeguard for Israel the possibility of continuing its traditional mission. Though inspired, however, by the particular situation of their own people, their struggle was universal implications. For what was really being defended was the principle that in a diversified society the function of the state is to embrace, not subordinate, the various constituent cultures, and that the complexion and character of the state must be determined by a cultural process of fusion on the one hand and selection on the other, and not by the arbitrary imposition of a single pattern on all elements.

Seen from this point of view, therefore, Hanukkah possesses broad human significance and is far more than a mere Jewish national celebration. As a festival of liberty, it celebrates more than the independence of one people — it glorifies the right to freedom of all peoples.

The real issue at stake was not the right of the Jews to be like everyone else, but their right to be different; and victory meant not the attainment of civic equality (which, after all, was what Antiochus was offering!) but the renewal, after its forced suspension, of that particular and distinctive way of life which embodied and exemplified the Jewish mission. The mark of that victory, therefore, was not a triumphal parade but an act of dedication — the cleansing of the defiled temple. Moreover, when the Jews wished to perpetuate the memory of their achievement, what they chose to turn into an annual festival was not the day of some military success but the week in which the house of God had been cleansed and the fire rekindled on the altar. There is an important meaning in this, one feels, for our own day, and especially in connection with the problem of safeguarding civil rights.

---

44. from *Hanukkah and Tradition: Feast of Lights*, pp 85ff.
45. *Festivals of the Jewish Year* by T.H. Gaster. NY: William Sloane Assoc., 1953, p. 244-246.

A Bukharan mother and daughter from southern Russia celebrate their first Hanukkah in Israel, using a menorah made from glasses with oil and wicks.
(December 1949, Central Zionist Archives, Jerusalem)

שְׁאֵלוֹת וּתְשׁוּבוֹת

Frequently Asked Questions and Answers

QUESTIONS AND ANSWERS:
HOW TO LIGHT RIGHT

SURVEYING THE RANGE OF OPINION IN TRADITIONAL LAW

by Noam Zion

INTRODUCTION

More than on any other holiday there is a contemporary consensus on how Jews of all stripes celebrate Hanukkah — candle lighting at home after sunset. Yet even according to the halacha there is latitude and multiple options on how, where, when, who and with what one lights Hanukkah lights. Traditional Jewish law defines the purpose of candle lighting as symbolic "publicity" *(pirsum hanes)* for the miracle of Hanukkah. The medium for that message is light. Yet there is a great deal of variety in how to personalize and to enhance the beauty and intensity of the mitzvah. That personal touch is called *"hiddur,"* special enhancement.

Below are most frequently asked questions and short but varied answers reflecting the complexity of Jewish Law.

1. Buying Candles and Menorahs

Q *Do the candles have to be multicolored?*

A No! The most recommended fuel is pure olive oil with a quality wick; however, all fuels are acceptable.[1] White wax candles became very popular in the 19th century because of their steady light. Colored candles first appear in 20th century America.

Q *How many candles are needed?*

A The **bare minimum** is one candle per household per night that burns for ½ hour each night. In theory one could use one Shabbat candle (that burns for 4 hours) and light it again and again every night for 8 nights (½ hour each). However, going back to **Hillel** (40 BCE), Jewish law has commended the use of **an additional candle added for each subsequent night, hence totalling 36 candles** for all

eight nights. Each candle must have enough fuel to burn for at least 30 minutes. Thus each night adds to the *Kedusha* (holiness) by adding more light *(maalim bakodesh).*[2]

Alternatively, or additionally, the Rabbis have encouraged every family member — men and women — to light their own menorah (or set of candles). Thus a family of five would need five candles on the first night and 20 candles on the fourth night of Hanukkah, not including the *shamash* — the extra candle used for light, which is explained below. The recommendation to add an extra candle nightly or to provide separate menorahs for each family member is called *mehadrin* from the term *hiddur,* meaning extra enhancement of the mitzvah.

Q *If we need 36 candles for each household, then why does the standard box of Hanukkah candles contain 44?*

A Since the 36 candles are wholly symbolic, their light may not be used in any other way. The ***shamash***, meaning the **"service candle"** provides the light by which to read the blessings or to eat or to maneuver in an otherwise darkened room, as well as to light the Hanukkah candles. **8 service candles plus 36 Hanukkah candles equals 44 per box.** Obviously one can rely on the electric lights or on a different type of candle to serve as the *shamash.*[3]

One way or another, a *shamash* is needed to provide useable light, and to show the observer that the Hanukkah candles are superfluous hence symbolic. Therefore the *shamash* should be set off from the Hanukkah candles in height or location.[4]

---

1. *Aruch Hashulchan Orach Hayim* 673:1
2. *T.B. Shabbat* 21b   3. *A.H.O.H.* 671:21   4. *A.H.O.H.* 673:9

Q *How many menorahs does a family need?*

A None! Until the late Middle Ages there were no special Hanukkah menorahs. People might use a series of ordinary individual cups of oil or a multiple wick device, the same lamps used for everyday lighting.

Today, the more *Hanukkiyot* the better. Each family member, as well as each guest of whatever age, may have their own 8-branched candelabrum with a special place for the 9th candle — the *shamash*. However, traditional Sefardi families follow the halacha that each household uses only one menorah lit by the head of the household, to represent everyone in unison.

The menorah can be improvised or professionally made. The rabbis felt that the more expensive the workmanship and material, the more the special *"hiddur"* (added aesthetic and personal investment); however a child's makeshift menorah can also be a spiritually significant example of *hiddur*.

Q *Isn't it true that a round menorah is prohibited?*

A Not really. **The wicks may not be clumped together to look like a bonfire, but as long as each separate flame is clearly distinguished, it is permitted to use a round menorah, as was the custom in many countries.** Of course, some rabbis urge that one avoid any round menorah lest it appear like a bonfire but that level of stringency is not obligatory.[5]

Q *If it is safer and easier to use an electric menorah, can we say the blessings over it as we plug it in?*

A Most contemporary Orthodox rabbis discourage the use of electric menorahs for a host of reasons. However, where there are no other alternatives, it may be acceptable, though it is dubious if a blessing may be said *(See the sidebar on electric menorahs below)*.

5. *A.H.O.H.* 671:13

When Are Electric Menorahs Permitted?
A Summary of Rabbi Nachum Rabinovich's Halachic Ruling for Israeli Soldiers[6]

Question — May one light electric flashlights to fulfill the obligation to light the Hanukkah light? (Please note that in the army, burning candles inside a tent may be dangerous.)

Responsum — Some rabbis claim that since electricity did not exist in the days of the Talmud, the Rabbis could not have intended to permit the use of electricity. Solid candles (wax or tallow) were only invented several hundred years ago. The Maharal of Prague, Judah Lowe, even forbade the use of wax candles "since the original miracle (in the Temple) was done with oil," while wax or tallow (fat) candles are not even called "a light" *(ner)*.

However Rabbi Moshe Isserles reports that "in some countries Jews light wax candles since they give out a clear flame like oil."

Can we imagine that wax candles are forbidden? After all, the *Shulchan Aruch*[7] establishes: "all the oils and all the wicks are kosher for the Hanukkah lights." Might this all include electric menorahs?

There are no proofs and no convincing theories to forbid or to permit the use of electric Hanukkah lights. Therefore, let the custom stand. Jews world over have preferred to use oil or wax candles to observe this mitzvah. Yet there is also a lovely new custom to light electric menorahs inside houses and courtyards and especially on the roofs of public buildings in order to publicize the miracle. Still we do not recite a blessing over these electric lights.

Therefore one should prefer wax or oil candles, but if the soldier for security reasons cannot light these kinds of candles, then s/he may light electric flashlights as long as it is clear that they are for Hanukkah. However, s/he should refrain from reciting a blessing and rely on others [his/her family] at home to say the blessing for the soldier (with him or her in mind) using conventional candles.

6. Based on N. Rabinovich, *Milumadei-Milchama — Responsa on War* (1994-1995).

7. *Shulchan Aruch O.H.* #673

2. Placing the Menorah and Timing the Candle Lighting — Multiple Options

Ideally the menorah should be placed **outside the front door** to the left of incoming guests in order to be visible to passersby on their way home after sunset. That serves best the purpose of publicizing the miracle. Next best is to display the Hanukkah lights on a **windowsill** no higher than 20 cubits, the usual height objects are visible in the normal range of vision of a passerby.[8] However, in time of danger the candles could be lit inside the house on the table for the benefit of the residents alone, at any hour of the evening when they are assembled. Ashkenazi European tradition ruled that we follow the lenient custom as if it were still a time of danger, especially since the weather is often inclement outside.[9]

Q *What about lighting the menorah in the synagogue?*

A It has become a custom to light the synagogue's menorah which is placed on the southern side of the synagogue just as the seven-branched menorah in the Temple was located on the southern exposure. However, **it is not sufficient to light the synagogue menorah even if the blessings are recited**. In addition to lighting the synagogue menorah, each person must light his/her home menorah for that is the original form of the mitzvah as a proclamation of the miracle by each household.[10]

Q *If we usually gather in the family room which has no window to the street or if we live in a high-rise apartment building, what should we do?*

A For Ashkenazim there is today no halachic requirement to let the menorah be seen by outsiders. However, in an era when Jews are proud of their identity and danger from anti-Semitic neighbors is minimal, there is no reason not to try to place at least one menorah in public view from the street or from other high-rise buildings across the way. The other menorahs in the house may be placed in more convenient locations in the house, but to keep the memory of the ideal alive, one should try to place at least one menorah in public view.[11] It is also recommended that there be a menorah facing *each* street upon which the house fronts.[12] Many Sefardim still follow the original ruling on the timing and placement of the menorah.

Q *Can we light the menorah first and then place it in the window?*

A Ideally Jewish law requires the menorah to be placed in public view **before** it is lit. "Lighting" — not "placing" *(hanacha)* — counts.[13]

Q *My children, spouse or guests will be coming late. Can I delay the candle lighting?*

A Yes, as far as the Ashkenazim are concerned, public display of the candles during the 30 minutes after sundown is no longer required. However, you may wish to light one menorah "on time" (either at sundown according to Maimonides or after the stars come out according to Rabbenu Asher) and in the proper location (facing the public domain outside the door or on the windowsill).[14] This will keep alive the memory of the original practice of the candle lighting. In many communities there is traffic (passersby) until well after sunset, so the "ideal time" might be extended beyond half an hour and longer candles might well be used. In any case, as long as residents of the household are awake, it is never too late — during the night — to light the candles.[15]

---

8. *A.H.O.H.* 671:20, 22, 23
9. *A.H.O.H.* 671:24 and 672:6
10. *A.H.O.H.* 671:26
11. *A.H.O.H.* 671:24
12. *A.H.O.H.* 671:27
13. *A.H.O.H.* 671, 675
14. *A.H.O.H.* 672
15. *A.H.O.H.* 672:6-7

3. Setting up the Candles for Family and Guests to Light

Though the minimum is one candle for the whole family, it is commendable to set up a menorah for each member and each guest, with the candles added — one per night — from right to left — even though they are lit from the newest candle — left to right.[16] Generally the Talmudic Rabbis recommend, "May all your turns be to the right,"[17] just as today putting one's right foot forward signifies starting off right.

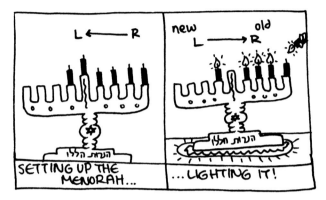

SETTING UP THE MENORAH... ...LIGHTING IT!

Q *What if we got mixed up and lit the candles from right to left?*

A Don't worry. A minority of rabbis, in fact, require that one light from right to left because that is the direction of Hebrew reading.[18] Besides, the absolute bare minimum requirement is simply to light just one candle per night per household.

Q *What if I am a guest and do not have my own menorah and candles?*

A A temporary guest may rely on their family lighting a menorah for them back at home. The mitzvah is primarily for the household, not the individual. However, a guest may wish to be included in the host family's candle lighting. By making a small monetary contribution, s/he can buy a "share" in the candles being lit by the host.[19] The host may then give the money to *Tzedakah*. Alternatively the guest can simply ask to borrow a menorah or make a makeshift one.

Q *Can I use one Hanukkah candle to light another?*

A Yes and No! Yes, one can light a Hanukkah candle with the flame of another Hanukkah candle. Both are holy and both are serving their symbolic function. No, one cannot light a *shamash* or an interim candle or match from a burning Hanukkah candle. (Of course, some rabbis urge stringency and forbid one to light one Hanukkah candle even directly from another.)[20]

4. The Order of the Blessings — Especially on Friday and Saturday Night

Brachot (blessings) must always be said before lighting the Hanukkah candles and after lighting the service candle — *shamash* — which should be lit first, so that its light is ready for use.

Q *On Friday night do we light Hanukkah or Shabbat candles first?*

A Hanukkah candles are lit first and then Shabbat candles immediately thereafter, so that the lighting precedes sundown and yet the Hanukkah candles burn after sundown. With oil lamps, extra oil is added so it will burn longer — both before and a full half hour after sunset.[21]

Q *What about Saturday night?*

A At home, Havdalah (the ceremony with a braided candle, spices and wine that marks the end of Shabbat and of its prohibition on doing work) precedes lighting the menorah. Hanukkah candles cannot double as Havdalah candles because Havdalah's light is for use and Hanukkah's is not.

Q *Can a woman light the candles and say the blessings not only for herself but for her husband?*

A Of course, women were part of the miracle — they were endangered and contributed to the rescue. They are equally obligated and may represent men in candle lighting.

Children under bar/bat mitzvah age should be encouraged to bless and to light their own menorah. However, if there is only one family menorah, a post bar/bat

---

16. *A.H.O.H.* 676:11   17. *T.B. Yoma* 15b
18. *A.H.O.H.* 676:12   19. *A.H.O.H.* 677
20. *A.H.O.H.* 674   21. *A.H.O.H.* 679

mitzvah man or woman should light the menorah. A child may sing the blessings for an adult if that adult so stipulates.[22]

Q *If I cannot light candles myself, but I see Hanukkah candles burning in a window, what blessings may I say?*

A Lighting is only one aspect of the mitzvah. Seeing the candles and remembering the miraculous victory are important in themselves. Therefore one who sees the candles, blesses *"al hanissim"* ("for the miracles") as well as *"shehechiyanu"* (on the first night only).

5. When Candles Blow Out

Candles need to burn for up to 30 minutes — the time it traditionally takes passersby to empty out of the marketplace after sunset. If the oil or candle does not provide enough fuel or the wind is strong and likely to extinguish the candles, then one cannot light that inadequate candle in that vulnerable location for Hanukkah.

Q *What if the candles go out?*

A The Hanukkah candles should be relit if they go out during the lighting ceremony itself. If, after the blessings and the initial ceremony, any of the Hanukkah candles go out or are blown out by mistake before burning for ½ hour, **it is not necessary to relight them**. If the *shamash* goes out at anytime and there is another light source in the room, from an electric light or the *shamash* of other menorahs, then it need not be relit.

Q *I need to leave the house. May I extinguish the candles?*

A Life threatening situations like a fire take precedence over candle lighting. But

"It's Too Cold Outside"

In medieval Germany Jews did not place the menorah outside because of non-Jews (who embarrassed them) and thieves, so they lit the candle inside their house next to the internal doorway of the "winter room," the one which had a fireplace so essential to family life during the European winter.[23]

---

23. Yitzchak Zemer, *Olam K'Minhago Noheg*, p. 292.

ideally one should let the Hanukkah candles burn for up to 30 minutes. Afterwards, one may intentionally extinguish them at any time and for whatever reason.

6. Time Out from Work — for Women Only — and Time for Publicizing the Miracle

It is customary, though not obligatory, for women to take a break from their work (which in medieval society meant cleaning, sewing and cooking) and concentrate on the candles for the ½ hour duration of their burning. (In fact, it is appropriate for everyone to take ½ hour off to reflect on the symbolic meaning of the candles before rushing on to everyday activities). Women are especially connected to Hanukkah, as the Rabbis explain, because of their central role in the original historical events.

Q *What readings are appropriate for Hanukkah?*

A There is no official *megillah* (such as the Scroll of Esther) and no *haggadah* (such as on Pesach) for Hanukkah. But there is an obligation **to publicize the miracle** *(pirsum hanes)* that is common to Hanukkah, Purim and Pesach. On Hanukkah the candles are the chief instrument to propagate the educational message to passersby as well as to household members. However, the candles are symbolic and therefore where knowledge is lacking they need to be accompanied by the historical tale.

In the early Middle Ages, the Jews wrote in Aramaic and read from a very concise abbreviation of the *Book of Maccabees* sometimes called ***"Megillat Antiochus"*** (written between 2nd-8th century CE). Sometimes it was read in the synagogue on Shabbat Hanukkah just as various *megillot* are read on Shabbat Pesach *(Song of Songs)* or Shabbat Sukkot *(Ecclesiastes)*. This scroll is no longer used but with the translation of the *Books of Maccabees* into Hebrew and

---

22. *A.H.O.H.* 675:5

Generally, the Talmudic Rabbis rule "that women are exempt from all time-bound positive mitzvot," those ritual actions that must be performed at a certain time.[25] Nevertheless, in direct contradiction to the rule, the Talmud obligates women to drink four cups of wine on Pesach, to read the Megillah on Purim and to light candles on Hanukkah. Each of these mitzvot are Rabbinic in origin and each one is explained by the Talmudic Rabbi Yehoshuah ben Levi with the historical rationale — *"even women were involved in that miracle."*[26]

The medieval German rabbis argued over the interpretation of this rationale. The German Tosafists argued that the phrase *"even women"* means only that they were secondarily involved since their lives were also "at risk," but Rashi and Rashbam argued vigorously "that the (miraculous) redemption was a Divine reward for the actions of righteous women in the generation of each event" — the Exodus, the fall of Haman and the Maccabean victory.[27] The word *"even"* in *"even women were involved in that miracle"* should be understood as "especially," for activist women were at the heart of triggering Divine intervention.

Which women are they referring to?

In the Megillah it is obviously Esther. In the Exodus it may be referring to the midwives and to Moshe's mother and sister. The Rabbinic midrash developed tales of female heroism associated with Miriam and with the Jewish women who aroused their husbands to procreate even though they were crushed with harsh labor and despair.[28]

But what about Hanukkah? Where is the heroine among Judah and his brothers?

In the *Book of Maccabees* IV 8:3 the heroine is a mother of martyrs. Hannah encourages her seven children to choose torture and death over obeisance to Antiochus and his pagan gods.

In the later Rabbinic midrash the Apocryphal book of *Judith* (who beheads the enemy general Holofernes) is identified with Hanukkah and her story becomes the rationale for eating milk-based foods on Hanukkah.[29] Medieval midrash also created the Hasmonean sister — Hannah, daughter of Mattathias — who triggers the revolt when she is forced by the Hellenist ruler to spend her first night as a married woman sleeping with the Hellenist lord.[30]

The rabbis took the principle of R. Yehoshua ben Levi seriously, so that women can represent men in reading Megillah, lighting Hanukkah candles, and saying Kiddush on Pesach. Later this principle was expanded to include saying Hallel and eating three meals on Shabbat.[31]

---

24. *"Af Nashim"* by Chana and Shmuel Safrai, *Yeshurun*, 1999.

25. *Mishna Kiddushin* 1:7

26. *T.B. Shabbat* 23a; *Pesachim* 108a; *Megillah* 4a

27. *T.B. Pesachim* 108a-b

28. See *A Different Night — The Family Participation Haggadah* by Noam Zion and David Dishon, p. 91.

29. *Midrash Hanukkah* in A. Jellinek, *Beit Midrash* 8 p. 133.

30. A. Jellinek, *Beit Midrash* 6: p. 2-3; *Megillat Antiochus.*

31. Rabbenu Tam, *Mordechai:* on *Shabbat* 39b

English, it is appropriate to read aloud from them. (See above *Maccabees' Megillah*, page 25).

Q *Isn't there also a Book of Judith for Hanukkah?*

A Strangely enough the rabbis identified Hanukkah (165 BCE under the Greek Syrian Empire of Antiochus IV) with the Persian Jewish or Hellenistic Jewish romance (historical novella) entitled *Judith* (attributed to the days of General Holofernes, representative of the Babylonian Emperor Nebuchadnezar, 586 BCE). The **Book of Judith** is preserved in Greek in the Catholic Bible. The rabbis identified Judith as a female heroine whose active role in saving the Jewish people from the Greeks justifies women's obligation to light candles and take a half hour pause from their tasks. Women in Jewish law are usually exempted from mitzvot requiring performance at a particular time like candle lighting on Hanukkah, but Hanukkah is an exception since women played an essential role in the redemption. (Read Judith's story in the *Maccabees' Megillah*, page 45.)

The Talmudic Rabbis insist that Hanukkah candles be lit **on time — at sundown** so that they will shine on the passersby on their way home from the market, approximately one half hour after sunset.[33] The latest they need to burn is when the last workers leave the public space. In their days "last workers" were defined as those who collected and sold fire wood and who remained in the market until people had gone home to light their hearth.[34] To publicize the miracle of Hanukkah, the menorah had to be placed outside the doorway of each house or, for second story dwellers, in the windowsill facing the street no higher than 20 cubits. Otherwise the normal passerby would not see the candles, since one generally looks forward — and not upward — while walking. Most Sefardim follow that tradition.

However, most Ashkenazim (Europeans from France, Germany and later Eastern Europe) are much more lenient on the timing of the lighting and placement of the menorah. This stems not only from modern times when people come home later because of electric lighting, but can be traced back to the little known persecution of Babylonian Jews in the 3rd century CE by the Zoroastrian rulers of Persia who worshipped fire, their god of light:

> "In the kingdom of the Persians they went through all the houses of Israel extinguishing candles and coals. Only fires dedicated to their gods were permitted. They carried pans of burning coals through the streets."[35]

Therefore the Talmudic Rabbis ruled: "In time of danger it is sufficient to place the menorah on one's table (inside the house)."[36]

The Babylonian Geonim expanded this exception: "If a strong wind is blowing (that can extinguish an outdoor menorah) or robbers may be attracted to one's house by the light, then place the menorah on the table and that is sufficient."[37]

In Ashkenazi lands the exception became the rule, and everyone was permitted to use an indoor menorah on their table. Some rabbis explained that even though it is no longer dangerous to light outside, the permission to light inside was never rescinded officially. The 19th century *Aruch HaShulchan* code summarizes Eastern European practice:

> "Since our lands are rainy and snowy with strong winds during Hanukkah, it is impossible to put the menorah outside unless it is enclosed by glass. However the rabbis did not ask us to go to such trouble. After all, an outdoor menorah might not be all that noticeable and the non-Jews might not allow it. Therefore we all light inside the house (on the table)."[38]

Since the candles are lit on the table inside the house, the only *pirsum hanes* (publicization of the miracle) is aimed at family members and no longer at passersby. Therefore the medieval German rabbis (12th century) ruled: "It does not really matter what time we light the candles, since it is only for inhabitants of the house" (as long as they are still awake) and "it does not matter if the candles are placed (in a window) above 20 cubits."[39]

Nevertheless, the authors of this book would recommend that, if possible, the menorah be lit on a windowsill facing the street as soon as family members arrive home during the period of time after sunset when people (or cars) are still passing by. Candles may be lit more than once if necessary, for example, at sundown and once again when the whole family gets home. In Israel, it is appropriate that the light of the menorah face the street, for Israeli sovereignty means that the public space is Jewish. Thus electric menorahs are lit on public buildings and giant oil lamps are lit at the Kotel (the Western Wall). In Christian countries, presuming that there is no persecution, it is appropriate that Jews let themselves and their homes be identified by the lights, just as Christians display Christmas lights. While many Jews in the Diaspora argue that the public space should not be dominated by Christian or Jewish symbols, at least individual families should feel proud and confident enough to make their religious commitments at home a matter of public record.

32. Based on sources collected by Daniel Sperber, *Minhagei Yisrael: Hanukkah* p. 43-49.
33. *T.B. Shabbat* 21-2   34. Rashi, *ibid.*
35. *Ozar Ha Geonim*, Babylonian heads of the Academies, 9th-11th century CE on *T.B. Gittin* p. 225).
36. *T.B. Shabbat* 21   37. *Halachot Kezuvot Hanukkah* 2
38. *Aruch HaShalchun Orach Hayim* 671:25
39. *Tosafot Shabbat* 21b and *Raviyah* #843

QUESTIONS AND ANSWERS
GETTING THE HISTORY OF HANUKKAH RIGHT

LEGENDS OR FACTS?

by Noam Zion

Q *Isn't it true that we celebrate Hanukkah for 8 days because the only cruse of pure oil found, burned for 8 days instead of its usual 1?*

A Not according to the best historical records of the time — **The Book of Maccabees** (125 BCE) and Josephus' **Antiquities of the Jews** (100 CE).

The 8 days are a "make-up" holiday for the 8 days of the previous Sukkot, which could not be celebrated in 164 BCE since the Greeks were still occupying the Temple. The *Second Book of Maccabees* calls our holiday **"Sukkot in the month of Kislev"** (December, instead of September-October, the usual date of Sukkot).[40]

"They celebrated for eight days with gladness, like Sukkot, and recalled how, a little while before, during Sukkot they had been wandering in the mountains and caverns like wild animals. So carrying wands (*lulav*) wreathed with leaves and beautiful branches and palm leaves too, they offered hymns of praise to God who had brought to pass the purifying of his own place. And they passed a public ordinance and decree that the whole Jewish nation should observe these days every year."[41]

In fact, Sukkot is originally a holiday celebrating the dedication of Solomon's First Temple.[42] The dedication of the Second Temple took place on the 24th of Kislev.[43] Thus, it was also appropriate that Hanukkah, the Maccabean Rededication of the Altar (defiled by Greek sacrifice of pigs to Zeus Olympus whose statue was erected in the Temple), should also last 8 days and begin on the 25th of Kislev.

The alternative explanation of the 8 day length of Hanukkah is the miracle of the cruse of oil which only appears in later sources like the Scroll of Fasts[44] quoted in the Talmud.

Q *Isn't it true that the 25th of Kislev, the first day of Hanukkah, is the day the Maccabees recaptured the Temple and lit the cruse of oil?*

A On the day of the military victory, the Maccabees may have lit a makeshift menorah described in the Scroll of Fasts:

"Why do we light candles on Hanukkah? For in the days of the Greek dynasty, the Hasmoneans entered the Temple with seven iron lances in their hands. They covered these (round hollow lances[45]) with wood and lit them (with oil) for the next 8 days."

Perhaps the miracle of the oil refers to this temporary menorah of seven lances.

However, the *First Book of Maccabees* describes no rush to light the menorah. The Maccabees did not capture Jerusalem on the 25th of Kislev, but at least a week earlier. The Maccabees had an enormous amount of work to do before they held the official Rededication Ceremony on the 25th of Kislev. They had to remove the defiled altar and build a new one, as well as prepare all new gold utensils including a new gold seven-branched menorah to replace the one plundered by Antiochus in 169 BCE. They recalled that:

Antiochus had entered Jerusalem with a strong force, and in his arrogance he went into the sanctuary and took the gold altar and the **lampstand (menorah) for light**, and all its furniture and the table for the Presentation Bread and the cups and the bowls and the gold censers and the curtain and the

---

40. *II Maccabees* 1:10   41. *II Maccabees* 10:6-8
42. *I Kings* 8 which lasted for twice seven days   43. *Hagai* 2:10, 20   44. *Megillat Taanit*
45. Daniel Sperber (*Minhagei Yisrael*: Hannukah p. 4-7) suggests according to Greek sources that the lances were sharp, hollow metal weapons also used as impromptu torches.

crowns and the gold ornamentation on the front of the Temple, for he stripped it all off. He took them all and went back to his own country.[46]

Q Is the miracle of the cruse of oil just an arbitrary invention of the Talmud?

A Yes and No.

When Jerusalem was liberated, Judah said:

"Now that our enemies are crushed, let us go up to purify the sanctuary and rededicate it." They purified the sanctuary and carried out the stones that had defiled it to an unclean place. They took whole stones, as the Law required, and built a new altar like the former one. They built the sanctuary and the interior of the Temple and consecrated the courts. They made new holy vessels and they brought the lampstand and the altar of incense and the table into the Temple. Then they burned incense on the altar, lighted the lamps on the lampstand and lit up the Temple.[47]

Finding a Name for Hanukkah: Names Change and the Essence Changes as Well

(1) **"SUKKOT IN THE MONTH OF KISLEV."** The *Book of Maccabees* notes that the 8 day Sukkot holiday celebrated in the Temple in Tishrei (Sept.-Oct.) was postponed until Kislev (Dec.) because the Greek Syrians still occupied the Temple during Sukkot, while the Maccabees hid in caves in the wilderness.

(2) **"FESTIVAL OF LIGHTS."** Josephus, the first century CE Jewish historian, is the first to use this term.

(3) The Rabbis of the Talmud ask — "What is **HANUKKAH**?" and explain it in terms of the **dedication of the new Menorah, the new Altar, and the rededication of the Temple.**"

(4) The Zionists renamed the holiday **"HOLIDAY OF THE MACCABEES OR THE HASMONEANS"** to emphasize the human heroes who recaptured Jerusalem and instituted a holiday celebrating their political independence.

Only when the Temple was wholly cleansed and new utensils prepared, could Judah and his brothers begin the rededication of the Temple. They probably had time to replenish the supply of pure oil as well.

Then they arose early on the twenty-fifth day of the ninth month, that is, the month of Kislev [December, 164 BCE], and offered sacrifice according to the Law upon the new altar of burnt offering which they had made. At the time and on the day the Greeks had polluted it, it was rededicated . . . .[48]

That date was not merely a function of the time it took to complete the refurbished Temple, but a direct reference to the date the Temple had first been defiled by the Greeks in 167 BCE.

Q *Is the miracle of the cruse of oil just an arbitrary invention of the Talmud?*

A Yes and No. Talmudic traditions are often carefully preserved oral traditions from generations previous. One way or another, the Rabbis needed to explain the observance of Hanukkah. The eight days of lighting candles is never mentioned in the *Books of the Maccabees*, Josephus, or Philo, and yet it seems to be an established custom before the destruction of the Second Temple.

Perhaps the story of the miracle of the cruse of oil sought to give Jewish roots to the pagan practices like the Dionysian torch processions that the Greeks forced on the Maccabean Jews:[49]

When the festival of Dionysus was celebrated, they were compelled to wear wreaths of ivy and march in procession in his honor."

Perhaps it is related to the festival of the sun's rebirth on December 25, celebrated by lighting fires.

46. *I Maccabees* 1:21-23   47. *I Maccabees* 4: 36,43-51
48. *I Maccabees* 4: 52-54, see also *II Maccabees 9:5*
49. *II Maccabees* 6:7

However, its Jewish roots may be much deeper. After all, the dedication of the *mishkan* (Tabernacle) by Aaron, involved a miraculous fire from the sky that consumed the sacrifices:[50]

> Fire came forth from before the Lord and consumed the burnt offering on the altar. All the people saw and fell on their faces.

Similarly, when Solomon dedicated the First Temple in Jerusalem, fire descended from the heavens:[51]

> When Solomon finished praying, fire descended from heaven and consumed the burnt offerings and the Presence of the Lord filled the Temple.

When Elijah dedicated a new altar to God on Mount Carmel, he called down a miraculous fire:[52]

> "O Lord, Let it be known today that You are God in Israel." Then fire from the Lord descended and consumed the burnt offering, the wood, the stones and the earth. When they saw this, all the people flung themselves on their faces and cried out: "The Lord alone is God!"

When the Second Temple was rededicated, the *Book of Maccabees* recalls, the miraculous fire of the Second Temple altar — a petroleum oil called *nephtai* — was rediscovered by Nehemiah.[53] (See *Maccabees' Megillah 6th Candle* sidebar, page 41).

In short, the combination of miraculous Divine fire and the rededication of the Temple suggests that the seemingly trivial, late legend of the cruse of oil continues an ancient tradition of Divine miraculous intervention. The miraculous fire is God's response to the human invitation to God to renew his dwelling in our cultic midst.[54] The Maccabees, no less than the Rabbis, sought a sign of Divine legitimacy to their new holiday, since it had no roots in the Biblical world.

---

50. *Leviticus 9:24*
51. *II Chronicles 7:1*
52. *I Kings 18:36-39*
53. *II Maccabees 1:18-23, 33-36*
54. Yariv ben Aharon, "Hanukkah," *Shdemot,* Tevet 5742

Appendix 3

HALLEY'S AND HANUKKAH

THE TALE OF A COMET AND THE ORIGIN OF THE NAME "FESTIVAL OF LIGHTS"

by Al Wolters[55]

Halley's Comet, the brightest of the periodically returning comets, may explain why Hanukkah is called the "Feast of Lights." According to our calculations, Halley's Comet was visible in Jerusalem at the time of the first Hanukkah.

Until the rise of modern astronomy, comets were almost universally regarded as supernatural portents, usually presaging some major historical event. They were often taken as a forewarning of some catastrophe, such as a great military defeat or the death of a ruler. As Shakespeare wrote in *Julius Caesar*: "When

---

55. Published by *Moment Magazine*, December 1995, p. 28-29, based on A. Wolters, "Halley's Comet at a Turning Point in Jewish History," Catholic Biblical Quarterly 55 (1993) 687-697. Al Wolters is professor of biblical studies at Redeemer College in Ontario, Canada. In 1994 his parents, Syrt and Lucinda Wolters, were honored by the Israeli ambassador to Canada as Righteous Gentiles. Used by permission.

beggars die there are no comets seen; the heavens themselves blaze forth the death of princes."

In connection with the last appearance of Halley's Comet in 1985, two astronomers and an Assyriologist announced that cuneiform records housed in the British Museum referred to the appearance of Halley's Comet in 164 BCE. The period of visibility for an observer in Baghdad in 164 BCE was from September 24 to November 10, after which the comet disappeared for more than three weeks during its swing around the sun. It then reappeared again at the end of November and continued to be visible for about three weeks in December. These dates would not be significantly different for Jerusalem.

In 164 BCE, the comet came unusually close to the earth, within 16 million kilometers. Its closest approach is usually between 25 and 73 million kilometers from the earth. Its appearance in 164 BCE must have made quite a spectacular display in the night sky. A month or two after the initial appearance of the comet, the Seleucid ruler of Syria, the Hellenistic tyrant Antiochus (Antiochus IV Epiphanes) died. The Syrians very likely regarded the comet's appearance as a portent of his death.

For the Jews it would have had another meaning. The Maccabees capped their military success by purifying and rededicating the Temple in Jerusalem three years to the day after Antiochus desecrated the Temple and triggered the revolt. The rededication of the Temple occurred on the 25th of Kislev, 164 BCE. The equivalent in our civil calendar is December 14 or 15.

The actual dedication of the Temple was preceded by its purification, which is described in some detail in I Maccabees 4:41-51. Not until completion of all this purification did the formal rededication take place on the 25th of Kislev, that is, in mid-December. Since the extensive work of purification was carried out by a select group of priests rather than by experienced tradesmen, it is reasonable to assume that it took a week or

two to complete. The purification therefore began in early December.

This means that the reappearance of Halley's Comet on December 3 would have come just before or right at the beginning of the work of purification and that the comet would have been visible on clear nights throughout the period in which the priests were preparing the Temple for the rededication ceremony on December 14 or 15. It was not until the rededication had taken place that the comet would have gradually disappeared from sight.

Why is Hanukkah called the Feast of Lights? The earliest mention of this name is found in the work of the first-century Jewish historian Josephus, who was already uncertain about its origin. In *Jewish Antiquities* he tells the story of the rededication of the Temple and the origin of the feast and then adds the following comment:

> And from that time to the present we observe this festival, which we call the **Festival of Lights**, giving this name to it, I think, from the fact that the right to worship came to light [or shone brightly] to us at a time when we hardly dared hope for it.

As the historian Ralph Marcus explains this passage, "Josephus here means that the deliverance experienced by the Jews 'was like a light appearing in the darkness of despair.'" Another explanation is that the name has something to do with a pre-existing pagan festival celebrated at the winter solstice.

It seems far more likely that Halley's Comet accounts for the name. The comet appeared as an unexpected bright light both at the purification of the Temple and at the death of Antiochus some weeks before. It is likely that many Jews would have been struck by the coincidence of this great light in the heavens and the great liberation celebrated in the festival thereafter called the Festival of Lights.

Doesn't the 25th of Kislev sound suspiciously like the 25th of December?

The 25th of Kislev was probably related to the 25th of December, the pagan solstice holiday which the Greeks probably chose for their rededication of our Temple to Zeus Olympus three years earlier on the 25th of December, 167 BCE.

The shortest day of the solar year in the Northern Hemisphere is also the first day when the hours of daylight begin to increase. That common natural fact may well have shaped the Jewish, the pagan and the later Yuletide Christmas holiday. However, it is pointed out in the *Book of Maccabees* that the 25th of Kislev, the day of the Greek desecration of the Temple, was chosen not as a continuation of the solstice theme but as a satirical lambasting and a nosethumbing reversal of the pagan date.[56]

In the 3rd century CE some of the church officials moved the date of Christmas from January 6 to December 25. A Syrian church Father explained that thereby they sought to draw Christians away from the pagan celebration of the rebirth of the Sun on December 25 by rededicating that date to the birth of their Lord. Both the Sun's birth and the birth of the son of god were celebrated by the lighting of a fire.[57] December 25 was both the Sun's birthday for the Iranian sun-god Mithra and the "Day of the Invincible Sun" for the Romans. Birth, resurrection and victory over darkness were reinterpreted in terms of Christ. "Christmas" is a development of the English term for Christ's mass.

Similarly, the Mishnah[58] reports that in the Second Temple on Sukkot morning after a night of acrobatics, dancing and juggling of burning torches, the Jews' procession "arrived at the Eastern Gate of the Temple. They turned their faces westward and said: 'While our ancestors turned their backs on the Temple and their faces to the East, bowing eastward toward the sun, we face west — our eyes are directed to You, God.'" That seems to indicate a conscious reformatory movement to adopt and yet polemically transform the solstice-related celebrations in a monotheistic direction.

Perhaps this solar solstice imagery lies behind the argument between the schools of Hillel and Shamai regarding the adding or deleting of one candle for each night of Hanukkah. Shamai's school says we begin with 8 candles and delete one a night (in reference to the decreasing days of the holiday) while Hillel's school says we add one candle a night (in reference to the increasing days).[59] Arye Ben Gurion, director of the holiday research division of the Kibbutz Movement,[60] suggests this parallels the Ancient Near Eastern solstice rituals which followed the "emptying" and "filling" processes of the sun. Those sympathetic rituals urged the sun on as it weakened or strengthened in its struggle with the forces of darkness, dying slowly or reviving slowly on the solar cycle of death and life.

The Rabbis were aware of the pagan fear underlying the Roman winter solstice holiday of Saturnalia that was celebrated in a carnival from December 17-24 annually.

> "When the Adam, the first human, noticed that each day [after his creation in Tishrei / September] grew shorter, he said: 'Oy! Poor me. Perhaps I sinned and now the world is darkened because of me and it is now returning to chaos. This is my death sentence decreed by the Heavens.'

> "So Adam stood and fasted and prayed for 8 days. At last he saw the day getting longer in the month of Tevet [immediately after Kislev] and he realized: 'The waxing and waning of the day is simply the way of the world, the natural cosmic order.' Therefore he went and celebrated for 8 days. The following year he established these 8 days of festivity as a permanent annual holiday."[61]

Here the Rabbis implicitly identify the eight-day winter holiday with a pagan holiday that originated in an unfounded ignorance and fear. However, once the reliable and beneficent ways of the Creator are recognized the festival is no longer tinged with the fear that the world may return to darkness.

---

56. *I Maccabees* 4:54-55
57. James Frazer, *The Golden Bough*, Chapters 37: 62-63.
58. *Sukkah* 8:5   59. *T.B. Shabbat* 21b   60. *Yalkut Hanukkah* 37-40
61. *T.B. Avodah Zarah* 8b

GLOSSARY

by Jeni Friedman

Acra — the fortress built by Greek Syrian soldiers in 167 BCE in order to control Jewish Jerusalem at the beginning of the Maccabean revolt. It was later recaptured by the Jews in 140 BCE.

Acropolis — the city center in a Greek-style city which contains the public buildings like the gymnasium.

Al HaNissim — the prayerbook's summary of the miracles and the political events of Purim and Hanukkah. It is recited during those festivals both in the *Amidah* (the Standing Prayer) and *Birkat HaMazon* (Grace after Meals).

Alexander the Great — the Macedonian general who studied under the philosopher Aristotle and led his native Greeks to a lightning conquest of the east from Turkey to India (332 BCE). His Hellenist successor-empires lasted some 300 years until they were swallowed up by Rome.

Antioch — the name of important Greek cities in the Greek-Syrian empire including the capital — all of which were named after King Antiochus. In 174 BCE, Jerusalem was renamed "Antioch" under the Hellenizing High Priest Jason.

Antiochus — King *Antiochus* IV, was the ruler (175-164 BCE) of Greek Greater Syria in the dynasty of the Seleucids. He considered himself a manifestation of God on earth, hence his acronym of "Epiphanes."

Apocrypha — a miscellaneous collection of sacred books, written by Jews and Christians from the third century BCE to the second century CE, which were not canonized, i.e., formally admitted to the Rabbininc or Christian Bible. The *Books of the Maccabees,* for example, were formally part of the Egyptian Jewish Bible, the Septuagint, and later the Catholic Bible, but not the Rabbinic or Protestant Bible.

Aruch HaShulchan — the expanded version of the traditional *Shulchan Aruch* (by Yosef Caro, 16th century), was written by Rav Yechiel Michal Epstein, a scholar of Jewish law in the late 19th century in Lithuania.

Beit Din — the Jewish court where legislative as well as judicial matters are decided.

Daniel — a Biblical prophet whose story is set in the days of King Nebuchadnezzar of Babylonia in 586 BCE. In fact, large parts of it were written during the Greek persecution of martyrs in Judea in 166 BCE. Daniel prophesied the fall of this great evil empire by supernatural intervention.

Diaspora — all Jewish settlements dispersed outside the land of Israel.

Dinah — daughter of the biblical patriarch Jacob, was raped by Hamor ben Shechem and was avenged by her brothers Shimon and Levi (*Genesis* 34). Their zealous vigilante activity was condemned by Jacob but praised by Judith.

Edom — the people that emerged from Esau, fraternal twin brother of Jacob, settled in southern Israel and southern trans-Jordan. Traditionally, Edom whose name means "red," like his ancestor Esau, the "ruddy" hunter and man of war, is identified with Rome, and the heirs to Rome, Christian Europe. *Maoz Tzur* refers to the Christian Crusaders as Edom.

Elazar — refers to two characters in the *Book of Maccabees.* Elazar the elderly scribe was martyred for his refusal to eat impure food, and Elazar the brother of Judah was killed in a suicide-mission trying to destroy the elephant of a Greek general invading Judea.

Gematria — an ancient system of equating letters of the Hebrew alphabet with numbers and establishing equivalencies between words spelled differently but equaling the same sum.

Gorgias — a supporter/friend of King Antiochus IV, who, along with General Nicanor, gathered Greek forces for the destruction of Judea in the days of Judah the Maccabee (ca. 164 BCE).

Gur/Ger — a village outside of Warsaw where the Ger Rebbe established his Hasidic dynasty.

Habad — the Lithuanian Hasidic movement led most

recently by Rabbi Menachem Mendel Schneerson, the Lubavitcher Rebbe, was founded in the village of Lubavitch in Lithuania. Unlike all other Hasidic groups, Habad is interested in outreach to non-observant Jews and therefore lights giant menorahs on Hanukkah in public squares.

Halacha — Jewish law

Hallel — a collection of the Psalms of praise recited on holidays of redemption.

Hannah — mother of seven sons martyred for their refusal to bow down to Antiochus' god — Zeus. Hannah is also the name of Mattathias' daughter who, according to medieval tales, instigated the Hasmonean revolt.

Hanukkiah — a modern Israeli term for a Hanukkah menorah with nine branches including one for the *shamash*.

Haredi — a contemporary term for Ultra-Orthodox Jews, both Hasidim and Mitnagdim (opponents of Hasidism), fearful of assimilation with anything from the western world.

Haskala — the 18th and 19th century Jewish enlightenment movement dedicated to the modernization of Jewish life in Eastern Europe.

Hasmonean — the term for the family and dynasty of the descendants of Mattathias the rebel priest, who are called also the Maccabees.

Hasidim — refer to the followers of any Jewish religious sect that goes beyond the letter of the law in its strictness and willingness to make sacrifices for observance of Judaism. The Hasidim of the Hellenist period refused categorically to violate Jewish law in any way; therefore they hid in the caves in the wilderness of Judea and later joined the Maccabean revolt. In the 18th century the Baal Shem Tov in the Ukraine founded a modern movement of Hasidism.

Havdalah — literally, "the ceremony of separation," marks the conclusion of Shabbat and other holy days at sunset.

Hellenism — the culture created by the integration of Greek and Oriental traditions resulting from the conquest of the Middle East by Alexander the Great from Macedonia. It differs somewhat from the original culture of the native Hellenes, the ancient Greeks.

Hillel — founder of the most influential school of rabbinic thought, lived in the land of Israel between 40 and 0 BCE in the reign of King Herod.

Holofernes — the enemy general who was beheaded by Judith when he sought to invade and conquer Judea. Holofernes is not necessarily a historical figure, but appears only in the *Book of Judith*. He is sometimes identified alternatively as a Babylonian general, an Assyrian general or a Greek king.

Hutzpah — Jewish daring, cheek.

Jason — the High Priest of Judea who won his office by bribing Antiochus the IV. He used Temple funds to pay his bribe and establish hellenizing institutions like the gymnasium in Jerusalem (174-171 BCE).

Josephus — the Jewish general who fought for the Jews against the Romans in the Great War, 66-70 CE. When captured, he became a historian of the Jewish wars and Jewish antiquities for the Emperor Vespasian and his son Titus from the house of Flavius.

Judea — the original area of Eretz Israel around Jerusalem, Bet Lehem and Hebron, which was the home of the tribe of Judah. After the exile of the northern ten tribes, Israel, Judea was the only remaining Jewish political entity. Hence all the remaining children of Israel became known as "Jews" rather than as "Israelites."

Judith — the heroine of the *Book of Judith*, who seduced and beheaded General Holofernes and thus saved Judea from destruction. The *Book of Judith* was written in the Persian or the Hellenist period and appears to be a historical romance.

Kabbalah — the Jewish mystical tradition which goes back to the period of the Rabbis of the Talmud. It was systematized in the Middle Ages in the book of the Zohar (13th century, Spain) and in many other works.

Kislev — the ninth month of the Jewish solar/lunar year during which the winter solstice generally falls.

Knesset — the ancient Jewish assembly and today the term used for the Israeli parliament.

Lamentations Rabbah — The Rabbinic explication of the biblical *Book of Lamentations (Eicha)*.

Lubavitch — a town in Lithuania, from which the original Lubavitcher Rebbe started his movement.

Maccabees, Books of — The four *Books of Maccabees* are preserved in the Christian Bible in Greek. Although they were written by Jews in the century after the Maccabean revolt, they were not made part of the Rabbinic Bible. The first two volumes are written by Maccabean historians and the second two volumes are written by Greek Jewish philosophers praising the Maccabean martyrs as philosophic heroes.

Maccabiah — the Olympic-style games inaugurated in 1932. Joseph Yekutiel convinced Meyer Dizengoff, mayor of Tel Aviv, to build Israel's first sports stadium and then convinced the Zionist Maccabiah sports clubs around the world to come to Israel to hold the first world Jewish Olympics in an era of extreme anti-Semitism that excluded Jews from interfaith competitions such as the 1936 Olympics held in Berlin.

Maimonides — the great Jewish philosopher, legalist, doctor, and political leader of the Jews of Egypt in the 12th century, integrated western philosophy with Jewish law. He wrote the *Mishneh Torah*, the most comprehensive code of Jewish law, and the philosophical *Guide to the Perplexed*.

Maoz Tzur — this 13th century European medieval poem about the historic rescues of the Jews is sung by Ashkenazim on Hanukkah.

Martyr — the Greek word *"martyr"* means "witness." The first recorded human beings to choose death over the public denial of their religion were the Maccabean martyrs who bore witness to their faith in a God who would ultimately defeat the evil empire of the Greeks.

Mattathias — this elderly priest of the Hasmonean family inspired the Maccabean revolt led by his five sons.

Megillah — a *megillah* means literally "a rolled up parchment." This was the typical "book" of the ancient world. All of the books of the Bible, as well as international letters, were called in Hebrew *"megillah/scroll."* Later in Jewish history, only five short books of the Bible were called *"megillot"* including *Megillat Esther* which is read on Purim.

Megillat Antiochus — an abbreviated Aramaic summary of the *Books of the Maccabees* which was written sometime between the 2nd and 8th centuries and used to be read aloud in the synagogue on the Shabbat of Hanukkah.

Megillat Ta'anit — this scroll of rabbinic dates lists days on which it is forbidden to fast. Written in the 1st century CE, it is the earliest written example of Rabbinic literature. Several of the dates are associated with Maccabean victories including Hanukkah itself.

Menelaus — the Hellenist Jew from Jerusalem who displaced the high priest Jason in 172 BCE by offering a larger bribe to Antiochus IV than his predecessor. He

was killed by the Greeks in order to appease the Maccabean rebels in 162 BCE.

Menorah — a "lamp" referring to the Temple menorah of seven branches, to household lamps, and to Hanukkah menorahs of eight/nine branches.

Midrash — any Rabbinic explication of the Biblical text is a *midrash*. Sometimes a *midrash* involves a liberal, literary re-writing of a Biblical story.

Mishnah — the first code of oral Jewish law, officially promulgated by Rabbi Judah Ha-Nasi (the Prince) c. 225 CE in Eretz Yisrael.

Mitzvah (pl. *Mitzvot*) — the commandments of the Torah as formulated by the Rabbis.

Modiin — a provincial town in the hills, on the road between Jerusalem and Jaffa, where Mattathias initiated the Maccabean revolt against the Greek religious coercion.

Nehemiah — a Jewish officer of the Persian court sent to the province of Judea to govern it and to rebuild the walls of Jerusalem (circa 450 BCE).

Ner Tamid — usually translated "the eternal light," refers to the seven-branched, gold menorah of the Temple. In fact, the *Ner Tamid* origianlly burned daily only from evening until morning. In today's synagogue, the *Ner Tamid* burns continuously during all hours of the day and night.

Nicanor — one of the Greek generals sent by Antiochus to put down the Maccabean revolt. His death in battle on the the 13th of the month of Adar was established as a Maccabean holiday.

Nike — the Greek goddess of victory, is often portrayed holding a palm branch.

Olympics — these ancient sacred celebrations and sports competitions were held every four years at Mount Olympus in Greece. Male participants would compete in the nude and victors earned fame and an olive wreath.

Philo — the 1st century Greek Jewish philosopher, was a student of Platonic philosophy and was the first to integrate Judaism and Hellenism in his interpretation of the Bible.

Pinchas — Aaron's great-grandson, Pinchas earned his position as the high priest by acting as a vigilante zealot to stop the public desecration of the covenant caused by the provocative act of public intercourse between a

Jewish leader and a non-Jew from the enemy nation in front of the Tabernacle. His zealous act served as a model for Mattathias.

Pirsum HaNes — the mitzvah of "publicizing the miracles" performed by God is achieved on Hanukkah by the lighting of the menorah in the doorway or window of the home at a time when passersby are likely to be out and about.

Rabbis — with a capital "R" refers to the Rabbis of the Mishnah and the Talmud (70-500 CE).

Reconstructionism — this movement for American Jewish renewal seeks to reconstruct Jewish civilization in the light of the growing ethical, scientific, and spiritual insights of the modern period. Its chief philosopher is Rabbi Mordecai Kaplan; its rabbinical seminary is located in Philadelphia, USA.

Reform — a German and later American movement for the reform of modern Jewish life which has emphasized ethics, progressive politics, and individual autonomy as a continuation of the Biblical prophetic tradition. It now has the largest synagogue affiliation in the United States.

Righteous Gentiles — a Rabbinic term for a non-Jew who performs moral acts above and beyond the call of duty. Today the term is used specifically to honor non-Jews who endangered their lives to save Jews during the Holocaust.

Sanhedrin — the legislative and judicial body of Judea at the end of the second Temple period and during the Mishnaic period.

Seleucus — one of Alexander the Great's generals who, after Alexander's death, won control over Greater Syria and established a dynasty that conquered Judea (200 BCE) and ruled it until the Maccabean revolt succeeded in gaining independence (140 BCE).

Sefardi (or Sephardi) — the Hebrew term for Spanish Jew, refers to all Jews who were expelled from Spain and Portugal yet retained their Spanish Jewish identity, often preserving the Judeo-Spanish language Ladino. This term is often used loosely and mistakenly for all Jews from African and Asian backgrounds even though most of them have no Spanish traditions.

Septuagint — the Greek Jewish translation of the Torah (c. 300 BCE) and later the whole Hebrew Bible prepared, according to tradition, by 70 (septa) scholars at the request of Ptolemy, king of Hellenist Egypt. It includes the first two *Books of the Maccabees*, even though they were not included in the Eretz Yisrael Rabbinic Bible of the same period.

Shamash — the "service candle" used to provide light for practical purposes and to ignite Hanukkah candles whose light may not be used for mundane purposes.

Shechinah — the feminine presence of God in the terminology of medieval Jewish mysticism.

Shehechiyanu — the Rabbinic blessing for new or annually renewed experiences of joy such as the reception of a nice gift on Hanukkah or the first night's lighting of Hanukkah candles for the first time for that year.

Shulchan Aruch — the basic medieval code of Jewish law written by Rabbi Yosef Caro in Safed in the 16th century. It was annotated by the Ashkenzai scholar Rabbi Moshe Isserles.

Solstice — refers to the longest and shortest day of the solar year. The winter solstice (December 21-22 in the contemporary calendar) falls close to or on Hanukkah. It is the 24-hour period of the longest night and the shortest day of the year and it is often celebrated with popular festivals of light.

Sufganiyot — jelly doughnuts eaten during the Hanukkah festival in Israel, symbolizing the miracle of the oil in which they are fried.

Sukkot — the eight-day biblical holiday of celebrating the harvest festival while residing in booths (*sukkah*) usually in the months of September or October. It also became the holiday of the dedication of the first Temple when dedicated by Solomon on Sukkot. It provided the model for the celebration of the new eight day holiday of Hanukkah established in the month of Kislev/December by the Maccabees.

Talmud — the comprehensive rabbinic discussion of oral Torah consisting of the code of the Mishnah, and its rabbinic explication in the Gemara.

TB — the Babylonian Talmud, completed in the year 500 CE, one hundred years after the completion of the Palestinian or Jerusalem Talmud.

Tanach — the Hebrew initials of the Bible made up of T=*Torah*, N=*Neviim* (prophets), and K=*Ketuvim* (miscellaneous writings).

Tur — the practical code of Jewish law written in Spain in the 13th century by Rabbi Yaakov ben Rabbenu Asher. It served as the model for the later 16th century *Shulchan Aruch*.

Tzaddikim — literally means "righteous human beings." In the Hasidic world the rebbe is called a *tzaddik* and he claims to have spiritual powers to invoke God's help for his people.

Tzedakah — literally means "an act of justice and mercy" performed by giving financial support to the needy. Unlike the Christian concept charity which means "free will offering of love," *tzedakah* is an obligation of Jewish law.

Yael — a non-Jewish biblical heroine who killed General Sisera, the enemy of Israel, when he forcibly took refuge in her tent when escaping from Deborah and Barak (*Judges* 4-5). Yael served as a prototype for Judith's beheading of General Holofernes.

Zealot — a Greek term referring to vigilante activists who seek to defend what is holy in their society against its desecration by internal traitors and external enemies. More specifically, the most radical rebels of the Great War against the Romans (66-73 BCE) were called Zealots and ended their lives in a mass suicide on Masada.

Zechariah –the 6th century BCE prophet of the rebuilding of the Second Temple. His messianic imagery includes an organic golden menorah and his prophetic chapter is read on Shabbat Hanukkah and concludes with *"Not by might, and not by power, but by My spirit, said the Lord."*

Permissions

"Don't violate the borders of your neighbor's property." (Deuteronomy 19:14)

We wish to thank all those who allowed us to use their creative work in **A Different Light**. We apologize to those whom we were unable to locate to request their permission and to offer them copyright fees. We have diligently sent many letters to publishers in order to obtain rights for all the photographs and articles contained in both volumes of **A Different Light**. In a small number of cases, we were unable to find a copyright holder. The creator of the text is acknowledged in the book, as well as the original publisher in whose volume the material was first discovered.

"Be warned! The making of many books is without limit . . . and very wearying."

— Ecclesiastes 12:12

ACKNOWLEDGEMENTS

Hanukkah is the Festival of Lights, where each evening more candles and lights illuminate the environment. So too this book is a Festival of Cooperation, in which as each chapter was added, more and more people helped illuminate the pages. Each one of the following professionals and friends added their own light to this production.

Barbara and I thank them all for their precious time, their tireless efforts, their much needed sense of humor, their loving criticism and encouragement.

First and foremost is our teacher Rabbi David Hartman who taught us to appreciate the world view implicit in the laws of Hanukkah and who gave us the mandate and the institutional backing of the Shalom Hartman Institute in Jerusalem to develop this two volume resource.

My beloved father, Rabbi Moshe Sachs, has been a very critical and constructive reader. Jeni Friedman was a God-sent volunteer literary editor. Tanya Zion created the family activities and many illustrations. Her artistic renditions of the Hanukkah heroes will make every reader smile. Joe Gelles, our very devoted and talented graphic designer, has been part of this book from its inception. Rivka Hillel typed every word.

All the translations from the Greek were made after studying the Septuagint with the generous help of Jonathan Price, professor of classics at Tel Aviv University.

And there were more: Daniel Abrams, Annette Bellows-Magnus, David Bernstein and PARDES students, Michael Brous, Eric Caplan, Jonathan Cohen, Rachel Cowan, Cliff Churgin, David Dishon, David and Jackie Ellinson, Naomi Eshel, David Estrin, Menachem Fish, Herb Friedman, Rhoda Friedman, Mordechai and Chaya Gafni, Shoshana Gelfand, Shlomo Gestetner, Aryeh Gol, Lisa Goldberg, David Golinkin, Daniel Gordis, Tom Hall, Susan Handelman, Lee Hendler-Meyerhoff, Elliot Jager, Brenda Jagod, Arlene Kantor, Edward Kaplan, Oren Kaplan, Simon Kaplan, Judith Kates, Yona Katz, Steven Kepnis, Yiftach Levy, Chaim Lauer, Levi Lauer, Leslie Litman-Rubin, Daniel Matt, Gabi and Naomi Meyer, Sharon, Jerry and Elisha Muller, Philip Munishor, Jane Myers, Benzion Netanyahu, Shlomo Naeh, Sharon Norrey, Morris Rosenfeld, Sherman Rosenfeld, Jonathan Price, Gabi Schein-Markovitz and JESNA students, Suzanne Singer, Danielle Upbin, David Wiener, Gary Wiener, Albert Winn, Jane Zeitlin and my in-house computer expert Mishael Zion.

We also want to mention the efforts of the professionals in the following institutions: The librarians at JTSA in New York and at HUC in Jerusalem, the staff at the Jewish Museum in New York City; the professionals in the photo archives of the Diaspora Museum in Tel Aviv, the Israel Museum, the Central Zionist Archives in Jerusalem and especially my sister Sharon Muller at the USHMM in Washington, D.C.

And last, but not least, my wife and partner Marcelle, who helped me give birth to this book. She proofread every page, consulted on every picture and has promised me to be there, with red pen in hand, when I start working on the next book. Giving birth to this book with my wife's help proves the truth of the adage *"Two is Better than One."*[62]

– *Noam Sachs Zion*

62. *Ecclesiastes* 4:9